Feliks Koneczny and Civilizational Fundamentalism in Poland

FELIKS KAROL KONECZNY, 1862–1949. Source: © Velogustik, CC BY-SA 4.0.

Feliks Koneczny and Civilizational Fundamentalism in Poland

Andrew Kier Wise

PIASA BOOKS

New York

Copyright © 2019 by PIASA Books

Published by PIASA Books, The Polish Institute of Arts and Sciences of America, 208 E. 30th Street, New York, NY 10016

http://www.piasa.org/pb.html

All Rights Reserved

ISBN 978-0-940962-75-0

Library of Congress Control Number: 2019944501

British Library Cataloging-in-Publication Data is available

Printed in the United States of America

FOR GLORIA

Contents

Preface

The origins of this book can be traced to research for my first monograph, a political biography of the Polish activist Aleksander Lednicki (1866–1934) that focused on his role in the Revolution of 1905. While his law firm flourished in Moscow during the final decades of the Russian Empire, Lednicki remained in touch with his home province of Minsk. He was one of the founders of the first liberal political parties in the former Kingdom of Poland (incorporated into the Russian empire) and in Russia, and he won a seat as a delegate for the Constitutional-Democratic Party (Kadets) in the First Duma representing Minsk. Lednicki travelled throughout the *kresy* region (the "borderlands," or eastern regions of the defunct Polish-Lithuanian Commonwealth) and to major Polish cities outside the Russian empire during the Duma electoral campaign in the winter of 1906. On one journey he made his way to Kraków, where on 20 January he delivered a rousing address entitled "The December Days in Moscow" to a receptive audience at the Slavic Club. Members of the club were anxious for reports about the bloody uprising in Moscow and the prospects for real political change in Russia. Lednicki preached a message of hope for the joint freedom of Russians and Poles—with Polish political and cultural autonomy—as an outcome of the liberation movement that he helped create.

Among the audience that evening was Feliks Koneczny (1862–1949), a leading member of the club and editor of its journal *Świat Słowiański* (Slavic World). Similar to Lednicki and others in attendance that evening, Koneczny was optimistic about the possibility of transformative political change in Russia and its potential impact on Poles. His hopes—and those of Lednicki, too—were dashed by the failure of the First Duma to build a constitutional monarchy during its brief seventy-two day lifetime. Nor did the following incarnations of parliaments in Russia (there were four Dumas between 1906 and 1917) fare any better. While Lednicki and Koneczny shared a dream of Russo-Polish kinship and espoused the slogan of "for your freedom and ours" during the heady days of 1905 and 1906, by the time Poles won their independence in 1918 the two men had taken radically different ideological paths.

The *kresy* Pole Lednicki fled Bolshevik Russia in 1918 and found sanctuary in Warsaw. But while he survived the revolutionary terror, he failed to adapt to the harsh political realities of interwar Poland. His message of compromise and conciliation fell on deaf ears in the increasingly radicalized political environment of interwar Poland. He finally committed suicide in 1934, distraught over his failure to implement his political vision. Meanwhile, the Cracovian Koneczny spent a decade (1919–29) teaching history at Stefan Batory University in Vilnius (Wilno). On the Polish frontier—or, as he perceived it, the civilizational frontier—Koneczny developed his "clash of civilizations" theory, which reflects the cultural and social anxieties of interwar Poland.

While my initial interest in Koneczny was restricted to his commentary on Russian history and Russo-Polish relations, over time I shifted my focus to his scholarship on world history. Beginning in 2001, I have regularly taught world history surveys at the University at Buffalo and at Daemen College. Broad reading on world history, the philosophy of history, and the historiographical debates of Koneczny's era brought new insights about Koneczny's work as a historian and his social, cultural, political, and intellectual contexts. From 2004 to 2014, my research on Koneczny extended to his legacy, especially the influence of his ideas on modern nationalist ideologies.

Although Aleksander Lednicki's contributions to cosmopolitan liberalism are all but forgotten in historiography and political thought today, the postcommunist Konecznian "renaissance" has flourished in Catholic fundamentalist and nationalist circles. As Rafal Pankowski (2010) wrote:

> Koneczny's works, popularized by successive generations of the Giertych political dynasty,[1] remain obligatory reading for the followers of the Polish extreme right today. . . . By the beginning of the 21st century, it was the obscure philosophy of Koneczny that counted as the ever-lasting endek[2] doctrine rivalling the influence of the more time-contingent (and hence losing some of its original influence) pieces authored by [Roman] Dmowski himself.[3]

This book is the first English-language monograph about Koneczny's theories and their reception in contemporary Poland. Ideological debates of the interwar period continue to shape political discourse in twenty-first century Poland, and right-wing nationalists in particular have turned to Koneczny's works for inspiration. While Koneczny's worldview—ethnocentric and grounded in fundamentalist Catholicism—seems outdated, he created a philosophy of history (or "science of civilizations") that provides a legitimizing framework for today's critics of globalization, cosmopolitanism, immigration, the European Union, feminism, homosexuality, and a myriad of other "threats" to traditional Polish society.[4]

In this book, I use the terms "civilizational fundamentalism" and "Konecznian fundamentalism" to refer to the ideology of Koneczny and his followers.

They desire a return to a pure "Latin" (Western) civilization. In the Konecznian worldview, Latin civilization possesses a peculiar "dynamism" and a pioneering spirit that make it special.[5] Koneczny believed that Latin civilization was the only one that allowed for the full and free development of human existence.[6] Ireneusz Białkowski adds that Latin civilization has generated several key ideas—"freedom of speech, thought and conscience"—that have become global in their appeal.[7] Jacek Barlik succinctly states that "[f]or Koneczny civilizations are not equal. One does not have 'better' and 'worse' civilizations, but 'higher' and 'lower.'"[8] And Koneczny deemed Latin civilization the highest.

I owe a great deal to the people and institutions who have provided funding and other support for this project. Daemen College granted me a sabbatical in 2006, as well as generous funding for multiple trips to Poland to conduct research and attend conferences. I wish to thank my colleagues on various committees for supporting my applications for funding. I am grateful to my departmental colleagues Penny Messinger and Lisa Parshall for their interest and support of my activities in Poland. Two colleagues in Poland—Sławomir Józefowicz and Tomasz Pudłocki—have provided great collegiality and advice over the years.

Koneczny's biographer, Piotr Biliński, kindly provided firsthand assistance to me during the early stages of my work in the archives in Poland. His encylopedic knowledge of the Koneczny collections proved invaluable to my research. Most important, over the years the late Robert Piotrowski provided insights about Koneczny that helped me shape my own conclusions. I am very grateful to these Koneczny scholars for their willingness to discuss my research. While I am indebted to them for their help, any shortcomings in the book are mine.

My first public presentation on Koneczny ("The Problem of Russian Historical Identity in the Thought of Feliks Koneczny") was at the 52nd Annual Conference of the New York State Association of European Historians in September 2002. This organization provides a welcoming environment for presenting research in its early stages, and I benefited greatly from constructive criticism at that forum. I had not planned on writing a monograph, but insightful commentary from Antony Polonsky and other attendees at the 62nd Annual Meeting of the Polish Institute of Arts and Sciences of America (PIASA) in Boston in 2004 enhanced my understanding of the Konecznian renaissance that was influencing Polish nationalist ideology—especially in the League of Polish Families (Liga Polskich Rodzin, or LPR, formed in 2001), which was beginning to experience electoral success. My research methodology consequently shifted: in addition to analyzing Koneczny's works within the interwar context, I began analyzing the discourse of Catholic fundamentalist, nationalist, and extremist media in order to understand their use of Konecznian concepts.

Conversations during this period with Charles Evans convinced me of the validity of reading Koneczny from a postcolonial perspective. I benefited greatly from insights offered by participants at two conferences in 2008 that addressed postcolonialism: "Reconsidering 'the Orient' and 'the Occident' in the 21st Century: Observing the 30th Anniversary of Edward Said's *Oriental-ism*" at SUNY Brockport, and "Beyond Imagined Uniqueness: Nationalisms in Comparative Perspective" at the University of Warsaw. Discussions at the latter conference opened up to me new ways to explore the intersection of national-ism and gender in my analysis of Koneczny's legacy. This resulted in my paper on "Cultural Fundamentalism and the Traditional Family in Poland," which was later included on the program at the 5th Biennial Conference of the AWSS (Association for Women in Slavic Studies) in 2011 in Austin, Texas. Participa-tion at this conference furthered my understanding of the role of gender in Konecznian fundamentalism.

I have published several works on Koneczny, and revised portions of the following articles and book chapters appear in various sections of this book:

- "The European Union and the 'Oriental Other' in Polish Nationalist Dis-course." In *Beyond Imagined Uniqueness: Nationalisms in Comparative Perspective*, edited by Joan Birbick and William R. Glass, 207–40. New-castle upon Tyne: Cambridge Scholars Publishing, 2010. Material from this book chapter is published with the permission of Cambridge Schol-ars Publishing.
- "Postcolonial Anxiety in Polish Nationalist Rhetoric." *Polish Review* 55 (2010), no. 3: 285–304.
- " 'Civilizational' Boundaries in Christian-Jewish Relations." *Studies in Christian-Jewish Relations* 5 (2010), no. 1. Avaliable online at http://escholarship.bc.edu/scjr/.
- "Russia as Poland's Civilizational 'Other.' " In *The East-West Discourse: Symbolic Geography and Its Consequences*, edited by Alexander Maxwell, 73–92. Bern: Peter Lang, 2011.

I am very grateful to the editors and publishers of these books and journals for granting me permission to use previously published material. I am also grate-ful to the anonymous peer reviewers who have provided critical and insight-ful commentary along the way, especially for an earlier manuscript version of this monograph. I would especially like to thank the editor of PIASA Books, Kathleen Cioffi, for patiently guiding this manuscript through the publication process.

In addition to the library staff at my home institution, Daemen College, I wish to thank the library staffs and interlibrary loan departments at the Uni-versity at Buffalo and the University of Illinois, where I conducted preliminary research for this project in 2003 as a participant in the Summer Research Labo-ratory at the Russian and East European Center. Ksenya Kiebuzinski, Slavic Resources Coordinator and Head of the Petro Jacyk Central and East European Resource Centre at the University of Toronto, has been extremely helpful dur-ing my research visits to the Robarts Library. The library staffs at the University of Warsaw and Jagiellonian University in Kraków provided excellent support. The staffs at several archives in Poland were welcoming and very helpful during my visits. These archives include Archiwum Uniwersytetu Jagiellońskiego, Biblioteka Jagiellońska—Oddział Rękopisów, and Archiwum Narodowe (Kraków); Biblioteka Narodowa and Żydowski Instytut Historyczny (Warsaw); and Biblioteka Zakładu Narodowego im. Ossolińskich (Wrocław).

Finally, I want to acknowledge my deep gratitude to my wife, Gloria. She has accompanied me on several research trips and has provided patient support for this project over the years. This book is dedicated to her.

Feliks Koneczny and Civilizational Fundamentalism in Poland

Feliks Koneczny (1862–1949) and the Science of Civilizations

This book provides an analysis of Feliks Koneczny's philosophy of history, referred to as the "science of civilization" or "science of civilizations" (I will use the latter term throughout the monograph). Koneczny believed that there has never been any sort of universal human civilization, nor will one develop in the future.[1] The study of world history does not reveal a convergence of cultural traditions on a global scale; rather, Koneczny declared that world history consists of "the struggle of civilizations and [failed] attempts at civilizational syntheses."[2] Koneczny developed his theories during a period of political, cultural, social, and economic transformations in Poland, as Poles adjusted to the challenges of modernity. During Koneczny's lifetime, Poles were emerging out of a long colonial experience with the revival of the independent Polish state (1918),[3] only to see that state dismembered in bloody fashion once again during World War II (1939–45). In his final years, Koneczny experienced the imposition of yet another "alien" system by the Soviet-backed communist regime.

Koneczny was born and raised in Habsburg-ruled Kraków. He also pursued his higher education in the medieval capital of Poland, receiving his doctorate from Jagiellonian University in 1888. While there his interests as a scholar and critic were piqued by courses with leading historians of the day.[4] At this time, Kraków was regarded as a cultural capital, hailed as the "Polish Athens" or the "Polish Rome."[5] The site of Wawel Castle and other remnants of medieval Poland, Kraków represented the traditional heart of Poland. During Koneczny's lifetime (and still to this day) it acted as a bastion of medievalism and a center of traditional Polish culture and the Catholic faith.[6] Undoubtedly inspired by his surroundings, Koneczny advised Poles to accentuate their Catholicism as a means of preserving their national identity.[7]

Kraków also served as a living symbol of Polish freedom, and it was home to a burgeoning public history movement that sought to commemorate Poland's glorious past.[8] Koneczny ascribed the better situation for Poles in the Habsburg Empire, as opposed to conditions they suffered in the Russian or Prussian partitions, to the dominance of Catholicism and "Latin civilization" among much of Austro-Hungary's population.[9] As a result of greater cultural autonomy granted by Vienna, the region of Galicia, "and especially the ancient Polish capital of Kraków, became the focal point for commemorative activity" for Poles after 1867.[10] Public celebrations of anniversaries peaked in the years just prior to World War I and the rebirth of the Polish state. In 1883 Poles celebrated the two hundredth anniversary of King Jan Sobieski's defense of Vienna against the Turks. In 1890 Poles celebrated the transfer of the poet Adam Mickiewicz's remains from Paris to Kraków; eight years later, they commemorated the hundredth anniversary of his birth with the erection of a statue in the medieval market at the center of the city. Anniversaries related to Poland's struggle for freedom during the period of partitions were also commemorated: in 1891 the hundredth anniversary of Poland's first constitution; in 1893 the hundredth anniversary of the second partition; in 1894 the hundredth anniversary of the revolt against the Russians; and in 1895 the hundredth anniversary of the third partition.[11] One contemporary observed that fin-de-siècle Kraków was "a city obsessed with 'ceremonies.'"[12]

As Keely Stauter-Halsted demonstrates, a notable aspect of this trend was that the peasantry "became increasingly active in public celebrations of national anniversaries."[13] In peasants' minds, anniversaries represented a key source of national strength. This related to "a conception of national vitality rooted in the soil"[14] that is still evident in nationalist thought today. In his theoretical works, Koneczny stressed the virtues of farming in comparison to commerce in various settings: he drew this dichotomy between ancient Rome and ancient Greece, and also between "Latin civilization" and "Jewish civilization." Just as "[p]hysical links between the soil and the nation typified one component of the peasantry's understanding of its role in the nation,"[15] Koneczny expressed an abiding concern for the fate of Polish farms and the persons who tend them, as have his followers. Koneczny believed that peasant culture was "one of the vital sources of national civilization, or in common parlance, of national progress."[16]

Fin-de-siècle Kraków certainly was steeped in the veneration of traditional culture and the commemoration of Poland's past. In the eyes of avant-garde writers and artists, however, the city seemed stagnant and bound by tradition in comparison with the vibrant and dynamic cosmopolitan imperial capital of Vienna.[17] Yet Kraków also became the heart of "Young Poland" (*Młoda Polska*), the modernist movement in Polish arts. A new municipal theater opened in 1893, and it quickly became a symbol of Kraków's new prosperity and the special role the city played in the national and cultural life of Poland.[18] Koneczny often attended the theater, and he wrote reviews of plays for *Przegląd Polski* (Polish Review) from 1896 to 1905. Cinemas began to appear, and the first special building for showing films—the "Wanda" theater—was built in 1912.[19]

Much of the inspiration for Kraków's traditions came from the Church, but noble landowners also contributed to the cultural mix. Many aristocratic families settled in the city when they fled the lands of the former Congress Kingdom or the *kresy* after the uprising against the tsarist regime in 1863, and others immigrated from Prussia. Many purchased old homes and refurbished them, while others built new palaces and villas.[20] These affluent Poles became active participants in Kraków's cultural life, both the traditional culture grounded in Catholicism and the new trappings of modernity that were transforming the city's landscape.

Larry Wolff finds that a sort of "cultural generational conflict"[21] was an important feature of life in Kraków at this time. His research on the response of the Kraków press to the September 1898 assassination in Geneva, Switzerland, of Austrian Empress Elisabeth finds that the conservative daily *Czas* (Time) was particularly vocal in its outrage. The actual assassin was Luigi Lucheni, an Italian anarchist, but *Czas* interpreted the killing "in terms of a cosmic struggle between Satanic and Christian principles, with nothing less than civilization itself at stake."[22] Despite their different perspectives, "the rival generations of fin-de-siècle Cracow, from the perspectives of decadent poetry and of conservative piety, acknowledged the same spiritual crisis" that many believed had led to the murder.[23]

It was in the midst of this manic milieu that Koneczny nurtured his reverence for Polish tradition in the face of perceived cultural threats—in the form of influences from alien civilizations or the cultural avant-garde—that fueled his imagination.[24] As a theater critic, Koneczny was at odds with modernism, with its "so-called symbolism."[25] He was especially critical of the "decadent" dramatist Stanisław Przybyszewski (1868–1927), claiming that there were no new ideas in his work. Rather, it seemed to be all form and no content.[26] He was not sympathetic to the decadents and their credo of "art for art's sake," pointing out that Polish artists had traditionally served a civic function.[27] Koneczny believed that historians also performed a sort of "public civic service" in Poland by clarifying the past as a means toward paving a path to the future.[28] Koneczny's search for authenticity in theatrical productions later appears as a key motivation for much of his thinking on civilizational issues.[29] His emphasis on the critic's responsibility to "truth" points to its later inclusion in his so-called quincunx of existential values.[30]

As Koneczny later recalled, Kraków in the first years of the new century was transforming not only culturally, but also materially.[31] There were dynamic tensions within the city between preserving its medieval traditions and the imperative to develop the technological infrastructure expected of a modern urban center. The first phase of restoration work on Wawel Castle—the medieval residence of Polish kings—was conducted from 1905 to 1914.[32] Yet this was also the time during which the city expanded its borders to incorporate neighboring towns and suburbs, becoming "Greater Kraków." As a result of this expansion, the population of Kraków increased significantly during Koneczny's youth, from about 55,000 in 1869[33] to 91,323 in 1900.[34] By 1910 the population was a little over 150,000.[35] In addition, the introduction of running water and street cars, electricity, and streetlights, along with other technological improvements, heralded a turning point in the city's history.[36] Interestingly, Nathaniel D. Wood finds that

> [i]n the popular imagination, Cracow was rhetorically positioned along an axis of civilization with "Europe" or "the West" at one pole and "Asiatic" backwardness at the other. Cracovians were confident that they belonged in the West but in the realm of urban infrastructure at least often feared that they were not yet fully there. . . . For many Cracovians, then, "Europe" represented modernity and progress.[37]

This tension between East and West is at the heart of Koneczny's theory about the inevitable "clash of civilizations." While this concept has become widely associated with the work of American political scientist Samuel Huntington (1927–2008), it was articulated sixty years earlier by Koneczny. Moreover, Koneczny developed a whole philosophy of history around this notion, as opposed to Huntington's more limited concern with the geopolitics of the post-Soviet era. This is indicative of Koneczny's concern with historicism, which implies a deep understanding of one's place in history that empowers one to engage in the present world and plan for future generations. He claimed that this heightened sense of historical awareness is uniquely developed in Latin civilization, allowing for the flowering of what he termed a "culture of action." As I. A. Vasilenko noted in 2000, many scholars continue to "proclaim Western culture to be unique, disregarding the cultural pluralism of contemporary societies."[38]

Early in his career, Koneczny's academic work was funded by the Polish Academy of Sciences. Most notably, from January to August 1890 he was a member of a research team that traveled to Italy. He primarily conducted his research in Vatican archives in Rome, but he also visited Florence and Venice, with a short stay in Paris, before returning home to Poland. Beginning in 1897 he worked as a librarian at Jagiellonian University in Kraków, and in 1900 he was appointed director of the manuscript division. Despite these duties, Koneczny found time to pursue an active publishing agenda. During his long career he published twenty-six major monographs and over three hundred articles and other shorter pieces.[39] Koneczny also wrote popular histories and gave public lectures, since he believed Poles had a weak understanding of their past. He undoubtedly sought to heighten their historical awareness, which in his thinking is a key feature of a thriving society.[40]

From 1905 to 1914, Koneczny also edited *Świat Słowiański* (Slavic World), which was a journal published by the Slavic Club (founded in 1901) in Kraków. Although the club had few members and was subjected to criticism in the socialist and *endek* (nationalist) presses, the journal exerted influence beyond Galicia.[41] Koneczny was an active player in the club, which initially possessed a Slavophile orientation and was rather anti-German in tone. According to Koneczny biographer Piotr Biliński, this was out of line with the attitudes of most Galician Poles, who preferred cooperating with Vienna rather than with Moscow.[42] Koneczny had already shown a concern about German ambitions in his *Dzieje Polski za Jagiellonów* (The History of Jagiellonian Poland, 1903). In this monograph, Koneczny depicted Jews as bringing German influence into Polish cities.[43] This was later viewed as a sort of "double negative," and a joint Jewish-German "conspiracy" against Poland appeared in a robust form later in Koneczny's posthumously published *Cywilizacja bizantyńska* (Byzantine Civilization, 1973) and *Cywilizacja żydowska* (Jewish Civilization, 1974).

Koneczny spent the war years (1914–18) in Kraków, but from 1919 to 1929 he taught history at Stefan Batory University in Vilnius (Wilno).[44] Selim Chazbijewicz jokes that during this time Koneczny's personal life was "in a word, monotonous. From work he came home, ate dinner, and wrote or read."[45] Koneczny taught courses related to Eastern Europe, medieval Russia, and the science of civilizations (a specific course on the "Science of Civilization" was offered first in 1925–26). Compared to those taught by other historians, Koneczny's courses suffered from low enrollments.[46] But contrary to Chazbijewicz's generalization, Koneczny also became active in public affairs; for example, he was an early advocate for the incorporation of Vilnius into Poland.[47] Life on the Polish frontier also helped shape Koneczny's views on the impracticality of cultural diffusion and the "synthesis" of civilizations.[48] He later recalled his transformative experience in cosmopolitan Vilnius in *Plurality of Civilisations* (1935): "I owe much to my ten-year stay in Vilno [Vilnius], whose narrow streets may be said to be full of broad problems of universal history."[49]

Koneczny's ideas were deeply influenced by the fate of Poland. Zbigniew Pucek notes that Koneczny's whole life was framed by national traumas: he was born shortly before the failed November Uprising of 1863 and died four years after the conclusion of World War II.[50] He came of age during troubled times: partitioned by three empires, Poland had long ceased to exist as an independent *state*. Yet Poles continued to cherish their *nation* in the form of a shared culture, which was defined in various ways. As Andrzej Bokiej explains, "[t]he basis of a nation is thus not in the conception of the state, but society. Thus it is possible for a nation to exist without a state, as it was in the history of Poland" during the period of partitions.[51] His emphasis on the primacy of the nation, rather than the state, is likely a product of Koneczny's experience as a stateless Pole. Moreover, Koneczny's foundational work on his science of civilizations was undertaken during a peculiar time of revolution and war that engendered great cultural anxiety.[52]

After his retirement from teaching in 1929, Koneczny returned to his hometown. He continued his work on the science of civilizations, and it was during this period that his major theoretical treatises were published. As he struggled to continue his work during World War II, part of his home in Kraków was occupied by the Germans, who had invaded Poland.[53] For Koneczny, this represented another period of domination of Poland by a "civilizational other." And after the war, Koneczny was confronted with a third colonial experience, this time in the form of the Soviet-imposed Polish People's Republic. In response, Koneczny developed a theory that explains and essentializes characteristics of various civilizations, with a particular emphasis on preserving the integrity of Poland's "civilizational ecosystem."[54] In the process, Koneczny explained Poland's special role in world history as a defender of "Latin" civilization in confrontations with occupiers from other worlds.

CULTURAL CRISIS AND THE SEARCH FOR ORDER

Scholars have identified a broader "crisis of culture"[55] endured by European intellectuals at the turn of the nineteenth and twentieth centuries. This entailed doubts about the system of values and the possibility of finding an absolute truth. The fin-de-siècle was also the period of "Young Poland," an era in which modernism and neoromanticism mingled in a creative atmosphere in such cities as Koneczny's Kraków. Sonia Bukowska has demonstrated that Polish neoromantic and neomessianic trends had an impact on Koneczny. As a result, he developed an axiological vision of a "historical mission" for Poland.[56] This is evident in his early (1897) discussion of the role of "Providence" (*Opatrzność*) in Polish history.[57] And in his later works he became more explicit in his vision of Polish exceptionalism.

Artists and intellectuals of Young Poland evinced a crisis of values in their works, and Koneczny's science of civilizations can be viewed as a response to the cultural uncertainty and questioning of traditional values. His attempt to impose order on history can be understood as a reaction to the intellectual and sociopolitical challenges of his time; this also helps us understand his popularity among contemporary Catholic fundamentalists.[58] Most important, Koneczny developed several key concepts that are central to his science of civilizations. His early theoretical works refer to the concepts of *logos* (theory) and *ethos* (practice).[59] In Koneczny's scheme "*logos* is a thought, an opinion, an idea, a conception. But *ethos* is the practical side of life."[60] Harmony between *logos* and *ethos*, between thought and action, is not constant, but it is required for a civilization to make progress.[61]

Koneczny also conceptualized the "quincunx of existential values" or "categories of being," which explain the innermost essence of each civilization: Health, Prosperity, Truth, Goodness, and Beauty. The first two categories belong to the "material world," while the next two belong to the "spiritual world"; the final, Beauty, belongs to both worlds. These categories refer to areas of human existence that Koneczny analyzed in great detail. The category of Goodness, for example, is associated with morality and ethics.[62] According to Koneczny, ethical considerations (rather than any bureaucratic imperative) provide the foundation for just laws.[63] He also asserted that a society "cannot have progress

without ethical progress"; without ethics a society would sink into "an acul-
tured state."[64] The categories of the quincunx have ancient origins; Koneczny
explained that the nations of Latin civilization share the ideals of Truth, Goodness, and Beauty that were adopted by Catholicism from classical culture.[65]

The quincunx of existential values validated Koneczny's Catholicism in
comparison with other ethical and moral systems. In a world of grays, with
people assuming multiple identities, he sought black-and-white clarity through
civilizational purification. He believed in a plurality of civilizations, each with
radically different value systems that developed over time. But he asserted that
Latin civilization, grounded in Catholic fundamentalism, was the highest human achievement. As such, it should be protected, purified, and preserved
against alien influences and the challenges of modernity.

Koneczny's science of civilizations was formulated in its full form during the
interwar period (1919–39). Despite Polish diplomatic and military successes
that led to the rebirth of the Polish national state in 1918, this period was a
time of great cultural anxiety. Koneczny evidently projected his fears regarding
Poland's fate onto the pages of world history. Civilizationally superior Poland
had been militarily conquered by civilizationally inferior Germany, Austria,
and Russia, and Koneczny's theories are infused with a critique of the lingering impact of Poland's colonial past. Koneczny saw threats everywhere: To the
east, there was "Turanian" Russia. To the west, there was "Byzantine" Germany.
Finally, there was the danger within, represented by the "flowering in Poland
of Jewish civilization."[66] These three civilizations threatened the existence of
"Christian-classical [Latin] civilization, represented in independent Poland by
Catholicism."[67]

Koneczny professed scholarly objectivity, but it is clear that he was also concerned with guarding Latin civilization against the dangers of other civilizations that might dilute its purity.[68] By the end of the nineteenth century, some
Poles had already developed a chauvinistic version of nationalism that taught
them "to hate"[69] the imagined cultural or civilizational "other." Koneczny contributed to this trend by blaming all crises that befell Poland and the West on
the dangers of civilizational mixing. Civilizational foes had conspired to destroy
the Polish *state*. The Polish *nation* only managed to survive by maintaining its
civilizational integrity. Koneczny strove to warn Poles about the continued civilizational threats, and also to offer a solution to this problem: the salvation of
Europe depended on its "return to a pure Latin civilization."[70]

Much of Koneczny's analysis reflects his reading of the Polish situation
within a broader temporal and spatial context. He commented on how artificial
any "nation" would be in some regions of Asia or Africa that are governed together only as a result of European imperialism. In this fashion, Koneczny anticipated postcolonial critiques of imperialism.[71] A tendency to theorize based
on the Polish experience can also be seen in his discussion of how an "inferior
order" can militarily defeat and colonize a higher civilization.[72]

However, the peculiar "dialectic of *colonizing and being colonized at the same time* that is characteristic of Poland"[73] also merits further attention. During the partition period (1795–1918), Polish nationalists could chafe at Poland's domination by "Asiatic" Russia, while simultaneously embracing Poland's messianic mission to spread civilization to the East.[74] Koneczny added a new twist: he created an Orientalist discourse of dominance that explained Poland's civilizational superiority, even during its occupation by more powerful neighbors. In his vision, Poland is the shining exemplar of "Latin" civilization in its struggle against other, inferior, and "Orientalized" civilizations that he defines and categorizes in his science of civilizations. As Paweł Skrzydlewski puts it, "[t]he only civilization of the West is Latin, while the others—although existing on European soil—have oriental origins."[75]

Koneczny's civilizational theories were emerging just as Poland regained its independence in the shadows of Russian Bolshevism and fascism in Italy and Germany. These alternative political systems were seen by Koneczny as alien to Latin civilization and its values, and his writings contain more than a bit of fear-mongering about their threat to Polish society. His search for "historical laws" and "order in history" can be viewed as part of a larger search for order and certainty at a time and place in which there was great anxiety. Thus, in Koneczny's thought we see a reflection of the Christian solidarism espoused in important papal encyclicals of the late nineteenth century (especially Leo XIII's *Rerum novarum* of 1891).[76] It also seems that Koneczny sought to "essentialize" various cultures and civilizations in a way that freezes them in time; for example, Piotr Grabowiec asserts that for Koneczny, Polish political culture was fundamentally formed by the fifteenth century.[77]

A PLURALITY OF CIVILIZATIONS

Koneczny's most important works deal with what he termed the "plurality of civilizations." He rejected the notion of any sort of overarching "supra-civilization" to which all humanity belongs, stating that "[m]ankind does not exist either historically or sociologically."[78] Rather than a single, unswerving path of historical development for all peoples, Koneczny concluded that different civilizations have emerged over the ages. According to Anton Hilckman (1900–70), Koneczny addressed two key questions in his theoretical writings: "1) On what is this [civilizational] diversity based and in what does it consist? 2) Where does it come from and by what factors of differentiation has it been brought about?"[79] Koneczny insisted that

> [t]here never was and there cannot be a common civilizational path for all mankind, because there cannot be any universal method of system of collective life. Civilizations do not connect the peoples of Earth but

rather divide them, and they never cease to divide them. World history consists of the history of civilizations and their mutual relations.[80]

He further explained that "there exist incomplete, defective, fragmentary civilisations . . . there is a great variety of defectiveness. . . . Civilisations may be complete and incomplete, one-sided, many-sided and universal, uniform and more or less mixed, original and derivative in whole or part."[81]

Koneczny identified seven existing civilizations: Brahman, Jewish, Chinese, and Turanian were ancient, while Latin, Byzantine, and Arab civilizations emerged in the medieval period. He dedicated most of his attention to analyzing Latin, Byzantine, Turanian, and Jewish civilizations and their impact on Polish history. But Koneczny searched for historical laws to explain diversity among all civilizations. Evidently he "had no doubt that the discovery of such laws would resolve the dilemma of whether history is a science on a par with the natural sciences."[82] Koneczny generally rejected the deductive method; he claimed that he did not have a priori assumptions, but rather employed inductive reasoning in developing his historical laws.[83] Koneczny used a wide array of evidence to support his arguments. But critics have challenged the claim made by Anton Hilckman that Koneczny, "so far as it is at all possible in the field of humanities," was "a thinker without preconceived ideas."[84]

Jan Skoczyński has suggested that Koneczny's laws of history are actually "de facto laws of civilization," since they really pertain to the rules that Koneczny believes govern civilizations: their structure, their functioning, and their relations with one another.[85] They include the following: all elements of the quincunx must be commensurable; all vital civilizations seek to expand and hence they will come into conflict; inequality is a natural state; civilizational syntheses are not possible; and civilizational mixtures are unstable and harmful. But the "law of laws is that it is not possible to be civilized simultaneously in two ways."[86] As noted earlier, Koneczny believed that world history deals with the struggles among civilizations and their attempts at syntheses.[87] Sonia Bukowska explains that "this conception does not entirely exclude the possibility of one civilization adopting a feature from another, but one must also state clearly that the assimilation process can only involve secondary features."[88]

For Koneczny, any "notion of . . . a synthesis [of civilizations] is absurd."[89] State and society must be civilized in a commensurable way.[90] Commensurability is the foundational "law" of history; functional syntheses are possible only between cultures of the same civilization. This historical law holds true throughout time. Koneczny could admit, however, that elements of one civilization might enter into another.[91] Yet these doomed mixtures possess a weaker "culture of action," since they consist of elements from different civilizations and consequently violate Koneczny's fundamental historical law that it is not possible to be civilized in two ways.[92]

As Zbigniew Kuderowicz maintains, for Koneczny any laws of history that he uncovered were certainly "not laws of universal progress."[93] However,

Koneczny's rejection of universal progress did not mean that he denied the possibility of advancement within a given society or its potential vitality. A sort of "internal enrichment" could be attained by following one's civilizational values to their utmost; a society could only maximize its potential if it remained true to its traditions.[94] It is important to note, however, that according to Koneczny only Latin civilization is a "personalist" civilization that allows civil society to flourish and generate societal progress. While the other "collectivist" civilizations might excel within the limits of their systems, they would still be hamstrung by innate, systemic flaws that Koneczny pointed out in his comparative studies.

Koneczny frequently posited that "it is not possible to be civilized in two ways."[95] He asked:

> For how is it possible to look in two ways, in three ways . . . on good and evil, on beauty and ugliness, on loss and gain, on the relations of society and State, of State and Church . . . ? Down this road the only possibility is decline into an a-civilisational state, which holds within itself incapacity for a culture of action.[96]

Defined by Koneczny as an "established capacity for intelligent actions,"[97] the concept of a "culture of action" is a key to understanding his science of civilizations. In the Konecznian worldview, a culture of action can only be found in Latin civilization.[98] Piotr Grabowiec agrees that the notion of a "culture of action" is vital to understanding Koneczny, since it represents a "connection between thought, word, and action, as well as internal convictions about the correctness of one's aims. Thinking in the context of goals creates a culture of action."[99] A culture of action flourishes when there is harmony between *logos* and *ethos*: "The relation between reason and will, thought and deed constitutes humanity. In the concepts of *logos* and *ethos* Koneczny tries to prove the need of commensurability between thought and action, reason and will in all areas of human existence."[100] According to Koneczny's "law of commensurability," a lack of cohesion among the different categories of the quincunx is the main source of societal decline;[101] societies can flourish only when all categories of the quincunx are in "civilizational harmony."

The concept of the quincunx of existential values has served Koneczny and his fundamentalist interpreters as a template for judging "others." Andrzej Bokiej identifies a mix of universalism and relativism in Koneczny's civilizational scheme. The five categories of the quincunx are universal, but the specifics within each and the relative weight accorded to each vary from civilization to civilization. This allows for a scientific framework for Koneczny's categorization of civilizations, yet it opens the way for a normative approach and his judgment of civilizations as underdeveloped or defective. The quincunx has functioned as a mechanism to construct a hierarchy of values that in turn allowed Koneczny to create a hierarchy of civilizations. He crafted an ideal type

(Latin civilization) that possesses the values of the quincunx that were chosen from his peculiar perspective.[102] Koneczny's fundamental argument was that a plurality of civilizations have developed distinctly different interpretations of the existential values of the quincunx. Koneczny explained that "the rules of the quincunx of humanity are set forth . . . in exclusive reliance on historical experience and so on the inductive method—we see that the categories of life may arrange themselves in very various relations, orders and proportions."[103]

Koneczny's concept of civilizational pluralism also allows for a multiplicity of interactive *cultures* within a given civilization. We find this in Latin civilization in the form of different national cultures. Latin civilization is unique, in that other civilizations do not produce *national* cultures, and they do not nurture "unity in plurality." Rather, the dictum of "unity in uniformity"—as in Byzantine civilization, which stifles societal diversity—is evident elsewhere.[104] Koneczny was skeptical of the concept of cultural diffusion across *civilizational* boundaries. Rather than the possibility of a synthesis of civilizations, Koneczny could only envision a healthy and mutually beneficial exchange between cultures of the same civilization.[105] Dismissing the possibility of a universal culture for all of humanity, he has provided fodder for contemporary Polish critics of globalization.

THE KONECZNIAN COMPARATIVE FRAMEWORK

Koneczny professed a desire to move the comparative study of civilizations from a chaotic approach to a scientific methodology. He warned against "mixing science of civilisation with history of civilisation. When there is talk of the history of civilisation it is necessary to ask which, for every civilisation has its separate history, whereas the science of civilisation must be concerned with all civilisations."[106] Koneczny's rejection of an overarching unifying civilization seems enlightened in one sense, since it called into question the assumption that "there is really only one civilisation, the so-called European, others representing only lower levels of the one, which is in any case spreading over the world. . . . Only the rungs leading to Europeanisation are seen, and the same point of view is applied in research into the past."[107] Koneczny conceded that "[i]t is not easy to get rid of learned superstitions" and that he might very well be criticized on this point.[108]

Koneczny also rejected the idea that older civilizations are more advanced than younger ones, as well as Oswald Spengler's (1880–1936) conception of the inevitable death of a civilization. He believed that there were ancient civilizations that were still robust and, in the case of the Jewish one, still a "threat" to the Latin world. Koneczny's position also allows for a civilizationally superior "Latin" Poland (which emerged in medieval times) in comparison to Jewish civilization, which was ancient.[109] In an attack on Spengler, Koneczny opined that there was no

> greater absurdity than the doctrine of the fall of civilisations as a result
> of old age: the Jewish and Chinese go on. The introduction into history
> of a biological point of view is a very gross philosophical error. . . . No
> civilisation need either decline or die of old age, but it may *poison itself
> with a mixture of civilisations* at any time.[110]

He noted that Poles had witnessed the collapse of the tsarist regime in Russia, and that had nothing to do with old age; he stated explicitly that the "biological view of history is mistaken."[111] This allowed for an optimistic outlook for the future of Poland, but only if it could preserve its civilizational integrity.[112]

Undoubtedly in response to Spengler and other theorists whose pessimistic visions foretold the inevitable "death" of civilizations, Koneczny provided room for adaptation in his system. He stated that "everything which is living is changing, and so civilisation is neither a brittle bone nor an immobile clod."[113] He posited that there are both "quantitative" changes related to the "levels through which every civilization passes," and "qualitative" changes in a civilization that represented "something quite different."[114] Progressive qualitative changes are "born naturally of the vital force of the civilisation," while regressive qualitative changes are the result of "influences of foreign civilisations."[115]

Koneczny identified a series of contrasting features that exemplify the persistent differences among the various civilizations. They include organic versus mechanistic organization of societies; a posteriori versus a priori modes of thinking; historicism versus improvisational meditation; societal unity that allows for diversity versus forced uniformity; and personalism versus collectivism. These reflect a hierarchy of values, with the first in each pair deemed superior. Koneczny concluded that all of world history "comprises the occilation between the two series of fundamental concepts."[116] The differences manifest themselves in a series of opposite values; for example, personalism is associated with freedom and a high degree of ethical behavior, and collectivism with brute force and a lack of ethics. Koneczny maintained that "[a]n association based on personalism constitutes an organism; those based on collectivism are mechanisms."[117] He identified two main types of civilizations: collective civilizations that share many features, most notably the insistence on forced conformity and the consequent stagnation of social life; and the personalist civilization that features people freely conforming to social conventions in ways that facilitate lively societal development. Only the Latin civilization is personalist.[118]

In his critique of other civilizations (which were all deemed to be "Oriental" in origin), Koneczny consistently dichotomized differences between them and Latin civilization. In a letter from 1935, Koneczny discussed how his recent book (*The Plurality of Civilisations*) was merely the latest in a long series of his works dealing with the East-West civilizational divide.[119] Along the way, he developed what Edward Said (1935–2003) called the "Orientalist vision," confirming "the Orient in his readers' eyes."[120] Other Polish historians were also writing critically about "the Orient." As Mirosław Filipowicz notes, during the second half of the nineteenth century an "Occidentalist tendency" dominated Polish historiography. For this school of thought, "the model and criterium of civilizational development was the West," and Poland was on the frontier of this experience.[121] A romantic and messianic view of Poland as the outpost of Western (Latin) civilization was certainly not unique to Koneczny.[122]

Nor was Koneczny out of step with contemporary historians when he concluded that "Byzantinism emerged from a mixture of the Orient and the ancient Roman civilization."[123] In his analyses of the relationship between Latin and Byzantine civilizations, Koneczny emphasized fundamental and unbridgeable differences, going well beyond the rift between Catholicism and Orthodoxy that was formalized in 1054.[124] He stressed that "not only was there a [religious] schism between Rome and Byzantium, but entirely different views on collective life, or differences of civilization."[125] In Koneczny's judgment, for example, the "Byzantine conception of the state is extremely totalitarian."[126] Koneczny dismissed the idea that Byzantine civilization represented a continuation of the Roman world in its basic values; rather, it had rejected the best of Rome. While Latin civilization nurtured the core virtues of the old Roman Republic, the Byzantine Empire embodied the worst features of an Orientalized Roman world.

Koneczny's Orientalist analysis of Russia was not unusual, either. Polish historians of the nineteenth and twentieth centuries displayed a broad interest in Russia, in part because there were frequent contacts and conflicts between the neighboring countries. Russia also figured prominently in Polish discussions about Poland's relationship with Europe and its place within Slavic culture.[127] Polish intellectuals frequently regarded Russia as their "Oriental Other," simultaneously situating themselves favorably along what Attila Melegh calls the East-West "civilizational slope."[128] This Orientalist discourse depicted Russia as less "western" and therefore culturally inferior. Writing in 1928, Koneczny concluded that "[g]eographically we [Poles] cannot stop being between East and West—but civilizationally it is not possible at all to be between East and West. . . . In the desire for an East-West civilizational synthesis is hidden for Poland cultural and political nothingness."[129]

Historical studies that engage in "East-West" comparisons are fraught with methodological pitfalls. As Jörn Rüsen points out, theories of cultural differences have "a dangerous tendency to essentialize or even reify the single cultures concerned."[130] Attila Melegh adds that "Othering structures" are devised by those engaged "in the fight for fixing borders on the slippery civilizational scale, especially by those who see this as a last resort to achieve a higher position in the imaginary of the world."[131] In the late nineteenth and early twentieth centuries, some Polish historians writing on Russia certainly fell into the "trap of dichotomies" described by Syed Farid Alatas, who finds that such Eurocentrism in the humanities and social sciences leads to "the essentializing and stereotyping of whole societies."[132] Feliks Koneczny's theorizing about Russia as Poland's "civilizational Other" illustrates these kinds of trends in the Polish context.

The roots of this cultural tension extend far back in time. According to Jiří Vykoukal, we need to look back at the second half of the fifteenth century, when post-Mongol Muscovy and the Polish-Lithuanian state were rivals in Eastern Europe. Muscovy's "gathering of the Russian lands" meant regaining lands of old Rus' that were provisionally under Polish-Lithuanian control. Vykoukal finds that this "struggle over territory established one of the major fields where the core of the Polish view of Russia was forged."[133] He contends that since the lands of the old Rus' state were

> located on the crossroads between "Europe" (Polish-Lithuanian Union) and the "East" ("Russia"), then "Russia" was interpreted as something located on the crossroads between the "East" and "Orient." . . . The fact that Russia could not be placed within a purely "European" or "Oriental" context made defining it problematic.[134]

The partitions of the late eighteenth century added a crucial new element to the discussion, as the Poles became colonized by the Russians. The need to explain how the colonizers were on a "lower civilizational level"[135] than the colonized encouraged Polish stereotyping of the East-West/Asia-Europe divide between the two countries. Religion also remained an important factor, as the independent predominantly Catholic Polish state was devoured in part by Protestant Prussia and Orthodox Russia.[136]

By the mid-nineteenth century, the "Occidentalist tendency" that stressed Poland's connections with West European culture dominated Polish historiography.[137] Building on the older messianic tradition of Poland as the "bulwark of Christendom" against the Tatars and Turks, Polish intellectuals now saw Poland as a shining beacon of Western culture and freedom on the civilizational frontier with Russia, along the dividing line between civilization and barbarism.[138] Polish historians frequently manifested elements of Orientalism in their emphasis on East/West dichotomies, with "the East" representing "a metaphysical evil and symbol of menace for their culture."[139] As Maria Janion has noted, Poles' self-identification as "true Latins, Catholics, Mediterranean Europeans" connoted a desire to situate themselves as civilizationally higher than Russians by eliminating any notions of common cultural traditions from Polish historical discourse.[140]

Polish scholars who sought to demonstrate a civilizational divide between East and West, between Russia and Poland, fit Jean-François Bayart's description of "culturalists, who claim to preserve the original purity of their identity from external pollution and the aggressions of the Other, if need be by reconstituting, in an authoritarian manner, 'their' culture."[141] Many Polish historians constructed binaries that essentialized Russians and Poles as belonging to different worlds. Bronisław Trentkowski (1808–69), for example, placed Polish-Russian relations within a larger "struggle of Europeanism and Asianism."[142] Others, such as Franciszek Duchiński (1816–93), engaged in a process of "deslavization" of Russians. Duchiński differentiated between Aryan Poles and Turanian Russians, so that the "Polish struggle for freedom became a fragment of a broader civilizational struggle" that imagined in racial terms "the higher Aryan and lower Turanian."[143] Wincenty Lutosławski (1863–1954) later also categorized Russians as neither Aryan nor Slavic, but savage Turanians. In this view, the Polish-Russian conflict becomes more than a political clash pitting freedom-loving Poles against autocratic Russia, but a biological struggle between two separate races.[144]

Koneczny's theories fit within this broader trend in Polish historiography of creating binary divisions between Poles and Russians. Like Duchiński, he labeled Russians as part of "Turanian civilization." However, Koneczny grounded his theories in civilizational distinctions that, while immutable, were not predicated on racial differences. Koneczny's concerns with purity led him to argue that "between civilizations a synthesis is not possible ... there are only poisonous mixtures,"[145] but he and his intellectual heirs have taken great pains to separate his worldview from biological racism.[146] Instead, Koneczny substituted the concept of "civilization" for "race."

Other Poles also believed that insoluble "civilizational differences" between Poles and Russians complicated Polish-Russian relations. Kraków historian Józef Szujski (1835–83) thought that "the cultural conflict of East and West was 'one of the fundamental certainties of history.' "[147] He saw no hope of accommodating European features with Russia, implying that there could be no mixing of cultures; he was apparently "convinced that the civilizations of the East and West are mutually exclusive."[148] Warsaw historian Władysław Smoleński (1851–1926) also saw a sharp East-West divide, and believed it was Poland's duty to prevent other Slavs from falling under eastern influences. His writings discussed the alleged "inferiority" of Russian culture. Smoleński posited that Russia and Poland will always be in conflict as representatives of "Eastern civilization" and the "Latin West."[149] The new Bolshevik threat, especially during and after the Polish-Soviet War (1919–21), intensified negative views of Russia. Jan Kucharzewski (1876–1952) saw a heavy Mongol impact on Russian history, assigning undesirable traits to eastern influences. He is best known for his work *From White to Red Tsarism*, which posited a great deal of continuity between tsarist Russia and the Soviet Union. Bogumił Jasinowski (1883–1969) also discussed the East and West as "two separate antithetical civilizations."[150]

Koneczny's own analysis of the Soviet Union was also harshly critical, especially after World War II. He rejected communism; while he conceded that "there is also a struggle for material existence in history,"[151] he remained adamant in his demand for the primacy of ethics and consistently emphasized morality as an essential part of our lives. Koneczny's contention that inequality is a natural state for humankind also helps explain his rejection of communism, not only the bastardized Soviet version but also even the notion of some sort of primitive communism in human history. Koneczny believed that "[f]rom the very beginning private property existed; there never was communism anywhere."[152] Any attempt at forced equality, as in the Soviet Union, would lead to stagnation.[153] Koneczny asserted that "[t]he historical progress of man begins not with communism and equality, but with property and hierarchy."[154] He claimed that "[t]he more highly developed the community, the more complicated the social set-up, the more marked the differences between the various systems of community life—and here is the source of the plurality of civilisations."[155]

CATHOLIC FUNDAMENTALISM

Polish intellectuals of the interwar period often discussed Soviet-Polish relations within a framework of civilizational differences and antagonisms.[156] For many nationalists, the "re-Catholicization of Europe" was an urgent task, with Poland renewing its historical role as the "bulwark of Christendom" against Bolshevik Russia. Koneczny gave Catholicized Poland a special place in his scheme, which is one reason for his renewed popularity in recent decades in some circles. In response to various totalitarian ideologies, Koneczny demanded "only one totalism, namely total ethics" founded on Catholic values in both private and public life.[157] "Catholic totalism" emerged during the 1930s as a popular theme, especially among the younger generation of nationalist activists who sought alternatives to socialism, liberalism, or "pagan" fascism.[158] A focus on culture is plainly evidenced by the rhetoric of commentators like Tadeusz Gluziński, who lamented that "our civilization is poisoned."[159] Increasingly, cultural cleansing was recommended during the interwar period as a remedy for societal ills in multicultural Poland. Although Koneczny's focus on empowering civil society fits well within a liberal democracy, he and his followers also have rejected the "moral neutrality"[160] and cultural pluralism that are often viewed as corollary features. In the context of twenty-first-century politics, this means that the state should not pass laws—such as those related to euthanasia or reproductive rights—that violate Catholic ethics.[161]

Nevertheless, Koneczny's followers have pointed to the "progressive" nature of his theories. For example, he disagreed with the racialist arguments of his day. Koneczny's rejection of race theory in its most explicit form was connected to his resentment of the hegemony of German scholarship. He complained that "the hierarchy of races assumed a dominating position in German science, which finally decided in the name of race to attach leadership in civilisation to Prussia."[162] In place of a German biological theory of race, Koneczny constructed a civilizational theory that privileged the very cultural traits that were evident in Poland and deemed to be at the heart of Latin civilization. Koneczny also directly critiqued Oswald Spengler; he debunked Spengler's predictions that Prussia would "assume hegemony of the world."[163] He ridiculed Spengler's use of what he termed a "theory of cycles" used by earlier theorists, such as Georg Wilhelm Friedrich Hegel (1770–1831), labeling it "an old error in new garments."[164]

As I stated in the preface to this book, I am using the terms "civilizational fundamentalism" and "Konecznian fundamentalism" to refer to Koneczny's ideology, since he advocated a return to the roots of a Polish national culture that is grounded in Latin civilization. But it is important to remember the central role of Catholicism in his worldview. Discussing the reborn Polish state, Koneczny urged Poles to recognize the indispensability of Catholic ethics and morality, which are at the heart of Latin civilization: "Our aim is to introduce morality into politics, to all politics, both internal and external, national and international."[165] Writing in 1938, Koneczny warned against "degeneration" in "art and all areas of life" unless civilizational purity were attained.[166]

During World War II, Koneczny provided a civilizational interpretation of the catastrophic developments. He completed *Państwo w cywilizacji łacińskiej* (The State in Latin Civilization) in October 1941, during the German occupation of Kraków.[167] Koneczny introduced his book by blaming all crises in Europe at that time on civilizational mixing and calling for "a return to a pure Latin civilization [as] a condition for the rebirth of Europe."[168] Not only was "the independence of Poland . . . only possible in Latin civilization," but Koneczny believed that the "rebirth of Latin civilization would be the best guarantee for the future of Poland and Europe."[169] The core problem in Europe was that three civilizations—Latin, Byzantine, and Jewish—were struggling for domination, and a fourth (Turanian) was also present in Eastern Europe. Koneczny urged that "European states must return decisively to Latin civilization."[170]

An unfettered mixing of various civilizations represented a "civilizational chaos" that had led Europe into "an acivilized state." Civilizational purity was the solution to Europe's problems, and for Koneczny it was "a question of life and death for European nations."[171] Koneczny warned that in Russia civilizational mixing "ended in nihilism and Bolshevism, in Poland in Piłsudskism, in Germany in Hitlerism. . . . All of Europe has been sick for a long time from a civilizational mixture; thus in all of Europe civilization has fallen."[172] A morbid fear of "stagnation" and "moral apathy," the sort of ethical chaos labeled as a "babel of ethics," is evident in Koneczny's pleas for civilizational purity.[173] Even during the war, Koneczny was seemingly still worried about Jewish influence on ethics, adamantly insisting that while "the ethic of our civilization is . . . religious," it is "not sacral, as Brahmanic or Jewish."[174] Koneczny's rhetoric reflects a fear of moral relativism,[175] which is still evident in civilizational fundamentalism today.

Despite his evaluation of "sacral" civilizations as defective in their one-sidedness, Koneczny still assigned a fundamental role for religion in his civilizational scheme. To ensure a return of ethics to politics in Poland after World War II, he even demanded that "[t]he state and the Decalog have to be in agreement!"[176] In Koneczny's worldview, Latin civilization was inextricably linked with the personalism that derived from Catholicism.[177] He also believed that "the more precisely and deeply we ponder Polish matters of the past, present, and future, the more we are convinced that Polishness and Catholicism are one."[178]

In the last years of his life, Koneczny clung to "the three great pillars of our [Polish] existence . . . Catholicism, Latin civilization, and Polishness."[179] They provided continuity, as well as purpose for a culture of action. He envisioned "Catholic totalism," in which "[t]he state must be dominated by ethics,"[180] and declared: "We want total ethics!"[181] He called for Catholic ethics to be the foundation for all aspects of life in Poland;[182] writing in 1947, Koneczny claimed that in this vision "each step of life, whether private or public, is based on Christian morality. Morality is foremost in all our thoughts and actions!"[183] Even economic policies should be grounded in Catholic doctrine, so that the "struggle for material existence will agree with ethics."[184]

POLAND'S ROLE IN WORLD HISTORY

Throughout his seminal work *Polskie logos a ethos* (Polish Logos and Ethos, 1921), Koneczny emphasized that one of his motivations for writing the book was to discuss Poland's importance in world history. Koneczny's dualistic system contains a series of opposing values, by which other civilizations are presented as inferior to Latin civilization. This whole system of binaries is related to the civilizational contrast between East and West; in this way, Koneczny "Orientalized" the other civilizations in contrast to Latin (western) civilization. He especially highlighted the special role of Polish Catholicism in his binary worldview. During the interwar period, he characterized Europe as "presently belonging to two civilizational camps: Christian and anti-Christian."[185] Koneczny also believed that the whole world was divided into "two civilizational groups: ours and foreign, that is Latin and all other civilizations."[186] Polishness could only be perfected within Latin civilization: hence, his call for its preservation. He maintained that "[c]ivilizational unity is the only way to the development of culture and a cultured state."[187] This vision exemplifies the sort of worldview described by Klaus Müller as

> composed of two antagonistic spheres: the endosphere of one's own world, the only sphere in which human existence appears as ideally realized, is surrounded by an outer-worldly exosphere, which represents the former's negative counterimage and is accordingly ruled by pernicous, destructive forces. This point of view allows for comparison only insofar as it serves the demonstration of one's own uniqueness; it thus tends to amount to "constructed dissimiliarity."[188]

Poland's geographical position between East and West has long influenced Polish ideas concerning civilizational differences, with the result that a sort of dualistic conception of civilization has emerged.[189] This phenomenon is evident in the Konecznian paradigm, in which Latin civilization is confronted by lesser "Oriental" civilizations. Koneczny contributed to the scholarly foundation for a Polish "ideology of identity," which Müller argues has "the tendency to render one's own sense of self-worth absolute."[190] Krystyna Kurowska asserts that for Koneczny "the question of the determination of the historical aims and problems of the Polish nation was more important than the idea of the unity of humanity."[191] She adds that for Koneczny the main aim for the Polish nation was "the defense of the purity of Latin civilization."[192] Koneczny explicitly discussed this task in relation to Poland's geographical location at the crossroads of various civilizations that are vying for control.[193]

But while Koneczny advocated "simple cultural expansion" as part of Poland's defense of Latin civilization, he rejected *political plans* for eastward expansion related to a "civilizational mission" as "absurd."[194] Koneczny's "law on expansion" states that healthy civilizations expand their influence at the expense of others, either physically through force or (more likely) spiritually and peacefully through the spread of ideas. The civilizational struggles that Koneczny perceived are mainly moral and ethical conflicts. Since a lack of expansion for a civilization was the result of a lack of "internal commensurability" or "internal harmony," we can perhaps better understand Koneczny's concern for civilizational purity and harmony. They were needed in order to avoid an "acivilized" condition; in other words, they were needed for progress and expansion. This all seems to derive from Koneczny's historical context and his perceived need to purge Poland of foreign elements in order to ensure internal cohesion.

According to Koneczny, the expansion of civilizations does not directly affect a whole civilization, but only those parts that are in direct contact with one another. This places a special burden on such border regions as Poland, where the responsibility to preserve civilizational purity is greater.[195] But in this Darwinian "struggle for existence," there seems to be no place for peaceful and healthy coexistence.[196] Sometimes two civilizations meet and exert influence in the same region, but they do not create a viable mixture. For example, there are elements of Byzantine and Latin civilizations in Germany, but they are in conflict for dominance.[197] Moreover, Koneczny held that lower civilizations generally emerge victorious in confrontations with higher civilizations. In the European context, this meant that Latin civilization required the most maintenance and was more fragile in comparison with its rivals.[198] Constant "civilizational vigilance" was required to ensure the purity and survival of Latin civilization in Poland.

But how could Koneczny have crafted a triumphalist theory of civilizations? His Poland had just emerged from a stateless existence, and during the interwar period he perceived constant civilizational threats to Latin Poland. Although

Latin civilization was allegedly superior in its values, one of its shining examples (Poland) had succumbed in its not-so-distant past to domination by non-Latin powers. This helps explain Koneczny's "law" that "higher" civilizations are prone to destruction by "lower" civilizations. Latin Poland was better than its neighbors, but this did not translate into military power. Koneczny had to recognize a plurality of civilizations as a reality in order to understand Poland's differences from its powerful neighbors, while his science of civilizations provided a theoretical explanation for its moral and ethical superiority. Poland was deemed special; Jolanta Kolbuszewska finds that Koneczny promoted the "history of Poland as an example of 'Latin civilization in action.'"[199] In this way, he contributed to an older messianic narrative that gives Poland a unique role in defending the integrity of the Latin world in its interactions with alien civilizations.[200]

OUTLINE OF THE BOOK

In chapter 1, I examine in greater detail select Konecznian themes. Koneczny's theories derived from his life-long search for order and harmony. Alienated from the power politics of his time, which were either imposed by external powers or Polish governments that seemed bereft of integrity, Koneczny explained these problems in the context of a grand vision of world history. The world was viewed through a civilizational lens, which Koneczny used to place current events within a broader temporal context. Delving back in time, he found historical parallels that helped make sense of Poland's present and future. For Koneczny, the solution for Poland's political and societal ills was simple: be true to one's civilizational values. This civilizational fundamentalism is at the core of Koneczny's vision. Koneczny also wrote a great deal about the need for self-government and civil society. These concerns are evident in his reading of world history; he especially praised societies in which individuals were allowed to exercise their free will.

In chapter 2, I analyze the classicism and medievalism evident in Koneczny's theoretical works. He admired the Roman Republic a great deal, but he abhorred the imperial system that later was necessitated by military expansion. The late Roman world was polluted by "Oriental" influences that filtered back to Rome as conquering generals and soldiers returned home with alien civilizational values. These included notions of divine rule and etatism that were at odds with Republican practices. The late Roman Empire, and the subsequent Byzantine Empire, represented for Koneczny bastardized and Orientalized distortions of Roman civilization.

His quest for purity led Koneczny back to antiquity, back to the roots of "Latin civilization." The Roman Republic was his classical ideal, and its values provided the foundation for a new Christianized Latin civilization that emerged under the auspices of the medieval Church. It is in the Middle Ages that Koneczny found another ideal: a new Polish nation that proudly defended Latin civilizational values. Koneczny's medievalism has proven attractive to audiences today, and his adherents create idyllic images of a purely Latin Poland. They harken back to a medieval world envisioned as a harmonious and orderly place. But only through constant vigilance and adherence to one's civilizational values can one find harmony and order. Koneczny's science of civilizations posits a need for civilizational purity as the most important "law" that governs human actions.

In chapter 3, I explain the threats to Poland's civilizational purity as envisioned by Koneczny. Orientalism is a major theme in Koneczny's thought, and it is analyzed in detail in this study. This is especially evident in my analyses of his scholarship on "Byzantine civilization" and "Turanian civilization." His emphasis on the East/West divide is central to all his works, whether the focus is the Greek/Roman distinction or the modern "Oriental" threats to Poland. This is also one of the most persistent aspects of Koneczny's intellectual legacy. Especially in the civilizational fundamentalist critique of the European Union, one sees a Konecznian Orientalist imprint.

In chapter 4, I situate Koneczny's science of civilizations within the scholarly developments of his time and provide an appraisal of his intellectual legacy. While Koneczny claimed objectivity in his research methodology, it is clear that his science of civilizations provides a justification for a civilizational hierarchy that places Latin civilization at the top. It allowed Koneczny to pass judgment on other civilizations, assessing their shortcomings and defective traits in comparison to Latin civilization. Koneczny and his intellectual heirs have been able to disavow any racism in the usual sense, claiming that he rejected the significance of biological distinctions. However, what emerged in Koneczny's thought was a fixation on civilizational purity that is similar to cultural racism. While condemning biological racism, Koneczny's scholarship effectively produced argumentation that casts "civilizational others" as pathologically inferior. Moreover, he rejected any notion of healthy cultural exchanges between civilizations that might alter basic civilizational traits associated with the quincunx of existential values. This is especially evident in his analyses of "Jewish civilization," which are anti-Semitic in tone.

In chapter 5, I assess the Konecznian influence on civilizational fundamentalism in twenty-first century Poland. His religious and ethical concerns are distinctly evident in contemporary fundamentalist commentary. A devout Catholic, Koneczny was also inspired by the Thomist revival of the late nineteenth and early twentieth centuries. His quincunx of existential values spells out the relationship between matter and spirit within our lives—as individuals and as societies. A deeply religious man, he posited that "abstracts" govern history, that spirit should dominate matter, and that ethical and moral considerations should be factored into all aspects of private and public life.

Koneczny's social theory is reminiscent of French and Polish "solidarism," which sought to foster an organically cohesive society that allowed for economic expansion without the horrific costs of social and cultural dislocation. He rejected the theory and the practice of communism, but he was also mindful of papal encyclicals condemning the unfettered capitalism that fueled class tensions. Mimicking papal decrees of the late nineteenth century, Koneczny likewise called for social harmony rather than class warfare. In his opinion, however, this could only be attained through civilizational purification. This concern for purity is the foundation for Polish fundamentalist ideology today.

There are important implications of a Konecznian public policy agenda, especially in connection with the peculiar intersection of nation and gender. These are explored in chapter 6. While a Konecznian agenda has not been implemented, there have been political movements that have consistently placed their proposals within Koneczny's civilizational framework. Foremost here is the League of Polish Families (LPR), which was heavily influenced by Konecznian ideals under the guidance of the Giertych family (most notably the ideologue Maciej Giertych). The Giertychs also provide a direct link to chauvinist and intolerant politics of the interwar period, when Jędrzej Giertych (Maciej's father) helped fuse Polish nationalism with fundamentalist Catholicism. Within the ranks of the LPR and extreme variants of radical nationalism, the Konecznian vision of civilizational fundamentalism found a home.

Koneczny developed his theories within a colonial and postcolonial context; in the conclusion I provide a postcolonial reading of Koneczny that helps the reader better understand the renaissance of his ideas in post-communist Poland. His arguments have found currency among nationalists who chafe at the regulations of the European Union that seem to restrict Polish sovereignty. Civilizational fundamentalists also mimic Koneczny's postcolonial anxiety in their warnings about "threatening others" from alien civilizations. These Konecznian critics have addressed the alleged demographic threat of Muslim immigration. While Koneczny provided relatively little analysis of "Arabic civilization" or the Islamic element within "Turanian civilization," his successors have updated his theories to take this most recent civilizational threat into account. As I demonstrate throughout this book, Koneczny's science of civilizations has proven to be remarkably resilient. Its theoretical considerations continue to serve as intellectual fodder for fundamentalist and radical right-wing movements in contemporary Poland.

Chapter One

Key Konecznian Themes

CIVILIZATIONAL PURITY

Writing in August of 1920, as the Battle of Warsaw raged during the Polish-Soviet War, Koneczny voiced an explicitly messianic message. "We are striving to be joint creators of a new historical epoch,"[1] he promised. "We are striving for something greater than independence, which for us never was the final goal but rather a means to a still greater goal. We have wanted and we still want to be a sentinel among the nations of Europe, in order to [herald] the development of a new historical epoch."[2] Later, after the "miracle on the Vistula" had secured Polish independence, Koneczny wrote of a "new order in Europe":[3] a "new blossoming of Latin civilization, a new method of socio-political organization for Christendom, a new concept of universal Good for the Christian family of nations. . . . We can think only of a new organization . . . a United States of Europe."[4]

This "United States of Europe" would only function, of course, if civilizational purity were guaranteed. Koneczny stated repeatedly in his works that one cannot be civilized simultaneously in two different ways. A viable European federation could not have competing ethical or legal values, since this would lead to stagnation and an "acivilizational condition."[5] Koneczny reminded Poles of his time that the "civilizational split, the cultural discord" that led to Bolshevism was not solely a Russian problem; there were signs of this discord in Europe, too, he warned.[6] Thus, broad international cooperation was not necessarily a solution to Europe's problems. Koneczny wrote in *Plurality of Civilisations* (1935) that "[a] supra-national association is an absurdity, because of the inescapable differences in homeland and native tongue. . . . Anybody who plans a supra-national association aims at the abolition of nationality, and so at the abolition of Latin civilization."[7] By the next world war Koneczny's mood had darkened even more. Writing under Nazi occupation in Kraków during World War II, he warned that "Byzantinism, Turanianism, Bolshevism, communism—this is one series of attempts to destroy all of Latin civilization; Poland is only a step along the way."[8]

It seems that Koneczny's vision of European unity entailed a revival of the old Polish-Lithuanian commonwealth on a grander scale, reflecting his belief in a romantic sort of "Jagiellonian idea" of peoples freely joining a union.[9] It is important to remember that, in Konecznian terms, a "free federation" is a uniquely Latin concept, and not present in other civilizations. Anton Hilckman explained, for example, that "[a] political conception such as federalism was unthinkable in Byzantium; whence derives the inability, until to-day, of all Byzantium-trained peoples to see the State otherwise as a centralistic unitarist body."[10] Hilckman added that the "medieval imperial idea" is "without any doubt of Byzantine origin"; the opposite concept promoted by Koneczny, "the idea of a family of free and equal nations . . . was really Western."[11]

For a brief period, at least, Koneczny had envisioned a grand defensive alliance within Latin civilization. He hoped that "a European United States, in connection . . . with the United States of America, would be able to ensure in the twentieth century the further development of Christian-Classical civilization and ensure its security against the pressure of other civilizations."[12] He believed that Christianity as a faith could exist in any civilization, but "in practice, both historically and today [1933], Catholicism must be connected in Europe with Latin civilization, for it is also its father."[13] Koneczny especially urged Poland to strive for Central Europe to be Latin. In a veiled reference to Nazism, he noted in 1933 that once again Vienna was under pressure, since Germany's own civilizational struggle was spilling over and threatened to spread the influence of Byzantinism. The fate of Catholicism was crucial in this regard, since it provided the ethical foundation for Latin civilization.[14]

From Koneczny's perspective, the application of Christian values in international relations had been long abandoned, as evident in the eighteenth-century partitions of Poland. A new way to realize Christian universalism was needed to prevent aggression: "a unity of the nations of Latin civilization in an international union within the civilizational boundaries—for the defense and development of universal good—[was] in the opinion of Koneczny the path to a new historical epoch. It cannot be an anti-national union. It ought to be pro-civilizational, based on nations."[15] An important component of this new order would have been an acknowledgment of Catholic morality as a foundation for international relations.[16]

As Radosław Brzózka correctly points out, the moral imperative was also important for internal enrichment. For Koneczny, "the question of the development of Latin civilization [was] the key problem."[17] From a Konecznian perspective, "[t]he moral life of society [in Latin civilization] ought to be . . . dynamic . . . it ought to rely on an active struggle with evil, which is present in foreign civilizational influences."[18] But nations engaged in the struggle must be "pure." Koneczny maintained that "[a] nation must belong in its entirety [sic] without the slightest reservations to the same civilisation. . . . The will of a society ripe for the shaping of a nation cannot be divided in the direction of two civilisations."[19]

Koneczny was not alone in his calls for purity, as other nationalist commentators in the interwar period complained about civilizational poison-ing.[20] The need for civilizational purification was becoming a key part of *endek* thinking,[21] and Koneczny's theories were used as "scientific" validation. The idea of a "Catholic state of the Polish Nation" emerged as a favorite *endek* slo-gan during the interwar period as the "re-Catholicization" of Europe became the ideal, with Poland renewing its historical role as the "bulwark of Christen-dom."[22] While nationalists commonly rejected biological racism as a materialist conception, they began to absorb theories that focused on spiritual, psycho-logical, or cultural differences.[23] Koneczny's science of civilizations filled this ideological need. His civilizational hierarchy rejected "others" as inferior and dangerous to Polish culture, but not in terms of biological racism. Rather, he stressed a sort of "civilizational fundamentalism" that advocated purity in the face of threats from inferior civilizations. As Koneczny opined, "It is not race that rules, but civilization."[24]

Koneczny insisted that "[t]here never was and is not any general European civilization . . . there never was and is not any 'Aryan' race . . . however, millions are moved by this fiction that is propagated by ignoramuses."[25] He believed that "civilizational unity is the only way to the development of culture," and as early as 1921 he was warning that foreign civilizational influences would lead to so-cietal problems and the collapse of the state if allowed to flourish in Poland.[26] He proposed that "each European must . . . choose from two Christian civiliza-tions: Latin and Byzantine, and two non-Christian: Turanian and Jewish."[27] For Poles yearning for ethics in both private life and public affairs, Latin civilization was presented by Koneczny as the only sound choice.

A Konecznian worldview does not prohibit all intercivilizational relations (such as technological exchanges), as long as the interaction does not jeopar-dize civilizational purity—that is, the commensurability of the elements of the quincunx. Nor was Koneczny directly concerned with interracial relations. He stated that "civilisations may cross without any anthropological crossing at all. The whole of Europe is today [1935] a testing-ground for exactly such a mixture of civilisations. For civilisations spread by their own roads, without needing ra-cial cross-breeding to clear the way for them."[28] Koneczny endorsed a hierarchy of civilizations, rather than a hierarchy of races. But he did believe that

> [a] certain analogy does occur between races and civilisations, on the issue of crossing. Just as only branches of races which are close to one another make successful crosses, in the same way advantageous cross-ing can only take place between cultures of the same civilisation—as the whole course of history witnesses. Despite the analogy, the real differ-ence is that race need not be pure, but civilisation must be pure.[29]

Despite Koneczny's claims, it therefore seems that he borrowed some aspects of race theory. Most important, Koneczny transfered the core concept of purity to his own philosophical framework.

A KONECZNIAN "ETHOCRACY"

Societal harmony is a fundamental feature of Koneczny's vision of Poland's future, and it relates directly to his insistence on civilizational purity and the compatibility of all aspects of the quincunx.[30] This should be the case for an individual, as well as a society.[31] According to his "law of commensurability," a lack of cohesion among the different categories of the quincunx leads to a society's decline. In order for societies to flourish, all categories must be in "civilizational harmony." Koneczny believed that Poland lacked this civilizational purity.[32] The historian Jacques Semelin posits that the need to "define oneself as 'pure' in fact implies categorizing some 'other' as impure."[33] Koneczny was especially worried about the growing "intellectual influences of Jewish civilization" and the consequent "Judaization" of Polish ethical values and other aspects of Polish culture.[34]

As many scholars point out, Koneczny frequently compared different ethical sytems as part of his science of civilizations.[35] Marian Bębenek labels Koneczny "ethocentric" and concludes that his ideal society represents a sort of "ethocracy."[36] From Koneczny's perspective, the mixing of ethical systems inevitably leads to "moral chaos"[37] and impedes societal progress. Koneczny claimed that a healthy society has civilizational commensurability of all the elements in the quincunx; without this, a "sickness" develops.[38] He repeatedly associated this sickness with "foreign bodies" in "our organism," since societal health directly results from civilizational purity. Above all, he argued that a "culture of action" is stymied when a foreign ethic is introduced.[39] Decrying the mixture of civilizations in Poland that threatened to destroy it, Koneczny declared in 1928:

> It is not possible to be civilized in two ways! Who will rescue Latin civilization in Poland from such a downfall? . . . In practice it is absolutely not possible to remain civilizationally neutral in Poland. . . . And thanks to the joint religious and civilizational ties in Poland, we Poles must with all our strength support the Church. Whosoever in Poland acts against the Church, acts slavishly against Poland.[40]

As Koneczny also put it, "Without solidarity one cannot have collective action."[41]

Writing in 1930, Koneczny despaired about Poland's "fatal multitude of civilizations (Latin, Byzantine, Turanian, and Jewish). A state cannot be civilized in four ways."[42] He lamented that the struggle among the four rival civilizations in Poland had created a "bedlam of ethics."[43] Koneczny asserted that "[e]ither Latin civilization regains public life and politics, or all is lost."[44] He complained that "[c]ommon today [1936] in Europe is a type of man, civilized a little with Latin, a little with Jewish, in Germany with Byzantine, and in Poland a little with Turanian—this is in fact acivilized."[45] In Europe this had led to "ethical anarchy,"[46] which he also consistently identified as "the main sickness of Polishness" in his later writings.[47] He posited that

> [w]henever a "synthesis between West and East" has been sought in Po-
> land, the East has always emerged the victor. . . . There are no syntheses,
> but only poisonous mixtures. All Europe is now [1935] ill of the mixing
> of civilizations: here lies the cause of all "crises."[48]

Robert Piotrowski identifies in Koneczny's works three possible outcomes
for attempted civilizational syntheses: a mixture, "circular madness" (*kołobłęd*
or *obłęd kołowy*), or an acivilized condition. All three outcomes are problematic.[49] Acting as "civilizational viruses,"[50] alien civilizational influences lead to
a "pathological loss of vital powers"[51] and eventual stagnation. The societal
ills of "civilizational apathy" and "sickness of spirit" are the results of civilizational mixing and civilizational confusion.[52] This confusion can be overcome
with more attention to traditional values that are passed on from generation
to generation through education. But there is always a cost related to overcoming civilizational pollution through an "immunological process"[53] that ensures
civilizational purity and a healthy society and state. Border cultures (such as
Poland) must devote lots of energy to this civilizational struggle, which requires
a heightened identity awareness.[54]

During the interwar period, Koneczny was persistently searching for "the
path to a better future. This does not relate to any sort of new party. This concerns something greater, significantly greater. The slogan of total ethics is a new
intellectual current."[55] "Total ethics" could only be attained, however, in societies where an ethical code was in harmony with the other civilizational elements
of the quincunx. To achieve "total ethics" in Poland, all schoolchildren must
be instructed in Catholic morality. Koneczny declared that even public schools
"cannot be areligious, nor acivilizational."[56] The same policy held for the legal
system: "Let God protect us from civilizationally 'mixed-up' judges! A court
cannot be civilized in two ways. . . . [T]he consciences of our judges" should be
based "on the ethics of Latin civilization, which is Catholic, having at the head
a Catholic interpretation of the Decalogue."[57] Koneczny insisted that:

> Harmony ought to prevail between state and society. The state cannot
> be acivilized; it must therefore belong to the same civilization as society,
> and the Polish state must also be a state in Latin civilization. Otherwise
> there would not be commensurability between the Polish nation and its
> state, and there are no exceptions to the law of commensurability. As a
> result, only adherents to Latin civilization, and thus only Christian Poles,
> are able to fulfill public functions in Poland.[58]

Progress in public life could only be possible with a "moral rebirth," and this
was contingent on societal harmony in Poland in the form of a purely Latin
civilization. Koneczny believed that it was not possible for a society belonging
to Latin civilization to allow a non-Catholic ethical system to have influence in

politics, law, and public policy. Such a situation would be nonsensical: "it is not possible to have two consciences, Catholic for private life and non-Catholic for public matters."[59] Koneczny concluded that "[i]n the Polish state Catholicism must be the dominant religion."[60]

A CULTURE OF ACTION

Koneczny's science of civilizations blended Catholic fundamentalism with a philosophy of history. In the Konecznian system, it is tradition that holds a society together; he called it "the backbone of all civilizations."[61] His concept of historicism was connected to the preservation of tradition and *polskość* (Polishness).[62] Historicism is an awareness of the continuity of history, while tradition is the fundamental tangible expression of this. Only with an awareness of the passage of time, of a society's place in history that is evidenced in the veneration of tradition and the efforts to work toward common goals, does one come to engage in a *culture of action*.[63] Historicism thus implies a high degree of control over time. Societies evolve as they gain more control over time, because this mastery is connected with abstract thought and the ability to make plans for the future.[64] Koneczny referred to this as an "active tradition";[65] he believed that one creates possibilities for concrete action in the present and the future through one's study of the past.

Similar to Koneczny, Jörn Rüsen points out that "concepts of time are the foundation of the sense of history."[66] But there is also an axiological aspect in Koneczny's discussion of time, since he believed that different concepts of time relate to different value systems. According to Koneczny, the more advanced the civilizational level, the more complexity is evident in notions about time and history.[67] In Latin civilization, historicism is not merely "the historical awareness of a society, but an *active and critical awareness*."[68] It is also directly linked to the formation of national identity.[69] Koneczny's understanding of historicism is similar to Rüsen's definition of "historical consciousness" as a "specific form of historical memory . . . in which the past is related to the present and—through the present—to the future." [70] Rather than marginalizing it, this gives the past a special importance in the continuum of historical imagination. We are able to reach back before our lifetimes, and also reach forward beyond our generation.

As Robert Piotrowski suggests, the concepts of "time surplus" and "time famine" provide contemporary parallels to Koneczny's notion of the "capitalization of time," which he finds most advanced in Latin civilization. Only Latin civilization has historicism, or an active tradition, which is the highest level of time management.[71] This is a key factor in societal development. In Koneczny's vision, a society without tradition cannot have culture, and all creative actions must be connected to some sort of cultural system. In Latin civilization, a basic condition of progress is the popularization of the national cultural ideal.[72]

Koneczny also emphasized free will and human agency, which enable individuals to intentionally cultivate a civil society: historicism, will, and purposefulness together shape the Konecznian "culture of action." As Zbigniew Pucek puts it: "The creative impulse of a society based on will and purposefulness is called Ethos. Without it one cannot have a culture of action."[73] Doctrinaire systems without historicism cannot have a culture of action, since they stifle human agency in setting goals.[74] Jörn Rüsen explains that historical consciousness "makes sense of past change which can then be applied to understanding the present, and thus enables people to anticipate the future, to guide their own activities by a future informed by the experiences of the past."[75] Koneczny made a similar argument, and he also believed that true historicism was unique to Latin civilization. This provided its members with an element of selflessness, since mastery of time leads to *moral* progress.[76] An awareness of the past also allows for further *social* development, for progress through practical action.[77] Historical awareness facilitates control over time, which Koneczny believed "exercises the will, fertilises the intellect and develops creative spiritual power."[78] Control over time is a crucial component of Koneczny's vision of a civil society that is concerned with the future: "In the interests of time-saving there emerge diligence, resource, thrift, circumspection, thought for the future and finally, consciousness of duty towards the succeeding generation."[79]

CIVIL SOCIETY

Koneczny's discussion of civil society also relates directly to his understanding of how the Polish nation survived its periods of statelessness. After World War II, Koneczny envisioned a "path to the rebirth of Polishness" through the resurrection of a robust civil society and self-government.[80] He had consistently maintained that any "state must be based on society. There is no other path for the public welfare."[81] Koneczny explained that unique developments in Latin civilization laid the foundations for civil societies in Poland and other parts of Europe. He often discussed the Cluniac movement of the tenth to the twelfth centuries that established Church autonomy from the state as heralding a "new epoch" for medieval Christendom;[82] for Koneczny, Cluny was the "smithy of History."[83] The reform movement not only promoted civil society in the form of religious freedom, but also helped confirm the dominance of Catholic ethics and Latin civilization in many parts of Europe. But due to the influx of so many non-Latin influences, Koneczny urged that modern Europe was in need of "a new Cluny."[84] Koneczny frequently cited this medieval episode as an inspiration for the moral rebirth—and salvation—of modern Latin civilization and Europe.

Koneczny believed that the question of the mutual relations between state and society was fundamental to understanding the differences among civilizations. In an analysis of Turanian civilization, he insisted that "[f]or them [Turanians] the State is all, although in miniature and caricature. . . . The community, however, experiences stagnation and disorder."[85] According to Koneczny, Turanian civilization is characterized by the domination of society by the state, evidenced in the arbitrary rule of a powerful leader and his or her bureaucracy. Exemplified by the "Oriental despotism" that prevailed in Russia, "[i]n Turanian civilisation the head of the State was always the sole source of law."[86] Koneczny used the term "political elephantiasis" to describe the domination of Russian society by the tsar and his bureaucrats, whose obsession with power and wealth stifled civic freedoms. In Europe (especially Poland) on the other hand, there are loftier goals than material existence.[87] Turanian civilization was alien to Poland, and Koneczny sharply distinguished Russian "Turanians" from Poles, who remained a vital part of "Latin" civilization.[88]

Koneczny especially contrasted church-state relations in other civilizations with the key role played in Latin civilization by the Catholic Church, which strove for "independence of the State, to prevent dependence by the spiritual factor on physical power."[89] "Everywhere in the East," and especially in the Byzantine and Turanian civilizations, "the moral element is subordinated to material strength"[90] and there is no true freedom, no recognition of the "unalienable dignity" of man.[91] Turanian Russia in particular had historically demonstrated a desire to expand through military conquests, rather than encouraging internal societal growth and enrichment. According to Koneczny, the state's thirst for military conquest was an integral feature of Russian history.[92]

The Konecznian ideal can be summed up this way: "A minimum of state, a maximum of civic freedoms."[93] Once again, "harmony" is the secret of success; Koneczny maintained that civil society can only be vital and thriving if all elements of a society develop in balance without one dominating another. Koneczny also distinguished between *administrations*, which emerge organically out of societies and are needed to help states function, and *bureaucracies*, which are artificial constructs and agents of oppression. Societies in Latin civilization feature administrations, while bureaucracies are products of the Byzantine and other non-Latin civilizations.[94]

Koneczny based his suggestions for independent Poland's political structure on this ideal: "We Poles must tend to a strong state, and to a society stronger than the state, and consequently we must contrive a state without bureaucracy."[95] This would require a parliament that controlled the administrative apparatus, but not excessive centralization of authority. Koneczny advocated provincial and local autonomy, as well as civil liberties that were fundamental to his vision of a functioning civil society.[96] But in order for a viable civil society to emerge in Poland or any other European nation, there must be a purging of non-Latin civilizational elements. In the Konecznian worldview, this is always the most urgent task in the ongoing struggle for survival for Poles.

MATTER AND SPIRIT

Koneczny believed that there was a triple struggle for existence—material, intellectual, and moral—and that the post–World War II regime in Poland ignored this.[97] Writing in 1947, he complained:

> Socialists only recognize historical materialism, that all historical actions and outbursts result from materialistic impulses. In this way, for example, King Jan III Sobieski set out in 1683 with the most courageous army not to "save Vienna and Christendom," but certainly specially for plunder from Turkish tents? And in the name of such historical materialism the final [1944] Warsaw uprising erupted? Nobody explains history with materialism.[98]

Koneczny placed a premium on the spiritual side of human existence. According to him, "not matter, but spirit"[99] governs the flow of history. Of all the binaries that Koneczny presents in his science of civilizations, the most significant is the opposition between physical power and spiritual power: "the struggle for supremacy in matters of humankind between physical forces and spiritual forces."[100] This view of the relationship of these two aspects of human existence was expressed by Koneczny long before he penned his main theoretical treatises. In one of his early works (1896), he stated his belief that "[t]he spirit is strong, but the body faint . . . [T]he goal is the spirit, and the means are the body; the ideals are the spirit, and the politics is the body."[101] Nearly forty years later, he reiterated in his *Plurality of Civilisations* that "from the very beginnings to the peaks of development, spiritual factors guide even concepts of the material. Here again we discover that abstractions govern matter."[102]

Significantly, Koneczny took the position that civilizational differences were not seen so much in the material world, but in the spiritual realm. He cleverly applied this argument to the story of Poland itself, holding that "the nation is the soul whose body is the state."[103] He distinguished between the nation (which evolves out of society in a natural way) and the state (which is an artificial construct ideally devised to serve society). As Joanna Nowak puts it, "a nation is thus a product of history."[104] Held together by spiritual bonds, the nation's strength derives from its moral foundation, while the state is founded as a legal institution.[105] A stateless nation for over a century, Poland nevertheless could claim civilizational supremacy over its colonizers, especially "Byzantine" Germany and "Turanian" Russia, where spiritual concerns were overshadowed by material ones.

According to Koneczny, Latin civilization is unique among civilizations in placing nonmaterial factors in a dominant role. He also found that the "[e]mancipation of spiritual forces from the ascendancy of the physical has occurred nowhere where the emancipation of the family has not been completed; so far and high reach the consequences of monogamy."[106] We see the influence of Koneczny's Catholicism here: monogamy allows for the development of a robust civil society in which spiritual forces have gained their "emancipation from the physical." In his mind, this was "the feature which above all others differentiates civilizations."[107] And this "emancipation" was most complete in Latin civilization. Koneczny seemingly eschewed scholarly objectivity when he concluded that in all ways that "we have attempted a systematization, Latin civilisation always holds a place apart, never in line with any other."[108]

Although Koneczny consistently articulated his rejection of biological approaches to the study of civilizations, he seems to have been inspired to some degree by developments in the natural sciences. Writing in 1948, he asked: "Order has already long ago been revealed in nature; can we not reveal it in history?"[109] His definition of "order" in the natural sciences was somewhat inappropriate, given the disorder evident in the theory of relativity and other concepts that emerged in the early twentieth century in physics. However, he managed to link these developments to his own civilizational concerns. He noted that "[n]ew physics regards matter and energy as identical," adding that "[t]he law of the preservation of energy is unknown in spiritual life."[110] Rather, he believed that

> [q]uantitative changes in spiritual energy are unlimited. . . . A new amount of spiritual energy may always arise, without connection with the quantities that already exist. It all emerges from "nothing." This sort of production we call creative power. Spiritual energy is creative, material is not. The creation of new spiritual energy makes up the main sort of spiritual work, which is distinguished from the physical by its creative power. . . . There therefore exist two separate energies, physical and spiritual; there thus exists a dualistic order. Monism contradicts reality, since man consists of body and spirit.[111]

And since "the spirit does not abide by the law of nature, then the law of death does not concern it."[112] As a spiritual construct (certainly in the case of Latin civilization), there is no need to regard a civilization's lifetime as finite. The same, of course, could be said about the Polish nation. Stefan Zabieglik interprets Koneczny's theories as a reaction to the cultural pessimism and predictions of the decline of the West that were common during the first decades of the twentieth century. Koneczny believed he had uncovered a path for the rebirth of Europe: "the restoration of a pure Latin civilization."[113]

Robert Piotrowski has noted that Koneczny's concern with the concept of "energy" should be understood within his historical context. The problem of energy was a point of great concern for naturalists and humanists at the turn of the nineteenth and twentieth centuries, as seen in fields ranging from physics to parapsychology.[114] As Piotrowski points out, Koneczny explored the ramifications of the findings of Albert Einstein and others developing the "new physics."[115] He was especially interested in the concept of the interchangeability of mass and energy. Koneczny concluded that "[u]ndoubtedly there also exists in the spiritual world potential and kinetic energy: usefulness and activity, possibility and result, intention and act, Logos and Ethos."[116] He believed that "in both domains, material and spiritual, energy is able to shift from one field to another."[117]

Koneczny explored the concept of energy within the context of the dualism of bodily and spiritual worlds and the way in which energy moved from one world to another. Such physical and spiritual energy has a potential form and a kinetic or actualized form. This relates to his concern about the linkage between *logos* and *ethos*, between thought and action, which is evident in his concept of a "culture of action."[118] The "activist option"[119] that is implied in Koneczny's concept of a culture of action is a key to understanding the Konecznian system. Koneczny contended that "the actual setting of the material and spiritual sides of life over against each other appears to me no more than a literary formula. It never happens in reality and never was in history."[120]

A core concept in Koneczny's science of civilizations is "the indissoluble knot" [121] of the three-dimensional struggle for existence: "material, moral, and intellectual." [122] Koneczny asserted that just as it is impossible to divide body and soul, one cannot separate the two aspects of culture—material and spiritual (moral and intellectual)—as seen in his quincunx. "The body is form, the soul is the essence of life; thus likewise is the essence of collective life spiritual culture, and material [culture] is the form."[123] This was an important feature in his comparative analysis of civilizations and their differences. He asserted that the "laws of material transformation are constant, but . . . in various civilizations it is possible to observe many symptoms of spiritual transformation. . . . [T]he laws of spiritual transformation are dependent on the civilization."[124] In Latin civilization, "social strength is very easily transformed into political power, but never the reverse; and there is no other manner in this civilization for the creation of political power other than with the support of societal development and the expansion of its functions."[125]

Koneczny believed that all persons have choice, or free will. However, from Koneczny's perspective one must choose civilizational purity if one wants to ensure societal progress and survival; a society's creative energies can only be tapped most effectively when its quincunx of existential values reflects harmony.[126] Personalism, found in Latin civilization, allows for the intellectual and moral emancipation of the individual and facilitates the conversion of spiritual energy into social action. This full emancipation of the individual provides a benefit to society, since it can manifest itself as selflessness that goes beyond egocentrism and leads to moral altruism and concern for the common good of future generations. It also allows for research and thinking of ideas and abstractions that are beyond oneself and certainly beyond the mechanistic collectivist thinking. This is central to a posteriori thinking and the "true science" that Koneczny found lacking outside the West.[127] Koneczny posited that "progress is more dependent on abstractions than on material factors; moreover . . . abstract ideas direct matter. Without abstract ideas physical matters would often come to a standstill."[128]

Despite the primacy of spiritual factors, however, Koneczny asserted that the "[i]dentity of civilisation and religion leads to under-development of civilisation; in such [an] over-close association standstill must be reached. . . . Significantly, only inferior religions produce out of themselves sacral civilisations. The higher the level of a religion the less of the sacral it imposes on communal life."[129] In his later years, Koneczny became more explicit in his contention that religious differences are important.[130] He emphasized that emanationist religions (such as Hinduism) were characterized by a collective relationship with God, while creationist religions (such as Christianity) entailed a personal contact with God. Creationism is the foundation of personalism, free will, a culture of action, and a viable civil society.[131] Conversely, he believed that emanationist religions could lead to despotic forms of government that claimed divine authority.[132]

Crucial for Koneczny was ethics. While Koneczny regarded "sacral" civilizations as defective and inert, he still believed that religious beliefs were an essential part of any functioning civilization:

> Life without religion cannot be complete—however many-sided, it will fall short of universality. . . . Because of the links between the physical and spiritual categories, any crippling of the latter brings in its train deficiencies and even abnormalities in material categories also. A civilisation which makes light of religion will begin to creak everywhere.[133]

Koneczny unabashedly proclaimed that "[w]e Catholics do not want science or art that is not in agreement with morality. Among us the supremacy of ethics must dominate."[134] He even maintained that in Latin civilization "[t]he whole economy must be based on Catholic ethics."[135] Latin civilization was firmly rooted in a Catholic Church that emerged out of the Roman world and provided the foundation for medieval Christendom. In the next chapter, I will explore the classical and medieval worlds envisioned by Koneczny and their place in his science of civilizations.

Chapter Two

Classicism and Medievalism in Konecznian Thought

GREECE VERSUS ROME

Koneczny's science of civilizations is grounded in antiquity. His quincunx of existential values (Health, Prosperity, Truth, Goodness, and Beauty) borrows from a classical concept of the nature of human beings that he applied to the highest level of collective life, or what he called "civilization." Koneczny's scheme is characterized by a holistic unity of spirit and body; just as an individual cannot simultaneously develop one side of one's being while ignoring the other, neither can civilizations be fully functioning and "normal" by ignoring one side of human existence.[1] Koneczny did impose a hierarchy by elevating spiritual values over the utilitarian side of life. This applies to both individual lives as well as societies.

Koneczny applied his theoretical framework not only to contemporary societies, but also to the ancient world. He notably argued that there was no common Greek civilization, since the various city-states, such as Athens and Sparta, had their distinct existential values. Koneczny used the case of the classical Greek city-states to prove his point about the need for commensurability: "Greek attitudes to the five categories of the quincunx were various to the point of being so full of contradictions that there can be no question of any commensurability. Even methods of regulating time differed."[2] Koneczny believed that the Greek city-states failed to consolidate into one unified state because of radically different existential values.

However, Koneczny was convinced that, unlike the Greeks, the Romans did have a common civilization. Moreover, he asserted that because of "the complete dissimilarity between the Roman and Greek methods, one ought to reject the notion that there existed some sort of joint Hellenic-Roman civilization, a so-called classical civilization."[3] Koneczny recognized commonality only in science and art, but there were many other areas where differences existed between Greece and Rome. In terms of commensurability, Rome represented the "antithesis of Hellas in more than one respect. Among the Romans consistency and logic permeated the entire system of communal life—so that in the whole vast territory of Rome there was in force the same concept of the State and society, the same attitude to the categories of being. . . . For a long period there was no slightest blemish on this harmony."[4]

In Koneczny's view, harmony is virtue, and lack of harmony means lack of virtue. From this perspective it would be difficult to develop a stable ethical foundation for a society under the influence of multiple value systems. In all times and places, civilizational harmony is also required for a culture of action to emerge. In the Roman Republic, this "ideally harmonious combination of thought and act in the sphere of the five categories of being would produce a harmony of unparalleled excellence, as well as a culture of action of unexampled power and endurance, an ideal and powerful society."[5] The Roman Republic would lose this harmony and culture of action as it became increasingly polluted with alien civilizational influences. This was understood by Koneczny as an early example of the debilitating effect that "lower" civilizations (in the Konecznian system they are all "Oriental" as well) have on "higher" ones in their encounters.

The glorification of Rome, of course, was not unusual among European intellectuals. While neither Koneczny nor the British scholar Christopher Dawson (1889–1970) cited each other's work, the two Catholic historians contemporaneously crafted similar visions of world history. In "Progress and Decay in Ancient and Modern Civilization" (1924), Dawson expressed views on the dangers of civilizational mixing that are remarkably similar to Koneczny's. Both focused on the Roman Republic as an early case study of decay caused by abandoning traditional values. Dawson stressed that "Rome, more than any other city-state of antiquity, was essentially an agrarian state. The foundation of her power and of her very existence was the peasant-soldier-citizen."[6] All this changed with empire building, as "[a] new type of agriculture based on the plantation system as it had been worked out in Carthage and the East, gradually took the place of the small yeoman holding."[7] This was a factor that changed the social and economic structures and helped lead to "a progressive degeneration and transformation of the characteristic Roman types. The fundamental peasant-soldier-citizen gave place—as farmer to the slave—as soldier to the professional—as citizen to a vast urban proletariat living on Government doles and the bribes of politicians."[8]

Koneczny also stressed the distinction between farmers and merchants, tracing this dichotomy back to antiquity. Like Dawson, he cited the small farmer-citizen as the backbone of the economy and the military in the old Roman Republic. Over time, he was replaced by slave labor and by a mercenary army. This development weakened the Republic and precipitated its collapse. Koneczny contrasted the Roman situation to that of Greece, where traders and merchants, rather than farmers, seemed to dominate the economy. Only in recent years has scholarly research rescued Greek farmers (the "other Greeks") from oblivion and corrected this misperception shared by many of Koneczny's contemporaries.[9] For Koneczny, a key "feature of Latin civilization, received from the Romans, is the recognition of the priority of real estate over movable property. At the source of this state of affairs stands personalism."[10] Related to each individual having a sense of responsibility, personalism is the fundamental feature of Latin civilization and was regarded by Koneczny as crucial to its identity.[11]

Like Koneczny, Dawson developed his reading of Roman history into a sort of historical law. He stated in 1924 that the decline of the Roman Republic

> is an extreme example of the perils that result from the urbanization of a society, but a similar morbid process can be traced in many other cases of cultural decline. . . . It is this process of urban degeneration and not Industrialism or Capitalism or Racial Deterioration or Militarism that is also at the root of the weakness of modern European Culture. Our civilization is becoming formless and moribund because it has lost its roots and no longer possesses vital rhythm and balance. . . . The essential need of our civilization is a recovery of these lost contacts—a return to the sources of life.[12]

Dawson optimistically held out hope for "the possibility of regeneneration,"[13] while Koneczny called for civilizational purity as the only solution.

Another world historian and contemporary of Koneczny disagreed with the glorification of Rome at the expense of Greece. In the twelfth and final volume (1962) of his *A Study of History*, Arnold Toynbee (1889–1975) addressed the tendency among some historians to place undue emphasis on the Roman heritage: "I suspect that the motive behind this Western insistence on magnifying Rome's place in history is a covert Western chauvinism. If the West is to be credited with a major role in history, Rome must be credited with a major role too."[14]

Koneczny fits the pattern described by Toynbee, since he was careful to accentuate the West's debt to Rome, rather than Greece. He believed that "[f]or the greater part Hellas and Rome are not materials for synthesis, but *opposites* which cannot be reconciled."[15] Koneczny idealized the Roman Republic as the true classical foundation of Latin civilization. But the Republic fell as a result of civilizational pollution from the Orient: "The fall of Rome began with the appearance of people who regarded as moral everything which was legal. . . . Honest people were obliged to withdraw to private life, since public [life] had become non-ethical. . . . In this way Rome grew easternised and fell into the ethical division between State and private life."[16]

ORIENTALISM AND ANTIQUITY

Andrzej Bokiej believes that as a Pole living on "the eastern border of the West [Koneczny] was especially sensitized to all that was foreign that western civilization met on the eastern Polish borders."[17] Koneczny's firsthand experiences convinced him of the impracticality of attempts at civilizational syntheses in Polish history. One can also infer that life on the civilizational frontier (especially in Vilnius) nurtured Koneczny's barricade mentality and inspired him to create his science of civilizations so that it contained laws warning about the dangers of mixing. Moreover, life in the borderlands likely contributed to Koneczny's Orientalizing tendencies. He extends the East-West divide far back into antiquity, and this shapes his reading of Greek and Roman history.

Koneczny is not unique in finding "Oriental" influences in Greek culture. But he is particularly persistent in regarding these as negative influences, which in turn were passed on to Rome and led to its downfall. A typical example of the Orientalization of the Greek world is evident in Alexander's (356–323 BCE) attempt to create a "universal state." Koneczny agreed with many scholars in contending that this idea was not *Hellenic* in origin, but rather *Hellenistic*, and represented an important step in the "orientalization of the Greek mind."[18] Alexander's particular plan for his empire was "an entirely new idea, a new ideal. . . . But the idea of a mixture of races was artificial. It was an a priori thought, an act of meditative method."[19] For Koneczny, Alexander's vision of a hybrid blend of Egyptian, Persian, Babylonian, and Attican civilizations was a "utopia" that was doomed to failure. No such effort to create a "new man" could ever succeed.[20] According to Koneczny, over time the eastern influences dominated Greek culture more and more, as the lower civilizations overcame a higher one. This reflects the Konecznian worldview that "degeneration" occurs when "mechanical" mixtures between East and West are attempted.[21]

While historians have long discussed an "Orientalizing period" in Greek culture from the late eighth century to the early sixth century BCE, Koneczny expanded on the way in which life in "Orientalized" Greek city-states was different from life in Republican Rome. He focused a great deal on the role in Greek economies of commerce, which he associated with "the East," compared with the central role of the landowner in Roman civilization. There were exceptions in Greece, of course, and he noted that "it is a most important fact for us" that Aristotle disliked commerce.[22]

According to Koneczny, over time commerce in Rome became increasingly dominated by a long list of eastern traders who extracted wealth from the West and concentrated it in the East: "Phoenicians, Greeks, Babylonians, Egyptians, Syrians, and Jews."[23] As commerce in Rome became increasingly Orientalized, "the wealth drawn from Italy did not serve Romans or Roman civilization."[24] Over time the incorporation of Rome into a universal trade network led to greater wealth for merchants, who were "Oriental," and the subsequent impoverishment of traditional Roman society. This economic transformation led to an increasing Orientalization of Rome with the "mixing of it with the civilizations of the Orient and the poisoning of the Roman spirit."[25] For Koneczny, this was the crucial factor in the demise of Roman civilization.

These creeping influences from the Orient were facilitated by Roman eastward expansion and the adaptations introduced to handle new challenges. For example, the so-called Marian Reforms launched in 107 BCE during his consulate by Gaius Marius (157–86 BCE) opened the ranks of the Roman legions to landless volunteers from the rural and urban proletariat. This reduced Rome's reliance on the small landholders who had provided most troops for the legions. In addition, these new recruits swore allegiance to the generals in the field, rather than the Senate, which further enhanced the association of military force with authority. Koneczny viewed this as a sign of Oriental influence.[26] Signs of Orientalization also included religious beliefs that soldiers brought back from their conquests abroad. Koneczny correctly identified Cato the Elder (234–149 BCE) as an important early critic of Hellenistic influences who mourned the loss of traditional Roman values. This was evident in the growing popularity of foreign religious movements, such as the cult of Cybele. Koneczny concluded that "Rome was divided into two camps: one friendly and another unfriendly with regard to the Eastern influences."[27] Koneczny is not alone in highlighting the influx of religious cults, along with Greek philosophy and other "eastern" influences. However, he is notable for his use of these developments for marking Roman (and later, Latin) civilization as distinctly different from eastern civilizations. Moreover, these eastern influences are invariably judged to be deleterious in their impact on the West. For Koneczny, the Roman civilization of the Republican era inspired the Christianized Latin civilization, while the hybridized mixture that emerged in the Roman Empire led directly to the formation of an Orientalized Byzantine civilization.

Koneczny asserted that Romans perceived this shift long before the collapse of the western empire in the fifth century. The Orientalization of the empire was also evident in the emperors themselves. Koneczny gave the example of Septimius Severus (r. 193–211), who was born into a mixed Roman-Carthaginian family and was married to a Syrian. He was "entirely foreign to the old Roman traditions."[28] For Koneczny, Gaul stood as a "counterweight for Rome against the pressure of the Orient. At the turn of the second and third centuries, the Roman intelligentsia began to emigrate there when the pressure from the Orient increased."[29] But the "lower elements" defeated a higher civilization. Over the course of its history, it was clear that Rome and then "Byzantium leaned more to Asia than to Europe"[30] with the emergence of a bureaucratic state and a cosmopolitan, artificial, and mechanistic society that was held together by force.

Koneczny posited that the expansion of the Roman empire eventually led to the death of the Roman state, which could not effectively absorb practices borrowed from Egypt, Persia, and other areas of the "Orient." He saw their influences in the mechanistic and bureaucratic state, the dream of a "universal" empire, and a cosmopolitan culture that spelled the demise for old Rome. As Koneczny concluded, "[c]osmopolitan universalism triumphed,"[31] and the Republican ideals were in retreat. Crucial to Koneczny's analysis of the Roman world is his contention that any version of "a universal state is completely cosmopolitan."[32] As the multicultural empire emerged, Romans lost their civilizational purity, and along with it their sense of national identity in the wake of wave after wave of "Oriental" influences. This culminated in the collapse of Rome in the West and the emergence of the bastardized, Orientalized version of "Rome" in Byzantium.[33]

Koneczny consistently viewed pivotal moments in Roman history through an Orientalist lens. A clash between the emperor's Praetorian Guard and the senatorial party that "represented the West" on the streets of Rome in 228 was deemed "the final struggle for Roman civilization in Rome."[34] Even the persecutions of Christians under Emperor Decius (r. 249–51) were interpreted in a similar way. True Romans were not to blame: "It appears that the Roman worldview did not at all lead to the persecutions; rather, they resulted from the hegemony of oriental worldviews."[35] According to Koneczny, Emperor Diocletian's (r. 284–305) reforms introduced bureaucratic and centralizing tendencies that were borrowed from Egypt and Persia. Diocletian's attempt to regulate trade was also part of a trend toward a more mechanistic society as in the East. Koneczny concluded that these reforms only served to "reduce the *culture of action* in society and finally led to stagnation. . . . All of Diocletian's reforms led to stagnation."[36]

LATIN CIVILIZATION VERSUS BYZANTINE CIVILIZATION

Diocletian formally restructured the empire in the third century for administrative reasons. Over time, however, the division of the Roman Empire into the Latin West and Hellenist East would provide the boundary between two rivals that emerged in Late Antiquity: the Latin and Byzantine civilizations. According to Koneczny, the division of the empire by Diocletian created a permanent civilizational gulf by the end of the sixth century, during the reigns of Justinian (r. 527–65) and his nephew and successor Justin II (r. 565–78).[37] Interestingly, Koneczny cited Justinian's notorious wife Theodora (d. 548) as an Orientalizing influence;[38] similarly, he blamed the Byzantine princess Theophano for introducing Orientalized Byzantine traditions into Germany after her marriage to Otto II in 972.

Koneczny sought to explain how the Republican traditions were preserved and merged with Christianity to create "Latin" civilization. While the term "Latin civilization" is not unique to Koneczny, his works provide a thorough analysis of its salient characteristics that are referenced by many civilizational fundamentalists today as they argue for a purification of Poland's culture. In Koneczny's mind, this process would entail purging Poland of influences from alien civilizations. During the interwar period, Koneczny strove to convince Poles to overcome delusions of a "historical mission" to bring about a synthesis between East and West. He feared this "literary cliché" would result in a "civilizational caricature."[39] Rather than decline into "cultural nothingness" and "political nothingness," Poles should acknowledge their membership in Latin civilization, grounded in Catholicism. Koneczny repeatedly warned: "Poland either will be Catholic, or it will not be."[40]

Like other civilizational schemes concocted in the twentieth century, Koneczny's science of civilizations is highly normative.[41] Koneczny even conceded that "it is difficult not to admit that a hierarchy of civilizations exists."[42] Latin civilization was the best, of course, and Jewish civilization was "at the very bottom."[43] Latin civilization was formed when the Church salvaged from the old Roman world those elements that were in agreement with Christian values.[44] Koneczny identified St. Ambrose (c. 340–97) as a key player in making Christian ethics obligatory in public life, as well as in private life. The requirement of ethics in politics and public policy would become a hallmark of Latin civilization.[45] Ambrose was in a unique position to bridge the dying Roman world and the emerging medieval Latin civilization. As a Roman official, and also a "father" of the early Church, he facilitated a melding of Roman governing practices and Christian ethics within Western Christendom.

Koneczny concluded that out of the ashes of the Roman civilization "[s]imultaneously two new civilizations were created, opposed to each other. A new western civilization . . . we will call Latin civilization."[46] In a sense, his focus on the so-called "dark ages" of the fifth–ninth centuries places him in good company; today scholars find that "it is increasingly difficult to deny that the long twilight period on the edges of Antiquity and the Middle Ages was fertile and even decisive for the destiny of medieval—and modern—civilization."[47] Koneczny credits St. Benedict (480–547) for creating a real foundation for a new civilization in 529 with the establishment of the monastery at Monte Cassino. For Koneczny, the monastery stood as a symbol of an alternative to Byzantinism, with its caesaropapism and dreams of a universal state.[48] In this context, Koneczny also discussed at length the contributions of Flavius Magnus Aurelius Cassiodorus (490–583). Over time, "Latin civilization was created in opposition to Byzantine," and Cassiodorus was a key architect.[49] Born into a wealthy Roman family, he served the Ostrogothic kings who ruled Italy after the collapse of Roman authority, thus facilitating some continuity between the Roman and Latin civilizations. As Małgorzata Dąbrowska points out, however, there is an ironic twist to the story of Koneczny's heroic founder of Latin civilization: Cassiodorus's family roots go back to the "Orient" itself, in Syria.[50]

But according to Koneczny, Cassiodorus recognized that Byzantium was essentially eastern and would not perpetuate the best elements of Roman civilization. Cassiodorus rejected the Byzantine state, instead choosing to serve the Ostrogoths. As a Roman intellectual, Cassiodorus sought to "Romanize" the Ostrogoths and simultaneously preserve classical culture for medieval Latin civilization. He also served as another link between classicism and Catholicism. Koneczny opined that "this is his greatest merit. All of us Latins, we are his progeny. Classicism has become revised by Catholicism through him."[51] And the new monastery schools that were founded—such as the one founded by Cassiodorus at Vivarium in southern Italy—were havens where the study of the classics was inspired and informed by the new Christian perspective.

Koneczny also cited the Cluniac movement, which began in 910 and persisted well into the twelfth century, as an important response to the Byzantine threat against the nascent Latin civilization. This is typical of Koneczny's methodology: he uses select episodes from history to highlight key moments in civilizational confrontations. He argued that "there is no doubt about the supremacy of the physical forces over the spiritual in Byzantine civilization; at the same time, Latin civilization had a directly opposite tendency."[52] This was evident in the Cluniac insistence on Church independence from secular authorities. Koneczny also maintained that the Cluniac movement created room in civil society for intellectual growth. As Byzantium stagnated, scholars emigrated to the West in search of greater freedom. Moreover, Koneczny claimed that those scholars who remained in Byzantium produced merely compilations and commentaries, with no real erudition or creative work as in the West.[53] Koneczny believed that a fundamental difference between Latin and Byzantine civilizations was that in "Western Europe, in our Christian-classical civilization, content prevails over form, in the Byzantine form is more important than content."[54]

An important criterion for distinguishing civilizations for Koneczny is whether a civilization nurtures spiritual strength in opposition to state power. The rift between the Latin and Byzantine civilizations is framed within this context, and Koneczny sees Byzantine statism as totalitarian in nature.[55] Koneczny believed that in "the whole Oriental world persists the supremacy of physical power over spiritual."[56] He conceded that a "few Oriental communities found a way out of this dilemma through a compromise in such a way that the highest spiritual authority was linked with the physical, religious authority with state authority in one hand. So it is in Islam, as it was in Byzantium and in Orthodox Russia."[57] While Latin civilization allowed for diversity in a civil society, the "Byzantine civilizational mission is identical with the introduction of uniformity, not understanding that there can be unity without uniformity."[58] Koneczny believed that "[t]here existed in Byzantium social organizations separate from the state, but they suffered from underdevelopment."[59] This was due primarily to the nature of "Oriental despotism" present there, but also to religious practices adopted from Asia, which were characterized by a person's rejection of society and a "yearning for nirvana."[60]

In discussing religious developments in the Roman world, Koneczny commented that "[t]he East possesses two fundamental psychic moments: either dissipation, or melancholy."[61] Such influences would serve to sap the vigor from Roman civilization in the form of eastern cults introduced first by the Greeks and then more significantly by Roman troops returning from their posts abroad. For Koneczny the Roman Republic laid the foundation for Latin civilization (which fully comes into being with the infusion of Christianity), while the Empire witnessed increasing "infection" from the East.[62] This tendency peaked with Byzantinism. Byzantium became the second attempt (after Alexander's) at an East-West synthesis that failed, only leading to a further Orientalization of the Roman world.[63] Koneczny asserted that "Byzantinism remains in a genetic connection with Hellenism; however, it stands as a separate civilization. It brought with it Hellenistic Orientalism. Rome also became infected with this Orientalism."[64]

Koneczny positioned Byzantine civilization to be in a struggle with Latin civilization for control of Europe. Byzantine civilization was "Oriental," despite having its obvious links to classical Greek and Roman culture. According to Koneczny, however, it was Hellenistic culture, an "Orientalized" version of classical Greek culture, which provided the foundation for Byzantine civilization.[65] Though it emerged out of Greek and Roman traditions, the eastern Roman Empire had come "under the influence of Orientalism and was changed into an Asiatic despotism."[66] Along the way the Romans lost their sense of nationalism, while the Byzantines developed a cosmopolitan autocratism.[67] Koneczny saw in Byzantium a "mechanical mixture" that sought to blend East and West, which in Koncznian terms always leads to "an a-civilized condition."[68] In his analyses, Koneczny consistently highlighted the debilitating "influence of the ancient East on Byzantine civilization."[69]

Another dominant theme in Koneczny's story of Byzantine history is etatism. As he stated in his most widely read book, *The Plurality of Civilisations*: "Western ideas on State and society developed in one way, Byzantine in another. In Byzantium society was only permitted to organise under the control of the State, in so far as the State, which prescribed both the competence and the form of the organisation, allowed."[70] Koneczny saw etatism (e.g., state-mandated price controls) in Byzantium in all aspects of life.[71] While old Rome was evolving into the new Latin civilization with a civil society and a vibrant "culture of action," the Byzantine world was sinking into what Koneczny termed "bureaucratic sclerosis."[72] Byzantium mimicked "the Orient" by establishing a dominance of the "physical forces" over "spiritual forces," even as the Church was creating Latin civilization by freeing religious authorities from state control. And between these two worlds—East and West—there could be no synthesis, but only conflict.

In Koneczny's works we see a manifestation of Byzantinism that is reminiscent of Said's concept of Orientalism. In Koneczny's view, many aspects of the

Byzantine world remained timeless; for example, he states that the "admini-stration of the Eastern empire did not change from the turn of the 3rd century onward."[73] More important, Koneczny dichotomized East and West by arguing that "[i]n the East the state became the goal, while in the West it became the means for attaining the goal."[74] The concept of caesaropapism is another core feature in Koneczny's analysis of Byzantine civilization. He argued that the ap-pearance of this "new idea" for the Roman world, which joined in one person both secular and religious authority, "stands as the first sign that a new sort of civilization was emerging."[75] Combined with the "fundamental Oriental law" to make sacral all elements of existence, this presented a situation in which the only mode of expressing opposition to a regime in the Byzantine world was heresy.[76]

Another deleterious influence that Koneczny associated with the Oriental-ization of the Roman world was the impact of eastern asceticism on early Chri-stianity. Koneczny claimed that according to "the oriental view, man can only come close to God in an abnormal state."[77] But according to his vision of the quincunx as a set of complementary existential values, "[t]he view that mutual exclusiveness between soul and body is something natural in the earthly life of man is entirely mistaken. On the contrary, such a formulation of the antithesis is abnormal. Wherever we meet it, we know that an unnatural, sickly condition exists."[78]

Koneczny contrasted the engagement of the western monks in all categories of collective life to the eastern ascetics' "escape from the world."[79] He assigned these tendencies in Orthodoxy to Brahmanic influences that had seeped into eastern Christianity.[80] Koneczny also claimed that monasteries in the East, such as Mount Athos in Greece or the Pechersk Lavra in Kiev, showed no precisely defined plan or goal. This was regarded as "anarchy"[81] in comparison with mo-nastic traditions in Western Europe: "Thus only in Catholicism did monasteries develop a culture of action. Thanks to this in Catholicism emerged a concrete program for rebuilding state and society" after the collapse of Roman civiliza-tion in the West.[82] Koneczny even explained that various saints have provided a model for Poles on how to be good Catholics and still remain engaged in public affairs.[83] He claims that this never developed in the Orthodox Church in Byzantinized areas of Europe.

The practice of engaging in public life, challenging accepted beliefs, and learning from experiences was identified by Koneczny as a fundamental feature of Latin civilization that emerged in medieval Europe. Koneczny professed a rejection of a priori assumptions that stifle intellectual creativity. As he claimed: "Out of doubt all progress is born."[84] Koneczny thus posited that

> amid the hard intellectual struggles of the Middle Ages and against a background of physical struggle for the supremacy of an ideal, a thought was born, the loftiest so far in the whole of history: that circumstances may arise in which resistance must be offered to material forces for the

good of the spiritual, resistance to the State in the name of society, resistance to law based on lawlessness in the name of ethics, resistance
to secular authority in the name of the Church. The supremacy of the
spiritual system of forces must be absolute.[85]

Medieval Latin civilization emerged from "the combination of a Catholicism
unreduced and uncompromising with a classicism cut according to Catholic
ideas."[86] As Koneczny put it: "The Gospel arrived, Christian ethics shone out,
the Church created Latin civilisation in the West."[87]

MEDIEVALISM, THOMISM, AND THE
KONECZNIAN QUINCUNX

Even as the Western Church incorporated the values of Republican Rome,
Koneczny contended that the Byzantine rulers gradually fully succumbed to
the "oriental influences (mainly Syrian and Persian)" that had "undermined
Roman civilization."[88] Just as civilizational mixing had led to the fall of Rome,
he believed that in his lifetime the same process was undermining the foundations of European societies. These concerns were also voiced by the Polish
radical nationalist youth movement of the 1930s, which was inspired by visions
of a "new medievalism."[89] A distinct Polish medievalism emerged, with a call
for a "return to the middle ages" invoking a time when Catholicism had greater
cultural influence.[90] Rafał Łętocha finds that even during World War II the nationalists continued to glorify medieval culture "as a source of harmony, justice,
and social peace."[91] Influenced by the French neo-Thomist Jacques Maritain
(1882–1973) and the English writer G. K. Chesterton (1874–1936), as well as
Polish thinkers such as Koneczny, the new generation of nationalists exemplified by Jędrzej Giertych (1903–92) looked to medieval Christendom as a model
for a society unified by faith and bound by the ethical tenets of Roman Catholicism.[92]

There were similar trends in other European countries. From the late nineteenth century onward, a medievalist revival appeared in France as a response
to contemporary fears of loss and degeneration associated with modernity, but
also to such national humiliations as the failed Franco-Prussian War (1870–71)
and the bloodshed of the Paris Commune (1871). In their joint study of French
medievalism at the turn of the nineteenth and twentieth centuries, Elizabeth
Emery and Laura Morowitz note that it is not surprising that "the medieval
world was conceived as the opposite of this fragmented modern era. Seen as a
period of unity . . . [t]his idealized image of a medieval world bound by social
cohesiveness surely comforted a period rent by bursts of anarchist violence,
worker demonstrations and battles between Church and State."[93] Medieval culture "seemed to weave a durable social fabric based on uncompromising and
uncorrupted faith."[94]

In France, the Middle Ages were also glorified in part because "medieval culture was perceived as alien to the Jew."[95] Laura Morowitz has found that

> during the fin-de-siècle, medievalism and anti-Semitism were often linked. Ideologies contributing to the spread of anti-Semitism—anti-materialism, anti-modernism, fanatical neo-Catholicism—could lead simultaneously to a glorification of the medieval era. Fear of modernity manifested itself in hatred of the Jew (who symbolized urbanism, indus-trial capitalism, the collapse of traditional Christian values).[96]

It appears that in French society often "multiple fears and hopes came together in medievalism: anti-Semites, for example, hailed the Middle Ages as a response to their longing for unity, to their anti-capitalist sentiment and to their religious dissatisfaction," while "Catholics celebrated its religious traditions."[97] In short, many French nurtured "a nostalgia for the purity and stability of the Middle Ages."[98] This sort of nostalgia is also evident in the Konecznian worldview, both in Koneczny's works themselves and in the commentary of his successors in contemporary Poland.

Another interesting parallel between French and Polish medievalism relates to wounded national pride. Koneczny's ideas emerged from his experiences liv-ing in an occupied nation, divided among the three great partitioning powers. Emery and Morowitz have concluded that in France "[o]ne of the primary rea-sons for the public's renewed interest in the Middle Ages after the Franco-Prus-sian war was that government leaders, intellectuals and journalists of all sides proposed the study of the Middle Ages as a cure for the moral, patriotic and political wounds of the defeated nation."[99] Like many Poles such as Koneczny, many French also saw the Middle Ages as a time when their nation originated. In both cases, it seems that attempts to create "a vivid medieval past helped rebuild the morale of a dejected, insecure nation."[100]

The dream of harmony was another reason for the appeal of the imagined Middle Ages in Poland and other European societies. Paul Robichaud points out that British Victorians "invoke the Middle Ages to articulate their desire for social harmony and cultural tradition. The Victorians imagine the medieval world as a time of meaningful social relations and authentic feeling, though one, like Camelot, threatened with disintegration."[101] Cultural memory seem-ingly had a medievalist tinge throughout Europe at this time. According to Stefan Goebel, cultural memory "constitutes a community's collective memory materialised in forms and practices and referring to a distant past."[102] He finds that during the long nineteenth century in Germany and Britain, "the idealisa-tion of the Middle Ages had pointed to dissatisfaction with the aesthetic, moral and social condition of contemporary society and a desire to return to (or at least to remember) the imagined harmony or purposefulness of the remote past."[103]

Confronted with a need to respond to the changing times, Catholic intellectuals looked to medieval models for ways to critique modernity.[104] Their revival of Thomism "identified the Middle Ages as the zenith of the Christian intellectual tradition, producing a similar tendency to idealize medieval culture in modern Catholic philosophical circles."[105] This movement was inspired in part by Pope Leo XIII (1878–1903), whose *Aeterni Patris* (1879) and *Rerum Novarum* (1891) were regarded as seminal documents. Koneczny cited Leo XIII's *Rerum Novarum* and Pius XI's *Quadragesimo Anno* (1931), issued in commemoration of the fortieth anniversary of Pope Leo's encyclical, as sources of inspiration for the Thomist revival.[106] There is a similarity between Koneczny's emphasis on social harmony and solidarism with Leo XIII's *Rerum Novarum*. That papal statement was a critique of both socialism and capitalism, expressing concern about class tensions in European societies that had intensified with economic modernization.[107]

Koneczny's civilizational theory was influenced by Thomism, which he explicitly cited as a foundation for "normality" in Latin civilization.[108] Leszek Gawor and other Polish scholars demonstrate that his concept of the quincunx of existential values fits nicely within the Thomist revival among Catholic intellectuals in Europe.[109] Koneczny explained this link between Thomism and his concept of the quincunx: "No broader or more many-sided generalisation of human affairs exists than that in the small catechism for children which teaches that man consists of soul and body. Let us take this as a starting point for our conclusions and discussions."[110] Tracey Rowland points out that Koneczny and other theorists of his time—such as Christopher Dawson—identified an emphasis on the spiritual over the material specifically with Catholic, as opposed to Protestant, Christianity. For them, Catholicism was characterized by a pursuit of spiritual perfection, implying that Protestantism by comparison displayed an "instrumental rationality and the priority of economic concerns."[111]

Wojciech Szurgot also asserts that "Koneczny was inspired by the Thomist ontology that regarded man as made of spirit and body."[112] Artur Soboń describes Koneczny's methodology as "neoscholastic induction" and points out that "the interest in Koneczny's thought among contemporary Thomists [he mentions Mieczysław Albert Krąpiec and Henryk Kiereś] should not seem strange to us."[113] Anna Frątczak also finds Koneczny's philosophy to be "closest to Thomist ontology" with its dualistic conception of human existence, and that his quincunx was "a natural consequence of such an ontology."[114] She believes that he was also "clearly inspired by Thomism" in his pursuit of perfectionism for Latin civilization—a sort of *civitas Dei*,[115] which in Konecznian terms also implies civilizational purity. It is understandable why Piotr Grabowiec concludes that Thomism was "the most persistent foundation of Koneczny's thought."[116] Koneczny undoubtedly was searching for a Catholic response to the challenges of modernity.[117]

A historian who focused on the medieval period, Koneczny joined other Catholic intellectuals who used Thomism as "an intellectual grid" to formulate a plan of action in modern Poland.[118] Koneczny also searched for the essence of Polish identity, and he once again turned to a medieval period in which Catholicism provided the basis for an emerging national culture.[119] During the tumultuous interwar period and through World War II, both Thomism and the medieval ideal of a harmonious and unified Christendom proved very appealing to Polish nationalists.[120] Although we can trace Koneczny's civilizational theories back to the pre–World War I years, his concern over the fate of Latin civilization intensified and his science of civilizations becomes fully formed during the interwar period.

This was a transformative time for other European Catholic intellectuals, too. For British medievalist David Jones (1895–1974), who converted to Catholicism in 1921, a "concern with European civilization emerges out of the cultural anxieties of the interwar years."[121] Jones was deeply influenced by Christopher Dawson; the two became friends in the 1920s as part of a group of British Catholic intellectuals who met regularly to discuss the fate of civilization in the modern age. Paul Robichaud concludes that it was "Dawson's holistic vision . . . that most appealed to David Jones, for whom historical continuity, unity, and synthesis are central thematic concerns."[122] This is reminiscent of the earlier Victorian medievalism described by Alice Chandler, who notes that

> behind all these varying expressions of a medievalizing imagination lay a single, central desire—to feel at home in an ordered yet organically vital universe. The more the world changed . . . the more the partly historical but basically mythical Middle Ages . . . served to remind men of a Golden Age. The Middle Ages were idealized as a period of faith, order, joy, munificence, and creativity. . . . The Middle Ages became a metaphor both for a specific social order and, somewhat more vaguely, for a metaphysically harmonious world view.[123]

Dawson, Jones, and many others concerned with the fate of civilization during the interwar period—such as Koneczny—resorted to medievalism as a palliative: "the Middle Ages were significant as a time when the spiritual and material needs of human beings were united in a fully sacramental culture."[124] Charles Dellheim finds that the "medieval search for usable symbols was part of a larger quest for cultural orientation . . . in an open-ended, unprecedented world."[125]

Koneczny's search for "usable symbols" led him to medieval Christendom, and he applied Thomist concepts and values in the formulation of his science of civilizations. He might well have agreed with Eva Ross's contention in 1940 that "Christian social concepts must have a place in sociology" and that Catholic sociology "would be both inductive and deductive. The deductive, or a priori, method would insure an appreciation of the ultimate source or cause of things and events in the social world."[126] Despite his protestations otherwise, Koneczny's own methodology in historical research mirrors this blend of the inductive and deductive, along with a comparative framework (the quincunx of existential values) that was steeped in Catholic philosophy. Moreover, his questioning of the anti-traditionalist aspects of modernism was consistent with his search for the essence of medieval Latin civilization. Rejecting alien civilizational influences that characterized the modern multicultural society, Koneczny pursued a quest for civilizational purity that led him back to the medieval world.

Koneczny's medievalism also was associated with his search for "usable symbols" from a harmoniously functioning civil society. Rejecting the atomizing effects of modernity, Koneczny was drawn to a vision of an organic and integral medieval past, whose social harmony was easily contrasted to the chaos of modern times. Abhorring the agnosticism of modern life, Koneczny also found the religiosity of the medieval world appealing.[127] Koneczny's civilizational theory manifested a yearning for harmony in the form of the quincunx and his law on commensurability. His search for an orderly society, in which all the parts functioned as a harmonious whole, is reminiscent of the angst that Alice Chandler has identified in Victorian medievalism. She detects "a sense of loss of connection within society itself. In contrast to the alienated and divisive atmosphere of an increasingly urbanized and industrialized society, the Middle Ages were seen as familial and patriarchal."[128] Koneczny's science of civilizations represents one of the attempts to create "a coherent world view"[129] that Chandler sees as part of the appeal of medievalism. In the next chapter, I will examine Koneczny's medievalism in more detail through an analysis of the medieval "clash of civilizations" that fired his historical imagination. Although Koneczny sought intellectual refuge in an idealized past, he also sought to explain the origins of Poland's contemporary civilizational threats.

Chapter Three

Civilizational Threats to Poland

GERMAN BYZANTINISM

In its essence, Koneczny's massive collection of works is dedicated to finding a formula for a harmonious and just society, one in which a free civil society controls a government that serves citizens through a responsive administration (not an oppressive bureaucracy). In short, Koneczny wanted morality in public life. In his view, this could only be found in a purely Latin civilization. He posited that "[t]he amorality of public life stands as a feature of all oriental civilizations and also Byzantine. . . . As a result it stood also in opposition to Latin Civilization."[1] In the wake of the collapse of a unified Roman world, the eastern Byzantine and western Latin civilizations emerged as rival heirs. Koneczny maintained that thereafter Byzantium represented a powerful "Oriental" threat to Latin civilization.

In his *Cywilizacja bizantyńska* and other writings, Koneczny provided an explanation for his fear of an Orientalized Byzantine threat to the *west* of Poland—in Germany, which, in Koneczny's view, had long been a battleground in the clash between Byzantine and Latin civilizations.[2] As in the earlier case of Rome, once again the civilizationally inferior East emerged victorious over the civilizationally superior West and weakened its influence in the poisonous mixture that emerged. For Koneczny, German Byzantinism represented another failed synthesis of East and West. As Andrzej Bokiej notes, "for Koneczny there exists a genetic and essential union of the Byzantine civilization in the East with German Byzantinism in the West."[3] Moreover, in Koneczny's mind Germany displayed "the highest level" of Byzantinism.[4] Koneczny spun a convoluted tale explaining this ongoing development, a story that many scholars have found unconvincing.[5] In contrast to Koneczny, for example, Arnold Toynbee held that Byzantine civilization had been "ossified" and then "extinguished" long ago.[6]

Koneczny's Orientalizing strategy in relation to Germany might seem peculiar and out of place. But Todd Kontje explains that "[b]ecause Orientalism has more to do with Western ideology than Eastern geography, the actual location of 'the Orient' matters less than the consistency of a certain Orientalizing discourse."[7] Iver Neumann's comments on constructions of the "East" and the "Orient" also offer insights relevant to understanding the construction of

Poland's "civilizational others." He also believes that "'the East' has been cut loose from its geographical point of reference and has become a generalized social marker in European identity formation. . . . 'The East' is indeed Europe's other, and it is continuously being recycled in order to represent European identities."[8]

According to Koneczny, "German Byzantinism" flowered after the marriage in 972 of a Byzantine princess, Theophano (960–91), to the son of German emperor Otto I (912–73).[9] Koneczny believed that Otto I wanted "to mimic the Byzantine emperors" in their pomp.[10] As wife of Emperor Otto II (955–83) and regent during the reign of her young son Otto III (980–1002), Theophano established Byzantine tradition at the German court.[11] But according to Krijna Ciggaar, the historiography of Theophano's role is problematic: "A tradition of hostility towards the Greek empress is discernible. Closely related is the problem of the so-called *Byzantinische Frage*, i.e. the influence of Byzantium on Western Europe. Xenophobia, historical and of recent date, may be part of such an attitude."[12] As Rosamond McKitterick notes, "Theophano, rightly or wrongly, has been regarded as a representative of Greek culture, and thus as the main source for the introduction of the indisputably Byzantine cultural influences at work in tenth-century Germany."[13] Koneczny asserted that from this point onward there existed in Germany a certain "civilizational duality."[14] He detected the coexistence of "a Byzantine-Germanic culture alongside a Latin-Germanic culture through the whole course of history to our day [1927]."[15] This weakened the whole, since "it is not possible to be civilized in two ways."[16] Moreover, Koneczny believed that Christianity in Germany in his day was still "hypnotized by German Byzantinism."[17]

Some scholars agree with Koneczny that the Ottonian dynasty sought to adopt the ways of the Byzantine emperors. As Karl Leyser states, there is "no doubt that Otto I, from an early date, wanted his recognition by the rulers of Byzantium to take the form of a marriage alliance for his son, Otto II."[18] And Ciggaar concedes that "[t]he marriage of Otto II to the Byzantine princess Theophano in 972 was another stimulus to introduce Eastern customs and thus enhance the prestige of the western rulers."[19] Otto II and Theophano were married by the pope in Rome on 14 April 972; Otto was sixteen or seventeen at the time, and Theophano was likely the minimum age of twelve.[20] The marriage certainly was used to build a diplomatic relationship, since "successful mariages could seal an alliance and ensure friendly relations probably better than any written agreement."[21] Since there was no fixed residence for the imperial court at that time, Theophano accompanied her husband on almost all his trips. Otto II died on 7 December 983, leaving three-year-old Otto III as king.[22]

It is during her reign as regent that Koneczny assigned Theophano a pivotal role in infusing the German court with Byzantine characteristics. He is not alone in ascribing a certain Byzantinization to this period. Odilo Engels concludes that for "Otto III's theory of rule the essential element was the antique example as it still seemed to exist in Byzantium."[23] It seems clear that as a youth Theophano was tutored in Byzantine cultural standards and traditions. As a niece of the emperor, she would have attended court, where she "might have observed some aspects of tenth-century political life. . . . All this helped her to train her son and to establish patterns of government in her own territories in the West."[24] According to Judith Herrin, she "inspired her son Otto III with visions beyond his father's ambitions" and "performed the task of Byzantine ambassador to an unprecedented degree."[25] Not all scholars agree: Leyser argues that "during her regency Theophano had not sought to introduce Byzantine ritual, let alone governmental practice. It was too dangerous."[26] Likewise, McKitterick finds "little evidence for any role played by her in the intellectual culture of her time, either in promoting the existing Latin culture of the German realm or in introducing Greek texts or authors to her adopted country."[27]

But for Koneczny, Ottonian Germany became a battleground between Byzantine and Latin civilizations. It is one of his historical "laws" that whenever East meets West, the "Oriental" civilization will come to dominate, since "inferior"—less demanding—civilizations always defeat "higher" civilizations. From a Konecznian point of view, Germany has long been a "civilizational problem" in this regard. As the Koneczny scholar Anton Hilckman mused:

> The question had to emerge in the West again and again, why it was that—at least since Prussia took over the leading role in Germany—Germany represented a permanent, provincial rebellion against the Western world. . . . Whenever we wish to answer this question, we must go back quite far in time: the roots which we seek are to be found in the Middle Ages.[28]

Koneczny was quite pessimistic about the fate of Latin civilization in Germany. There the heart of Byzantinism was Prussia, whose kings and statesmen crafted a unified state in the nineteenth century. From that time onward Byzantine influences had come to dominate the German lands, and Koneczny posited that German-Byzantine culture drove a civilizational wedge into the heart of Europe and presented yet another "Oriental" threat to Poland and Latin civilization.[29]

Koneczny also claimed that "Protestantism strengthened and deepened Byzantinism in Germany and at the same time significantly weakened Latin-German culture."[30] Sonia Bukowska explains that in this regard Koneczny had "a rather original view," since for him "the term 'Byzantinism' also emphasized the Protestant relationship of society to the state," especially in Germany.[31] Indeed, Koneczny claimed that Protestantism borrowed the doctrine from Byzantine Orthodoxy that states "the one who rules determines the faith."[32] Koneczny also found traces of Byzantine "uniformism and lack of recognition for freedom and social pluralism" in German Protestantism.[33] This faith tradition became yet another civilizational pollutant from "the East."[34]

THE "GRUNWALD THEORY"

The Polish-German civilizational conflict thus was conceived as being deeply rooted in the Middle Ages. Koneczny maintained that during the medieval period Poles constructed a society and culture that was based on Christianity, but nevertheless was different from that in other European countries. He pointed out the lack of feudalism in Poland as a factor that distinguished it from other Western European societies. Koneczny found that concepts of private property held sway, rather than feudal landholding practices.[35] He also stressed that Poland did not borrow Byzantine patterns of absolutism that were "Oriental" in origin. From his perspective, Poland seemingly was the only place where Augustine's ideal of "the city of God" came close to realization.[36] Most important, Koneczny presented the Polish war with the Order of the Teutonic Knights in the fifteenth century as an exemplar of a clash between a nation embracing Latin civilization and an imperial power infused with Byzantine values.

The Teutonic Knights were the third military order established during the medieval crusades, after the Templars and Hospitalers. The Order was originally founded in 1190 in the Middle East, but the Knights later shifted their focus to Northern Europe—with new headquarters in Marienburg (Malbork)—after the fall of Acre in 1291 ended their role in the Holy Land. Their effort to spread Christianity among the pagans of the Baltic region was in effect sanctioned by papal commands that urged northern Europeans to "make war on their own heathens" as a continuation of the knights' crusading mission.[37] As the knights enjoyed military successes and expanded their possessions, German settlers followed in their wake. But as Todd Kontje cautions, "What nineteenth-century Germans would describe as the spread of civilization to barbaric Eastern lands naturally looked somewhat different from the Slavic perspective, particularly since the Teutonic Knights continued their depredations long after the Poles had accepted Christianity [in 966]."[38]

The original purpose of the Order had been to spread Christianity, rather than to extend German authority in the Baltic region. But Koneczny asserted that the Teutonic Knights in reality attempted to build "the first total state in Europe."[39] Consequently, Poles were fighting a two-front war at the pivotal Battle of Grunwald (15 July 1410): not only one against the Teutonic Knights on the field of battle, but also a "struggle of two views about the organization of states and societies."[40] Koneczny posited that the Battle of Grunwald was one of the most important battles in European history, in part because it was one engagement in the long war between the forces of the Polish-Lithuanian lands and the Order that lasted a whole generation. He maintained that the conflict had economic dimensions, too. Poles were fighting for all of Pomeranian society—"in the name of work and productivity"—while the Knights sought to enrich themselves, "in the name of parasitism."[41] Koneczny also promoted Polish exceptionalism; he maintained that while other Slavic nations were assimilating Byzantine influences and building on Christianity only in a "quantitative way," Poland alone "enhanced it qualitatively."[42] The Polish war with the Knights—the "great war"[43]—represented a war to determine the future for all Slavs, since Poland was uniquely original in its cultural creativity.

Despite Poland's contributions to Latin civilization, Koneczny lamented that "in the dispute between Poland and the Knights the sympathy of Europe was constantly on the side of the Order. For Poland, this struggle was not only with the Knights but also with Europe."[44] According to Koneczny, Poles' "aspirations and . . . progress [were] a puzzle for the people of the West," who believed the Knights were fighting a valid crusade in defense of Christendom against the pagans of northeast Europe.[45] Therefore, as "the two armies neared Grunwald, the sympathies of Europe were not on our [Polish] side."[46] Rather, "European opinion was on the Knights' side, on the side of 'the apple of the eye of Christendom.'"[47]

Koneczny was not the only Polish scholar concerned with this episode from medieval history. Especially during the interwar period, Polish historians regarded Germans as an "element of foreignness" that had affected the development of Polish national identity. Some scholars believed that medieval German expansion was the key factor in spurring the formation of Polish nationalism, while others held that it merely enhanced an already existing self-awareness. But an increasingly popular view was that medieval Poles' consciousness of a distinct identity developed at least in part as a reaction to their German neighbors. This directly challenged the previously widely accepted theory that Polish nationalism was a modern construct. As a result, during the interwar period the idea of a medieval origin for Polish national identity became prevalent in Polish historiography.[48] According to this view, Poles' sense of national awareness appeared especially early in comparison to other European peoples.

Poland was also special, even within Latin civilization, since it rejected imperialism as a viable option for expanding its own influence. This is the essence of Koneczny's "Grunwald Theory": Poland was at odds with the Teutonic Knights and much of Western Europe, which viewed with approval the Knights' forcible conversion of pagans as part of its imperial expansion. Koneczny stressed that Poles sought to insert morality into politics through the contention that Christian powers should not be free to convert pagans by force. This infusion of politics with morality—the need for morality in public life as well as private—was promoted by the Polish delegation at the Council of Constance (an ecumenical council held from 1414 to 1418).[49] According to Koneczny, the Polish proposal of a "law of nations" offered a radically different vision than the imperialist one represented by the Knights. Paweł Gondek believes that this is important for Polish (and European) history and culture because it represents "an intellectual victory for Latin civilization over the expansion-oriented Byzantinism, especially German."[50] Building on Koneczny's analysis, Maciej Giertych adds that this episode at the Council of Constance exemplifies the long Polish tradition of tolerance.[51]

Interestingly, this focus on the Teutonic Order and the Battle of Grunwald was evident in German historiography, too, especially after World War I. Historical research during the nineteenth century helped bring the history of the Order into the German national consciousness. Todd Kontje points out, however, that "[a]lthough the medieval Order of the Teutonic Knights was largely German, it was not a nationalist organization in the modern sense of the term."[52] But later German scholarship and German popular memory distorted its history, as they "gradually appropriated the Teutonic Order into Germany's national history."[53] This trend is important to remember, for it was in this context of heightened German glorification of the Order and its clashes with Poles that Koneczny developed his "Grunwald Theory." In 1862, Henrich von Treitschke's *Das deutsche Ordensland Preußen* (The Prussian land of the Teutonic Order) "introduces a new belligerence into the discourse.... He celebrates the Germanic conquest of the Slavs, whom he denounces as a culturally and racially inferior people."[54] This work had an impact on early twentieth-century German scholarship; Kontje finds a "German prejudice against the 'Asiatic' Slavs is already firmly in place in German accounts of the battle of Tannenberg of 1914, which was viewed as the long-overdue German revenge for the humiliation of the Teutonic Knights in 1410."[55]

Stefan Goebel also credits the commemorative politics of Emperor Wilhelm II (r. 1888–1918) for the growing German interest in the Teutonic Order. In 1902, he gave a speech at the restored castle of Marienburg (Malbork) in West Prussia. At this former seat of the Grand Master of the Teutonic Order (from 1309 to 1457), the German emperor reminded his audience about ancient German-Polish tensions in the east. Among the special guests were members of the remnant of the Teutonic Order from Vienna.[56] In that same year, Henryk Sienkiewicz's novel *The Teutonic Knights* (*Krzyżacy*) made a huge impact in Poland. Patrice Dabrowski credits the novel for helping "the scene of the victory at Grunwald ... work its way into collective memory."[57] Readers could imagine that "the oppressors of the Poles in the new Germany were modern Teutonic Knights."[58]

During year-long celebrations of the five-hundredth anniversary of the battle in 1910, nearly sixty memorials were unveiled in Galicia. These included the massive statue of Władysław II Jagiello on a horse that was erected in Koneczny's Kraków.[59] Over 150,000 visitors travelled to the city for the grand commemorative celebrations in mid-July, at which the statue (funded by the famous pianist Ignacy Jan Paderewski) was unveiled to rave reviews.[60] In a speech in honor of Grunwald, historian Oswald Balzer issued a judgment similar to Koneczny's: "Here two worlds stood face to face, two cultures were at grips with each other, two political and ethical ideas, two distinct, collective spirits, which had been formulated on two completely different bases, and which contradicted each other at every point."[61] All these commemorations were related to even larger Polish concerns; fueled by the spirit of Grunwald, by 1910 "Polish unification rhetoric was virtually unchecked."[62]

In a peculiar way, Koneczny's Orientalizing strategy against the Germans was a scholarly reply to derogatory German depictions of the backward "Asiatic" lands—including Poland—to their east. Todd Kontje asserts that "the conviction of German cultural and, increasingly, racial superiority could later be extended beyond eastern Europe to German colonies in other parts of the world."[63] German accounts of the Teutonic Knights provided one aspect of "an anticipatory vision of their destiny as a nation of conquerors and colonizers: today Poland; tomorrow, the world."[64] Koneczny would perhaps have agreed with Kontje's assessment of German commentary after 1914 about "Asiatics" and "half-Asiatics" threatening Europe with their barbarism:

> From here it is a fairly short step to Adolf Hitler's proclamation in *Mein Kampf* (1925) that if "land was desired in Europe, it could be obtained by and large only at the expense of Russia, and this meant that the new Reich must again set itself on the march along the road of the Teutonic Knights of old, to obtain by the German sword sod for the German plow and daily bread for the nation."[65]

Kontje points out that "Heinrich Himmler envisioned the SS as a reincarnation of the Teutonic Knights,"[66] and their eastward march of conquest did indeed result in the invasion and occupation of Poland during World War II.

As chance would have it, in World War I, "Germany's greatest victory in the entire war happened to take place not far from the ancient battlefield [of Grunwald], a coincidence which gave rise to the most powerful German myth of the war: the Tannenberg myth."[67] A Tannenberg memorial was unveiled on 18 September 1927 in a ceremony that Stefan Goebel describes as "an ostentatious display of nationalist sentiment and arguably a prelude to future Nazi ceremonies at Tannenberg."[68] The site was declared a Reich memorial by Hitler on 2 October 1935. President Paul von Hindenburg (the victorious general at the battle in World War I) was buried there as "the Nazis coupled two interlinked yet not identical myths, the myths of Tannenberg and Hindenburg."[69] The Grunwald site subsequently became important for Nazi propaganda, too. Goebel notes that "[f]or Nazi ideologists, the endeavours of the Teutonic Knights perfectly exemplified the necessity of German territorial expansion into eastern Europe at the expense of Slavic *Untermenschen*."[70] Moreover, "in contrast to the earlier writings of nationalist scholars, the Nazis regarded the Teutonic crusaders as racial warriors in pursuit of *Lebensraum*."[71] During the 1930s there was also a mobilization of "Polish cultural memory" and a "resurgence of Grunwald nationalism in Poland."[72] This commemorative battle took on bloody dimensions with the destruction of the Grunwald memorial in Kraków during the German invasion of Poland in 1939. (It was restored in 1976.)

In this context of conflicting historical memories, one can better understand why Koneczny perceived a palpable threat from Byzantine Germany. In addition, there was growing concern during the interwar period about the fate of Polish culture among Poles who were "surrounded on all sides by Germans" in such areas as northeast Saxony and Lower Silesia.[73] Koneczny was a member of an organization that was interested in their fate. One of its goals was to raise funds for Lusatian students to study at Polish schools and universities as a way to preserve their Polishness.[74] This had long been an area of interest for Koneczny. In one of his early monographs (*Dzieja Śląska* [History of Silesia], 1897; republished 1931), Koneczny sought to teach Poles living in Silesia about their past through his general history of the region, with a special emphasis on its historic ties to other parts of Poland.[75] In an address at the Slavic Club in Kraków in 1905, Koneczny had predicted that the direction of Polish consolidation and expansion in the twentieth century would be toward the Baltic, rather than the Black Sea. He maintained that "for us [Poles] Silesia is worth more than all of Ukraine; not the Dnieper, but rather the Oder will be the ideal political goal."[76]

THE RUSSIAN CIVILIZATIONAL THREAT

While the German state might enjoy an advantage in political, military, and even economic assets, Koneczny proclaimed the superiority of the Polish nation because of its moral and cultural capital. Poland also has a similar advantage in comparison with Russia. Poles enjoy moral superiority over "Turanian" Russians, since Latin civilization is characterized by the supremacy of "spiritual forces" over "physical forces," including the application of ethics in public life. This insistence on connecting moral and political ideals recalls older messianic depictions of Poland as a "bulwark of Christendom."[77] Indeed, in Koneczny's discourse the vision of a purified Polish society "has a mystical, quasi-religious character."[78] By comparison, Koneczny depicted Russian society as deficient in many ways. Ezequiel Adamovsky has demonstrated that intellectuals in the West frequently "constructed [Russia] as a 'land of absence' . . . the absence of certain elements that were considered fundamental to civilization."[79] Koneczny likewise saw a sort of "syndrome of abnormality"[80] in Russian history, which he blamed on civilizational mixing. In his assessment of Koneczny's concept of Turanianism, Selim Chazbijewicz also hears "the echo of medieval descriptions of Tatars, the echo of heroic anti-Islamic literature."[81]

Koneczny did look to ancient and medieval history to find earlier episodes of civilizational clashes. For example, he focused on the "Orientalization" that sullied the civilizational purity of the classical Roman Republic. Roman civilization fell because Oriental pollutants diluted national consciousness, and the same fate could befall Poland and other nations of Latin civilization. In

Konecznian terms, "returning to old Rome" was a call for civilizational purity. Poland could become purely "Latin" only if it eliminated alien civilizational influences. In doing so, Poles would avoid the social mayhem and identity crises of Russia. Koneczny frequently pointed to Russia as a place of civilizational chaos. He believed that in the nineteenth century Russia's logos derived from the Latin civilization of Western Europe, while its ethos was steeped in Turanianism.

This is the crucial point for understanding Koneczny's theory of history and how it relates to Polish-Russian relations. As representatives of two distinct civilizations, Poland and Russia were prone to confrontation rather than cooperation. Moreover, any attempts to blend the two worlds would prove disastrous. As the Konecznian scholar Anton Hilckman explains, "One can be civilized for instance in a Turanian way; but it is impossible to introduce principles and forms of Turanian civilization into the Latin civilization; they do not fit in here, in the same way as forms and principles of the West, introduced into the domains of other civilisations, act as elements of decomposition."[82] Writing in 1935, Koneczny reflected on the long period of occupation by empires from other civilizations: "By hard effort we have returned to Latin civilization, having lost our independence in the struggle."[83]

Long before Koneczny wrote those words, the Polish mood had been darkened by the failure of the January Uprising in the Russian-ruled Kingdom of Poland (1863) and the subsequent repression and Russification by the tsarist regime. Increasingly, Polish intellectuals cast Russia as a civilizational foe that was fundamentally different from Latin Poland. Koneczny even opined that "after 1863 a real new Mongol invasion oppressed our land."[84] This was a "true civilizational catastrophe"; for Koneczny, Russification represented an attempt by "eastern Turanianism" to squash Latin influences in Poland.[85] Koneczny's search for civilizational purity thus can be seen as a response to alien influences in Poland that were forced on Poles by foreign occupation.

Koneczny's science of civilizations reflects the fears and resentments, the demonization of "others," and the quest for purity that have been identified in other postcolonial discourses. Caught up in the "neo-messianistic trends" that flourished in Poland at the start of the twentieth century,[86] Koneczny developed a vision of two neighbors whose civilizational differences were unbridgeable.[87] These were not biological differences, as Franciszek Duchiński had maintained, but rather reflected a sort of cultural racism. The concept of a civilizational divide had already emerged in Polish debates about Polish-Russian relations, with an emphasis on Poland as part of Europe providing a logical corollary of the "Orientalizing" of Russia.[88] Over time, Koneczny would place Polish-Russian relations within a fully developed world historical theory that privileged Poland as a cornerstone of Latin (Western) civilization in its struggles with the East.

The Russian Revolution of 1905 was pivotal in challenging Polish intellectuals to reevaluate the stormy history of Polish-Russian relations. Buoyed by the hope of political change in the former Kingdom of Poland, more Poles became willing to talk of close ties between kindred Slavic peoples.[89] The best hope for Polish freedom was envisioned as a democratic Russian government that would seemingly soon replace the tsarist regime. Motivated by the ideas of progress and just treatment for their Polish brethren, surely the Russian Duma (the newly created parliamentary body that first convened in St. Petersburg in 1906) would grant Polish autonomy as a logical step toward independence. However, the ultimate failure of the Duma to bring about an effective check on tsarist absolutism called these assumptions into doubt.[90] The failure of Poles to gain political autonomy reverted discourse to the familiar binary depiction of Poland and Russia as opposite worlds.[91]

Koneczny showed a keen interest in Russo-Polish relations during this period. Excited about the prospects for real political change during the tumultuous years of 1905 and 1906, he wrote extensively in the journal *Świat Słowiański* (Slavic World) about Polish-Russian cooperation in the struggle to bring down the tsarist autocracy. An announcement for the new journal claimed that "[t]he Slavic question takes on a greater and greater importance" due to the growing power of Germany and the need for Poles to reach out to sympathetic Russians.[92] The journal was published by the Slavic Club in Kraków, and Koneczny ran the editorial board meetings from his home.[93] Members of the club frequently discussed the latest political developments in Russia; this was possible since there was greater freedom of speech in Galicia than in the lands of the former Kingdom of Poland.[94]

Koneczny and his colleagues placed their faith in "unofficial Russia," especially the congresses of representatives from municipal assemblies and local *zemstva* (organs of rural self-government), as well as gatherings of the Union of Liberation (*Soiuz Osvobozhdeniia*).[95] At meetings in 1905, the *zemstvo* activists and *osvobozhdentsy* (liberationists) recognized Polish demands for autonomy within the Russian empire.[96] With the collapse of absolutism, Koneczny hoped the "new" Russia would at last grant Poles their freedom.[97] Throughout this period, calls for Slavic brotherhood frequently appeared in Koneczny's editorials.[98] He insisted that Poles had never hated Russians, but only the tsarist regime that oppressed both peoples alike.[99]

But in the years after the failed Revolution of 1905, his scholarship and commentary in the press increasingly indicated that Russians and Poles were separated by a cultural chasm that presaged a "clash of civilizations." Jolanta Kolbuszewska notes that in Koneczny's theories "we find elements of cultural determinism,"[100] and this is certainly evident in his writings on Russia. Crucial to this changing attitude was his view that "Eastern" Russia's culture was radically different from that of "Western" Poland. As early as 1907, he noted that Poles and Russians had different concepts of freedom: "when a Pole says 'freedom' [*wolność*], a Russian hears 'rebellion' [*bunt*]."[101] As late as 1913, he was still hopeful that Poland had not yet become a helpless mix of various civilizational influences.[102] Obviously, Poland had been *politically* dominated by Russia, yet Koneczny enhanced the existing Orientalist paradigm to explain Poland's *civilizational* superiority to Russia.

The events of 1917, especially the success of the Bolsheviks in October, bolstered Koneczny's contention that "Latin" Poland did not share a common civilization with "Turanian" Russia. Moreover, the Bolsheviks perpetuated civilizational mixing, in Koneczny's view a never-ending problem in Russia.[103] Koneczny saw cosmopolitan Bolshevism as civilizationally weak, but nevertheless he believed it posed a threat to Poland. Poles could defend themselves against this danger by purifying their "Latin" civilizational traits;[104] Koneczny complained in 1921, however, that "we are already too cosmopolitan in our daily life."[105] Koneczny regarded the cultural question as extremely important for the history of Russia,[106] and he sought to demonstrate "Latin" Poland's *civilizational* and *moral* superiority to "Turanian" Russia. This notion of *moral capital* is at the heart of Koneczny's thinking, which is permeated with a traditionalist Catholicism.[107]

As noted in the introduction, from 1919 to 1929 Koneczny taught history at Stefan Batory University in Vilnius (Wilno). His scholarship seems to have been inspired by his time on the civilizational frontier; for example, Koneczny posited that medieval Muscovy and Lithuania were not only the centers of two rival political systems, but that they represented two rival civilizations. While the medieval boyar state of Lithuania saw an increase in political and individual freedoms, Muscovy became more and more a part of Turanian civilization, with its suppression of society by the state. In Koneczny's view, for example, Ivan II (r. 1353–59) behaved as a Tatar khan, rather than a Byzantine tsar.[108] Modelling its behavior on Turanian bureaucratic methods, Muscovy under Ivan III (r. 1462–1505) sought to extend its control over the autonomous city of Novgorod. He was opposed by the "Lithuanian party" in Novgorod in 1470, which proclaimed: "We don't want the Muscovite Grand Prince! We are not his patrimony! We are free people!"[109] Koneczny asserted that Lithuania was distinctly different from Muscovy: its boyars were citizens, rather than *kholopy* (servants), and this tendency was accelerated after the Polish-Lithuanian merger.[110]

Life in the *kresy*, the "borderlands" that had long been the focus of conflict between Russia and Poland, also made Koneczny more pessimistic about relations between Poland and its eastern neighbor. As noted earlier, Koneczny held that "[e]very civilisation, while it remains vital, aims at expansion; so that wherever two vital civilisations meet they *must* fight each other. Every vital civilisation which is not dying is aggressive. The struggle lasts until one of the fighting civilisations is destroyed."[111] "Universal history," he declared, "is the struggle of civilizations and [doomed] attempts at civilizational syntheses."[112] Poland and Russia, representing two distinct civilizations, were prone to confrontation rather than cooperation. As Koneczny put it: "Our struggle with Russia has always been a constant civilizational struggle, a struggle in defense of Latin civilization."[113]

Those who hoped for Polish-Russian amity were mistaken, and those who worked for a sort of "synthesis" of East and West were doomed to failure.[114] Koneczny believed that attempts to blend together various aspects from different civilizations inevitably led to failure and that Russian history plainly revealed this problem.[115] Russia, Koneczny asserted, exemplified the impracticality of merging various cultural influences—Slavic, Viking, Mongol, Byzantine,[116] and Latin—into a coherent, organic whole.[117] This Russian mélange became especially messy over time, as different civilizational elements were merely pieced together "mechanically" without any organic development. This created internal societal "chaos," which Koneczny regarded as "the fundamental sickness of Russia."[118] Russia was unable to experience "internal enrichment" because there was no harmony among the different elements of its quincunx of existential values;[119] that is, Russia was incapable of sustainable development because it was a civilizational mashup.

In the Russian context, the concept of *dvoeverie* (dual belief) that is associated with the coexistence of Christianity and paganism is a shining example of the blending of civilizations that Koneczny considered so problematic. He argued that much of Russian culture exhibits the influence of many civilizations.[120] Over time, he posited, Russian culture became a "real civilizational *dvoeverie*."[121] "Since the dawn of Kievan history," he asserted, "Latin and Byzantine civilisation have been in combat there, with the victory going to—Turanian. The upper hand was taken by those who served Polovtsians, then Mongols and Tartars, until in the end towards the close of the reign of Ivan III the struggle ceased for a long period, for Turanian civilisation had won complete victory."[122] Curiously, Koneczny believed that it was "an error to include Muscovy in Byzantine civilisation. In Turkey there was incomparably more of Byzantium than in Russia."[123] He observed that Muscovite Russia was more influenced by the Mongols than the legacy of Kievan Rus'.[124] And Koneczny argued that the "Turanian" influences go even farther back in Russian history. He pointed to 1054 as a pivotal year: Yaroslav the Wise died, the schism within Christianity occurred, and the Polovtsy ("a Mongol people") first appeared as an integral part of life in Rus'.[125]

Koneczny's later writings on Russia increasingly defined its culture as eastern, decisively belonging to the "Turanian" civilization since the Mongol conquest of the thirteenth century. Koneczny believed that in Russia "a mixed civilization developed, but with a background which always remained Turanian. The Turanian mark lasts to this day [1935]."[126] Turanianism was the culprit for every "aberrant" feature of Russian life: the plague of drunkenness;[127] Muscovite court rituals with "all their barbarous oriental pomp";[128] and the "oriental despotism"[129] that came to characterize Russian political life. For Koneczny, the "tatarization of Muscovy"[130] was complete by the end of the sixteenth century. He regarded the reign of Ivan III as a turning point. He stressed that Ivan III imitated those Mongol rulers who had ruled the lands of old Rus' for two centuries.[131] In his analysis of the significance of Ivan's second marriage (to Zoe, a Byzantine princess whose family resided in Italy after the fall of Constantinople to the Turks in 1453), Koneczny claimed that the tsar only superficially linked Moscow to the most progressive region in Europe (Italy). The Renaissance may have arrived earlier in Moscow than Kraków, as Koneczny notes, but Ivan was not interested in humanism. Rather, setting a precedent for Peter the Great's later interaction with the West, he sought primarily military technology.[132] Turanianism prevailed, not least in the guise of high-ranking Mongol servitors of the Muscovite prince, who rivaled in numbers the boyars of Slavic background.[133] Even when Mongol rule had ended, Muscovy thus remained part of Turanian civilization.[134]

For Koneczny, Russia's core civilizational attributes remained immutable. He was unconvinced that the reforms of Peter the Great (r. 1682–1725) really altered the situation. Russia still "belonged to the Turanian civilization,"[135] and the state continued to dominate society, which was as geared for military conquest and territorial expansion as before. Peter's reforms sought only to introduce European technical culture for military uses, and nothing more. In addition, Peter's borrowings from Western Europe included Byzantine-inspired bureaucratic practices; as Koneczny put it, Peter's reforms in this area led to the "Germanization of official Russia."[136] Of course, in the Konecznian worldview this meant yet another Oriental (Byzantine) influence. But conditions worsened in another respect: Peter's "westernization" of Russia introduced the influence of yet another civilization—Latin—into the messy mixture that characterized Russian culture. Any successful blending of civilizations was impossible, according to Koneczny, and Russia presented a perfect example of the failed attempts to integrate European and Asian cultures into a coherent synthesis.[137] European cultural influences did seep into Russia after Peter, and especially after the partitions of Poland during the long reign of Catherine II ("the Great," r. 1762–96). But Peter's reforms did not really "guide the Muscovite world to Europe."[138] Instead, the bureaucracy he established made possible "a more Asiatic relationship of the state to society," and Koneczny argued that the decades after Peter were the "time of the most monstrous orientalism."[139] The Bolshevik threat of the interwar period represented merely the latest in a long line of civilizational monstrosities born in Russia.

THE JEWISH CIVILIZATIONAL THREAT TO POLAND

In his major theoretical treatises of the interwar period, Koneczny consistently defined Poland's basic problem as a lack of civilizational purity. Koneczny's commentary on "Jewish civilization" is best understood within this context. In his posthumously published *Cywilizacja żydowska* (Jewish Civilization), Koneczny opined that

> One cannot be civilized in two ways. . . . Either we must de-Judaize or we will perish miserably in Judaization. There is not any anti-Semitism in this thesis, but only a warning about civilizational mixtures. . . . [T]he Jewish question is neither religious nor racial, but civilizational. In the civilizational sense of the word, who will not be an anti-Semite? . . . In any country, who will thirst for civilizational Judaization?[140]

Koneczny averred that anti-Semitism was a defense of Latin civilization "against the claims of Israel for world domination."[141]

As discussed in the introductory chapter, Koneczny's Kraków was a city undergoing great change during the late nineteenth and early twentieth centuries, and the Jewish community there was also experiencing a transformation. Jews increasingly lived and worked outside the traditional Jewish district in Kazimierz. When the Habsburg monarchy restored self-government to Kraków in 1866, twelve of the sixty members of the newly elected city council were Jews.[142] These electoral results indicate the emergence of the Jewish bourgeoisie and intelligentsia in public life at century's end. Constitutional guarantees in 1867 for "freedom of conscience and other civic freedoms" also "radically changed the situation of Cracow's Jews."[143] In Galicia and in other Polish lands, such developments were viewed with concern in some circles.

This concern was evident in the writings of Koneczny and some other fundamentalist Catholic intellectuals. According to Brian Porter-Szucs, by the early twentieth century in Poland "Catholic rhetoric and modern antisemitism became increasingly compatible. The key shift came in the period immediately before World War I [with] . . . a slow but steady accommodation between Catholic authors and the theories of modern antisemitism."[144] He finds that by the 1930s "a great deal of undisguised antisemitism had penetrated the Church in Poland."[145] Porter-Szucs cites a passage from a pastoral letter (1936) by August Cardinal Hlond, Primate of the Roman Catholic Church in Poland:

> It is a fact that the jews are struggling against the Catholic Church, that they are penetrated by free-thinking, that they constitute the avant-garde of godlessness, of the Bolshevik movement, and of subversive activities. It is a fact that jewish influences on morality are pernicious, and that their publishing enterprises propagate pornography. It is true that in the schools the influence of the jewish youth on the Catholic youth is, in general, religiously and ethically harmful.[146]

Dariusz Libionka also finds that during the 1930s, "and particularly in the second half of that decade, the Church as an institution was tolerant of expressions of antisemitism in public life."[147] Although mainstream clergy and

Catholic writers distanced themselves from the most strident anti-Semitism, Libionka points out that "[t]heological argumentation was increasingly supplemented by reasoning from the fringes of the philosophy of history" and other disciplines.[148] The issues of "Judeo-communism" (*Żydokomuna*) and the "Jewish conspiracy" were especially prominent. Libionka asserts that

> on the eve of the war [World War II] advocates of the "de-Judaization" of culture and the economy, of the introduction of religious schools and *numerus clausus* at universities, of Aryan sections at public institutions, and finally of the emigration of Jews, whether voluntary or forced, dominated among the Polish clergy.[149]

Anti-Semitism intensified in many areas of public life in Poland during the interwar period. The campaign by the All-Polish Youth (*Młodzież Wszechpolska* or MW) and other groups for the *numerus clausus* to limit the number of Jewish students led to violent conflicts at institutions of higher learning. The issue of limiting Jewish enrollment in higher educational institutions was first promoted by the MW in 1922, leading the Sejm to address the issue as early as January 1923. Parliamentary action was postponed, but the Ministry of Religion and Public Education issued a statement that hinted at future quotas. The issue was dropped in early 1927, as a result of the Piłsudski coup of May 1926.[150] But in 1923, Koneczny—along with many other faculty—had supported the introduction of a *numerus clausus* at Stefan Batory University in Vilnius.[151]

Renewed anti-Jewish pressure from extremists in the 1930s had an impact. Szymon Rudnicki finds that "[a]s a result of this systematic anti-Jewish campaign, the number of Jewish students in institutions of higher education fell from 20.4 per cent in the 1928–29 academic year to 7.5 per cent in 1937–38."[152] New anti-Jewish measures included the "bench ghetto" policy of segregated seating for Jews and Christians in lecture halls. It was first introduced at the Lwów Polytechnical Institute in December 1935, and it was soon copied elsewhere.[153] The MW campaign for "ghetto benches" resulted in universities being granted this power in 1937.[154] Jews feared that this was just the start "along the road to segregation in other walks of life. Such concern had a real basis," concludes Rudnicki, since a variety of measures were introduced to separate Jews and "Aryan" Poles in markets and parks, and exclude Jews from professional organizations.[155] Such restrictions applied to certain groups or activities; however, no universal laws separating Jews from mainstream Polish life were promulgated.[156]

Endek thinking about Jews was part of a broader European pattern of the interwar period. William W. Hagen sees "central and eastern European anti-Semitism in the early twentieth century as a broad regional phenomenon rather than as a set of nationally bounded histories."[157] The *endek* electoral organization (*Stronnictwo Narodowe* or National Party) passed resolutions during the interwar period "declaring that it considered 'the Jews to be its chief enemy' and

that 'its main aim and duty must be to remove the Jews from all spheres of social, economic, and cultural life in Poland.' "[158] *Endeks* proposed curtailing Jews'
civil liberties, including the right to vote. They also suggested forced emigration as a solution to the Jewish "problem."[159] The Polish government responded
with its own radical proposals. Hagen contends that "the anti-Jewish policies
enacted by the post-Piłsudski regime [after 1935] inflicted severe disabilities
on the Jewish community and in important respects bore strong resemblances
to prewar Nazi practices."[160] The Camp of National Unity (*Obóz Zjednoczenia
Narodowego*, OZN or OZON) was created in 1937; while in control of parliament in 1938, the party discussed drafting anti-Jewish laws similar to those adopted in Germany, Romania, and Hungary during the 1930s. The OZN and the
government also considered plans for Jewish emigration to Palestine, Mada-
gascar, or Africa. The OZN even discussed legislation similar to the Nuremberg
Laws in January 1939, although it was tabled.[161]

Paranoia about "Judaization" was not an isolated phenomenon. This term
was used as early as 1869 in France, and also by Richard Wagner in reference to
"Verjüdung" in modern art. The word entered into Polish as *zażydzenie,* which
was a concept that Koneczny and others used to refer not just to economic competition but also to the alleged threat that Jews posed to Catholic culture; over
time the word came to mean the broader challenge of secularism.[162] Ronald
Modras finds that rhetoric in the interwar Catholic press called for a "cultural
war,"[163] just as Koneczny claimed that a civilizational struggle was at hand in Poland. Modras adds that for "the Catholic church leadership at least, the Jewish
question in interwar Poland was cultural rather than economic."[164] The "nationalist obsession with the necessity of the 'defense' of the nation and the 'purity'
of its culture" was a growng factor that reinforced "the traditional conviction
that religious conversions would lead to the 'judaizing' of the Church."[165] This
fueled a hostile Catholic attitude to Jews, including those who had converted
to Christianity. But Dariusz Libionka also identifies a "racist logic" that was
expressed in the Catholic journal *Ateneum Kapłańskie* (Priestly Atheneum), to
which Koneczny contributed; according to an article in the journal from 1939,
for example, a Jewish convert "*racially* and *ethnically* . . . remains a Jew even
after undergoing baptism."[166] Koneczny made similar arguments about the *civilizational* immutability of Jews living in Poland; Jews therefore represented a
threat to the integrity of Polish identity.

Brian Porter contends that the "Catholic framework for understanding modernity did not mandate any specific antisemitic ideas, and it certainly did not
lead directly to biological racism, much less to any genocidal desires. None-
theless, it did offer a Manichean worldview that fit antisemitism nicely."[167] The
Konecznian worldview is similar, with its system of binary contrasts that pits
Catholic Poles against their civilizational enemies. Koneczny's influence on extremist thinking goes back to the interwar period, especially among the so-
called youth who eagerly sought to combine their Catholicism and nationalism

into a coherent ideology. Rafał Łętocha has proven the undoubted influence of Koneczny on the *endek* vision of history that emerged before and during World War II, and his "clash of civilizations" theory can also be found in their wartime analyses.[168] His influence is evident in concepts and terms, such as "Latin civilization," which were borrowed from his works. Also, *endek* rhetoric has a Konecznian emphasis on ethics as a key factor in distinguishing civilizations.[169]

Koneczny's most notorious treatise on the alleged Jewish threat to Poland and Latin civilization is his *Cywilizacja żydowska* (Jewish Civilization), but his other works from the interwar period also consistently addressed the supposed civilizational boundaries between Poles and Jews. As Robert Piotrowski points out, Koneczny was much closer to a culturalist perspective than a racial one in his analysis of Jewish civilization.[170] Moreover, he was concerned primarily with the way in which Jewish ethics purportedly represent something totally opposite to the Catholicized morality of Latin civilization.[171] Koneczny's substitution of "civilization" for "race" in his theoretical writings is evident in his opening sentences of *Cywilizacja żydowska*: "The Jewish question among nations is not a racial one, nor is it a confessional one. The question of Jewry is one of an entirely different civilization, or separate method of collective life."[172] More succinctly, he stated: "*The Jewish question is neither racial nor religious, but civilizational.*"[173]

Koneczny was not alone; *endek* thinking of the interwar period had also become focused on Jewish culture rather than race, and its threat to Catholicism's "moral-cultural code."[174] Analyzing the rhetoric in the Catholic press from the interwar period, Anna Landau-Czajka also finds that for commentators what

> distinguished Jews from Christians was not their blood, but the character or psyche which resulted from their religion or customs. It was a psyche completely different from that of Catholics, such as to rule out completely the possibility of the two peoples, Polish and Jewish, inhabiting the same territory. Jews were different not only because of their religion and customs, but also because of the way they thought, their morality, culture, and principles.[175]

In his *Cywilizacja żydowska*, Koneczny also addressed the alleged Jewish dreams for a "state within a state," or Judeopolonia, which he traced back to the seventeenth century in the form of the autonomous Jewish *kahal*.[176] He argued that during the eighteenth century, Jews played the role of parasites, as this "state within a state became stronger, even while the Polish state weakened."[177] Koneczny viewed the contentious Jewish demands for autonomy during the Revolution of 1905 that nearly toppled the Russian Empire as further evidence of plans for a separate Jewish state within Poland.[178] As Jerzy Jedlicki notes, it was "especially in the wake of the 1905 Revolution" that "the Jew" became "a powerful personification of a mysterious 'enemy from within,' conspiring to deprive the Poles of their expected self-rule."[179] Tsar Nicholas II's October (1905)

Manifesto granted concessions to Poles, but also to Jews, who now seemed to be in competition with their Polish "hosts." Demands for Yiddish rights led to fears of a future bilingual Polish state, a variant of the Judeopolonia imagined by Koneczny.[180] There emerged a "Polish national feeling of uncertainty and the fear of being manipulated—as a national entity—by the great powers, secret societies, or other forces beyond people's knowledge and control. The image of the conspiring Jew made this mysterious world clearer, simpler, and more comprehensible."[181] Over time, the *endeks*—and even some "liberals" and "progressives" after the failed revolution of 1905—would come to identify Jews "not only as a cultural and religious 'other' but as an alien internal enemy."[182]

Koneczny regarded the Germans as allies of the Jews in their civilizational assault on Latin Poland. As Joanna Michlic notes, "[t]he theme of the Jewish conspiracy against Poland was not limited only to one external enemy, namely the Soviet state, but also referred to an older external enemy, Germany."[183] Long before the Bolshevik threat appeared as a Jewish plot, Koneczny explored the German support for alleged Jewish designs in Poland. In a review of a book (*Sprawa polska*, 1912) by Eugeniusz Starczewski, Koneczny discussed the author's analysis of the German Ministry of War's alleged plans for creating a Jewish state in Poland. Koneczny noted that "Judeopolonia is not the invention of our Jews, but Berlin's idea, going back twenty years."[184] This fear of a "nation within the nation" was a key component to Polish anti-Semitism of the late nineteenth and early twentieth centuries. During World War I, even the progressive Warsaw activist Aleksander Świętochowski (1849–1938) expressed the fear of an autonomous Judeopolonia that would threaten Poland's future.[185]

Koneczny also detected a German-Jewish alliance against Poland during World War I, with Jewish financial support for the German war machine offered in exchange for the promise of a Jewish state carved out of Polish lands. He contended that while Warsaw was under German occupation, German military leaders and Jewish rabbis—"two powers hostile to Polishness and Christian civilization"—met "within the walls of the great synagogue" to discuss mutual interests.[186] From Koneczny's perspective, the Bolshevik Revolution was also Jewish in origin: Marxism was a product of Jewish civilization, and the revolution itself was financed in part by American Jewish bankers.[187]

During the interwar period, Joanna Michlic finds that Polish-Jewish relations were increasingly depicted in hygienic terms as "a zero-sum conflict,"[188] as in the case of Koneczny's "law on mixing." As a precaution, extreme nationalists called for the "purification of the Polish nation from the physical presence of Jews and from Jewish spiritual and cultural influence."[189] They sought the "dejudaization of the Polish state," which even nonviolent "cultural anti-Semites" supported.[190] During the interwar period,

> [t]he thesis found in nationalist ideology and journalism that the nation is an organism of a psychophysical nature, led to the use of expressions and phrases connected with disease and health. . . . Jews were the most

dangerous elements threatening the cohesiveness of the national body
and were compared to many kinds of diseases.[191]

Malgorzata Domagalska writes that "[t]he imaginary Jewish threat was described not only in medical, but also biological terms." [192] Jews were equated
with snakes and rats, and the "fear of communist Jews was induced by the
metaphor of a pack of rats on assault."[193] As in Nazi rhetoric, "[t]he invariably
negative connotations of the diaspora were to be achieved through the use of
the word 'parasite.' In the process of creating a pejorative image of Jewish existence, parasites included flies, bedbugs, fleas and lice."[194] Domagalska notes that
another metaphor used was "vermin"; this served to create revulsion "and to
change the perspective from the human world to the animal one."[195] This rhetoric found an audience in the growing public debate in interwar Poland about
the dangers of Jews spreading a "spiritual disease" within Polish culture; even
radical nationalists were more concerned about negative influences on Polish
culture emanating from the "dangerous Jewish *soul*" rather than the "dangerous
Jewish *race*."[196]

   One of the most insidious of these imaginary effects could be found in the
Jewish emphasis on law before ethics, or what Koneczny called "the Jewish
method of legal thinking"[197] that he feared had come to dominate in Europe.
This resulted in law losing its moral compass. He believed that Jewish civilization inverted the relationship between law and ethics in comparison to Latin
civilization, in which laws are created in response to ethical determinations of
situations as they arise. By contrast, in Jewish civilization there was a reliance
on the "letter of the law."[198] Koneczny here depicted Latin civilization as the
antithesis of Jewish civilization; thus, he noted that "we Latins, we follow the
Romans" in legal views.[199] He contended that there was a direct link between
Roman civilization and Latin civilization, "for it was among the Romans that
law first ceased to be sacral. The Church accepted this state of affairs, giving the
faithful a free hand in the secular development of law."[200]

   There are peculiar twists in Koneczny's analyses of Jewish civilization and
Judaism, especially in regard to Jewish influences in Germany. As early as 1921
Koneczny was explaining that Jewish funding of German militarization cleared
the "path to domination for Judaism, but it was the ruin of Christian-Classical
civilization."[201] He saw a continuation of the old conflict between Judaism and
Christianity, except now in the guise of a civilizational struggle. The connection between German militarism and opportunities for Jewish domination was
most evident to Koneczny in the alleged German-Jewish plan for "Judeopolonia," a Jewish state on Polish territory.[202] Forestalled by Germany's defeat in
World War I, Jewish hopes had since turned eastward, to Bolshevik Russia.
During World War II, Koneczny lamented that "[w]e Poles are only waiting
for the time when they [Jews] will not be among us, but we among them."[203] In
October 1945, Koneczny noted that all of Poland had in fact come under Jewish control in the form of communism. Seemingly dismissive of the horrible

realities wrought by the Holocaust, Koneczny concluded that Judeopolonia was being created by the Russians.[204]

Koneczny's insensitivity is perhaps most evident in his discussion of the impact of Jewish culture in Nazi Germany. Koneczny believed that Adolf Hitler's vision of German world supremacy developed under the influence of Jewish notions of the "chosen people" and collective predestination. He concluded that "Germans have assimilated Jewish civilization most visibly. Hitler murders Jews, but he thinks and feels in the Jewish manner."[205] Koneczny was not alone in voicing these assertions, as other commentators in Poland also found "striking analogies between the Talmud and *Mein Kampf*."[206] As Rafał Łętocha points out, *endek* writers also linked Jewish messianism with Hitler's vision of world domination.[207] Konecznian commentary still makes these offensive connections. Controversial historian Dariusz Ratajczak (1962–2010) cited Koneczny on this theme, noting the shared "rebellion against Christianity and Latin civilization" found in the "ideas of Jewish civilization" and "the Hitlerite worldview."[208] Konecznian pundit Andrzej J. Horodecki not only assigns the origins of Hitler's fantasy of Germans as a chosen people to Judaism, but he also blames it for Stalin's revulsion to Christianity. In this way, he seems to have unearthed Jewish roots for two totalitarianisms.[209]

Koneczny and his successors have focused on what they regard as issues of civilizational (rather than racial) differences between Jews and Poles. Since Jewish civilization is deemed "sacral" in the Konecznian paradigm, however, the distinction between it and Judaism is difficult to draw and criticism of Jewish civilization can easily devolve into a critique of the Jewish faith. And while Latin civilization is not "sacral," the pervasive influence of Catholicism is frequently cited as a source of its strength and appeal. Koneczny's construction of civilizational boundaries between Latin and Jewish civilizations, therefore, has a corollary effect of erecting barriers between Catholics and Jews. Discussing the early history of the Church, Koneczny bluntly declared that "Judaism did not exert any essential influence on Christianity in matters of faith."[210] As Rafał Łętocha finds, *endek* literature from the interwar period shared similar views. *Endeks* also sought to separate themselves from Jews by severing the ties between Judaism and Christianity. This was done in part by minimizing the impact of the Old Testament on Judaism; the Talmud was seen as the true source of Jewish beliefs, especially its "ethical relativism." This tactic of separating Judaism from the Old Testament and focusing on the Talmud is seen in the writings of Józef Kruszyński (1877–1953) and Stanisław Trzeciak (1873–1944), who were influential in *endek* circles.[211]

One of Koneczny's key authorities on early Christian-Jewish relations was Tadeusz Zieliński (1859–1944), who posited in *Hellenizm a Judaizm* (1927) that early Christianity connected "psychologically" more readily with the classical pagan world than with Judaism.[212] As Zieliński put it, "Christianity emerged from Judaism—this is often written and stated—but despite this it is false."[213]

There "was no psychological continuity between Judaism and Christianity"; rather, "continuity existed between Hellenism on the one side and Christianity on the other. This means that the religion of the Hellenes was better prepared mentally to receive Christianity than Judaism."[214] A "paradox" emerged: "the true Old Testament of our Christianity is the religion of the Hellenes."[215] Zieliński insisted that this was not heretical, since he simply identified the obvious "psychological continuity."[216] This understanding of the theological boundaries between Judaism and Christianity was not uncommon in Polish nationalist circles during the early twentieth century and the interwar period.[217] Koneczny blamed earlier misunderstandings on faulty historiographical approaches that placed undue emphasis on ancient Israel as the center of attention for pre-Christian history. He blamed Jacques Benigne Bossuet (1627–1704), in particular, since due to his efforts, "the history of Israel became as if the essential component of our religion."[218] Bossuet stressed the unity of religions, which Koneczny asserted paved the way for the notion of a "historical unity of the Christian and Jewish faiths."[219] In this way, "Bossuet became the father of judeocentrism."[220]

Koneczny feared the "moral and spiritual Judaization of Europe,"[221] which he envisioned might lead to a sort of religious "synthesis" of the two faiths.[222] He even claimed that "[t]he Judaization of the Church would be the pinnacle of success for Israel."[223] It is important to note that he regarded Protestantism as a Judaized version of Christianity; he plainly stated that "Protestantism is, in general, rejudaization."[224] In *Cywilizacja żydowska* and other studies, he insisted that while Protestants had become "rejudaized" by emphasizing the teachings of the Old Testament, Catholicism remained critical in its stance toward Judaism.[225]

Koneczny was quite explicit in his judgment of "Jewish civilization." In his opinion, since its origins it had been "an incomplete civilization, defective, not possessing all the categories of being, without Truth and Beauty."[226] He detected only "the tiniest provision of the intellectual categories of being."[227] As an example of these shortcomings, Koneczny noted that for Jews "historical thought itself is very, very difficult. From my own experience, I know that for Jewish students it is difficult to acquire this sense, difficult to understand the historical nature of people and things."[228] He consistently maintained in his works that the civilizational question is more a matter of mentality than one of race; the key danger posed by Jewish civilization was the threat that the "Jewish way of thinking" would exert an influence on Latin civilization.[229]

For Koneczny, Jewish civilization was frozen in time. Already in his *Plurality of Civilisations* (1935), Koneczny was maintaining that "the whole of community life—the whole structure of Jewish civilisation with a mass of detail—is contained in the rules of the Old Testament. It is a sacral civilisation."[230] Similar to other interwar scholarly critics of Judaism, Koneczny placed great emphasis on Jewish "legalism" that he traced back to Mosaic law and the "contractual" agreement between Jews and their god. Koneczny found that "over the course of centuries there emerged here and there *a priori* law. It imparted sanction not to existing circumstances and was not created in a natural manner, but it was imagined, invented . . . Mosaic law was a prototype of *a priori* law."[231] Koneczny added that there later appeared

> a second source-book of Jewish religion and civilization—the Talmud. . . . It may safely be said that there is nothing in heaven or earth which is not debated there, but always exclusively from the sacral angle. . . . Jewish civilisation would become even more strongly sacral.[232]

Koneczny believed that this focus on a priori law is a fundamental feature of Judaism and Jewish civilization. He stressed that "[a]mong Jews . . . law is not based on ethics, but precisely the opposite: ethics are based on law."[233] He theorized that this sacralized law became the regulator for all aspects of Jewish life, leaving no room for the natural development of ethics. An "elephantiasis of law" later emerged, with the motto "the more law the better!"[234]

From a Konecznian perspective the fundamental flaw in Jewish civilization is that it is "sacral," which leads Jews to become mired in "a priori thinking" and a suspiciousness toward secular learning.[235] As early as 1926, Koneczny was writing in *Ateneum Kapłańskie* (the most important organ for the Polish clergy during the interwar period)[236] that "of all religions the Jewish one is most identical with a civilization. The Talmud is this civilization, because it contains the method of collective life in all its details, not neglecting a single category, but with several huge defects (such as the lack of scholarship). . . . In Jewry religion and civilization are the same."[237] He asserted that while religion "is the most important part of a civilization . . . only religions of a lower order create civilizations and these are also of a lower type."[238] Koneczny contended that in sacral civilizations "religion acts as a brake on progress. . . . Where everything is established *a priori*, where there is no doubt and no inquiry, progress is excluded and instead there is danger of stagnation."[239] For Jewish civilization, this meant that there was no creative originality.[240] Koneczny asserted that Jews did not possess a sense of historicism, which implies a creative and critical engagement with the past as part of a mastery over time.[241] Koneczny also believed that Jews might give up their faith far more easily than giving up their civilizational values, such as the dream of Jewish world domination,[242] in exchange for Latin civilizational attributes, such as historicism and personalism.[243]

Another important factor for Koneczny was the notion of Jewish "chosenness."[244] He concluded that this special relationship with God and the "faith that all must end with the Jews ruling the world"[245] was the most immutable, distinguishing characteristic of Jewish civilization. This concept of "the chosen people" was also transmogrified in *endek* thought into a threatening vision of Jewish aims to control the world.[246] Koneczny also identified an "ethic of exclusivity" that "generated contempt, then hatred, for foreigners. In all of universal history, Jews have developed hatred to the highest degree."[247] He asserted that Judaism's doctrine of "collective predestination" reflects its diminution of the individual, and precludes the personal relationship with God that is found in Christianity.[248] This all highlights the "defective"—and threatening—nature of Jewish civilization.

Koneczny conceded that even while Jewish civilization promoted an "ethic of exclusivity," Jews have been forced to live among other peoples and to live within other civilizations. According to Koneczny, "Jewish civilization experienced significant changes among other 'nations,' but what is most interesting is that the changes occurred for the better: the supplement of a defective civilization in many directions and lifting it to a higher level in each case."[249] For example, Jews learned other languages in order to express a higher order of abstract thought, since Hebrew was itself "a language able to facilitate civilizational development only to a certain level, beyond which it becomes a brake on higher development."[250]

Jewish civilization allegedly only developed in the diaspora, as this "defective" civilization was elevated by exposure to the higher civilizations among which Jews lived.[251] Koneczny suggested that "[a] Jew understands a lot . . . but almost exclusively deductively, and the basic conceptions become for him dogma."[252] This resulted from "Talmudic studies" that stifle individual creativity; Koneczny maintained that the only creative Jews have been influenced by non-Jewish civilizations. According to Koneczny, "The factors of Jewish civilization (collectivism above all) do not encourage creative originality, which everywhere and always depends on two conditions: strong personalism and also a philosophical formulation of the question."[253]

Koneczny insisted that "[w]ithout personalism one cannot have creativity,"[254] and he presented an argument reminiscent of the anti-Semitic trope of Jewish parasitism. Koneczny contended that "Jews never were pioneers,"[255] asserting that "Jews take in intellectual culture when the non-Jewish surroundings are highly developed, but when the surroundings are at a lower level, they are too."[256] In other words, Jews have achieved more culturally when surrounded by another well-developed civilization, such as Latin civilization, and fared poorly when surrounded by another "defective" civilization.[257] These changes were limited in scope, however, since Jewish civilization was a sacral one and the changes ultimately were superficial; in Koneczny's words, "the essence of things remained unchanged."[258] But Jewish influences on their "hosts" were seemingly more lasting; Koneczny claimed that it would take a separate volume to fully discuss all the ways "our [Polish] life" has been Judaicized.[259] Koneczny depicted Jews as chameleon-like at best, and at worst, as culture-stealing parasites.[260]

Koneczny's attitudes resembled those of German scholars who influenced Nazi Jewish studies. Similar to Koneczny, Hans F. K. Günther described Jews as "artful traders" who possessed a variety of traits that allowed them to exploit others. Their "commercial spirit" was characterized as a menacing feature.[261] Both Fritz Lenz and Koneczny agreed that Jews had a propensity to "mimic" and blend into host cultures. Lenz depicted Jews as parasites, and Koneczny also viewed Jews as guests who took advantage of their hosts. Koneczny also cited Eugen Fischer in his works; while Fischer ascribed key Jewish traits to race, Koneczny focused on immutable civilizational characteristics.[262] Another prominent German scholar, Gerhard Kittel, warned like Koneczny that Jews "harbor a deeply rooted, 'fundamental hatred of non-Jews,' a hatred that is sanctioned and encouraged in the Talmud."[263] And Polish scholar Tadeusz Zieliński contrasted "Greco-Roman society with its fundamental and universal tolerance, with its boundless love for the very idea of humanity"[264] with that of the Jews, who had a more exclusive approach to others. He puts forth this quality as a cause of anti-Semitism: Jews rejected others, who then rejected them. Zieliński also asserted that "the [pagan] Greek religion was a religion of love; the religion of Israel and Judea was a religion of fear."[265] For him, "the fundamental feature of Judaism—[was] that it was a religion of fear."[266]

Koneczny, like these contemporary German and Polish scholars, took Talmudic passages out of context and manipulated them to prove a point. Scholars such as Karl Georg Kuhn found the Talmud possessed a "spiritually empty, legalistic, textual literalism" that "had been the essence of Judaism from the very beginning."[267] Similar to Koneczny, Kuhn believed that "Judaism was founded as a religion in which the 'word of God had to be fulfilled with the most precise exactitude.'"[268] Zieliński also commented on the "basically legalistic character of Jewish morality."[269] Similar to Koneczny's critique of Jewish apriorism, Kuhn asserted that Jewish use of the Talmud was

> a fundamentally dishonest intellectual process. Rather than analyzing a text in order to discover what might logically follow from it, Midrash [a form of textual analysis] did the exact opposite, seeking to establish a textual basis for a predetermined legal outcome. Midrash operated according to mechanical principles of reasoning that resulted in 'purely formalistc thinking' that was divorced from the concrete reality of the issues.[270]

This sort of description is still used by authors inspired by Koneczny. Writing in 2007, Wojciech Szurgot pointed out that Jewish "sacralization of the law" hinders Jews' civilizational progress. He restates Koneczny's idea that "[a]s soon as the law is given by God, then it cannot be subject to any change. In this way the a priori law introduced at the beginning of Jewish civilization is also a brake on the development of this civilization."[271]

For Koneczny, the well-being of Poland was inextricably linked with the purity of Latin civilization and the integrity of Catholicism. He resorted to using the metaphor of infection to argue that "Judaization" would threaten the civilizational health of Poland, as would a disease.[272] This was the case in the economy, for example, where a lack of ethics was blamed on the "spiritual influence of Jews."[273] Koneczny maintained that Jewish civilization in Poland flowered in the second half of the fifteenth century, with a strong economic foundation.[274] Over time, Poland suffered as Jews gained control over commerce. And with economic decline came a loss of a "culture of action."[275] Jewish civilization supposedly became more influential in Poland from the time of the "Deluge"[276] onward. Koneczny suggested that Jews seemingly benefited from Polish misfortunes. He emphasized that their role in commerce grew during times of war and unrest, such as during the "Deluge." Since Jews were not engaged directly in the fighting, he asserted, their economic standing improved. Jews flourished and gained more autonomy even as Poland declined.[277] As a result, by "the nineteenth century Poland had become the classic land of Jewish civilization."[278] Koneczny saw Jewish civilization competing with "Christian-classical" (Latin) civilization from this time onward more and more successfully in all aspects of Polish life.[279]

Writing in 1928, Koneczny explicitly summarized his perception of a clash in Poland between Jewish and Latin civilizations. He feared that "Christian-classical civilization" would cease to function in a recognizable form, instead "becoming gradually a kind of strange mixture. How many purely Jewish notions are running rampant among us! Our literature, legal ideas, political views—all of them have been subjected to judaization. A civilizational mixture endangers us—and with the same sort of results as in Russia."[280] Jewish civilizational influences in Poland were dangerous, according to Koneczny, because this would violate the "law of laws" that for him represented "the achievement and outcome of the labours of an entire life. . . . *It is not possible to be civilised in two ways.*"[281]

In the next chapter, I will further explain the intellectual context that influenced Koneczny's thinking as he developed his laws of history and his science of civilizations. I will also explore the scholarly reception of his ideas and place them within a broader theoretical context.

Chapter Four

Koneczny's Intellectual Context and Legacy

A HISTORIOGRAPHICAL TRANSFORMATION

Koneczny's theories emerged out of a historiographical crisis at the turn of the nineteenth and twentieth centuries. This was the result of a broad challenge to the Rankean model of historical scholarship,[1] which included a research focus on states, governments, and their activities. Koneczny certainly challenged the Rankean model in two ways: he focused on the history of the *stateless* Polish nation in much of his work, and he moved away from narrow case studies toward a new "science of civilizations" on a global scale.[2] The ferment in Poland especially affected young scholars, who were anxious about history's relationships to other social sciences that were also undergoing methodological transformations, such as sociology, ethnology, anthropology, economics, and psychology. Koneczny used these other disciplines in creating his science of civilizations.[3] Polish historians' horizons broadened in a geographical sense, too, as they began looking not only to German historiography for inspiration, but also to French, Italian, and even Russian models.[4]

This emergence of a plurality of research methods is termed a modernist "mutation" by Andrzej Grabski, who finds that the reaction against the old methods took place not in a constant flow of change, but rather in spurts and phases.[5] For example, Jolanta Kolbuszewska points out that a "neoromantic period" peaked from 1900 to 1918. She cites Koneczny as a historian who took "an extreme neoromantic position" that was sometimes associated with the rising popularity of a "heroic conception of history."[6] Koneczny's emphasis on human agency reflected his rejection of historical determinism;[7] he explicitly stated that "[w]e . . . possess free will."[8] (But he believed that only in Latin civilization could free will be fully exercised, allowing individuals to act freely in a "culture of action.")[9] Selim Chazbijewicz, however, asserts that Koneczny's works anticipated those of Fernand Braudel (1902–85) and other French historians of the Annales school, who believed that "history is the sum of daily labor and work of thousands of anonymous people" who struggle for a better life.[10] Paweł Milcarek also argues that "Koneczny distances himself from the 'heroic' type of historiography"; rather, the main hero for Koneczny is society itself, which is the organic and authentic generator of progress for a nation, while the state is merely a mechanism that serves society in achieving its goals.[11] But while the Annales school was secular in its approach, Koneczny emphasized the key role of Christianity in the formation and history of Latin civilization.[12]

In this complex historiographical milieu, there was also tension between speculative and empirical methodologies. In Poland and elsewhere a veritable "cult of science" emerged after the mid-nineteenth century that took up the empirical methods of positivism and spurned philosophical tendencies in historical research. However, by the end of the nineteenth century a backlash against positivism led to a reconsideration of "reflection" in historical research. There was growing doubt about positivism's "laws" of progress, which included assumptions about the improvement of humankind's intellectual abilities and moral values. And there was also growing skepticism about history as a discipline that could be objective in the same sense as a natural science. A new appreciation for reflective history emerged as a result of this reevaluation of methodologies. Koneczny was engulfed in this "process of reorientation" or "mutation" in historiography, but Kolbuszewska identifies a process that was more complex than an abrupt "antipositivist turn."[13] She finds elements of positivism in Koneczny's work—for example, his search for historical laws and his defense of the scientific method—while at the same time he challenged positivism with his desire to broaden the horizons of the discipline of history, his departure from the "cult of the fact," and his questioning of the potential existence of a global civilization.[14]

Koneczny frequently addressed methodological questions related to his science of civilizations. He condemned a priori (deductive) thinking as detached from reality. Moreover, he posited that "[a] posteriori is the law of evolution, a priori—revolution or stagnation."[15] He believed that a priori thought appears characteristically in utopian ideologies or as the motto of revolutionaries; a posteriori thought relates to a critical review of the past.[16] Koneczny also made a distinction between a priori assumptions that are bestowed on humanity from on high, as in "sacral" civilizations, and a posteriori ideas that are derived from historical experiences and grounded in tradition.[17]

Koneczny touted a posteriori thinking as a good civilizational attribute.[18] And he believed that he engaged in unbiased critical research as he gathered mounds of specific data and generalized his findings into a science of civilizations and a series of historical laws. But while Koneczny may have criticized the speculative approach, his theoretical work moves in just such a speculative direction over time.[19] Jan Skoczyński refers to this mixed methodology as a sort of "third path,"[20] while Sonia Bukowska adds that "the ambivalent attitude of F. Koneczny to positivism not only was not something exceptional, but clearly placed him within certain general tendencies within historical scholarship."[21] Koneczny also refuted biological interpretations of history, Social Darwinism, and anthropological evolutionary schemes that were racist in nature.[22] Evolutionism may have deeply influenced historical thought after Darwin's revelations, but contrary tendencies appeared by the end of the nineteenth century. This new trend fed Koneczny's doubts about the unity of mankind, which led to his theory about a plurality of civilizations.[23]

For Koneczny, civilizations were "the key to understanding human reality and the essence of the historical process,"[24] and he regarded the science of civilizations that he devised as "quite simply the highest level of historical science."[25] As Kolbuszewska notes, Koneczny was not the first or only Pole working on civilizational issues at the time: Erazm Majewski (1858–1922), Jan Karol Kochanowski (1869–1949), and Adam Szelągowski (1873–1961) were contemporaries of Koneczny who were working in this same field. But Koneczny's ideas continue to resonate into the twenty-first century, in part because of his central thesis that world history "was the terrain of the struggle for hegemony and influences among civilizations."[26] It seems ironic today, since Koneczny's science of civilizations is frequently deemed quaint at best and chauvinistic at worst, but Kolbuszewska makes the case for reading him as a pioneer of his time who sought to modernize the discipline of history.[27]

KONECZNY'S CONTEMPORARIES

While today Koneczny may seem dated in his quest for a holistic understanding of world history, he should be credited for challenging the widely held belief that all of mankind was moving forward in a pattern established by Western civilization. He was not alone: Erazm Majewski, Arnold Toynbee, and Christopher Dawson also followed this reasoning.[28] In his thinking Koneczny was influenced by Majewski, who had also proposed that there was no such thing as "mankind" and that there was in fact a plurality of civilizations.[29] Koneczny admired his fellow Pole, whose work he deemed "by any standards—remarkable," in part because Majewski was "a resolute opponent of materialism."[30] Although the two men were contemporaries, their relationship was not one of mutual influence. While Majewski influenced Koneczny, the reverse is not evident.[31] Majewski published the first volume of his *Nauka o cywilizacji* (Science of Civilization, 1908) a decade before Koneczny presented his civilizational theory in some detail.[32]

Arnold Toynbee also derided "the misconception of 'the unity of civilization'" in the first volume of his epic, *A Study of History*. In 1934, he wrote that

> [t]he misleading feature in the social environment has been the fact that, in modern times, our own Western Civilization has cast the net of its economic system round the World. . . . This economic unification on a Western basis has been followed up by a political unification on the same basis which has gone almost as far. . . . [T]his explains how

Western historians have come to exaggerate both the range of these facts and their import.[33]

Critiquing the notion of "Westernization" in post-Soviet Russia, I. A. Vasilenko points out that "[t]he conception of a single civilization spawned the fallacious interpretation of social progress as a system of originally universal impulses, operating automatically in any cultural milieu. Hence there was no problem of a choice of civilization: all nations had the same fate, all would be irresistably drawn up the escalator of progress to a preordained future."[34] This echoes Toynbee's earlier complaint that the

> thesis that the present [1934] unification of the World on a Western basis is the consummation of a single continuous process which accounts for the whole of human history requires a violent distortion of historical facts and a drastic limitation of the historian's field of vision.... While the economic and political maps of the World have now been "Westernized" almost out of recognition, the cultural map remains to-day substantially what it was before our Western Society ever started on its career of economic and political conquest.[35]

Although Koneczny and Toynbee came to some similar conclusions, Andrzej Piskozub believes that they represent different approaches.[36] And it seems that Koneczny constructed his science of civilizations independently of Toynbee. Early signs of Koneczny's theories are evident in the first volume of his *Dzieje Rosji* (History of Russia, 1917), and certainly his two-volume *Polski logos a ethos* (Polish Logos and Ethos, 1921) puts forth his theoretical framework in an introductory way. This is earlier than Toynbee, who published his first volume of *A Study of History* in 1934. Koneczny's comprehensive *Plurality of Civilisations* appeared the next year.

Polish scholars today have delivered a mixed verdict in their assessment of Koneczny's methodology. Sonia Bukowska believes that despite the fact that "today some of Koneczny's views are anachronistic, the theory formulated by him certainly is notable."[37] Zbigniew Pucek contends that over time Koneczny's methodology transformed "from historiography to sociological historiosophy."[38] He stresses that the impact of World War I, including the emergence of an independent Polish state, served as a key trigger for Koneczny's shift from empirical research to a philosophy of history that sought to address Poland's fate in the world. Jan Skoczyński concludes that Koneczny may have started out as an empiricist and positivist, but he ended up as a romantic who embraced a priori assumptions to fit his axiological framework for the comparative study of civilizations.[39] Pucek also believes that Koneczny "only partially remained true to the positivism of the Kraków School"[40] as he sought new methods for his historiosophical works of historical synthesis. But Piotr Bezat, author of a glowing synopsis of the Konecznian worldview, insists that Koneczny never renounced aposteriorism.[41]

In the conclusion of his most important theoretical work, *Plurality of Civilisations*, Koneczny expressed his grand vision for a new approach to researching world history. He declared that historians would

no longer yield in anything to the "exact knowledge" of the natural sciences. History is capable of discovering and demonstrating her "axioms" and "laws" *by her own method*. . . . I believe I have succeeded in indicating the direction of a new road for those on the pilgrimage to Truth.[42]

It is evident, however, that Koneczny and some of his contemporary world historians relied heavily on a priori philosophical and religious assumptions, rather than the methodologies of the social sciences.

For example, Christopher Dawson's concept of civilizations as "spiritual unities" seems similar to Koneczny's vision of ethical values as an important foundation of civilizations. In "Sociology and the Theory of Progress" (1921), Dawson defined "civilization" as "essentially the co-operation of regional societies under a common spiritual influence."[43] Dawson's comment on imperialism also fits with Koneczny's own postcolonial attitudes: "Unlike civilization which is a spiritual co-operation of regional societies, Imperialism is an external forced unification, which may injure or destroy the delicate organisms of local life."[44] In an essay from 1942, "Vitality or Standardization in Culture," Dawson expressed other concerns that were shared by Koneczny. He believed that while the "modern planned society" might have greater power and wealth, "it has two great weaknesses: (a) it seems to leave little or no room for personal freedom, and (b) it disregards spiritual values."[45] Similar to Koneczny's medievalism, Dawson idealized what he termed the "older type of culture. . . . On the whole there was a lot of freedom and no equality, while today there is a lot of equality and hardly any freedom."[46]

Like other twentieth-century pluralist-relativist conceptions, the Konecznian scheme has a normative element that comes into play in distinguishing civilizations and serves to create a hierarchical framework for understanding cultural differences. As Janusz Mucha points out, "religious thinking was very strong in Polish . . . humanities and social sciences,"[47] and this is evident in Koneczny's theories. The British historian Dawson also pined for the religiosity of medieval culture, which "had very clearly defined spiritual standards and was rich in cultural values. These were of course primarily religious, for religion was the supreme unifying force in the old type of society, but they were also cultural in the narrower sense."[48] He believed that "[s]ooner or later, there must be a revival of culture and a reorganization of the spiritual life of Western society."[49] Like Koneczny, he chided "our intense and one-sided preoccupation with the economic issue" and sought the sort of balance evident in Koneczny's quincunx of existential values with an "organized social effort and thought to the development of the noneconomic functions. In this respect it would mark a return to the traditions of the pre-industrial age" and help "open this new world of apparently soulless and soul-destroying mechanism to the spiritual world which stands so near to it."[50] Dawson asserted that "[m]an cannot live in a spiritual void; he needs some fixed social standards and some absolute intellectual principles."[51] Attention must be paid to "the spiritual and social as well as to the economic needs of human nature."[52]

While Koneczny developed his ideas independently of Dawson's influence, he certainly was fully aware of Oswald Spengler's theories, and he presented a direct challenge to them. Koneczny faced a dual dilemma in his project, since he sought to avoid both speculative history and the naturalist reductionism of Spengler.[53] Koneczny's originality stems in part from his reaction to these methodologies. As Skoczyński points out, Koneczny began his work as an empiricist, primarily using the inductive method in his research. He modified his position over time, and his works dealing with civilizational theory reflect a use of the deductive method that he described in disparaging terms so often—especially in his earlier works—"as meditative, speculative, *a priori*, abstract, schematic, presumptuous, synthetic, and generalizing."[54] Alas, Koneczny would eventually express a modified opinion that an exclusively inductive approach makes the construction of a universal history impossible and that something more than empirical material is needed: a schematic of sorts that is evident in his science of civilizations. Skoczyński also finds that Koneczny's optimism about the inductive method fades in his later commentary.[55] For example, Koneczny claims in *Prawa dziejowe* (Historical Laws, 1943) that even though his laws are the result of inductive research, one does not have to dismiss deduction entirely. Later, writing in *O ład w historii* (On Order in History), which was finished just eight months before his death in 1949, Koneczny explicitly proclaimed: "Abstracts govern history!"[56] Skoczyński believes that this indicates a revision of his earlier stance on the use of a priori assumptions when conducting historical research.[57] Indeed, Robert Piotrowski points out that "the pillar of his [Koneczny's] doctrine is the a priori principle of commensurability."[58]

The popularity of efforts to create all-encompassing syntheses of world history waned in the decades after Koneczny's death. But the works of Toynbee continued to generate lively debate about the need for "big history." Commenting on debates among historians in 1964, Othmar Anderle noted that "[a]t the root of these complaints against the remoteness, irrelevance, and uselessness of historical writing is a wish for synthesis, synopsis, or integration."[59] He added that a "majority of those in the debate, even those who reject Toynbee's theory of history and consider his treatment of historical particulars unsuccessful, agree not only with his attacks on specialization but also with his attempt to achieve a synopsis."[60] Anderle was concerned about "whether the methods of contemporary historiography are sufficiently developed to permit the step from specialized research to a synopsis."[61] He identified a conundrum in such efforts, noting that "such a world-picture is not simply the product of a quantitative summary of particular insights, but requires reworking of a qualitative sort, which not only comprehends its material but fuses and integrates it."[62] Koneczny struggled with this same methodological problem, which he hoped to solve with his science of civilizations.

In his discussion of Koneczny, Toynbee, and other philosophers of history, Anderle opined that "[a]ll these men are . . . outsiders, iconoclasts and revolutionaries in oppositon to the aims, methods, and standards of the official academic discipline. They constitute an 'Historiographical Fronde.'"[63] Referring to these men as the "Opposition," Anderle pointed out that

> according to their mood, they are empirical or a priori. . . . They cross boundaries of the discipline and . . . combine or confuse areas which the academic discipline has clearly distinguished. . . . All this is done with little hesitation, if it helps or seems to help in attaining their goal of . . . a comprehensive historical world-picture. [64]

On the other hand, John Lukacs adds that although "we may have transcended the phase of our interest in philosophies of history . . . we ought not dismiss all the philosophers of history out of hand. . . . [T]hey represented at times the highest intellectual aspirations of a certain period."[65]

Koneczny certainly had high hopes about creating a new method of historical research, but he eventually resorted to a priori assumptions about civilizational values. His system resembles a "metaphysics of morality," a "practical metaphysics," or a "historiosophical realism" that is linked to his search for the foundations of a just society based on the traditional values of a given civilization.[66] Moreover, since Poland was a "nation without its own state" during Koneczny's early career, his "most important 'social task' was . . . to contribute to regaining the national and political sovereignty. Sovereignty and freedom (not liberal individual freedom but national, collective freedom, the independence from other, external, political bodies) were the most cherished social or even moral values."[67]

Koneczny's emphasis on morality is similar to Toynbee's (in his later volumes) and Jacques Maritain's (1882–1973) in that his concept of a "plurality of civilizations" represents "an attempt at reconciling the tradition of Christian historiosophy with the modern postulates of historical-cultural relativism."[68] Most important, it is clear that "[a] Christian worldview gives his conception an axiological perspective."[69] For Koneczny, values are formed over time through concrete historical conditions, and this is a crucial feature of his cultural relativism. Moreover, the "relativizing interpretation of the quincunx allows for the introduction of the idea of defective civilizations . . . that developed weakly in general or did not develop in certain areas."[70] As Pucek correctly notes, this allows for the creation of "an ideal type," which for Koneczny is Latin civilization. All others prove to be incomplete and "defective" in some fashion as they neglect some aspect of either the spiritual or material side of life.[71] Koneczny labeled various features of other civilizations that he disliked as "civilizational deviations."[72]

An intellectual construct that reflects the concerns of his time and place, Koneczny's science of civilizations also addressed the three crucial issues that Janusz Mucha identifies as the primary concerns for Polish social scientists at that time: the concept of "the nation," the problem of cultural identity, and the search for societal harmony and autonomy. Mucha states that such "crucial issues were raised, during this period of time, by non-academic, non-institutionalized social sciences (sociology). This kind of early sociology was done by some academics who worked professionally in other fields, like philosophy, economics or history, by political journalists and writers."[73] Koneczny certainly fits within this group of researchers working on the periphery of a discipline—for much of his career he also worked on the periphery of established academia—who contributed a great deal to the intellectual discourse on these weighty issues. While these persons were well-educated and were fluent in many European languages, they "were 'independent' from the foreign intellectual traditions and took advantage of originally Polish conceptual categories and confronted originally Polish (or, rather, non-Western European) issues."[74] Moreover, Koneczny and other Polish social scientists

> were not afraid of the normative concept. They did not differ from their Western colleagues in their ideological and reformist attitude, but understood reformism differently. When Western social sciences worked on the development of scientific foundations of institutional social policy and social work, the normative Polish sociology intended to address the moral attitudes of Poles, to shape the "spirit of the nation."[75]

The sociological component of Koneczny's theories is evident in his analysis of civil society, especially in his distinction between *społeczność* and *społeczeństwo*. The former (community) is more rudimentary and "mechanistic" in nature, while the latter (society) is more highly developed and differentiated and is more "organic" in nature.[76] Skoczyński sees similarities with Emile Durkheim's (1858–1917) emphasis on an organic unity within society among different social groups.[77] While its "clash of civilizations" thesis is better-known, Koneczny's science of civilizations can also be viewed as an attempt to explain the role of social harmony in history.[78] This emphasis on social harmony, the primacy of nation over state, and civilizational purity can be understood as another contribution to Polish social theory in the same vein as Aleksander Świętochowski's (1849–1938) positivism or Jerzy Kurnatowski's (1874–1934) solidarism. The solidarist Kurnatowski believed that a healthy "organic" society thrives on differences within the population, similar to the way Durkheim called for harmonious relations among all societal groups.[79] Koneczny also saw the "unity in variety" that developed in Latin civilization, which allowed societies to evolve in "organic" ways. All other civilizations represent a contradictory tendency, with a "mechanical" uniformity imposed that creates "monotony" in society.[80] An important corollary in Koneczny's theories is the "law of inequality"; in Koneczny's worldview, inequality feeds progress.[81] Koneczny believed that societal progress leads to more variety but inevitable inequality, as opposed to forced uniformity and equality. As Stanisław Jedynak points out, in the Konecznian worldview all efforts to create equality go against natural societal processes.[82]

One can read Koneczny's works as a response to Karl Marx's (1818–83) theory of class struggle. While the Marxist dialectic requires conflict to move history forward, Koneczny emphasized civilizational harmony within society as the key for progress. In contrast to artificial or mechanical changes forced on people, Koneczny sought moral progress through valid change that preserved civilizational authenticity.[83] The goal for Poland was the "moral regeneration of statehood" that is reminiscent of the nineteenth-century Polish romantic linkage of moral progress and action.[84] Above all, Koneczny advised Poles to stay true to one's civilizational values.[85] Societies move forward only through a culture of action that emerges from an understanding of one's civilizational roots. Ignorance of one's heritage, or apathy, inevitably leads to regress and decline.[86] His "law of commensurability" states that societies need uniform values to avoid mayhem and moral decay. This could only happen if there was civilizational purity attained by purging a society of its alien civilizational influences.[87]

Scholars have debated the merits of Koneczny's "science of civilizations" for over half a century. Reviewing the English-language translation of Koneczny's *Plurality of Civilisations*, which first appeared in 1962, Jean Floud commented that it was

> better than its auspices. It is an anachronism in 1964, representing a dead mode of sociological discourse. But the mode was not quite dead in 1935 and the book could then have been reasonably regarded as a serious effort by a scholar working off the European mainstream and subject to the peculiar pressures and seductions of Polish nationalism.[88]

Anton Hilckman wrote extensively in the 1950s and 1960s about Koneczny's ideas, especially his quincunx of existential values and the need for civilizational purity. The German scholar explained that "[t]he attitude towards these values, the valuation of them and the determination of the relation between them can be very different. The understanding of these differences gives a key which opens the riddle of the diversity of civilizations."[89]

There has been a renewed interest in Koneczny's works in the past three decades, and scholars and journalists have addressed the Koneczny "renaissance"[90] in critical fashion. Most notably, Jan Skoczyński's edited work, *Feliks Koneczny dzisiaj* (Feliks Koneczny Today, 2000), brought together in one volume multiple perspectives on a variety of Konecznian themes. As one reviewer put it, the contributors explore the "depths and shallows of Feliks Koneczny."[91] Janusz Goćkowski analyzes Koneczny's "ethnocentrism and xenophobia."[92] Marian Bębenek explains Koneczny's "ethocentrism," which is evident in his emphasis on ethics in public life. He predicts that in practice Konecznian policies would reject equality before the law by distinguishing among people based on their "civilization."[93] Interestingly, this very issue has been raised by some Polish pundits, who argue that "guests" from other civilizations who reside in Poland should not be afforded full citizenship. Zbigniew Kuderowicz is another contemporary scholar who shares Bębenek's concerns; he also questions the process of "internal enrichment" Koneczny prescribed, which required one to follow one's civilizational values to their utmost. Kuderowicz also sees in Koneczny's advocacy of an "ethical unity of a civilization"[94] an element of xenophobia and an unwillingness to recognize the creative role of cultural diffusion or the vital role of immigration in world history.

While some scholars acknowledge that all efforts at historical synthesis place some order on the material according to some preconceived concepts,[95] others are more critical of the fundamentalist Catholic viewpoint that permeates Koneczny's historical and theoretical works.[96] Although he consistently railed against apriorism in all realms of scientific research, it is clear that Koneczny's theoretical works are colored by his own preconceptions and biases related to an intense nationalism and devout Catholic fundamentalism. Some critics have labeled Koneczny a "neoromantic and mystical" historian,[97] whose ideas are out of line with mainstream historiography. However, the Polish medieval historian Henryk Samsonowicz concedes that Koneczny "continues to play a great role. Possibly not in the studies of scholars, but in the visions of Jędrzej Giertych, for example, and other authors whose creations have repeated certain stereotypes."[98] In recent years, Koneczny continued to exert an influence among nationalist activists; LPR leader Wojciech Wierzejski recalls that he read Koneczny while in middle school, and he continues to view the world through a Konecznian lens.[99]

Perhaps Koneczny's science of civilizations can be better understood as historiosophy or philosophy of history.[100] Stanisław Jedynak argues that although Koneczny claimed to be an empiricist and does cite a great deal of evidence, it merely "serves to illustrate" a certain preconceived philosophical worldview. He detects a series of a priori assumptions that are axiological and indicative of the traditional Catholic views held by Koneczny. Jedynak concludes that "Koneczny was, moreover, intolerant in regard to other civilizations."[101] And Janusz Tazbir detects a "strong anti-Semitic, although not racist accent" in Koneczny's works.[102]

EXPLORING THE "OTHER"

Not unlike other Polish social scientists of his day, Koneczny "underlined the separateness, conflictual character of neighboring cultures."[103] This approach reflects the "dichotomizing tendencies" described by Jacques Semelin. He posits that

> identity is conceived through the perception of a difference, giving substance both to One and the Other. And this One can enter into peaceful relations with this Other: History provides enough examples. But it is also true that this identity "open" to another can retreat and withdraw into itself by establishing a criterion of exclusion from this Other.[104]

For Koneczny, the "criterion of exclusion" is "civilization" rather than race or ethnicity. This confirms Leonidas Donskis's contention that "[t]he concepts of culture and civilization can . . . become tools of symbolic exclusion. Whenever we hear a voice raised in defense of the paramount values of civilization, we may have no doubt that 'civilization' here means a unifying ideological principle to mobilize 'us' against 'them.' "[105] In Koneczny's quest for civilizational purity, we find that "others" were marginalized in the process. As Iver B. Neumann asks, "The other upsets order, simply by being other, and what is one to do when there is a multiplicity of others?"[106]

In this regard, Koneczny's science of civilizations clearly presents certain methodological problems. Scholars such as Jörn Rüsen have explored the "difficulty of applying specialized research skills to different historical cultures," which makes comparative studies difficult.[107] He finds that "[n]egative, menacing, disturbing aspects are repressed and pushed away towards the 'other.' . . . It is part of the utility of historical memory."[108] According to Rüsen, "the formative power of the normative factors of historical identity remain prevalent. Even a historiography based on methodologically controlled research is determined by the political and social life of its time and by the expectations and dispositions of its audiences."[109] Koneczny undertook his comparative studies using western historiographical methodologies, and he tended to view the world through his peculiar lens. If "[e]very comparison needs an organizing parameter,"[110] then Koneczny supplied such a mechanism in his science of civilizations in the form of the quincunx of existential values. This device reflects the influence of his Thomist thinking and represents an artifact of the Catholic fundamentalism that is central to the worldview of Koneczny and his followers.

Rüsen cautions that "[i]ntercultural comparison is a very sensitive matter. It touches the field of cultural identity and it is therefore involved in power struggles among different countries."[111] This is especially evident in Koneczny's critiques of Byzantine, Turanian, and Jewish civilizations, which in his mind represented threats to the purity of Latin civilization in Poland. He constructed a discourse of dominance that makes Poland's Latin civilizational traits more

valid and more worthy than those of its rivals. Koneczny's science of civilizations also appears as an attempt to understand the imperial project from the
perspective of the colonized subject, especially in his works that deal with German Byzantinism and Russian Turanianism.[112] Despite Poland's occupation by
Byzantine (German) powers and Turanian Russia, and the threat of the Jewish
internal "Other," its true national wealth thus rests on its foundational values of
Latin civilization steeped in Catholicism.

In the works of theorists like Koneczny, it seems that intercultural "contact
increases awareness of difference between civilizations and invigorates animos-
ities."[113] As Rüsen also points out, in comparative efforts "there is an epistemological difficulty with enormous conceptual and methodological consequences
for the humanities: every comparison is done in a given cultural context, so
the culture is involved in the subject matter of the comparison itself."[114] Ezequiel Adamovsky's commentary on "Euro-Orientalism" might also be applied
to Koneczny's civilizational theories. Adamovsky contends that "[t]he counter-
part of the liberal-bourgeois narrative of Western civilization is the narrative
of its 'others,' for in every binary construction of identity the excluded 'other'
and the self that gained consistency by means of that exclusion depend on each
other; both identities are part of the same discourse."[115] This resembles the sort
of "discourse of misrepresentation" and "trap of dichotomies" that has been
described by Syed Farid Alatas.[116] Equally important, Adamovsky reminds us
of David Cannadine's argument about the role of class, in addition to race, in
shaping visions of empire.[117] This tells us that "otherness" need not be solely
about race. In the case of Koneczny, it is "civilizational otherness" that shapes
his vision of the world and allows him to construct a hierarchy that places Latin
civilization at the top. Civilizational fundamentalists in contemporary Poland
share a similar worldview.

Koneczny could more appropriately be regarded as "Latin-centric" rather
than "Eurocentric," since he does acknowledge the existence of other civilizations in Europe. But his quincunx and its existential values are defined in ways
that privilege Latin civilization. In the process of comparing civilizations within
his framework, moreover, Koneczny undertakes the sort of "essentializing and
stereotyping" described by Alatas.[118] While Koneczny recognized a "plurality of civilizations" and implicitly accepted the "authenticity of non-European
systems, ideological orientations, culture and religions,"[119] this did not prevent
him from judging them to be "incomplete" or "defective" in some fashion in
comparison to Latin civilization.

Koneczny's attempt to comprehend world history manifests itself as a series
of misunderstandings of "others." His science of civilizations, unfortunately,
has also provided validation for the diminution of "others." Leonidas Donskis
posits that

> it might be suggested that hatred often originates as the will to misun-
> derstand. Stereotyping and thinking in clichés are related to our need for

mental security and predictability of the world. Hatred always signifies the loss of our sense of certainty and security. Those who overcome in themselves the propensity to think in polarities, to jump to extremes or to rely on safe stereotypes are a minority.[120]

This would seem to relate especially to Koneczny's formative years, at a time when Poland was still stateless and as traditional Polish culture was threatened both by foreign occupation and the challenge of modernism. Plagued by what Donskis terms a "troubled identity," people in times of cultural flux are "inclined to create the imagined gallery of the heroes of history, culture, and self-hood. . . . [C]ulture becomes a mode of discourse and also the collective hero of our troubled imagination."[121]

Koneczny's tendency to essentialize "others" by assigning them immutable traits brings the risk of "freezing" civilizations in a static state. But how does one create a comparative framework that avoids the diminution and possible demonization of "others?" Jörn Rüsen proposes a solution:

> We avoid ethnocentrism if a specific culture is understood as a combination of elements which are shared by all other cultures. Thus the specificity of cultures is brought about by different constellations of the same elements. Such an approach has the following virtues: it presents the otherness of different cultures as a mirror facilitating better self-understanding; it thus includes otherness rather than uses it as a principle of segregation; it encourages recognition and mutuality in people of different cultures.[122]

Koneczny's quincunx of existential values would seemingly allow his science of civilizations to reach such levels of objectivity. This is not evident in his works, however, or in the commentary of those successors who use his scholarship as "scientific" validation for their chauvinism.

Moreover, Koneczny's commentary frequently reflected a superficial understanding of the various cultures that he analyzed. For example, he claimed that "negro Africa is becoming deforested. Once felled, the forests do not renew themselves, and negroes do not plant trees, while missionary efforts to reafforest with European seeds have only local importance."[123] He also stated that "negroes know nothing of fishing, of which there is a good deal among Indians."[124] Koneczny's ignorance was due in part to his use of poor source material, which was often subjective in nature (such as missionary accounts of lands far removed from his personal experiences).[125] Koneczny also relied on missionaries' experiences to explain different ethical systems—such as that among the First Nations in Canada.[126] Elsewhere, he cited the random impressions of a Polish pilgrim to the Holy Land in 1934 as evidence.[127] Closer to Koneczny's Polish home, we still detect a curious tendency to rely on anecdotal evidence. When commenting on bathing habits in various cultures, he claimed that "the average

Slav countryman cares more for the cleanliness of his clothing than of his body."[128]

Koneczny may have rejected race theory, but he did make racist observations based on dubious logic. This was often the result of his poor selection of sources.[129] He commented that "experience confirms a thousand-fold that the brunette passes on his features more strongly than the blonde, and the negro twice as strongly as the white. . . . [C]hildren of a Japanese woman and a German tend to be delicate, while the offspring of a Japanese woman and a Frenchman may be healthier than those of two Japanese parents."[130] This leaves the reader with an impression that Koneczny is concerned with race-mixing;[131] these asides serve as a distraction from his main concern, which is the explication of the categories of being as useful in comparing civilizations. In this context, race is not regarded by Koneczny as relevant: "It is certain that there is no *permanent* relation between race and civilisation. And a quite primitive knowledge of history is sufficient to bring realisation that within one civilisation there may be different races—and in one race different civilisations."[132]

While Koneczny rejected any claims based on alleged racial superiority, he clearly used other ways to explain levels of civilizational development.[133] As Sonia Bukowska notes, the quincunx allowed Koneczny to assess and judge civilizations for their "completeness." Moreover, the concept of harmony that is so central to Koneczny's civilizational vision also applied to all categories of existential being within a person. The same "law of commensurability" held sway: the greater the agreement, the stronger the person or collective life. The highest order of collective life, as defined by Koneczny, was a civilization.[134] In Koneczny's judgment, Latin civilization was the only complete and "ideal" civilization, while all others were defective.[135] As Bukowska correctly notes, "for F. Koneczny Latin civilization was the most splendid method of organization for collective life."[136]

DEFENDING LATIN CIVILIZATION

Koneczny's quincunx is not unique. Rüsen cites the example of Johan Galtung's "Six Cosmologies: An Impressionistic Presentation," which has some elements that remind one of Koneczny's system. Galtung compares six different cultures by using eight basic concepts: nature, self, society, world, time self, time society, transperson, and episteme.[137] Rüsen argues that the

> idea that cultures are pre-given units and entities is committed to a cultural logic which grounds identity on a fundamental difference between inside and outside. Such a logic conceptualizes identity as a mental territory with clear borderlines and a correspondingly sharp division between self and other. This logic is essentially ethnocentric.[138]

An ethnocentric tendency is clearly evident in Koneczny's scholarship. I agree with Jolanta Kolbuszewska's contention that even Koneczny's early historical research on Poland and Russia—such as the first volume of *Dzieje Rosji* (History of Russia, 1917)—did not produce "simple diachronical narratives, but analyses of the past of these states from the point of view of civilizational and cultural transformation occuring in them, and also the consequences deriving from them. The author evaluated their histories through the prism of the theory of civilization that he was gradually creating."[139] Here Kolbuszewska identifies the roots of Koneczny's civilizational theory that appeared in full form in *Plurality of Civilisations* (1935). She also detects the growing influence of cultural determinism in his works as Koneczny developed his theories over the years. This is evident in Koneczny's use of abstract concepts, as in the quincunx, that evoke certain values. Each civilization creates its own rules that govern human coexistence as a whole; in essence, each civilization has its own "method." From Koneczny's perspective, these various methods were not compatible, and they were in constant conflict as civilizations interacted with one another.

As Radosław Brzózka reminds us, Koneczny completed the work on his science of civilizations during the era of two world wars; undoubtedly, the global conflicts affected his thinking on the tendency of civilizations to be locked in perpetual struggles for dominance. As a result, Koneczny identified alien civilizational influences as the cause of Europe's decline into dysfunction. He concluded that its recovery was contingent on "a return to a pure Latin civilization."[140] Even today, in the Konecznian worldview international relations are often placed within the context of civilizational conflicts. Following Konecznian reasoning, Brzózka also finds that "[t]he theory of empire was a vital and topical problem" during the medieval period, and "Poland emerged on the foundation of Latin civilization, but rejected feudalism and imperialism."[141] According to Koneczny, this explains the absence of a Polish absolutist tradition. He credited the Church for its resistance to state power in Poland, which exemplifies his persistent emphasis on the constructive role of the Church in Latin civilization.[142]

Koneczny's historical laws also indicate that in civilizational struggles the "lower" or less-developed civilization will usually defeat the more advanced and complex one. Constant vigilance is needed to maintain higher civilizations against these threats. A "higher" civilization, such as the Latin one, bears a burden of sorts, since its more complex nature requires a great deal of effort to maintain.[143] Jan Skoczyński finds that this vision is both "pessimistic and tragic at the same time."[144] It is pessimistic since it implies the possibility of regression in collective life; it is tragic because the values of a higher civilization could be destroyed by a lower one.[145] There is a certain "civilizational fatalism" in this reasoning, since it burdens the defenders of a higher (Latin) civilization in Poland with a great responsibility in their confrontation with the threats of lower (Byzantine, Turanian, and Jewish) civilizations.

MEDIEVALISM

An important component of Koneczny's position on civilizational differences is that technology and other "material" factors are far less relevant than "spiritual" matters of ethics and morality.[146] As Tomasz Wituch opines, "Feliks Koneczny categorically rejected the materialist conception of human history."[147] Koneczny believed that technology could change the outside trappings of life, but not the inner workings of man.[148] Technological change is not the key for Koneczny's vision of progress, which relates more to ethical and moral behavior. Moreover, technology transfers do not disrupt civilizational purity.[149] New technologies emerge and spread from civilization to civilization, but this does not mean that fundamental differences are bridged; rather, ethical factors distinguish civilizations from one another.

Andrzej Bokiej sees a close connection between morality and historical development in Koneczny's theory, since morality is the most important part of the quincunx. One cannot mix civilizations in part because one cannot mix moral codes—this would lead to ethical chaos.[150] Koneczny maintained that "[t]here does not exist, to be sure, any 'ethical unity of humanity,' because each civilization has its own ethic."[151] Leszek Gawor also identifies morality as a key for understanding Koneczny's reading of history:

> The fall of the Roman Empire, the partitions of Poland, the cultural crisis of the first decades of our [twentieth] century were in Koneczny's thinking above all the result of changes in the sphere of morality. These changes, and their subsequent catastrophes, were due to the departure from a uniform and coherent moral foundation that is harmonized with the rest of the quincunx—in this case, of Latin civilization—and the acceptance of values that are appropriate only for another civilization.[152]

From Koneczny's perspective the crises of his time were the result of weakened civilizational foundations, and he looked to medieval Christendom for clues about how to solve the crisis.[153]

The concept of "medievalism" is central to understanding Koneczny's appeal to contemporary readers. Clare A. Simmons points out that differences

> between Medievalism and medieval studies might be summarized as oppositions: *Medieval Studies*: Professional; within the academy; research-based; objective; committed to discovering the authentic past. *Medievalism*: Amateur; outside the academy; based on cultural preconceptions; subjective; shaped by the individual's needs and desires.[154]

She cautions, however, that these distinctions are not so clear-cut: "medieval studies cannot, at least in hindsight, be entirely free of Medievalism."[155] This blurring of distinctions is evident in Koneczny's work. Early in his career, he strove to conduct empirical research on medieval topics, especially related to

Polish-German relations and Russian history. Over time, however, his work reflected a certain medievalism as he moved from empiricism to a more normative approach. In his commentary on medieval history, we see signs of his shift to the very aprioristic method that he so often condemned.

Koneczny was not alone; in his monograph *Inventing the Middle Ages* (1991), Norman Cantor demonstrates how scholars of the interwar period "injected their own personal circumstances into their reading" of the past.[156] Cantor effectively illuminates several examples of what he calls "'retromedievalism,' the desire to return to a past that seems more attractive than the present."[157] He focuses on scholars who "fashioned their interpretations of the Middle Ages out of the emotional wellsprings of their lives, and these lives were in turn conditioned by the vast social and political upheavals of the twentieth century, especially during the dark times from 1914 to 1945."[158] Likewise, Koneczny's medievalism emerged out of his quest for refuge from troubled times, and he found a safe haven in medieval Poland. Koneczny regarded Poles as the first people since the ancient Romans to possess a national consciousness. This consciousness emerged as Poles were developing a national state, which occurred by the fourteenth century, in contrast to the prevalent dynasticism of the time.[159] For Koneczny, the "national idea is a peculiarly Polish concept."[160]

In the field of nationality studies there are broad distinctions between primordialists (like Koneczny), who trace a long national history, and modernists who argue that nationalism emerged much later.[161] Mieczysław Ryba draws attention to the key Konecznian concept that the nation predates the state, that the national state is the natural form for organizing social life in Latin civilization, and that it reflects a vital and organic ethical union. Ryba contrasts this "natural" union to mechanical bureaucracies, an argument frequently used by Konecznian pundits to denounce the German-dominated European Union.[162] Koneczny's analysis of the fifteenth century "great war" between Poland and the Order of Teutonic Knights thus inspires twenty-first-century critics of Germany. His "Grunwald Theory" goes well beyond the recognition of the importance of Germany in the formation of Polish national consciousness, as he also highlighted Polish advocacy for a new international system. Koneczny maintained that Poles laid the foundation for a theory of the "brotherhood of nations, a system of union, and also the notion that public law flows from society and not from dynastic rule."[163] Thanks to the outcome of the "great war," Koneczny believed that these key ideas took hold in other parts of Europe.[164]

Koneczny clearly found solace in Polish traditions, and he sought to explain to readers their historical context. Discussing his use of the concept of historicism, Sonia Bukowska points out that he defined it not only in the context of the relationship to time, "but also in connection with reflection on the problems of morality and tradition."[165] She notes that for Koneczny the whole realm of ethics could not be grasped by those who do not have historical consciousness, because this means they lack a sense of responsibility for future generations.

Koneczny stressed continuity, and those who do not comprehend a person's place in the flow of history cannot envision a need to preserve civilization for the future. Defending tradition is the key, but Koneczny also distinguished between a passive and active relationship with tradition. The former he associated with primitive cultures and sacral (Jewish and Brahmanic) civilizations. Koneczny's depiction of their stultifying reliance on tradition brings to mind Friedrich Nietzsche's admonitions about "antiquarianism" and the unhealthy reverence for the past that stifles actions in the present.[166] On the other hand, in Latin civilization an *active tradition* "stimulates acts, calling them forth and giving them direction. In other words, it ought to influence practical life."[167]

ORIENTALISM

One of Koneczny's historical laws stated that civilizational mixing leads to moral and psychological damage and a general decline in the "culture of action." Another indicated that "lower" civilizations generally overcome "higher" civilizations in confrontations.[168] In historical terms, the Roman civilization declined as it became culturally Orientalized; likewise, modern Latin civilization has been confronted with a variety of "Oriental" threats. Koneczny believed that "the Orient" had no culture of action; rather, it merely flashed its "self-satisfied smile."[169] He also feared that contacts with the East would sap Poles of their vitality. Robert Piotrowski has detected hygienic ideas in Koneczny's civilizational discourse, with a pathological aspect being an important feature of intercivilizational contacts.[170] Konecznian historian Dariusz Ratajczak pointed out that Koneczny was "a passionate advocate of western or Latin civilization" who maintained that "this civilization developed in its most pure form in Poland," which was "for centuries . . . a defensive bulwark of the Western Christian world."[171] He endorsed Koneczny's argument that Latin civilization had been weakened by "three aggressors attacking the West"—Turanian, Byzantine, and Jewish civilizations—and that Poles should take measures against further pollution from these "lower" civilizations.[172]

One of these Oriental threats was Byzantinism. Koneczny completed his monograph on Byzantine civilization in March 1947, but the problematic book was already partially finished at the time of the publication of *Plurality of Civilisations* (1935).[173] Waldemar Ceran finds that the book has "a huge number of factual errors."[174] Andrzej Bokiej stresses the mass of material presented in his *Cywilizacja bizantyńska*.[175] Yet, he manipulated existing knowledge to fit within his theoretical framework. Maciej Salamon thus contends that Koneczny selectively used existing scholarship that fit his worldview.[176]

As Małgorzata Dąbrowska demonstrates, Koneczny sought to present "Byzantine civilization" as deficient in comparison with the Latin world.[177] This tendency to essentialize Byzantium and to cast it as the polar opposite of "the

West" is reminiscent of Edward Said's concept of Orientalism.[178] One also sees in Koneczny's work an example of a different sort of "Byzantinism" defined by Dimiter G. Angelov as the attempt "to designate a representation of Byzantine civilization as an antipode and an imperfect reflection of Western historical experiences and values."[179] According to Angelov, Byzantinism tries

> to present a variation within the construct of European civilization and to portray the other "within." Byzantinism is both a specific discourse about Byzantium with a long history stretching back to the Middle Ages and a reductionist approach which essentializes Byzantium through the application of analytical categories derived, explicitly or indirectly, from Western historical experience.[180]

Angelov notes that the "methodological fallacy of Byzantinism is not unique in itself. It is also the fallacy of reductionism and of simplistic comparative history, which both tend to prejudge issues."[181] He finds that "the essentialization of Byzantinism as a polar opposite, or an imperfect reflection, of the West has been a tradition within Western intellectual history."[182] In this sense, Koneczny reflected the biases of his age. Michael McCormick notes that "it must be emphasized that modern scholarship's very positive appraisal of Byzantium's creative role in the formation of early medieval culture is a recent development. . . . By applying new methods and newer questions, today's Byzantinists are exploding the image of a culture frozen in time."[183]

In his depiction of Byzantine civilization as a defective and incomplete amalgam, Koneczny highlighted the negative influences of "inferior" Oriental civilizations.[184] Koneczny fits Said's description of an "Orientalist at the barricades, where in his professional work he confronted the East . . . and held it at bay on behalf of the West."[185] He believed that "in Byzantium a separate civilisation developed which certainly did not become a continuation of the Roman. It was a compromise creation between Rome, Greece and the Asiatic Orient with Syrian influences weighing increasingly in the scales."[186] He thus claimed to understand how civilizations are formed and are distinguished from one another. Isaiah Berlin's critique of such efforts surely fits Koneczny: "To understand is to perceive patterns. . . . The more inevitable an event or an action or a character can be exhibited as being, the better it has been understood, the profounder the researcher's insight, the nearer we are to the one ultimate truth."[187]

The "truth" was that Latin civilization was substantively different from the Orient. Anton Hilckman sought to clarify Koneczny's vision in relation to civilizational differences between Latin Poles and Byzantine Germans.[188] He maintained that "[o]nly in the light of a science of civilisations is it possible to understand the present [1962] antinomy of East and West. . . . We do not hesitate to consider the doctrine of Koneczny to be one of the sharpest weapons which can serve in the struggle for the defence of the West."[189] As Hilckman inadvertently implied, at the core of Koneczny's thinking is an Orientalist assumption of a dichotomous and antagonistic relationship between the "West" and "East." Of course, one might argue that Koneczny's science of civilizations is "not Eurocentric, and thus it does not exclude other non-European civilizations as separate civilizations."[190] But he obviously established a hierarchy in which Latin civilization held a special place.

Turanian civilization, especially in its Russian guise, represented another Oriental threat to Latin Poland. Koneczny's analysis of Russian history was hailed by Hilckman as one of his "greatest merits."[191] Hilckman later updated Koneczny's analysis of Russia, adapting it for the Cold War. Writing in 1957, he argued that totalitarianism was not new; rather, in the thirteenth century Ghengis Khan had created a "totalitarian state."[192] Hilckman explicitly analyzed Bolshevism as a continuation of this Turanian statist tradition.[193] But this "Turanian" interpretation of Russian history is laden with Orientalist assumptions. In his seminal work, Edward Said noted that one of the "principal dogmas of Orientalism" is the emphasis on an "absolute and systematic difference between the West, which is rational, developed, humane, superior, and the Orient, which is aberrant, undeveloped, inferior."[194] Hilckman identified this same phenomenon in the works of Koneczny, for whom Turanian Russia was the polar opposite of Latin Poland. As Hilckman put it: "*Between the West and Turan, there is a contrast, an opposition that is absolute.*"[195] Hilckman expanded on this theme: "In the Turanian civilisation and in its descendant, Muscovy-Russia, there is, legally, no such a thing as a 'society' in existence: the State is everything. The European lives *also* in the State, the Turanian lives *exclusively* in it."[196] As Koneczny had explained, "[i]n the contrasts of Turanian and Latin civilizations appears the whole opposition of East and West."[197]

ANTI-SEMITISM

Another striking feature of Koneczny's theory is his "monadic" vision of closed civilizations that are resistant to fundamental changes. This is perhaps most evident in his discussion of Jewish civilization, which also represented a threat to Latin Poland. He asserted that it had

> passed through changes which in any other [civilization] would certainly be regarded as basic, and which despite this has nevertheless remained itself. . . . [C]hanges have taken place without touching the supreme principle that they are a privileged nation, called to rule over the whole earth (Jewish Messianism). If this feature were to collapse, Jewish civilisation would collapse.[198]

He did concede that "[c]ivilisations obviously exercise a reciprocal influence on one another, and the Jewish has left its imprint on societies of Latin civilisation."[199]

As Sonia Bukowska puts it, Koneczny's "views . . . on the theme of Jewish civilization particularly arouse lots of emotions."[200] Koneczny's treatise on "Jewish civilization" represented what an early reviewer termed "'high anti-semitism' revived."[201] Other Polish scholars have also criticized Koneczny's works on Jewish civilization, including his "completely grotesque" depiction of Jewish influences on Nazism.[202] When Koneczny's *Cywilizacja żydowska* (Jewish Civilization) was published in London in 1974, it seemed like a blast of fear and intolerance from the past. In a critical review of the book, S. L. Shneiderman judged that while "Hitler had his racial purity, Koneczny has his cultural purity. . . . Obsessed with defending the purity of Latin civilization, Koneczny looks into the crystal ball and predicts that when the War [World War II] ends, 'Jewish influence in Europe will have grown immensely.'"[203] Koneczny even addressed the issue of ritual murder as a legitimate topic, hypothesizing that there could have been a fanatical Jewish sect that endorsed such a practice.[204] Nationalist ideologue Jędrzej Giertych excused Koneczny's insensitivity to Jewish suffering during the Holocaust by noting that his book was finished by 1943, that he was already eighty-one years old by that time, and that he had no access to the ghettos to document their horrors.[205] But in a recent essay, Richard Pipes opines that Koneczny "espoused a rabid anti-Semitism. His writings on the subject of Jewish civilization border on the demented."[206] Commenting on *Cywilizacja żydowska*, Pipes notes that "as he was writing this, the Holocaust was at its peak, and Jews from his home town were being rounded up and gassed by the thousands in Auschwitz, a mere fifty kilometers from Kraków."[207]

Koneczny's ideas reflect the extremist mood of nationalist discourse about the "Jewish question" during the interwar period and wartime. This included rhetoric about "'the dangerous physical exposure' to Jews and the 'Jewish way of thinking.'"[208] In his introduction to Koneczny's book, Jędrzej Giertych discussed the so-called "Lublin plan" for concentrating Jews in Poland that Germany devised during the first years of World War II before the "Final Solution" was implemented. Giertych saw this as another incarnation of a Jewish state within Poland, another manifestation of Judeopolonia.[209] Writing in 1974, he also dredged up old arguments that Jewish communists were instrumental in the installation of a Stalinist regime in Poland after the war, heralding another era of domination by aliens. Giertych asserted that "it is possible to say that Poland was under Jewish domination."[210]

POSTCOLONIALISM

Koneczny's theories thus can also be understood within the framework of "postcolonial Poland."[211] In the Polish context, this means "outsiders" are to be blamed for Poland's problems in the past and in the present. There is a rich history of debating whom to blame for Poland's ills. In Koneczny's time, colonized Poles deliberated about the causes of the death of the Polish Republic and the partitions that led to occupation by three empires. Historians from the "Kraków school"—the so-called "pessimists"—developed narratives of "national suicide" that placed responsibility on Poles themselves. In contrast, critics of the Kraków school—"optimists"—concluded that Poland's rapacious neighbors were at fault.[212] Koneczny clearly belonged to the "optimist" camp, and Andrzej Wierzbicki regards his *Polskie logos a ethos* (1921) to be a lengthy polemic with the Kraków school.[213] Koneczny's theories, and the commentary by fundamentalist critics today who cite his authority, reflect the sorts of fears, anxieties, and quests for cultural purity that have been identified in other post-colonial discourses. Moreover, postcolonial theorists posit that "culture can be seen to be not only a site of struggle, but also a mode of struggle and that for which the struggle is waged."[214] And Maria Janion reminds us that "transformation" and "modernization" in postcolonial societies relate not only to economics, but also to culture. Commenting in 2006, she detected a "cultural crisis" in Poland, which was evident in debates about national identity. For Janion, the application of postcolonial theory to Poland enables us to better understand this phenomenon.[215]

Koneczny's focus on cultural or civilizational matters continued a pattern that emerged earlier in Polish history in response to the Russian threat.[216] In coming to terms with the Russian military colossus, Tomasz Zarycki finds that "the insistence on the cultural, 'civilizational,' and moral qualities of Poles . . . may be seen as an element of a wider strategy that could be theoretically described as the compensation for economic and political weakness through the reliance on cultural capital."[217] Zarycki's notion of "cultural capital" can be supplemented with Attila Melegh's concept of the "civilizational or East-West slope."[218] Melegh asks, "Can we explain coloniality on the basis of a civilizational slope? To what extent can the East-West civilizational slope . . . be linked to colonial or postcolonial patterns? . . . By coloniality I mean a system of power understood as a complex form of domination . . . most importantly the *colonization of consciousness*."[219]

TRADITIONAL VALUES

In twenty-first-century Konecznian scholarship, the influence of alien civilizations in Poland is also interpreted as weakening traditional rural culture. Tomasz Banach draws on Koneczny's analyses of the pernicious influence of Orientalized Hellenistic culture on Roman traditions. Especially significant is Koneczny's discussion of the way in which trade was controlled by foreigners who drained the Roman economy. Koneczny cites this as a factor in the demise of the small landholding system that had been the foundation of the Roman Republic's society and the military. Banach sees parallels in contemporary Poland in the various threats to the family farm. He argues that today there is "a life-and-death civilizational struggle playing out before our eyes. In order to win, we must turn to old Rome" for inspiration.²²⁰ Fundamentalist pundit Andrzej Horodecki agrees; he adds that Byzantine and Jewish civilizations show preference for "*the city at the expense of the village*."²²¹ Koneczny himself emphasized Polish ties to the soil, claiming that "in all of Europe there is not a nation that is more in love with the rural life than us; every Pole is by nature a peasant."²²² He also drew a distinction between the important role that landownership played in early Polish history, compared to the nomadic and trading tendencies introduced by the Vikings into Kievan Rus'.²²³

Some recent scholarship develops this Konecznian argument even further. Paweł Skrzydlewski posits "nomadism" as a contemporary phenomenon of people who have no ties to a particular location or culture. Essentially, this is a variant of "rootless cosmopolitanism," and he positions Latin civilization as one that nurtures a tradition based on the close connection of people to their homeland. This reflects some of the concerns about the issues of "landedness," property ownership, and agriculture that are part of the Konecznian paradigm.²²⁴ Skrzydlewski finds "Oriental" roots for all this contemporary nomadism; it represents another "pressure of the Orient on the West"²²⁵ that so concerned Koneczny.

While Koneczny's ideas are not widely accepted among academic historians, his theories are used in some academic analyses in such fields as sociology and philosophy. Koneczny certainly is not mainstream, yet his ideas have survived and have been revived despite their methodological haziness and strident chauvinism. For example, Koneczny's civilizational theory has been applied to election results as a means to understand regional voting patterns in Poland,²²⁶ and his thesis concerning the role of the marriage in 972 of the Byzantine princess Theophano to Otto II has been cited to help explain supposedly persistent Byzantine cultural influences in Germany.²²⁷

The author of an introductory world history text, Jan Kieniewicz, was inspired in part by Koneczny's science of civilizations. In *Wprowadzenie do historii cywilizacji Wschodu i Zachodu* (An Introduction to the History of Eastern and Western Civilizations, 2003), he discusses the ways in which many societies are rediscovering their traditional values in the wake of the collapse of hegemonic ideologies (such as communism in Eastern Europe) and in the face of new threats (such as globalization).²²⁸ Kieniewicz suggests as the "fundamental question, clearly present in contemporary debate about the crisis of European civilization, but fundamental for all civilizations: Can values from the past be recovered?"²²⁹

Kieniewicz's work is a good example of scholarship that shares some common concerns with Koneczny but nevertheless uses him in a critical manner and goes beyond his original areas of interest. For example, Kieniewicz consistently integrates environmental factors in a more sophisticated way than

Koneczny did. At times, he rejects Koneczny's interpretations, as in the matter of the influence of Byzantine culture in Muscovy.[230] Nevertheless, both historians agree that Russia is Poland's "civilizational other"; Kieniewicz even asserts that "Russia as a civilization appeared later than Europe and in explicit opposition to it."[231] Kieniewicz's debt to Koneczny is also evident in another essay in which he states:

> My assumption is that there are many civilisations. Their confrontation is a natural state. Civilisations do not strive for unification, there is no global civilisation, and its emergence is not desirable. . . . Civilisation does not give people a separate identity, it offers them a new space of identification, an awareness of affiliation. In the European civilisation, values originate from Christianity.[232]

CATHOLICISM

Koneczny's emphasis on the role of Catholicism in promoting civil society has also inspired philosophers and historians. Arkady Rzegocki explains that the philosopher and Solidarity activist Mirosław Dzielski (1941–89) took up Koneczny's emphasis on the rule of law as an argument against the arbitrary use of force by "alien" regimes that both men abhorred.[233] Like Koneczny, Dzielski identified crises in Poland that resulted from deviations from key civilizational values. Dzielski denounced Marxism as an example of a new "constructivist Promethean credo" that was at odds with the foundations of Latin civilization: the family, monogamy, law, religion, and morality.[234] According to Dzielski, this credo emerged during the Enlightenment and developed further in the nineteenth century as "elites lost their faith in God and believed in Man as an independent designer of his own fate, his own creative, spontaneous development."[235] As Rzegocki points out, Dzielski regarded constructivism as "the universal sickness of our times"[236] that affected Poland especially. The People's Republic was out of sync with the tenets of Latin civilization, since the religious and moral teachings of the Church were displaced from Poles' lives. Dzielski and Koneczny both believed that the Church was vital to the preservation of Latin civilization.[237] They sought to explain the role of Catholic ethics in public life, especially in the construction of a viable civil society that could oppose arbitrary governmental power.[238] For Dzielski, Pope Saint John Paul II was a heroic figure who would lead a "revolution of the soul" in Poland. This was an aspect of the "civilizational turn" and spiritual reawakening that would overcome the excessive materialism promoted by the French and Bolshevik revolutions.[239]

Dzielski sought to understand the internal situation in Poland in the 1970s and 1980s within a broader historical and theoretical context. His rediscovery of the science of civilizations offers us further explanation for the Koneczny renaissance: Koneczny's theories allow Poles to analyze current events within some grand scheme that helps them understand Poland's challenges and its place in the world. The key point for our discussion is the way in which Dzielski was drawn to Koneczny's notion of fundamental differences among civilizations due to historical conditioning. As Miłowit Kuniński notes: "Inspired by Koneczny, he [Dzielski] viewed the political problem from a civilizational perspective"; he began to find the "civilizational differences between East and West . . . at the foundation of political differences."[240] Dzielski came to believe that "Latin civilization appeared to be the civilization in which an individual could develop most fully, thanks to which nations and societies also flowered."[241] This observation bears a remarkable Konecznian imprint.[242] By the late 1970s, Dzielski envisioned the Polish national interest as an expansion of Latin civilizational influences to the East.[243] He promoted a consolidation of Latin civilization that would bind European peoples (East and West) against the Russian threat. For Dzielski, the tension between Poland and Russia was not only political in nature but also due to civilizational incompatibility.[244]

Like Kuniński, Arkady Rzegocki argues that Dzielski's civilizational vision was shaped by his reading of Koneczny. Rzegocki also points out that both men spent most of their lives in Kraków and both are buried in the Salwator cemetery. However, there were key differences in their analyses: most important, Dzielski incorporated developments after Koneczny's death into his own theory in order to promote the concept of sustainable civilizational borrowing. While Japanese and American cultures remained quite different by century's end, for example, they nevertheless seemed to be civilizationally closer than during Koneczny's lifetime.[245] Dzielski also identified fundamental changes in the ancient civilizations described by Koneczny; for example, in his view both Israel and Taiwan had transmogrified into "bastions of Latin civilization."[246]

As this discussion indicates, Koneczny's ideas have been interpreted in various ways by Poles. Mainstream scholars often critique the provocative nature of Koneczny's attempts to create a holistic vision of history, while civilizational fundamentalists tend to accept the anachronistic and chauvinistic Konecznian worldview in a less critical manner. Part of this attraction to Koneczny relates to his methodology; in his major work on the science of civilizations, Józef Kossecki (b. 1936) even claims that "[o]ne can compare the role of Koneczny in the social sciences to that of Linneus in biology."[247] More important, the religious component in fundamentalist rhetoric is as important as ever, echoing the call for "Catholic totalism" that Koneczny voiced in the interwar period.[248]

Following Konecznian reasoning, the scholar Paweł Gondek argues that the Church not only has played a religious role in Poland, but it has provided a civilizational foundation by introducing law and order and demanding ethical behavior in politics and public policy. Hence, Gondek supports Koneczny's contention that Poland (and Europe as a whole) will suffer if it strays from the teachings of the Church. Catholicism is intimately linked with Latin civilization in Europe, so that "anyone in Poland who acts against the Church—acts in essence against Poland."[249] Gondek is quick to note that there is no sort of "clerical government" or theocracy implied; rather, the key is that any party or government in Poland must adhere to the teachings of the Church rather than succumb to the temptations of "neocommunism and neoliberalism" with their materialism and "moral relativism."[250] With a Konecznian sense of urgency, Gondek warns, "Before our eyes emerges a new [global] civilization, whose broad flow of lava threatens to destroy from the inside classical culture and Latin civilization" through its opposition to Catholicism. He reminds readers of Koneczny's dictum: "Poland either will be Catholic or it will not be at all."[251]

The teaching of Koneczny's ideas has also become more widespread at some institutions, especially Catholic University of Lublin (KUL). Most important there is the Lublin School of Philosophy,[252] where Father Mieczysław Albert Krąpiec (1921–2008) was a leading figure in the "renaissance of Koneczny's thought" in the 1990s.[253] According to Radosław Brzózka, Krąpiec studied the theories of both Toynbee and Koneczny and applied them in his own teaching and research.[254] Koneczny has advocates at KUL because he strove to make the Christian-classical tradition relevant for the contemporary world.[255] Historian and Konecznian pundit Mieczysław Ryba directly attributes the resurgence of interest in Koneczny at KUL to the efforts of Krąpiec. He regards this as one of Krąpiec's most important legacies.[256] One student from the 1990s, Mirosław Król, recalls that he and colleagues from the History Department attended Krąpiec's lectures in order to learn more about Koneczny. Król had purchased reprints of Koneczny's publications in Warsaw and brought them with him to Lublin. He remembers that Krąpiec lectured on Koneczny even though his ideas were not popular at that time in scholarly circles. Krąpiec professed that Koneczny's analyses were timeless and they aided him in his own search for truth about man and the world.[257]

KUL Professor Henryk Kiereś states plainly that the "plurality of civilizations is a fact."[258] He frequently uses Konecznian reasoning in his argumentation, as in the preface to his book, *Man and Civilization* (2007):

> The whole story of mankind can be pictured as a battlefield, where various civilizations were and still are fighting against each other, and this is a mortal struggle, without taking prisoners—that's what Feliks Koneczny once noticed and tried to demonstrate. . . . The struggle of civilizations is always on, even right now and right here.[259]

Some pundits have even detected Konecznian themes in the thinking of the former Cardinal Ratzinger (now Pope Emeritus Benedict XVI), such as the contention that one cannot be civilized simultaneously in two ways and the belief that civilizations are in constant conflict for supremacy.[260]

While Koneczny's works have been critically reviewed by mainstream scholars, his theories have been enthusiastically revived by many nationalist, fundamentalist, and extremist commentators. In the next chapter, I will analyze Konecznian themes that were evident in public discourse in the first decade of the twenty-first century. My analysis focuses on key Konecznian pundits who were actively publishing their commentary during this time period in books, websites, and blogs. My methodology also includes an analysis of articles in the newspaper *Nasz Dziennik* and the periodicals *Myśl Polska* and *Nowy Przegląd Wszechpolski.*

Chapter Five

The Konecznian Revival

KONECZNY IN PUBLIC DISCOURSE

Writing in 2009, Karol Brandt declared that the complaint that Koneczny had been "forgotten" by Poles was no longer valid, citing the many recent monographs, book chapters, articles, and dissertations that deal with his theories. He defends Koneczny's legacy, noting that his commentary on "Jewish civilization" was no harsher than many scholarly observations of the interwar period. He points out that many "nonessentialists" balk at Koneczny's search for the fundamental and distinct "essence" of each civilization, but he believes there is no reason to marginalize Koneczny for his views.[1] Inadvertantly, Brandt actually gets to the heart of the controversy about Koneczny's renaissance in post-communist Poland: his theories emerged from a milieu of extraordinary chauvinism. While there has been critical scholarly commentary on Koneczny in the past three decades, his theories have also been used by present-day civilizational fundamentalists to validate their own brand of intolerance. For example, Koneczny is often cited as an authority by those who seek to marginalize the Jewish roots of Christianity and create civilizational boundaries between the two faiths.[2] As Brandt attests, it is Koneczny's "essentialist" critique of multiculturalism and cosmopolitanism that retains a certain appeal for some of today's readers.[3]

Poland is perceived by civilizational fundamentalists to be threatened by the forces of economic and cultural globalization. Moreover, from their perspective political independence has been forfeited in return for membership in the European Union. Koneczny's theory, born at a time of war and revolution, once again provides a template for Poles to understand their place in an uncertain world. As Maciej Kociuba points out, in times of crisis an axiological theory seems to serve to reassure people.[4]

Koneczny's "axiological vision of Europe" certainly is well-suited to meet this need.[5] Stanisław Jedynak sees in Koneczny's theories a vision of a "utopia of purity and sterilization of Latin-Roman-ecclesiastical civilization."[6] He believes that "[t]he description and estimation of Latin civilization by Koneczny further advances the idealization of a certain sketchy cultural type. This idealization was treated in his exclusion and closure as a utopia seen in the past, as a specifically *new medievalism*. The task of this new utopia is the defense of the West."[7]

Renewed interest in Koneczny among some intellectuals is a result of the attractiveness of "Koneczny's retrospective optimistic utopia" that also gives Poland a certain messianic role in the defense of Latin civilization.[8] Konecznian ideologues consistently warn against cosmopolitanism as a sure sign of civilizational decadence. In their analyses, they frequently restate the key Konecznian historical law: "Civilizational syntheses are not possible."[9] Michał Wolnicki even suggests that Koneczny's works should be translated into "all languages" so that anyone concerned about the decline of the West can become familiar with his work.[10]

Writing in 1994, Mirosław Dakowski proposed that Koneczny's "science of civilizations is . . . the key to understanding the present world situation."[11] He warned that "we" must decide to which civilization "we" want to belong. Drawing on the then-recent examples of the dissolution of Yugoslavia and Czechoslovakia, he reminded Poles that Koneczny's dictum about the instability of "artificial" states that were civilizationally mixed still held true. Dakowski infused his appeal with a sense of urgency, since he believed influential circles in Poland were promoting a "melange of various moralities"[12] that would only lead to a loss of civilizational identity. As a way to save Latin civilization in Europe he called for the dissemination of Koneczny's ideas in Poland and abroad.[13] Apparently, Dakowski's call was heeded; by 1996, leading Konecznian fundamentalist Maciej Giertych could proclaim, "We have a renaissance of interest in the creations of Feliks Koneczny!"[14] And Giertych insists that all Polish schoolchildren should be taught Koneczny's ideas.[15]

Marcin Dybowski, the owner of the Antyk publishing house, which has republished many of Koneczny's works, goes even further. He believes that Koneczny has become "indispensible for the rescue of the Polish spirit."[16] Through his press, Dybowski has successfully contributed to the dissemination of Koneczny's ideas. In an interview from 2006, extreme nationalist blogger Jan Bodakowski shared how he enjoyed discussing Koneczny's works with other customers during his thrice-weekly visits to the now-defunct Antyk bookstore in Warsaw. There he encountered a wide range of interested readers, from "simple workers to professors."[17] In supporting the contention that Koneczny is still valid for the twenty-first century, pundits emphasize that he made an important contribution to Polish scholarship by placing Polish history within the broader history of the Church and the world.[18]

Koneczny's influence has often been evident in fundamentalist rhetoric. An editorial from 2005 in *Nowy Przegląd Wszechpolski* (New All-Polish Review) explicitly states, "Thanks to Feliks Koneczny, we are able to better understand the Germans."[19] Wojciech Reszczyński likewise argues that Koneczny's concepts have validity for today's world, especially in relation to his observations about German Byzantinism.[20] He regrets that Polish leaders during the communist period, and still in 2008, have neglected Koneczny's legacy. Reszczyński seeks to educate the Polish public on Koneczny's ideas, as he does in an article explaining the Konecznian quincunx in detail, weaving together references to Koneczny's works and also commentary from scripture and popes that seemingly agree with the science of civilizations.[21] In this way, Koneczny's ideas are made to seem an integral part of Polish Catholicism. They frequently have been discussed in commentary aired on the controversial fundamentalist Catholic Radio Maryja and in editorials in the daily *Nasz Dziennik* (Our Daily).[22]

Koneczny's books have been readily available in Poland for years in a variety of venues, from the popular Empik chain outlets and academic bookstores in major cities to the controversial Antyk bookshop in Warsaw already mentioned.[23] Koneczny's ideas also have been widely debated at nationalist gatherings. At a discussion hosted by Stowarzyszenie Patriotyczne Serenissima (The Serenissima Patriotic Society) in October 2004, Sławomir Lisiecki and Artur Gawiński spoke on Koneczny's civilizational theory based on their reading of *On Order in History* and *Polish Logos and Ethos*.[24] In a lecture commemorating the sixtieth anniversary of his death (2009), Karol Stehlin addressed the role of Koneczny's thought "for the preservation and development of Latin Civilization in our difficult and turbulent times."[25] Reporting on the speech, Mirosław Dakowski added that Koneczny's theories are a good way to analyze and understand the current "acivilized condition" in Russia resulting from a mixture of civilizational influences, as well as the problematic attempt of the European Union to create an artificial conglomeration of peoples from different civilizations.[26]

In an open letter written to then-President Lech Kaczyński in February 2007, Dakowski defended Koneczny and Maciej Giertych, whose Koneczny-inspired booklet *Civilisations at War in Europe* was under attack in the Polish and foreign press. He claimed that the concept of a "war of civilizations" had been plagiarized from Koneczny and used by Samuel Huntington, but nobody had attacked Huntington in such a manner. Dakowski stressed that Koneczny's ideas are not the sole property of *endeks*, but rather belong to a broader global public. He concluded that "[i]f the promotion of the thought of Koneczny is rebuked and condemned in Poland, then with happiness and pride for my deeds I will go to prison. For certain, I will not be alone."[27] Piotr Jaroszyński bemoans the ignorance of Poles about Koneczny, blaming the "pervasive terror of 'political correctness'" that has marginalized his ideas and excluded them from public discourse.[28] Sebastian Pasławski admits that "[t]he works of Feliks Koneczny are extremely politically incorrect."[29] But he complains that just because Koneczny's works are not appreciated by "ignorant editors of liberal papers" or "university scholars with Marxist roots," it does not mean that they are without merit.[30]

THE EUROPEAN UNION AND GLOBALIZATION

All these Konecznian critics would agree that Poland has struggled to adapt to the "new world order" of the post–Cold War era. An important part of this process of adjustment has been the search for new international partners. However, the establishment of closer ties with new military allies (with NATO membership in 1999) and an active engagement with the broader Western European community (with EU membership in 2004) has met with criticism. Konecznian critics have insisted that the end of Soviet hegemony has not eliminated the threat of colonial domination, especially in the form of a German-dominated European Union. In *Dokąd Polsko? Wobec globalizacji i integracji europejskiej* (Whither Poland? In the Face of Globalization and European Integration, 2002), Włodzimierz Bojarski repeatedly connects the EU with colonial designs on Poland, arguing that it is a source of "neocolonial exploitation."[31] He fears that Poles are once again under a civilizational assault: "The attack of international financial and economic imperialism as well as the globalist, secular-cosmopolitan structure of evil has already caused significant losses in the Fatherland. Poland is becoming more and more an area of neocolonial exploitation."[32] Perhaps Maciej Giertych most succinctly expressed Konecznian fundamentalists' postcolonial anxiety during his 2005 presidential campaign: "We believe in Poland, we believe in the Polish Nation. . . . However, we do not believe in the good intentions of 'non-Polish forces,' either foreign or international."[33]

In his research on Polish nationalism at the turn of the twenty-first century, Grzegorz Tokarz found the fear of German control (via the European Union) over Polish farmland to be a prominent theme.[34] For example, Andrzej Horodecki revived memories of German colonization of Polish lands in the nineteenth century, spreading fears about future German designs.[35] Soviet-inspired collectivization was also remembered as yet another attempt by a colonial power to destroy Polish rural traditions.[36] As Poles debated entry to the EU, it was viewed as the main threat to the Polish farmer. Here, however, Horodecki's concern went beyond the loss of territory or civilizational traditions. He feared that the "natural agriculture" (organic farming) of Poland's independent farmers would be replaced by harmful practices of industrialized farming.[37] Jan Piwowarski also linked his concern about the fate of family farms to environmentalism and opposition to the EU. The small Polish farmer is thus seen as a guardian of "purity" in another way, since he uses "biological methods that are in agreement with the laws of nature."[38] Small family farms are promoted as the opposite of the large-scale "industrialized farming" encouraged by the EU that uses chemicals, produces genetically modified organisms, and creates such ecological nightmares as mad cow disease.[39] Maciej Giertych also cited Koneczny to support his theses about the sale of farmland, the fate of the small farmer, and the purity and safety of the food supply.[40]

The imperative to preserve Polish rural life as a repository of *polskość* (Polishness) and values of Latin civilization is a prevalent theme in Konecznian postcolonial rhetoric. During the interwar period, *endecja* ideologues had also been concerned about the endangered Polish peasantry, who were regarded as paragons of traditional virtues. Peasants who worked on farms were judged to be more immune to cosmopolitan modernity than urban intelligentsia, remaining true to Catholicism.[41] Farmland itself was regarded not only as an economic resource, but "was also invested with cultural significance. Geopolitical thought posited a necessary and mutually defining relationship between 'culture' and a nation's agricultural working of the land."[42] Farmland devasted by World War I was also in need of ecological purification.[43] These same concerns are evident in twenty-first century commentary that praises the relationship between farmers and their land as a special mix of "spirit and body" that is manifested in greater care for Polish traditions. And globalization is viewed as a new threat to this way of life.

Konecznian commentators have persistently stressed the importance of keeping Poland's farmland in Polish hands.[44] A League of Polish Families (LPR) campaign brochure for elections to the European Parliament in 2004 featured the "image of a Polish, idyllic, summertime, countryside, landscape."[45] Before Poland's entry to the EU in 2004, Euroskeptics exploited the fear of Germans buying land in territories annexed by Poland after World War II.[46] And Father Tadeusz Rydzyk played to his listeners' fears on Radio Maryja by voicing concerns that "rich EU citizens" would buy up Polish land.[47] Worried about the possible "liquidation of the Polish village," Andrzej Horodecki has pointed out that Koneczny, Cardinal Wyszyński, and Pope Saint John Paul II had voiced similar concerns about the fate of the Polish countryside.[48] He believes that there is a "reserve of spiritual energy in the Polish village,"[49] which is relatively free from the influences of globalization and thus relatively pure in civilizational identity. Dariusz Kosiur jolted readers by erroneously claiming that only 5 percent of American farmland is owned outright by farmers, with the rest controlled by banks. He warned that the same fate will befall Polish agriculture, as the "oligarchy of the financial-economic world" extends its influence into Poland.[50]

For Andrzej Horodecki and other Konecznian fundamentalists, defending Polish agriculture morphs into a defense of Latin civilization. To fend off the "disease" of foreign civilizational influence, which is most evident among urban intelligentsia, he has proposed that the village's traditional family-centered lifestyle "ought to become the *model for the entire nation*."[51] Horodecki also contends that in Latin civilization private land ownership has been a foundation of societal stability. This is threatened in the new global economy. Jerzy Pawlas agrees, asserting that in the modern global economy "business is business" and all is a commodity, including land.[52] Building on Koneczny's theoretical works, Piotr Jaroszyński argued that the attitude to land as a commodity reflects the influence of Jewish civilization, where "land is not loved, money is loved."[53] He points out that for Koneczny attitudes to "the land above all depend on the type of civilization to which one belongs."[54] Jaroszyński has regularly provided commentary from a Konecznian perspective as a contributor to *Nasz Dziennik* and other nationalist media outlets. In an address from 1999, he quoted Koneczny at some length: "The economic ideal of Latin civilization is fixed property; generally speaking, the least movable property means the most stability and continuity . . . All that facilitates the transfer of property from hand to hand is contrary to our civilization."[55] Also citing Koneczny, Pawlas posits that land ownership "gives the greatest spiritual independence."[56] "In our Polish tradition," Jaroszyński adds, "love of one's land was a particularly characteristic feature."[57]

Prior to the EU vote, Jaroszyński also expressed anxiety about the so-called "Recovered Territories" (*Ziemie Odzyskane*) that had been heavily populated by Germans prior to World War II. He sensed a lack of ties to the land among Poles living there, in part because they were transferred from the *kresy* after Poland's boundaries were moved westward on Stalin's orders after the war. And this problem has been exacerbated by new economic values that promote the commoditization of land. This presents what Jaroszyński regards as a "fatal threat" to Poland: "This threat is also the result of a thousand-year tendency of our western neighbors for expansion to the east, as expressed in the well-known formula *Drang nach Osten*."[58]

This contention that Poland is threatened with foreign domination is the most persistent sign of postcolonial anxiety in Konecznian discourse. Magdalena Nowicka points out that Poland is now linked to NATO, the European Union, and the United States in a number of ways that provide fodder for critical commentary about the compromise of Polish sovereignty.[59] Konecznian critics would agree with Židas Daskalovski, who prior to the eastward expansion in 2004 concluded that "the EU treats the nations of Eastern Europe with just as much 'compassion' as the Spaniards treated the indigenous peoples in the 'New World.'"[60] Citing Koneczny's condemnation of "civilizational mixing," Włodzimierz Bojarski attacked the "barbaric and neocolonial European Union" and called upon the Polish nation to fulfill its mission of saving Latin Civilization.[61] But Mariusz Kowalski warned that if countries from Latin civilization leave the EU, then it would be left totally in German control. This would allow the emergence of a sort of "new empire"—a "Byzantine empire."[62] And Maciej Giertych pledged in his 2005 presidential campaign that despite its membership in the EU, Poland would not sacrifice national sovereignty to any outside power in "the Kremlin, in Berlin, in Brussels, or in Washington."[63] Interestingly, Giertych would actually serve as a Polish representative in the EU Parliament (2004–9). Having opposed Polish entry into the EU, he justified his seat with an explicit reference to earlier colonial times. Citing Roman Dmowski's participation in the Russian Duma, Wojciech Korfanty's seat in the German Reichstag, and Wincenty Witos's role in the Reichsrat in Vienna, Giertych stated that his function would be much the same: to defend Polish national interests.[64]

Central to national interest, of course, is the preservation of Poland's civilizational identity and integrity. In *Europa bez Ojczyzn?* (A Europe without Homelands?), Piotr Jaroszyński described the various phases of the destruction of Polish national identity.[65] He emphasized that "the EU is not the first, but the latest phase in the process of the denationalization of Poles."[66] The first phase was the partitions, which brought the plagues of Germanization and Russification. The second phase was communism, during which a "civilizational degradation" took place in Poland under the influence of the Soviet Union, with "its Asiatic-communist face."[67] Integrating the latest phase of colonialism into his analysis, Jaroszyński opined that

> both communism and liberalism are alien to the Polish tradition, which at its core is Catholic or Latin. Communism was introduced by force as a continuation of the Russian partition, while presently so-called liberalism to a great degree is promoted by a second partitioner—the Germans, although an international consortium also enters this game. One cannot forget that geopolitically we are constantly between Russia and Germany and through these states are realized further, alien interests.[68]

Elsewhere, Jaroszyński refers to this alien interest as "colonial globalism."[69]

MULTICULTURALISM

In Koneczny's vision, clarity of civilizational identity ensures societal vitality.[70] Koneczny would have undoubtedly rejected the concept of "hybridity," which allows for the possibility that a person can have multiple identities. His theories leave no room for the possibility of "additive identities and additive assimilation,"[71] which would allow a person or a society to add layers of new civilizational identities on top of others. While it may be true that multiple identifications is a growing trend, Koneczny's sentiment from an earlier era still resonates among some Poles. His heirs in twenty-first-century Poland reject notions of hybridity as "multi-kulti" nonsense.

Koneczny's laws banning "civilizational syntheses" and "civilizational mixes" both relate to his obsession with civilizational purity. Such amalgams represented "pathological phases of social evolution"[72] for Koneczny. Jan Skoczyński detects hygiene metaphors in Koneczny's rhetoric, which associates alien civilizational influences with impurities that ruin a society's health. Much like Mirosław Dzielski, Skoczyński also finds Koneczny outdated in some of his assumptions about cross-civilizational contacts. He observes that Israel and Japan appear to be functional societies that blend together various civilizational traits.[73] But despite the anachronistic nature of the Konecznian ban on borrowing from other civilizations, there are fundamentalists in Poland who cite Koneczny's laws as justification for their opposition to a "multi-kulti" society. They cite similar examples as Koneczny, especially the gradual Orientalization of the Roman Republic and its consequent collapse, as evidence that artificial mixtures weaken tradition and lead to societal chaos.[74]

Citing Koneczny, pundit Adam Wielomski argued in 2003 that Poland must avoid becoming a civilizational mixture. He contends that "Europe is not a geographical idea and is not identified with a boundary line of the European continent. Europe is a civilizational idea."[75] For Wielomski and other civilizational fundamentalists, Europe is the "antithesis" of multiculturalism: "as Feliks Koneczny instructs us—it is not possible to be a member of several civilizations simultaneously."[76] Wielomski professes that as "a Catholic, a Roman Catholic, I am compelled to be above all a member of Latin Civilization, whose capital for two thousand years has been Rome. Only then am I a Pole. St. Peter's Basilica is the acropolis of our civilization. . . . I am therefore first a Catholic-European, and then a Pole."[77]

The Konecznian attacks on cosmopolitanism and yearning for civilizational purity are important components of postcolonial resentment in Poland. This is not unique to the ethnocentric variant of contemporary Polish nationalism, which reflects an older trend in European history of "creating purity out of impurity" and "elevating homogeneity to an imperative of nationhood."[78] For decades Konecznian critics have decried a perceived civilizational chaos in Poland caused by an "open society" or "guests from other civilizations."[79] The problem is obvious: "Cosmopolitanism is synonymous with the resignation and renunciation of the idea of Latin civilization."[80] The solution is equally clear: Poland needs to spearhead a "reevangelization of Europe"[81] based on the values of Latin civilization that will lead to its rechristianization.[82] Only with a return to the ethics of Latin civilization and a "moral reconstruction"[83] can Poland—and other European societies—be healthy.

This need for a robust and healthy "culture of action" is a Konecznian concept that has appeared frequently in civilizational fundamentalist discourse. Writing in 2004 in wake of the terrorist attacks in Madrid, Mieczysław Ryba lamented that "[t]oday Europe appears to be totally defensive, while Asia [he specifically mentions India, China, and Islamic fundamentalism] has civilizational dynamism."[84] Citing Koneczny's historical law that inferior civilizations destroy more advanced ones, as well as the historical example of ancient Rome falling to barbarians, Ryba concludes his essay on a note of warning: "If contemporary Rome [Latin civilization] does not return to its Christian civilizational roots, sooner or later the barbarians will conquer it and conquered Europe will lie in the rubble for years to come."[85]

KONECZNY AND HUNTINGTON

Polish and American commentators have observed that Koneczny's theory is very similar to Samuel Huntington's famous thesis presented in his "clash of civilizations" essay in *Foreign Affairs* in 1993, and the book-length exposition in *The Clash of Civilizations and the Remaking of World Order* (1996). Writing in the *National Interest* in 1997, Neil McInnes briefly discussed the "Polish philosopher Feliks Koneczny" and his "clash-of-cultures" theory as espoused in his book *Plurality of Civilisations*. McInnes correctly observed that decades before Huntington's book appeared, Koneczny had warned that in cross-civilizational encounters a "[p]eaceful interpenetration could lead only to bastardization."[86] McInnes noted that "Huntington revived these notions in less bellicose form in his 1993 article in *Foreign Affairs*."[87] Some Konecznian fundamentalists, such as Mirosław Dakowski, regard Huntington as a plagiarist. Dakowski finds that Koneczny's ideas "were, however, deformed," and that intellectuals in the United States and Europe need to pay more attention to Koneczny's original argument.[88] Historian Piotr Biliński agrees that there are similar themes in the works of Huntington and Koneczny. However, he sees a key difference in their aims: while Huntington seeks to provide a practical guide for understanding post–Cold War international relations, Koneczny sought to create a theoretical framework to understand all of human history.[89]

Koneczny's renaissance in recent decades should perhaps not be suprising. He believed that the struggle for existence, and the clash between rival civilizations, had three elements: moral, intellectual, and material. Societies in more developed civilizations are more complex, thereby making them more difficult to preserve and protect in struggles with rival civilizations.[90] This sort of argument seems to resonate in today's world. Paul Rich explains that "[p]rofessional historians and scholars of International Relations in the years since 1945 have generally been wary of trying to understand global political conflicts through differences of 'civilisation.' . . . In the post–Cold War era, however, there are growing signs that issues of civilisational rise and fall have re-entered scholarly debate."[91] This was certainly the case in the United States, at least for a brief time after the publication of Huntington's works on the "clash of civilizations." In Poland the debate also emerged in the 1990s, in part as a response to Huntington's argument, but also in wake of the republication of many of Koneczny's works and a rediscovery of his ideas in both the scholarly and popular press. And Rich contends that "the study of civilisations in world history has the potential to offer a lot to social science debates."[92]

Jacinta O'Hagan explains that Huntington presents a picture of a fragmented world, in which the "West should abandon its universalist pretensions which are false, immoral and dangerous."[93] This mimics Koneczny's vision of a plurality of civilizations that are constantly striving for expansion. O'Hagan observes that Huntington's thesis regards civilizations "as largely incommensurable;

their capacity to understand each other is limited. It rejects any suggestion that humanity forms, or is converging towards, a single, universal civilization."[94] O'Hagan notes correctly that this sort of approach "does not seek to escape grand theory itself. It posits an overarching theory aimed at reducing the rich and bewildering complexity of world politics to a clear and simple pattern."[95] The attractive scholarly framework simultaneously provides a level of "accessibility" for nonspecialists with its "appealing lens through which to view world politics."[96]

O'Hagan's commentary about Huntington seems to apply to Koneczny, too. In Huntington's thesis she finds "conflict as the predominant form of relationship. . . . [T]hese disputes are ancient and primordial. . . . [T]he 'clash' metaphor implies that cooperation is more likely amongst peoples of a similar civilization."[97] This same worldview is evident in Koneczny's science of civilizations, and it appears in the anti-EU and anti-globalization rhetoric of his heirs. For Koneczny, world history "is above all the history of the expansion of civilizations and the struggles among them"; these clashes constitute a "historical necessity" and a sign of civilizational health.[98] The expansion of a civilization does not necessarily mean war, but could also manifest itself in the form of competition in the "spiritual" realm through the spread of ideas.[99] This, too, can be threatening and dangerous. For example, in the Konecznian worldview, Jewish influences in Poland represent alien ethical concepts that challenge the traditional values of Latin civilization.

Both Huntington and Koneczny would agree on "the importance of norms and values to conceptualizations of civilizational identities."[100] Huntington believed that the spread of western values and institutions has been superficial and has relied on a preponderance of western military and economic power. O'Hagan notes that "this is an argument not uncommon in postcolonial and some postmodern perspectives. Huntington's analysis led him to conclude in 1996 that the promotion of western norms and values as universal was false, immoral and dangerous."[101] The "clash" metaphor is essentially "reductionist" in its treatment of civilizations, "portraying them as rigid 'hermetically sealed' and largely incommensurable communities."[102] Moreover, in this vision "the outsider is always a potential enemy."[103]

In many ways, it is evident that Huntington's vision of "a plurality of incommensurable civilizations"[104] is very similar to the Konecznian model. O'Hagan finds in Huntington's work an argument "that globalization and modernization do not necessarily lead to cultural homogenization or Westernization."[105] Rather, Huntington's thesis suggests that "[m]odernization contributes to dislocation and alienation from traditional community and structures. This leads to people seeking a renewed sense of identity in their own culture or religion."[106] Koneczny's renaissance in Poland is related to a similar backlash against perceived threats to political, economic, and cultural autonomy, especially in the form of globalization and the European Union. Koneczny's followers demonstrate that it is possible that "the forces of modernization and globalization lead to fragmentation rather than integration."[107]

Polish scholars and critics have commented extensively on the similarity of Koneczny's theories to Huntington's "clash thesis."[108] However, there are similarities to be found with Huntington's later work, too. In *Who Are We? The Challenge to America's National Identity* (2004), Huntington focused on threats posed by immigrants (especially Mexicans) to a national culture based on the "American Creed" that emerged out of the Anglo-Saxon tradition. He complained that the "term 'nativism' has acquired pejorative connotations among denationalized elites on the assumption that it is wrong vigorously to defend one's 'native' culture and identity and to maintain their purity against foreign influences."[109] This complaint is also clearly evident in Polish commentary inspired by Huntington's "clash theory" and (more importantly) Koneczny's dictum that "one cannot be civilized simultaneously in two ways." O'Hagan contends that in his *Clash of Civilizations*, Huntington is not concerned with immigration so much as the issue of "cultural heterogeneity," the fear "that multiculturalism is undermining the homogeneity of Western society."[110] But Huntington addressed immigration more thoroughly in his later work, where he expressed a fear of "becoming swamped by peoples of other cultures."[111] His ideas fit well within the Konecznian paradigm, including his contention that "[m]ulticulturalism is in its essence anti-European civilization. . . . It is basically an anti-Western ideology."[112]

Commentators continue to debate the role of civilizational pluralism in contemporary societies. Some point out a persistent and widely held delusion in the West about a universal world civilization in which all humans share a common set of values. For example, Mislav Kukoc finds that "the concept of a universal civilization is a distinctive product of Western civilization, which helps justify Western cultural dominance of other societies. Universalism is the ideology of the West for confrontations with non-Western cultures. The non-Wests see as Western what the West sees as universal."[113] The Konecznian worldview is radically different: there is a plurality of civilizations, each with different values and different historical trajectories.

Just as civilizations have different pasts and presents, so do they possess different futures. From I. A. Vasilenko's perspective, "[t]he West's cultural aggression has led to a powerful de-Westernization of other civilizations, which are returning now [2000] to their own roots."[114] This is a process taking place in Europe, too, as the Konecznian fundamentalist movement in Poland demonstrates. Rather than a sense of triumphalism after the collapse of communism, Koneczny's heirs are fearful of the constant threat to Poland by non-Latin civilizations. As Vasilenko notes, "[t]he most controversial question is that of communicability, that is, whether the cultural elements of one system can penetrate into other systems. For [Nikolai] Danilevskii, [Oswald] Spengler, and F. Konechnyi, the integrity, uniqueness, and self-sufficiency of civilizations served as weighty arguments for establishing their closure."[115]

Vasilenko's commentary about post-Soviet Russia has relevance for understanding the way in which Konecznian fundamentalists in Poland evince postcolonial anxieties about globalization. He contends that in today's information age "the strategy of dominance of strong civilizations has changed fundamentally—it has become extra-institutional."[116] This would seem to make the culturalist argument more legitimate. Vasilenko identifies a process of "informational imperialism," whereby "[a]lien information invades all spheres of social life through numerous communication channels. The result is a rejection of one's own culture, its norms and traditions, and a loss of civilizational identity."[117] Konecznian fundamentalists in Poland would likely agree with Vasilenko's assertion that "[t]here is only one way out of the situation—a quest for new paths of national spiritual renewal and the acquisition of our own civilizational identity."[118]

CATHOLIC FUNDAMENTALISM AND LATIN CIVILIZATION

In their search for a civilizational identity, Konecznian fundamentalists especially recall the medieval era with a touch of nostalgia. Andrzej Horodecki has dreamed of a more civilizationally pure medieval period. As he puts it, "Hatred of the Middle Ages is a hatred of a time when Jewish civilization did not yet have a decisive influence on life in Christian states."[119] Koneczny, too, looked to the Middle Ages as a time when the Catholic foundation of Latin civilization was unchallenged. In his "Forty Fundamental Theses," which he put forth in 1927, Koneczny maintained that "Poland will either be Catholic, or it will not be."[120] He also noted in these theses that "our religion and civilization" is opposed to class struggle,[121] warning Poles that Bolshevism must be contained to prevent Europe from depravation. Medieval models are often contrasted with the divisive horrors of the French Revolution and the Bolshevik Revolution, which serve as examples of the devastation wrought by upheavals of the modern era. Grzegorz Tokarz points out that contemporary Polish nationalists talk about the "medieval, organic social order" with emotion. They see a well-ordered society whose development was disrupted by Renaissance humanism, the Reformation, and the Enlightenment.[122] In response to these debilitating (and secularizing) forces, Koneczny and his successors have called for a return to the Church and its teachings as a remedy for the ills of modernity.

In their rhetoric, Konecznian pundits place a primary significance on Catholic morality and ethics. As Arkadiusz Robaczewski states: "Without virtue there cannot be the development of morality, and the development of morality must encompass all of life."[123] This means that one must strive for ethical behavior in both private and public life. Koneczny also repeatedly asserted that ethical progress is the key to civilizational development.[124] He insisted that the "issue of civilization—the psychical issue—is not dependent on the bodily, the racial. We see that here the spirit is stronger than the body. The independence of civilization from race is a valuable *contribution to the problem of the superiority of the soul over matter*."[125] Spiritual concerns are central to Koneczny's scheme, and Jan Skoczyński concludes that for him "the final aim of history is the realization of values. A sense of history in this context is thus the discernment of values and the justification of their existence."[126]

The resurrection of Koneczny's theories in recent decades, especially his medievalist construct of civilizational boundaries that separate Christians and Jews, has proven problematic for Catholic intellectuals. Some pundits have attempted to make it seem as if Koneczny's worldview is an integral part of Catholicism. Krzysztof Nagrodzki finds parallels between the thinking of then-Cardinal Ratzinger (now Pope Emeritus Benedict XVI) and the Konecznian laws of history: one cannot be civilized simultaneously in two ways, the inevitable clash of civilizations, and the contention that "lower" civilizations will dominate and defeat "higher" civilizations without constant vigilance in defense of traditional values.[127] Commentators also discuss Koneczny's ideas in the context of the teachings of Pope Saint John Paul II.[128] For example, the term "Latin civilization" is sometimes equated with the "civilization of love," a concept espoused by Popes Paul VI and Saint John Paul II.[129] Jarosław Paszyński explicitly claims that the "civilization of love" is "nothing other than a new name for Latin civilization."[130]

Konecznian rhetoric, however, is not filled with love for "others." Leonidas Donskis's general commentary certainly seems appropriate in helping us understand the Koneczny revival among civilizational fundamentalists and also right-wing extremists in Poland over the past three decades: "In Western societies, hatred comes in the guise of conspiracy theories, militant moral stances, and radical political ideas—from the struggle against globalization to the clash of civilizations, not to mention ideological, political, and racist hate groups."[131] Donskis argues that hatred should not be assigned solely to totalitarian regimes:

> Instead, it proliferates its forms in the modern troubled imagination, assuming such sophisticated forms of interpretation of the human world and of self-comprehension as the philosophies of history and culture, the comparative study of civilizations, literary scholarship, and fiction. Hatred of the modern world is manifest in myriad abuses of religion, spirituality, scholarship, and humanity.[132]

A Konecznian perspective on "others" is evident in the teachings of some prominent Polish clergy. Wojciech Giertych—Maciej's younger brother—was appointed as Theologian of the Papal Household in December 2005. In a lecture delivered in March 2006 at the Warsaw Dominican monastery, Father Wojciech cited Koneczny in the first sentence. He pointed out that Koneczny would regard current attempts to create civilizational mixtures as "absurd."[133] His article on "The Moral Natural Law" (2007) also includes extensive references to Koneczny's science of civilizations:

> Koneczny claimed that it is not possible to be civilized in two differing ways at the same time, because it is common ethical convictions that generate social cohesiveness and condition civilizations. . . . Today, however, Western Europe is rapidly losing, or totally transforming, its age-old Christian ethical convictions, and in this it is drifting away from the moral foundations in which for centuries it was anchored.[134]

Other Polish clergy have been less receptive to Konecznian concepts. Father Romuald Jakub Weksler-Waszkinel (b. 1943) is particularly critical of Koneczny's rejection of the Jewish roots of Christianity and the influence this view has had on Catholic fundamentalists.[135] For example, fundamentalist Andrzej Horodecki cites Koneczny as an authority as he flatly rejects any "Judeo-Christian tradition" in Europe. In his mind, this tradition connotes "civilizational chaos."[136] Weksler-Waszkinel is disturbed in part because this is contrary to doctrine that emerged as a result of decisions made at the Second Vatican Council (held 1962–65, and also known as "Vatican II")—as well as the teachings of Pope Saint John Paul II—which held that Judaism was a root religion for Christianity.[137] An advocate of Christian-Jewish amity, Weksler-Waszkinel laments that "according to Koneczny, *Jewish civilization* was supposed to be the greatest enemy of *Latin civilization*."[138]

Archbishop Józef Życiński (1948–2011) alluded to this attempt to separate Christianity from its Jewish roots when he condemned the way some Poles regard Koneczny as more relevant than Abraham in their understanding of Catholicism. He believed that this "leads to painful consequences" for the "disoriented person" who focuses on materials that "have nothing in common with the Catholic tradition."[139] A disparity of views toward Jewish-Christian relations was an element of the tensions found in Poland at the turn of the twenty-first century between the progressive "Open Church" and the "Closed Church," which supported a more traditionalist approach "based on the pre-1939 model of Polish Catholicism."[140] Critics accused the Closed Church of failing to adopt the pronouncements of the Second Vatican Council that "upheld the view that Jews were Catholics' 'elder brothers in spirit' with whom 'Christianity has a special bond.'"[141] As pointed out in chapter 4, the teaching of Koneczny's ideas also appeared at Catholic University of Lublin (KUL). Joanna Michlic finds that the "support of the Closed Church in the post-1990 period by members of the university faculty is intellectually disturbing, because in the 1980s the Catholic University of Lublin was known for its liberal and progressive traditions."[142] Weksler-Waszkinel adds that the KUL case is especially discouraging, since Pope Saint John Paul II taught there during an earlier progressive period.[143]

Koneczny's ideas on "Jewish civilization" are still circulating in twenty-first-century Poland, thanks in part to the republication of his works in recent years. In an interview with an elderly man in Sandomierz, for example, Joanna Tokarska-Bakir found that his misinformation about Jews came from Koneczny's book on Jewish civilization.[144] One fundamentalist pundit, Stefan Kurowski, explains that Koneczny's analysis is very useful in understanding the important role that Jews play in the world today. Kurowski contends that Jews' growing power is the most important development of our time, more significant than either the collapse of the Soviet Union or the rise of China.[145] Commentator Andrzej Szydlik also praises Koneczny for identifying Jewish civilization as a globalizing force.[146] Jewish civilization is thus still imagined by Konecznian fundamentalists as a direct threat to Poland. For example, Andrzej Leszek Szcześniak explains that "[t]he project for the creation of Judeopolonia is a classic example of Jewish egoism, ruthlessness, and lack of any sort of scruples."[147]

Pundits also embrace other aspects of Koneczny's analysis of Jewish civilization. Radical activist Zbigniew Lignarski, for example, concedes that Koneczny's argument about the Jewish inspiration for Hitler's ideas "[a]t first glance . . . might appear absurd, particularly for adherents of political correctness."[148] But he asserts that the connections are real. Moreover, he uses Koneczny's analysis of Jewish influence around the world to explain the seemingly paradoxical connections between Nazism and Bolshevism: the disregard for private property, the monism of public law, and the hatred of Christianity, especially Catholicism.[149] And these complaints about Jews can apparently be transferred to other "others." Analysts of anti-immigrant (usually anti-Muslim) discourse from the turn of the twenty-first century found that it borrowed tropes from Konecznian commentary on Jews. The new complaint about immigrants as civilizational "others" who do not integrate into Polish society is similar to the old contention that Jews cherished a distinct identity that was at odds with Polishness.[150]

An alleged cost of the continued interaction with Jewish civilization is the "moral schizophrenia" that is associated with civilizational mixing.[151] Koneczny's followers today reject any efforts at civilizational compromise as "naive ecumenism"[152] that would result in what Koneczny termed a "civilizational caricature."[153] Bemoaning Poles' ignorance about the immutable differences between Latin and Jewish civilizations, Andrzej Horodecki reminds readers that the two are incompatible and cannot be partners in any sort of civilizational dialogue.[154] Even conversion to Christianity from Judaism does not mean an automatic membership in Latin civilization, since it is so radically different from Jewish civilization.[155] Rather than decline into "cultural and political nothingness,"[156] Poles should cherish their role in Latin civilization, which is grounded in Catholicism. Early in the Communist period, Koneczny once again voiced his commitment to the three "great pillars" of an authentic Polish existence: Catholicism, Latin civilization, and Polishness.[157] In post-communist Poland, his heirs have revived this credo as a rallying cry to construct civilizational boundaries between Jews and Christians. Konecznian fundamentalist Andrzej Horodecki warns that between Latin and Jewish and Byzantine civilizations: "A state of war continues!"[158]

Fundamentalist commentators use Koneczny's framework in a variety of ways to explain world history and current events. In one clear rendition of Koneczny's key ideas, Witold Kowalski mimics his mentor's argumentation. He accepts Koneczny's glorification of the Roman Republic and emphasizes that the Roman world endured "Oriental influences, especially Jewish, Greek, Syrian, and Egyptian."[159] Here Kowalski repeats Koneczny's tendency to Orientalize the Greek world in contrast with Roman civilization, which in his vision provided one of the foundations for the emergence of Latin civilization in medieval times. Kowalski firmly places the Byzantine empire within the "Oriental" cultural orbit, and he also repeats Koneczny's peculiar emphasis on Byzantine influences on German cultural and political history. The derogatory nature of Kowalski's commentary is especially evident in his discussion of an alleged lack of civic culture in Turanian civilization, where subjects behave more like "a mound of termites or rats scurrying for the mercy of the ruler" rather than an empowered civil society.[160] And in a judgment that is derived from Koneczny's writings on Jewish civilization, Kowalski states that "Jews are ambivalent in their alliances. In armed conflicts or social conflicts, we always see them on both sides of the barricades."[161] Moreover, he contends that Jews "never" fully assimilate within any society, remaining distinctly aloof from host communities.[162] This sort of rhetoric is frequently seen in Konecznian commentary on the history of Polish-Jewish relations.

Konecznian followers consistently warn against cosmopolitanism as a sure sign of "civilizational decadence," and Koneczny is often cited as an authority on the "civilizational" history of this problem. In one essay, Adam Wielomski concisely argues in Konecznian terms that one cannot belong to two civilizations at the same time.[163] Such statements reflect what some scholars identify as a "persistent polarity"[164] in metageography that pits "Europe" against the rest of the world. Rafał Dobrowolski reminds his readers that "Prof. Koneczny already in 1937 warned against the pressure of the Orient on our continent, which is more visible in Europe today [2003], especially in its western part."[165] Other publicists contend that "'Europe' does not have a geographical meaning, but a cultural one."[166] This is not an unusual contention, nor is it inherently hostile to "others." But Koneczny's spiritual heirs consistently discuss Poland's relationship with the broader world as a binary one that assesses "others" in a negative way.

KONECZNIAN CULTURE WARS AND THE POLISH FAMILY

A Konecznian judgment of "others" is also apparent in anti-immigrant, anti-gay, and anti-feminist rhetoric. The common denominator seems to be unease about persons whose identities do not fit within the traditional paradigm of "normality." Immigrants threaten Poles with different civilizational influences, while gays and feminists challenge the patriarchal vision of society promoted by Catholic fundamentalists.[167] Konecznian fundamentalists do not welcome an open, tolerant, and multicultural society. Piotr Jaroszyński contends that the "[e]thic of tolerance promotes other models of a 'family,'" including the promotion of "'homosexual marriage.'"[168] This is merely another example of "political correctness" that he contends threatens traditional Polish culture.[169] Jaroszyński also sees a "modern neocolonialism" in the world today that threatens Poland. This takes the form of alien values that seep in via the media. As Teresa Zawojska puts it, he regards the television as a "Trojan horse in each Polish home" that weakens the traditional Polish family.[170]

A key feature of the fundamentalist vision in Poland is the view of the traditional patriarchal family.[171] According to his grandson, Koneczny was "an advocate of old patriarchal customs" that were part of the "natural" hierarchy.[172] He assumed that women would generally not work outside the home, and that if they did work outside the home, most would not return to those careers after having children.[173] He believed that the traditional nuclear family was the foundation of Latin civilization, and the rearing of children ensured the preservation of tradition and culture.[174] Another important point is that Koneczny was suspicious of state power, and preferred that parents rather than the state have the primary role in educating children.[175] He was convinced that one "who holds the young in one's hand controls the future."[176] Vested by nature with this authority, Polish fathers and mothers have an extraordinary responsibility to the Polish nation and to Latin civilization.

Preservation of the Polish family was thus important to Koneczny; he posited that since the "family is at the center of the circle of collective life,"[177] its decline "brings with it the dangerous stagnation of public life."[178] Traditionalists often draw a close relationship between the concepts of "family" and "nation," and Piotr Grabowiec confirms in his analysis that in Koneczny's vision the family is also the bedrock of Latin civilization. This helps us understand his popularity in contemporary Poland among Catholic fundamentalists, who detect a variety of threats to the traditional Polish family.[179] For example, Paweł Gondek blames divorce and abortion for weakening marital ties, and also sees "all sorts of sexual deviants" destroying families.[180] Using a Konecznian paradigm, Jerzy Bajda explains that the family in Poland is under assault from "anti-Polish, anti-Christian, and anti-humane groups" with their "materialistic, liberal, secular, and consumer ideologies."[181]

Konecznian fundamentalism thus emphasizes the sanctity of "normal" family life, which entails the fulfillment of "natural" gender roles. For women, this places a premium on the biological and cultural reproduction of the nation. This can be seen as a response to perceived threats to Polish political autonomy (in the form of the European Union, which Poland joined in 2004) and Polish cultural identity (posed by creeping globalization). Fueled by fear, fundamentalist rhetoric is peppered with blatant expressions of sexism, bigotry, and chauvinism.

Agnieszka Graff and other scholars have detected in Poland a sort of "cross-cultural logic of gender and nation, one of idealization and control that intensifies in periods of transition, war, and real or perceived instability."[182] In addition, the Polish case demonstrates how "the nation is often symbolically figured as a familiar domestic space, a family, with a corresponding distribution of gender roles and hierarchies."[183] In this vision, women "are needed for reproduction: not only for biological but also cultural, as bearers of the collectivity's identity and honor."[184] This is clearly the case among Konecznian fundamentalists, who believe there is a perpetual "clash of civilizations" that threatens Poland's identity and sovereignty. Women play an integral role in this conflict: they must reproduce new generations of Poles, and raise them in the spirit of Polish patriotism and civilizational purity.

Tamar Mayer has identified this longing for purity as a common theme in many "national narratives of gender, nation and sexuality."[185] This is plainly seen in the rhetoric of Konecznian fundamentalists, for whom traditional gender roles have become "a guarantee of stability in an otherwise unstable world."[186] Catarina Kinnvall points out that in a "globalized world . . . devoid of certainty, of knowing what tomorrow holds," there is a temptation to go back "to an imagined past by using reconstructed symbols and cultural reference points . . . to recreate a lost sense of security."[187] The category of "home" is one such "bearer of security."[188] And women must be there to provide a refuge for children who are bombarded elsewhere by alien civilizational influences. Fundamentalists in contemporary Poland agree with Koneczny's contention that a woman's most important responsibilities are in the home.[189]

Graff states that the concepts of "nation" and "gender" are "both culturally constructed categories; moreover, they construct each other via notions of what is 'natural' and what is 'cultural.'"[190] Polish fundamentalist discourse is filled with "the yearning for a natural order" and the "fantasy of familial bliss" featuring a "hierarchical couple with many children."[191] The "natural" role of woman is in the home, raising children and perpetuating Poland's civilizational identity. Such traditional gender roles are desired by pundit Janusz Parada, who pleads for the recognition of the "psycho-physical differences between men and women" within a family that is "based on the natural hierarchy of authorities, where each [member] has obligations."[192]

Leading up to Poland's entry to the European Union in 2004, fundamentalist discourse about the role of women became increasingly associated with anxieties about national identity. Graff explains that

> the obsessive "gender talk" of this period is best understood as displaced narrative about the national identity: an effort to contain ambivalence about change and construct a notion of Polishness stable enough to accommodate, or perhaps even outweigh, European Union accession. It is hardly surprising . . . that the "bearer" of this stability was an idealized vision of femininity.[193]

The Polish Church's initial skepticism about the European Union also stemmed in part from concerns about gender roles, because of a perceived secularization and decline in family values in Western Europe.[194] Konecznian politician Maciej Giertych expressed a fear that there would "not be a place for the Church [in the EU]. There is also no place for the traditional, Catholic, and national Poland."[195] These anxieties about Polish membership in the EU were "projected onto, and resolved within, the realm of gender."[196] Konecznian fundamentalists asserted that women's primary obligation is to have children, and to raise them as good patriots in an era when Poland is confronted with the civilizational chaos of the European Union.

In the rhetoric of civilizational fundamentalists, "the family is portrayed as the core social institution, and women serve as the maintainers of religion and tradition. Women come to represent the timeless quality of status quo, of tradition, in the name of religion."[197] Writing in 2008, Maciej Giertych reflected back on the legislative agenda that the LPR promoted during its time as a coalition partner in the Polish government. He noted that its "main policy platform was on family issues. After all we are the League of Polish Families. . . . The League of Polish Families was the only party with 100% of its parliamentarians voting in defence of unborn life. This is also well remembered in Poland."[198]

Abortion had been legalized in Poland as early as 1932, but only in cases where the pregnancy resulted from a crime or when a woman's health was at risk. The communist regime adopted a more liberal abortion law in 1956, with abortion on request granted in 1959. Abortion on demand was banned in 1993, and despite a brief period of liberalization (1996–97) and continued efforts to expand a woman's right to choose, the Polish abortion laws remain restrictive.[199] Graff sees conservative Catholic efforts to ban abortion as part of an ongoing effort to "build a solid link between antichoice politics and Polish national identity."[200] Rachel Alsop and Jenny Hockey point out that since abortion was allowed by the communist regime, opposition to abortion became a symbol for opposition to the regime, and support for greater reproductive rights became associated with anti-nationalism and anti-Catholicism.[201] Wanda Nowicka adds that the "current [2007] position on abortion can be attributed in part to the fact that the almost 40 years of legal abortion under communism was based on instrumentalist and needs-based approaches rather than on the concept of rights."[202] This legacy hinders any movement today that calls for reproductive "rights." Moreover, public debate about national identity has been dominated by fundamentalists, "whose rhetoric abounds with references to 'true woman-hood.' This puts feminism in the position of nationalism's natural opponent."[203]

Pundits in *Nasz Dziennik* and other fundamentalist media have followed this reasoning to the conclusion that feminists are "enemies of our nation."[204] Feminism is viewed by fundamentalists as a phenomenon that is alien to Po-land; Barbara Bubula even blames foreign money pouring into Poland as the source of funding for feminist and other liberal causes.[205] Feminists' support for women's reproductive rights is further proof of a lack of respect for mother-hood and a lack of loyalty to the Polish nation.[206] This issue is central to the fun-damentalist argument, as voiced by Maciej Giertych: "Drawing pleasure from sex life remains in the life plans of the feminists, but drawing pleasure from maternity does not."[207]

During the first years of the twenty-first century, it seems that in Poland the abortion issue also represented a "coded discourse" for larger concerns.[208] Opponents to liberal abortion laws claimed that they represent an affront to Catholic values, and since Catholicism has become so integral to Polish identity among fundamentalists the demand for abortion becomes unpatriotic.[209] Na-tional survival is at stake, according to the traditionalist argument, and women have a civic obligation to the larger community.[210] They also have an obligation to defend Latin civilization. For example, Katarzyna Gawlicz identifies in *Nasz Dziennik* a tendency to place Poland within its civilizational context: a country founded on the values of Catholicism, it belongs to "Latin civilization"—"the civilization of life."[211] In this discourse, Polishness is equated with Catholicism and includes "the conviction that human life begins at the moment of concep-tion and, as a consequence, the defense of the fetus is an integral part of the defense of life itself."[212]

THE POLISH MOTHER

Konecznian fundamentalists insist on "permanent" monogamous unions with dedicated fathers and mothers, which implies that divorce is not an option. Koneczny claimed that "in all communities where there is divorce . . . a mar-ried woman becomes her husband's first servant. . . . Any marriage subject to notice, if the right to give notice applies only to the husband, lowers the posi-tion of the woman in their life together."[213] Koneczny believed that permanent monogamous marriage was the original source for the equality of women;[214] in his view, women were elevated and emerged as man's equals as a result.[215] Konecznian pundit Jerzy Bajda adds that divorces should be outlawed because a fruitful marriage preserves and passes on cultural identity from generation to generation.[216] After all, Koneczny claimed that "[a]ll discoveries and inventions . . . would have been worth nothing had it not been possible to transmit them to later generations. Nothing is worth anything without tradition, which is the backbone of all civilisation."[217] Paweł Skrzydlewski concludes that monogamy "strengthens the dignity of woman and thus her freedom. The indissolubility of a marriage not only protects and strengthens the woman, but above all it serves the child who in the long and difficult period of upbringing needs stability and support from both sides of the family."[218] Mothers play the key role in this process, not only as biological reproducers but culture bearers who raise children in the traditions of Latin civilization. Bajda opines that "divorce is a crime against marriage, which is also a crime against humanity because it kills the very source of those values that determine the meaning of its existence."[219] According to Maciej Giertych: "For the proper development of a child parents are needed, parents in a permanent matrimonial relationship."[220]

A potent component of the fundamentalist discourse on family and marriage is the image of the "Polish Mother" (Matka Polka). This motif emerged in a powerful form during the partitions.[221] It defined the ideal Polish woman as devoted to family and nation, a patriotic domestic who raised children in a traditional Polish home. As Wanda Nowicka points out, this "led to the position of women being elevated; procreation was more than a private family act—it was a patriotic act on behalf of the nation."[222] This notion is dear to fundamentalists; at the First Congress of the Women's League of Polish Families in 2006, delegates stressed that mothers play a crucial role in teaching children about patriotism.[223] It is important to note that

> the long tradition of occupation by outside forces in Polish history has meant that, while public spaces and institutions remained overwhelmingly occupied by non-Polish forces, the private sphere became the focus for maintaining national heritage and pride and for resisting occupation. The "Polish Mother" thus took central stage in the symbolic representation of Polish patriotism.[224]

The Church has traditionally played a leading role in burnishing this image;[225] this adds an important religious imperative to a woman's role in Polish society.

While this model idealized them, it also "made it very difficult for women to realize their ambitions outside of family. Any attempt by a woman to liberate herself from family roles was treated as betrayal of the nation and the Church."[226] Women were tasked with reproducing the nation, and nothing could undermine this. Thus, there is another side to the Polish Mother image: if a woman does not engage in the biological and symbolic reproduction of the nation, then she is demonized as an enemy of the people.[227] Konecznian fundamentalists also place the Polish Mother image within a larger civilizational struggle: Polish women must give birth to a new generation of Polish patriots, steeped in Polish tradition and culture, who will defend the ideals of Latin civilization in the face of alien civilizational threats.

In contemporary Polish fundamentalist discourse, "nostalgia for tradition, identity and authenticity" has produced "a conception of gender whereby women become symbolic markers as guardians of the nation in their capacity as biological reproducers."[228] This helps explain fundamentalists' attraction to Koneczny, who emphasized traditional Catholic values and an authentic and pure civilizational identity. He called upon women to play a key role as reproducers of the Polish nation and bearers of its culture. Maciej Giertych's analyses fit within this Konecznian framework, since his concern for demographic decline and intermarriage are part of his overall obsession with preserving Polish civilizational purity. He admonishes women for not having enough children, which has contributed to the "demographic crisis of the Western world."[229] He defines abortion as "the most antifeminist deed one can imagine, one directed against maternity, against the ultimate essence of femininity."[230]

In her book *Gender and Nation*, Nira Yuval-Davis elaborates at length on women's key role in nationalist agendas as guarantors of the "biological reproduction of the nation."[231] In this way, nationalist ideologues have a special regard for women who fulfill "the so-called 'natural' role of women—to bear children."[232] These concerns have led in Poland to a political manipulation of reproductive rights as a symbolic marker of larger national concerns. Indeed, Alsop and Hockey note that "women's reproductive health has ceased to be an issue in its own right. . . . An interweaving of nationalism and Catholic doctrine frames the debate on women's reproductive choice, with the powerful symbol of the 'Polish Mother' exploited in anti-abortion campaigns."[233]

Moreover, Yuval-Davis has found that "the effects of globalization on contemporary politics of belonging have been such that in many places we see new kinds of conservatism and tribalism which, under the claims of returning to 'authentic' culture and tradition, radically enlarge the differential ways in which manhood and womanhood are constructed."[234] Not only men, but "women, too, participate culturally in reproducing the nation, defending the 'moral code' and partaking in controlling the Other."[235] Women are often viewed as preservers of "culture and tradition," and Yuval-Davis finds that the "freezing of cultures in a selective manner beneficial to the patriarchal leadership is often one of the major tactics of fundamental leaderships."[236] This phenomenon is evident in the rhetoric of civilizational fundamentalists in Poland. For example, Piotr Jaroszyński uses a Konecznian argument to promote the use of education to defend Poles against globalization and the loss of national identity. The situation today, he fears—with the denationalizing impact of the European Union and globalization—is similar to that in the partition period.[237] Wojciech Wierzejski, a leading figure in the LPR, also uses a Konecznian framework to explain that the proper education of children according to traditional Polish values is the key to Poland's future.[238]

A declining birthrate until recently compounded anxieties about the decay of traditional cultural identity and exacerbated fears about the loss of political autonomy within the European Union. Fundamentalists highlight the history of Poland's near destruction as a nation during the partition years, as well as the more recent memories of Soviet domination.[239] Their position is clear: "We will be stronger as a Nation and State if there are more of us."[240] And women who "reject" their "natural" role as mothers are traitors; for example, readers of *Nasz Dziennik* complain that the legalization of abortion is an act against the Polish nation.[241] In an article dedicated to a Konecznian exploration of the status of women in various civilizations, Ryszard Polak explains that the nature of women is different than that of men. Women are better suited to raise children, and society would be better served if men could support a family on one income.[242] Women would be free to raise the children in a way that is central to the survival of cultural traditions. A key component of opposition to reproductive rights is thus the "ideology of female domesticity";[243] in contemporary Poland, fundamentalists still believe that "[a] woman's mission is to deliver children because the society needs more children."[244] They assert that "[w]omen's aspirations for professional and/or scientific careers are secondary to their primary role of having children."[245] Andrzej Horodecki opines, "A love for children stands at the heart of Latin civilization."[246]

The Konecznian ideal is thus "the natural, monogamous family that is based on the union of one man with one woman."[247] A monogamous patriarchy provides a stable environment for the education of children in the traditional values and faith.[248] But this way of life is weakened by the debilitating effects of modern culture. For example, soap operas on Polish television erode traditional family values with their depictions of different lifestyles and broken families, which Piotr Jaroszyński terms "pathological." He fears that depictions of characters with multiple marriages or homosexual relationships will eventually follow.[249] Fundamentalist rhetoric is "filled with moral certainties, aversion toward 'equality' and 'tolerance,' and a deep commitment to what it calls 'normality.'"[250] Agnieszka Graff recalls a "Normality Parade" that took place in Warsaw on 18 June 2005, which was a response to recent "Equality Parades" that were organized by gay rights' advocates. She characterizes the event as "a proud promotion of home-grown 'natural' heterosexuality, threatened by minorities, which are perceived not only as aggressive and powerful, but also, crucially, as foreign."[251]

As Anika Keinz explains, the concept of "nationalism as a form of resistance informs contemporary conservative arguments against ideas perceived as 'foreign,' including gender equality stemming from a 'foreign'—Soviet—system or later the European Union."[252] Koneczny acolyte Andrzej Horodecki consistently warns of the "disease" of foreign civilizational influences in Poland. In one message rife with populist appeal, Horodecki explains that foreign influences are more evident in cities, especially among the intelligentsia. Condemning the "enemies of Poland," he calls for "a return to Latin civilization."[253] This begins in the home, with parents raising their children according to Poland's appropriate (Latin) civilizational standards. Traditional family life, anchored by a permanent monogamous marriage, also nurtures a love of Poland. Horodecki even devoted a section in his draft Polish constitution to this issue; it stated that patriotism has its source in family life.[254] This ideal family is situated in the Polish village; however, he believes that this ideal is under assault.[255]

In the Konecznian fundamentalist vision, the "West" has become decadent, filled with cosmopolitanism and materialism.[256] Horodecki also finds that "Poland is in a state of civilizational mixture, and thus chaos, in which the still remaining elements of Latin civilization are more easily destroyed."[257] In a Konecznian messianic statement, Maciej Giertych claims that it is Poland's historical mission to defend Latin civilization: "Our civilizational awareness predestines us to struggle for the victory of Latin civilization in the world. We ought to strive for this."[258] But first, Poles must achieve civilizational purity at home.

Just as society as a whole must avoid foreign civilizational influences, Konecznian fundamentalists see a need for commensurability of the different elements of the quincunx within the family. Koneczny even questioned the viability of "mixed marriages" because "[n]either in marriage, nor in family life, nor in private life in general, nor in public life is it possible to be civilized in two ways."[259] He maintained that "[a] married couple coming from different civilizations will always be mismatched (as long as one of the sides does not abandon his or her civilization)."[260] Konecznian fundamentalists in contemporary Poland still believe that marriage partners should be from the same civilization, or children will be raised with mixed values, mired in a state of epistemological chaos.[261] From a Konecznian viewpoint, children raised with multiple civilizational influences will not thrive, for they will not develop a culture of action.[262]

MACIEJ GIERTYCH

The fundamentalist ideologue today who is most responsible for propagandizing Koneczny's vision is Maciej Giertych. He has sought to "update" Koneczny's framework to help explain the civilizational challenges of the twenty-first century. In his controversial treatise, *Civilisations at War in Europe* (2007), Giertych addresses the issue of mixed marriages: "Someone may have a Jewish father and a Chinese mother but in terms of civilisational affiliation, he will belong to either one or the other or altogether to a different one but he can never be civilised in both ways."[263] Giertych warns that children born into mixed marriages run the risk of experiencing confusion that inevitably devolves into an "acivilized" condition. He recommends that "spouses can be from different races, or different nationalities, but they must be of the same civilization."[264]

Giertych expressed similar views in the mid-1990s in a regular column dedicated to popularizing the ideas of Koneczny ("Z nauczania Feliksa Konecznego," or "The Teaching of Feliks Koneczny") that appeared in his monthly journal, *Opoka w Kraju* (The Bedrock in the Country). Navigating an intellectual minefield, Giertych posited that couples coming from different civilizations are "always ill-suited, unless one of them abandons his or her civilization and accepts the civilization of the other."[265] Civilizational identity thus functions in much the same way as race in earlier constructs that warned against alien influences. In both cases, purity is needed. Giertych clarifies his position on this matter in *Civilisations at War in Europe*: "In human societies, inter-civilisational marriage does occasionally occur but it is a rare phenomenon and the less it occurs the more biological differences will develop between civilisations. However, it is not the race that makes a civilisation. It is civilisation that can make a race."[266]

Giertych hypothesizes that a Polish woman marrying a "Negro" would have a "chocolate child" that would nevertheless share its mother's civilizational values. "This colored Polish child is a Pole by its upbringing, by its civilization. The color of the skin has no significance. In Africa, and even in the USA, it would be mentally in a foreign world."[267] Giertych's commentary fits within a broader rhetorical tendency of fundamentalists, who consistently assign to women an important "symbolic status, connected to their reproductive roles, as representatives of purity. Only pure and modest women can re-produce the pure nation; without purity in biological reproduction the nation cannot survive."[268]

Fundamentalists in contemporary Poland believe that the family is threatened by a variety of "pathological pressures" that are anti-Polish and anti-Christian in nature. Jerzy Bajda, for example, fears that "the nation is dying, marriages are falling apart."[269] Confronted by the "encirclement of the global conspiracy against Church and family," the solution is to "purify what is defiled in [Polish] customs and culture."[270] In essence, this entails purging Poland of alien civilizational influences and returning to what is "pure," "natural," and "normal" in Polish culture. This begins at home, where the mother is primarily responsible for passing on Polish traditions and values from one generation to the next. Maciej Giertych develops this line of reasoning extensively in his brochures. He maintains that "[i]n the civilisations where a mode of family life is so organised that mothers are at home all the time, the civilisation is perpetuated. In places, where the mother is absent most of the day, the children risk being educated in a set of values alien to the parents."[271] He warns that "[o]ur [Latin] civilisation has to be actively defended. Even at the risk of poverty, we must insist on having control over our children."[272] Giertych believes that it is "absurd" for Polish households to need two incomes. He argues that the "social system must be reorganised to make it possible for a family to live on a single income and to have a living home with a mother always ready to control children and be available to them."[273] Polish women must recognise their specific value, respond to their natural vocation, accept their femininity for what it is and live accordingly. They must also demand from the society at large an acknowledgement of their natural value when doing the most important task in the world, the rearing and upbringing of children.[274]

In his booklet *European Values* (2007), Giertych posits that the "monogamous, autonomous, nuclear family composed of a husband and wife and any children their union will be blessed with"[275] is the core institution of Latin civilization. He also defines marriage as a "permanent union of one man and one woman;"[276] in *Civilisations at War in Europe*, Giertych reminds us that "[i]n the Latin civilisation, monogamy is obligatory."[277] This demand for permanent monogamous marriages is grounded not only in Catholicism, but also in the theories of Koneczny. He, too, believed that a permanent, monogamous marriage was the foundation of Latin civilization. He explained that "at the beginning [of human existence] there was monogamy. It is no longer possible to talk of an alleged original unordered group without exposing oneself to ridicule."[278] He linked monogamy with other values promoted by fundamentalists today in Poland: sexual restraint, which can be maintained within a monogamous marriage; and the sanctity of private property, which emerged with monogamy.[279] Koneczny found that the "basis of all associations is the combination of the human couple.... Sex is thus a highly beneficial factor for humankind. But under one condition.... It must be controlled, otherwise the beneficial force may become mischievous. All the senses must be controlled, and sex is no exception."[280]

Maciej Giertych promotes these same Konecznian family values. He frequently bemoans the alleged social costs of feminism, which he believes belittles women who work as homemakers. In the labor market, meanwhile, women pose special problems related to "their biological functions."[281] This includes not only maternity leave, but also the alleged natural tendency of women to think about home while they are at the workplace. He advocates a "return of women to the home, of mothers to children"[282] as a way to relieve the labor market, but also to ensure the correct upbringing for children. This "would not only limit such pathologies as divorce, drug abuse, and wasteful spending, but would also reduce the need for retirement homes and orphanages and restore dignity to women who are working in accordance with their calling."[283]

Giertych is greatly concerned with what he terms the "defeminisation of women and demasculinisation of men in Europe and their consequences for the family.... In view of her biological role traditionally a woman performs the majority of jobs at or near the home, while the man performs those that require a longer period of absence from home."[284] Giertych believes that men and women "differ but we also complement each other. Thank God we differ and thank God we complement each other. This is the way God has created us and He knew what He was doing."[285] He laments that "[t]oday most commonly the paid work a father does is insufficient to maintain the family, thus also the mothers seek employment."[286] For fundamentalists, this tends to blur the "natural" distinctions between the parents and diminish patriarchal authority. Worse yet, Giertych concludes that the

> priority of the professional career will result in children being brought up by somebody else . . . often an *au pair*, from abroad, possibly passing on to the child ideas from an alien culture. The natural bond between the mother and the child will be missing. And it is on this bond that the transfer of values from generation to generation is based.[287]

Fundamentalists call for a return to the "natural" order that serves to glorify the unique "natural" contributions of women to the nation. Giertych asserts that women "are of exceptional value and this stems primarily from their biological functions of carrying, giving birth to and nursing the next generation."[288] He believes that feminism diminishes the value of women's "natural" role in society, insisting that

> the so called "feminist movement" leads to loss of feminine characteristics in women, and therefore in fact it is an antifeminist movement. . . . [A woman's] primary role is to maintain the family hearth, to supply the heart, the warmth, the feeling of security, the remembering about everyone and about everything.[289]

Giertych calls for a broad cultural transformation that would create a more positive image for the traditional family lifestyle. In a concise summation of the fundamentalist definition of womanhood, he opines, "Women should be judged more by their family life than by their professional achievements. Women whose families broke up should be shown for what they are—failures."[290]

A defense of the traditional patriarchal family is not Maciej Giertych's only concern. On a variety of social and cultural issues, Giertych has been the most outspoken Konecznian fundamentalist contributing to popular debate in Poland. In *Civilisations at War in Europe*, a booklet published in February 2007, Giertych expressed his worldview as a true "konecznianista":[291] "Civilisations differ so much that it is not possible to be civilised in two different ways. . . . Civilisations, by their very nature, must be at war with each other. This war has nothing to do with military activity or force. It is a war of ideas."[292]

Giertych endured broad public criticism at home and abroad for his booklet, which was published in English in order to expose an international audience to the ideas of Koneczny. Most of the commentary targeted his discussion of "Jewish civilization," which repeated many of the same themes expressed by Koneczny during the interwar period and in posthumous publications (especially *Cywilizacja żydowska*).[293] Rafał Pankowski of "Never Again" noted that the booklet was "consistent with his [Giertych's] previous writings, as disappointing as that may be."[294] Piotr Kadlcik, president of the Union of Jewish

Religious Communities in Poland, did not find explicit anti-Semitic comments, but added that the booklet contained "dangerous thoughts that could elicit anti-Semitism."[295] Writing in his periodical *Opoka w Kraju* in April 2007, Giertych explained that he wanted to popularize Koneczny's ideas outside of Poland. As a result, he "was proclaimed an anti-Semite, a racist, a xenophobe, a violator of the values on which the European Union was constructed, etc."[296] Despite the criticism, he was glad for the publicity in a way, since it might "build interest in the works of Koneczny, and finally this author will gain the international recognition that he deserves."[297]

Critics have detected in Giertych's ideas the echoes of a discourse from the interwar period that replaced the concept of "race" with the euphemism of "civilization."[298] In an interview with *Gazeta Lubuska* conducted after the publication of his Koneczny primer, Giertych was directly asked by the reporter, "Pan Professor, are you a racist?" Giertych replied, "Of course not."[299] But in response to another question about whether he would object to his son marrying a Jewish woman, Giertych voiced reservations about "intercivilizational marriages."[300] While he would not oppose such a union if she "belonged spiritually to our civilization and professed our values," he noted that if she were not Catholic it would be very difficult for this to be the case.[301]

Giertych has commented at some length on how a civilizational boundary is drawn between Christians (particularly Catholics) and Jews. Basing his commentary on Konecznian ideas, Giertych posits that

Jews do not represent any specific race. It is a great misunderstanding to consider anti-Semitism as racism. . . . However, the fact that they stick to their own community, their own civilisation, their own separateness, results in biological differences developing. It is not the race that forms the Jewish civilisation but the civilisation can cause a biological separateness.[302]

This is all for the best, it would seem, since Giertych argues that aspects of Jewish civilization, especially its "situational ethics," pose a "spiritual threat" to Latin civilization and must be avoided.[303] This concern is shared by other civilizational fundamentalists who have warned Poles about the need to regulate interaction with "lower" civilizations.[304]

Some pundits have defended Giertych and Koneczny against charges of racism by correctly noting that Koneczny rejected biological definitions of a Jewish "race."[305] Others have questioned why Koneczny's ideas should be marginalized, since many prewar authors wrote more harshly about Judaism.[306] Piotr Bezat has defended Koneczny against charges of chauvinism by using Konecznian reasoning: "On the basis of the theory of the plurality of civilizations anti-Semitism does not mean hostility toward anyone—it is simply an attitude of opposition to the contamination of the Latin method of collective life."[307] Mirosław Dakowski wrote an open letter in February 2007 to President Lech

Kaczyński, in which he made clear that Giertych's booklet was based on Koneczny's ideas, which were explicitly "anti-racist."[308] Piotr Jaroszyński of the KUL
Faculty of Philosophy frequently comments on Koneczny in *Nasz Dziennik* and
on Radio Maryja. He has warned that "Jewish civilization is a very sensitive
topic, because to a certain degree today it is embraced by the censorship of *political correctness*" and there are consequences if one is labeled an anti-Semite.[309]
He added that "Koneczny does not attack a race, a nation, or a religion. For
Koneczny was neither a racist, nor a fascist, nor a xenophobe; he was an analyst
of civilization. It is possible to agree or not with this analysis, but it is not possible to classify him as *anti-Semitic.*"[310]

Maciej Giertych carefully grounds his argumentation in Koneczny's science
of civilizations and promotes the concept of civilizational purity for Polish society. He is a controversial public figure who has been at the center of controver-
sies about Koneczny's intellectual legacy. In the next chapter, I will examine the
Giertych family's role in greater detail as part of my analysis of the influence of
Konecznian fundamentalism on political movements in Poland through the
first decade of the twenty-first century.

Chapter Six

Konecznian Fundamentalism in Politics

POLISH NATIONALISM

Konecznian fundamentalism emerged as an important component of nationalist ideology in post-communist Poland. In the twenty-first century, Koneczny has become a member of the "'pantheon' of Polish nationalism."[1] While Koneczny's works fell into disfavor in communist Poland, several key manuscripts were published in exile by Jędrzej Giertych. Giertych's Catholic-centered ideology is sometimes referred to as "Christian Nationalism," which is the title of a brochure that he published in 1948.[2] His Catholicism has been favorably described by followers as "complete," "consistent," and "traditionalist."[3] Much like Koneczny, Giertych stressed that Poland was a Catholic nation and should be a Catholic state; Poland should also be a leading representative of Latin civilization in Europe, confronting destructive threats from "anti-Catholic centers and foreign civilizations."[4] He mimicked Koneczny's historical vision in his own writing, and Piotr Piesiewicz concludes that one may even "consider Giertych's historiography as the manifestation of Koneczny's theories in the realm of politics."[5]

Jędrzej Giertych's thinking exemplified the attitudes of the nationalist "youths" who came of age in the interwar period. Jarosław Tomasiewicz argues that the "integral Catholicism of the so-called 'young' nationalist faction in the '30s" is an important influence on nationalism today:

> Geopolitical "realism" was replaced by ideological vision. . . . [T]his is caused by an influence of Koneczny's "theory of civilizations," according to which [the] whole social life should be based on Catholicism. We can see Koneczny's influence in all aspects of neo-nationalist doctrine. "Theory of civilizations" made nationalist ideology more coherent and gave nationalists [a] quasi-"scientific" fundament but on the other hand made this ideology more dogmatic and anachronistic.[6]

Jędrzej Giertych's brand of "Christian Nationalism," which blended the thinking of Koneczny and Roman Dmowski, has now been passed on to the current generation of nationalists.

The most prominent nationalist ideologue in interwar Poland, Roman Dmowski (1864–1939) reacted to the youth movement by showing more concern for the relationship between Polish nationalism and Catholicism; this is evident in his 1927 book *Kościół, naród, i państwo* (The Church, Nation, and State). This concern marked a shift away from the more secular brand of nationalism of Dmowski's earlier years.[7] His former rationalist approach to politics "was yielding to fundamentalist radicalism, seeing politics as a Manichean struggle between Good and Evil."[8] Andrzej Walicki has identified the influence of Dmowski's new thinking on contemporary Catholic fundamentalists, who

> are obsessed with the idea of an essential similarity between communism and liberalism, as equally godless and antinational, and with the alleged Masonic threat to Catholic Poland. Hovering in the background is, of course, the widespread fear of "aliens in our midst," manifest in a suspicious attitude towards people of Jewish origin and in the tendency to enormously exaggerate their numbers in Poland.[9]

Jędrzej Giertych's son Maciej cherishes his family ties with the old interwar movement, and he consistently promotes policies that bear a Konecznian imprint.[10] I have already discussed his dedication to Konecznian fundamentalism in chapter 5. Maciej has served as the leading ideologue for the League of Polish Families (Liga Polskich Rodzin, or LPR, formed in 2001), and as a deputy to the European Parliament (2004–9). Another Giertych—Maciej's younger brother, Wojciech—has already been mentioned in the context of Koneczny's influence on Polish Catholicism. Father Wojciech was appointed as Papal Theologian in December 2005.[11] And Maciej's son, Roman, served briefly (May 2006–August 2007) as Deputy Prime Minister and Minister of Education in a coalition government. Maciej, in particular, has elevated Koneczny's science of civilizations to a new level of importance in nationalist ideology. Ulrich Schmid concludes that the Giertychs blended Dmowski's national democracy with Koneczny's Catholic philosophy of history to create the foundation for their political ideology.[12]

Maciej Giertych has explicitly linked Koneczny's science of civilizations with Dmowski's nationalist ideology. Writing in 1999, he marked the fiftieth anniversary of Koneczny's death and the sixtieth anniversary of Dmowski's death by emphasizing their common features.[13] Although the two men did not work together in their lifetimes, their ideas have now become mutually complementary components of contemporary Polish nationalism.[14] Giertych believes that Dmowski would agree with key elements of Koneczny's theories, including the impossibility of syntheses between civilizations and the need for "total ethics" in Polish society.[15]

Another Konecznian pundit cited in this monograph is Andrzej J. Horodecki; he also refers to interwar authorities, frequently pairing Dmowski and Koneczny as key foundations for the contemporary nationalist movement.[16]

With the exception of Maciej Giertych, among fundamentalist ideologues Horodecki has been the most consistent in his application of Konecznian principles. In 2005, he even penned a new draft constitution for Poland, in which he peppered his prose with Konecznian phrases and concepts. There are frequent references to "Latin civilization," and in the preamble he discusses as a second foundation ("personalism" is the first) of Latin civilization the "harmonious development of the five categories of social existence: *truth* and *goodness* as transcendental categories, *health* and *well-being* as worldly categories, as well as *beauty* as the capstone of it all."[17] These are—verbatim—the five components of Koneczny's quincunx of existential values that are at the heart of his civilizational theory.

Horodecki has been active in the nationalist movement since his days as a member of the *Polski Związek Katolicko-Społeczny* (Polish Catholic-Social Union), which was founded in January 1981.[18] He and other Catholic fundamentalists find Koneczny appealing in part because during his lifetime he "rejected the materialist interpretation of history" that was promoted during the Communist era.[19] Horodecki also cites Koneczny to deflect charges of bigotry, claiming that he is not anti-Semitic or anti-German, but rather does not want civilizations to mix for fear of harmful results.[20] He maintains that Polish politicians ought to have a knowledge of Koneczny's civilizational theories in order to better understand threats to Poland, especially in the form of German-Jewish or German-Russian alliances.[21] Other pundits put forth similar Konecznian xenophobic fears. Employing a Konecznian framework, Mieczysław Ryba argues that "the key period for a resolution of the direction for the development of Poland in the twentieth century was the twenty-year interwar period, and the fundamental terrain of the struggle was the civilizational conflict."[22] He and other Konecznian fundamentalists insist that the oppressive systems that dominated Poland for much of the twentieth century were forced on it by alien civilizations—German Byzantinism, Russian Turanianism, and Jewish civilization.[23] Koneczny offers binaries, closed worlds, and polar opposites with no room for confusion. He provides clarity and comfort in his prohibition against civilizational mixing, which is a core belief of Polish civilizational fundamentalists.

KONECZNY'S RESURRECTION AS NATIONALIST ICON

After the marginalization of rival political parties by the Communists—the Polish United Workers' Party (*Polska Zjednoczona Partia Robotnicza* [PZPR])—from 1948 onward, the prewar nationalist parties were cast into the political wilderness. Over time, however, they began to regroup, and the *Liga Narodowo-Demokratyczna* (National-Democratic League) resurfaced by 1958. During the 1959–60 academic year, the party attracted several dozen people in the Warsaw area alone, especially among law students at the University of Warsaw.

Two or three times a week the Warsaw group held meetings at which members discussed a variety of topics, including Koneczny's theory of civilizations. According to Jarosław Tomasiewicz, this group was dedicated to the "orthodox" version of *endecja* represented by Jędrzej Giertych, Adam Doboszyński (1904–49), and the later ideas of Roman Dmowski that sought to wed Polish nationalism with Catholic fundamentalism.[24] One of the leaders was Józef Kossecki (b. 1936).[25] Active in underground nationalist politics, Kossecki was an advocate of Koneczny's theories. Trained as an engineer and a student of "social cybernetics," he has published works on civilizational theory and also Konecznian commentary on current affairs.[26]

Another key player in the nationalist revival was Bolesław (Bernard) Tejkowski (b. 1933), who was active in the Political Discussion Club at the University of Warsaw in the mid-1960s. He later became involved in extremist movements in the 1990s. Tejkowski was also drawn to Koneczny's ideas. Apparently, Tejkowski collected several unpublished works of Koneczny, which he subsequently passed on to Maciej Giertych. He, in turn, smuggled them abroad to his father in London, where his publishing house printed the volumes long after Koneczny's death. These works included *Cywilizacja bizantyńska* (Byzantine Civilization, 1973); *Cywilizacja żydowska* (Jewish Civilization, 1974); *O ład w historii* (On Order in History, 1977); and *Prawa dziejowe* (Historical Laws, 1982).[27] According to Maciej Giertych's recollections, this was a laborious and risky process.[28]

T. David Curp has demonstrated that from the 1960s to the 1980s, Poland's communist leadership also "created new movements or re-created nationalist organizations similar to those that existed after the war and mobilized public opinion to support the regime."[29] Some of these groups, such as the Association for the Development of the Recovered Territories, focused on potential threats to Poland's lands returned from Germany after World War II.[30] The group nurtured the sort of nationalist rhetoric that would emerge in more vocal form in the 1990s. The communist regime recruited former nationalist activists, who joined such efforts simply to counter perceived German threats rather than because of an ideological transformation. The association was closed down after the recognition of Poland's western border by West Germany in 1970 (the border had been recognized by East Germany in 1950, and it was reconfirmed in 1990 by the unified German state); nevertheless, "[a]nti-German fear and animus did not disappear from Polish society (or from the state's reformulation of Polish history) during the 1970s."[31] Later organizations, such as the Grunwald Patriotic Union (founded in 1980) also recruited nationalists.[32] This organization included the Koneczny popularizer Józef Kossecki as a leading member.[33]

More important than traces of Konecznian influence in state-sanctioned organizations, however, were the ways in which opponents to the regime created arguments based on Koneczny's theories. As Piotr Bezat reminds us, Koneczny "was above all a Catholic philosopher."[34] This made his arguments for civil society even more attractive to activists seeking an alternative to communism. By the 1970s, the Church had assumed its familiar role as defender of the authentic Polish "nation" against an alien "state." It provided an institutional infrastructure for the opposition movement, as well as connections with the international community that brought in financial and moral support for Solidarity.[35] Writing in October 1981, Solidarity activist Jan Józef Lipski noted that Koneczny's civilizational theories were once again being discussed among intellectuals as a way to explain the "Turanian" and "Byzantine" aspects of Russian culture.[36] Koneczny's theory of the plurality of civilizations was also being employed as "an argument against the 'unifying theory of progress,' or totalitarianisms."[37] At that time, this meant a rejection of the Marxist vision of historical progress of all humankind through definite stages. Today, it means a rejection of globalization as an inevitable end to national distinctions. Koneczny is an inspiration to pundits in the extremist nationalist press who seek to justify the division of the world into different camps. His theory of a plurality of civilizations that are in constant conflict is an important part of the fundamentalist worldview, which tends to assign negative traits to "civilizational others."[38]

Koneczny's ideas were important components of nationalist ideology among a new generation of Polish activists that emerged in the late 1970s and early 1980s. Curiously, Koneczny's science of civilizations has played a more central role in contemporary nationalist ideology than during his lifetime, as new generations of activists and publicists have found new applications for his theories. Kazimierz Janusz (1925–2014) quite explicitly applied Koneczny's "science of civilizations" in his underground classic, *Konfrontacje Rosja-Zachód: Zderzenie dwóch cywilizacji* (The Russia-West Confrontation: A Clash of Two Civilizations, 1974). Janusz became a leading ideologue in the *Ruch Młodej Polski* (Polish Youth Movement), which was founded in Gdańsk in late July 1979. Its members were inspired by Koneczny's theory of civilizations.[39] Interestingly, Janusz claimed that he was not a true "koneczjanista," since his analysis went beyond Koneczny and developed new arguments.[40]

Yet Janusz's book actually speaks to the vitality of Koneczny's thought and the ease with which it can be manipulated to explain the shortcomings of the "other." Janusz praised Koneczny for his quincunx of existential values, which addresses both material and spiritual aspects of life with an explicit effort to connect them into a holistic vision. He opposed this to the dreaded materialism of the official Marxist ideology, in the process demonstrating the civilizational superiority of Latin (Catholic) Poland compared to Byzantine-Turanian Soviet Russia.[41] It is true that Janusz attributed far more Byzantine elements to Russian/Soviet culture than did Koneczny. Perhaps this was a sign of the times: exhibits in Warsaw in May 2008 recalled that the events of 1968 included contemporary denouncements of the vulgar "Byzantinism" reflected in the pomp and display of the communist regime.[42]

Koneczny himself provided plenty of criticism of communism. He poked fun at the way in which observers seemingly found communism in every aspect of human existence: "If [several families] living in one building is a manifestation of communism, towns are populated entirely by communists!"[43] He also derided Bolshevism as an "Asiatic" presence that appeared on Polish soil during the Polish-Soviet War: "We in Poland had ample opportunity to become acquainted with it when the Bolshevik hordes cut up into strips furniture-covers, curtains, carpets, etc. in order to share them 'justly.' What was received from the share-out became personal property; there was absolutely no question of any kind of communism."[44]

The collapse of the communist regime in 1989 allowed the revival of old nationalist parties, as well as the mushrooming of new organizations. The *Stronnictwo Narodowe* (National Party) was reactivated in July 1989 by members of an older generation who sought to continue the interwar *endecja* tradition. This was evident in the choice of Maciej Giertych to head the party's chief governing body. Giertych is undoubtedly the man most responsible for integrating Koneczny's theories with contemporary nationalism in Poland; he bases his commentary on Koneczny's theoretical works, and his controversial brochures published in recent years have declared this linkage more explicitly.[45] His efforts at propagandizing Koneczny's ideas were also an important part of his campaign for the presidency in 2005.[46]

As Grzegorz Tokarz notes, the new National Party "regarded itself as a modern national movement, based on the values of Latin Civilization and Polish Catholic traditions."[47] Tokarz also indicates that the revival of Koneczny's ideas reflects a persistent tendency within the nationalist movement to revive debates from the interwar period within the changed context of the late twentieth and early twenty-first centuries.[48] The anachronistic arguments frequently evident in fundamentalist rhetoric reflect the intellectual gymnastics required to make Koneczny's ideas seem applicable to the world today. Yet contemporary observers, such as Wojciech Szurgot, confirm that the fall of communism and the emergence of a new geopolitical situation raised the interest in Koneczny.[49] In a series of articles published in the nationalist monthly *Szczerbiec* (The Jagged Sword) from 1992 to 1994, Michał Poradowski followed Konecznian reasoning to address the problems confronting Poland. For example, in one article he discussed how land and humankind's connection to it are viewed differently in various civilizations. This is a favorite Konecznian theme—the unique bond between "Latin" Poles and their land and the way in which other civilizations have commoditized the environment. Poradowski also followed Koneczny in his critique of "Jewish civilization," focusing on how its "sacral" nature serves as a "brake" on its development.[50] Warning Poles against the dangers of losing one's spiritual roots, Poradowski concluded that a "worldview is . . . the most important civilizational factor in determining a civilization. Other factors can be changed without a fundamental change in the civilization . . . however, when a worldview is changed a civilization must undergo a transformation."[51] Moreover, he asserted that "there exist only two fundamental worldviews: pagan and Christian."[52]

Jarosław Tomasiewicz suggests that "the influence of Koneczny on the contemporary *endecja* is difficult to overestimate. The 'theory of civilizations' is a sort of 'metatheory' for the Catholic nationalism of the *endecja*."[53] While Koneczny was not a member of the *endecja*, "the notion of 'Latin [Western] civilization'—which is a key to his theory—has become the standard for the new *endeks*."[54] Other scholars, such as Marian Bębenek, also find that Koneczny's views are embraced by extreme Catholic nationalists in Poland.[55] Stefan Zgliczyński of *Stowarzyszenie Nigdy Więcej* (Never Again Association, an anti-racist watchdog group) identifies Koneczny as the "unquestioned authority" today among nationalist ideologues who construct defenses against "civilizational threats."[56] One of these ideologues, the scholar and pundit Piotr Jaroszyński, prescribes the thought of Koneczny as an antidote against the corruption of Polish culture.[57]

ALL-POLISH YOUTH (MW) AND THE LEAGUE OF POLISH FAMILIES (LPR)

In December 1989 the interwar organization All-Polish Youth (*Młodzież Wszechpolska* or MW) was revived in Poznań by Roman Giertych, who also served as its first president.[58] Its ideology is grounded in prewar ideas, especially those of Roman Dmowski and Feliks Koneczny. In a 2006 profile of the Kraków chapter (which met at the local office of the League of Polish Families), journalist Małgorzata Olszewska described the reverence the youth displayed for figures from the interwar period. The hall featured a portrait of Roman Dmowski, as well as books by Dmowski and Koneczny. Favorite topics for lectures and discussions included Koneczny's science of civilizations.[59]

The civilizational fundamentalist League of Polish Families (LPR) was formed in 2001 by uniting over twenty parties. The MW played a key role in its formation, and the personal links between the two organizations proved important. In its first parliamentary elections in 2001, the LPR received 7.87% of the vote. This gave the LPR 38 out of 460 deputies to the Sejm (Polish parliament). In 2005 the LPR received 7.97% of the vote and 34 seats in the Sejm.[60] The issue of Polish integration into the European Union was a key factor that prompted the formation of the LPR, which sought to fight Polish membership.[61] Once Poland entered the EU, the party pledged to defend Polish national interests within the European Parliament. In EU elections in 2004 the LPR received 15.92% of the vote and 10 out of 54 Polish seats in the European Parliament. The years 2004–5 represent the peak of LPR popularity, and in the 2007 elections the party failed to gain any seats to the Sejm, receiving only 1.28% of the vote. By 2009, the LPR was no longer represented in the Sejm or European Parliament, although its members continued to hold some local and regional offices.[62] In an interesting commentary in the nationalist weekly *Myśl Polska* (Polish Thought) after the electoral disaster in 2007, Stanisław Stojanowski-Han suggested that party leaders, ironically including Roman Giertych, had strayed from Koneczny's teachings. In his opinion, they had deviated from the tenets of Latin civilization and drifted toward the excessive centralization and neglect of ethics in politics that characterize Turanian and Byzantine civilizations.[63]

Scholars have noted that "[f]rom the beginning, the key role in the party [LPR] was played by the Giertych family—Maciej (father) and Roman (son) who proclaimed themselves to be heirs to Roman Dmowski's national camp tradition of the 1930s; Roman's grandfather—Jędrzej Giertych—was one of the founders of the camp." [64] Fabian Chropski claims that when Poles speak about orthodox nationalist thought, they "have in mind three figures, whose views create the foundations of this ideology. They are Roman Dmowski, Feliks Koneczny, and Jędrzej Giertych himself."[65] Especially in the Giertych connection, the LPR and MW truly represented what one author calls "dinosaurs of the traditional extreme nationalist groups."[66]

Sarah de Lange and Simona Guerra offer insights into the brief period of electoral success for the LPR. Their research indicates that "the Polish historical legacy has created a fertile breeding ground for RRPs [radical right parties] in general, and for a party that campaigns on a programme that combines Catholic conservatism and nationalism in particular."[67] The LPR was one fundamentalist party that "positioned itself strategically in the Polish political space."[68] As de Lange and Guerra point out:

> The transition from communism to democracy has provided Poland with an opportunity to redefine its national identity, while exposure to the processes of globalization and European integration have increased awareness of Poland's "Polishness." Both developments have paved the way for the resurgence of nationalist sentiments and the emergence of nationalist movements.[69]

An important aspect of the LPR's rejection of the communist past was its attack on the old regime's "cosmopolitan universalist ideology."[70]

During its heyday, leaders of the LPR consistently used Konecznian terminology in their analyses of Poland's societal problems. This is evident in many phrases, such as "the unbridgeable civilisational difference," "the law of the impossibility of the civilisational synthesis," "the law of harmfulness of the merging of civilisations—civilisations cannot coexist," and "contact of different civilizations is the greatest challenge for society."[71] Hanna Kwiatkowska has found similar echoes of intolerant rhetoric from the interwar period in the pages of the fundamentalist daily *Nasz Dziennik*, noting "an ideological continuation from the thoughts of the pre-WWII nationalists such as R[oman]

Dmowski and Prof. F. Koneczny, whose writing[s] are very much promoted in the newspaper. The newspaper never sees the Jews who lived in Poland as Poles but as strangers or guests who abused the Polish hospitality."[72]

Konecznian fundamentalist critiques consistently raise concerns about "cultural" or "civilizational" crises. Writing for a regional LPR website in 2006, Daria Łatkowska lamented the "crisis of western civilization"[73] that Koneczny had also fretted about during his lifetime. She blames the cult of relativism, which she associates with the Enlightenment tradition, for its challenge to the fundamental values of Latin civilization. She urges societies in Latin civilization to return to the core civilizational values that Koneczny identified in his works. Koneczny had warned of this problem over seventy years earlier, but she believes that the erosion of traditional values has nevertheless continued unabated into the present century.[74]

In his blogs and his brochures, former MW and LPR leader Wojciech Wierzejski suggested reading Koneczny as a way to understand current affairs.[75] One of the burning issues confronting civilizational fundamentalism is globalization, which is defined as having two elements: cultural and economic-political.[76] In an interview from 2004, Wierzejski stated that the "National Movement has always been opposed to globalization. Globalization is a threat to the identity of nations and therefore we also oppose the idea of a European Union. The unification of various cultures and civilizations is not possible, unless on the way to totalitarianism."[77] Wierzejski also defends the preservation of Polish culture in areas of the interwar Republic that were lost as a result of boundary changes after World War II. Claiming that an important element of Poland's foreign policy is "the question of Polonia in the east," he has asserted that Poles "have there [Ukraine and Belarus] after all a civilizational mission and it is not possible to forget about this."[78]

In addition to the LPR, other fundamentalist groups have explicitly acknowledged their intellectual debt to Koneczny in their party statements. The president of the Popular-National Alliance (*Przymierze Ludowo-Narodowe*) claimed in 2004 that his party endorsed "the political ideas of R. Dmowski, J. L. Popławski, F. Koneczny, and W. Witos."[79] The party program used Konecznian rhetoric, stating that the "Polish state and Poles were formed in the personalist Latin civilization, which all our enemies have tried to destroy, this is the Germans—formed in the Byzantine civilization, the Russians—in the Turanian civilization, and the Jews, formed in the collectivist, religious Jewish civilization."[80]

Fundamentalist youth organizations have also engaged in the Koneczny revival. Many regional MW homepages provided links to Koneczny books online.[81] In a report about the MW from 2005, investigative journalist Anna Fostakowska found Koneczny to be a popular topic among the youth she interviewed. As one interviewee noted, "civilizations never are in agreement," with different views on beauty, goodness, and other categories of the Konecznian quincunx.[82] Gatherings of MW activists frequently featured programming related to Koneczny's science of civilizations; at a camp in spring 2006, for example, youth were instructed on "Civilizations According to Feliks Koneczny."[83]

During its peak of popularity, LPR leaders used MW meetings as a way to proselytize. Koneczny's ideas provided common ground for these encounters. The featured guest at a 2006 meeting organized by the local MW group in Biała Podlaska was LPR parliament deputy Andrzej Mańka. An audience of around one hundred persons was in attendance for a presentation on "Methods of Political Activity in the Thought of Feliks Koneczny" and their application to the current political scene.[84] A year earlier, at an MW meeting in Radom in May 2005, the topic of interest was "Credibility in Politics." Special guest Andrzej Fedorowicz (LPR Sejm deputy) provided a Konecznian analysis, reminding his youthful audience: "Feliks Koneczny wrote, 'Poland either will be Catholic or it will not be.' And this is our fundamental problem."[85] Undoubtedly, Koneczny's devout Catholicism has been one reason for his great popularity within contemporary civilizational fundamentalism.[86] His ideas provide fodder for the "radical conservative Catholics" in Poland who "allow themselves to judge and criticise everything and everyone they disagree with," while simultaneously "criticism of (or sometimes merely skepticism about) their views and conduct is labelled as 'antichurch' or 'animosity' towards the church."[87]

KONECZNIAN EXTREMISM

Koneczny has also been revered in the most extreme political settings. The website for *Obóz Narodowo-Radykalny* (ONR, or National-Radical Camp) has featured commentary that explains the world from a Konecznian perspective. For example, in "Prawdziwa Tożsamość Europy" (The True Identity of Europe, 2010), the values of Latin civilization are presented as the opposite of those associated with the European Union: "materialism, militant atheism, the atomization of society, democratic socialism, cosmopolitanism, decadence, relativism, and hedonism."[88] From May until September 2003, the fascist International Third Position funded summer camps in Poland (*narodowa akcja letnia*, national summer campaign) for radical activists. Thousands of youth from such groups as the National Rebirth of Poland (*Narodowe Odrodzenie Polski*, or NOP)[89] attended free of charge, since Polish neo-fascists received financial support from western counterparts. Another source of funding came from the sale of propaganda, including Koneczny books sold through the NOP website.[90]

Beginning in February 2007, members of the NOP gathered in Kraków each year to commemorate Koneczny's life and work. The annual "Koneczny Conference" was always scheduled around the anniversary of the historian's death (10 February 1949), and after the proceedings a small group marched to his grave in the Salwator Cemetery to pay homage to the man dubbed by one admirer as the "Copernicus of the Third Millenium."[91] Participants at the inaugural event discussed the need for "wiping out" in contemporary Poland the influence of the same non-Latin civilizations identified by Koneczny as threats in the inter-war period: Turanian, Byzantine, and Jewish. Central to this vision is the belief that these civilizations aim to diminish Catholicism, which is at the heart of Latin civilization. One young activist, Marcin Jendrzejczak, concluded that it is "necessary in our hard times of culture wars to cooperate with Catholics and Latinists from all western regions in a sort of 'white international.'"[92]

At the inaugural Koneczny Conference, Dariusz Tarnowski sought to make Koneczny relevant for today. He reminded his audience that a "civilization is either pure, or it does not exist; it is not possible to be civilized in two ways. Po-land fell because it sought some sort of synthesis between West and East, which formed it into a sort of civilizational caricature," and it will fall again if it fails to purge itself of non-Latin civilizational traits.[93] Part of Koneczny's appeal is the way in which he "speaks" to audiences today, providing a scientific framework for analyzing and understanding the complexities of the twenty-first century. Following Koneczny's reasoning, Tarnowski argued that the rivals of Latin civi-lization are also enemies of Catholicism. The immediate threat today is global-ization and the intrusion into Poland of alien values, such as those associated with liberal ethics. Quoting Koneczny, he reminded his audience that "Poland will either be Catholic or it will not be."[94]

There are other timeless "threats" that were discussed at these meetings. At the 2008 Koneczny Conference, Kamil Sawczak delivered a paper "On the Res-olution of the Jewish Problem." Citing Koneczny as an authority, the speaker contended that the "Jewish problem" is not a racial or religious issue, but a civilizational one. Sawczak's diatribe was filled with resentment about the "civi-lizational sickness" that accompanies the "Judaization" (zażydzenie) of Polish thinking.[95] As we have seen in chapter 3, this is an old complaint that was voiced frequently by fundamentalist Catholic critics of the interwar period.[96] Linked in a new conspiratorial vision with the "new world order," Sawczak identified Jewish influence in the bureaucratization of Polish society, the proliferation of pornography,[97] and most significantly, in the focus on the "letter of the law" rather than its ethical content. Echoing Koneczny's fears from an earlier era, Sawczak proclaimed, "The Judaization of Polish society has become a fact; thus the problem of the solution of the Jewish question stands before us."[98] The Konecznian inspiration for this rhetoric is not unusual; Katarzyna Stańczak-Wiślicz finds that Koneczny's Cywilizacja żydowska is "a source of arguments for contemporary anti-Semitic discourse."[99] She contends that Koneczny's vi-sion of "anti-Semitism as a positive program leading to the 'dejudaization' and rescue of Latin civilization" provides a "scientific" basis for similar arguments today.[100]

The theme of the third annual conference in 2009 was "Cywilizacja Cza-sów Próby" (Civilization in Trying Times). Rafał Szydlik discussed articles by Koneczny about religion that were published in Tygodnik Warszawski (Warsaw

Weekly) in 1946, including "O nierówności religii" (On the Inequality of Religions). Piotr Leń delivered a paper on Koneczny's book *Święci w Dziejach Narodu Polskiego* (Saints in the History of the Polish Nation, 1937), in which he explained the historian's vision of the inseparable ties between Catholicism and Polishness. Artur Ślósarczyk also presented a paper dealing with the role of the Catholic Church as the political caretaker of the nation, and Bartosz Biernat spoke on the fatal effects of Protestantism on societies.[101] The Eighth Koneczny Conference was held in Kraków in February 2014. Among the presentations was Michał Padacz's paper on the relationship of Koneczny's theories to the Third Position's stance on racial segregation. At the conclusion of the conference there was once again a march to the Salwator Cemetery to lay flowers at Koneczny's grave.[102]

A KONECZNIAN CRITIQUE OF THE EUROPEAN UNION

As we have seen, Koneczny's civilizational theory has greatly influenced fundamentalist critiques of the European Union.[103] His fear of German hegemony makes Koneczny quite relevant to his followers who reject the German-dominated EU. Koneczny's musings on shortcomings of the League of Nations and other international organizations also fuel criticism of the civilizationally mixed European Union. Basing his argument on Koneczny's thinking from the interwar period, Włodzimierz Bojarski claims that in the post–Cold War era, *"the strategic goal of Poland ought to be the desire for Central Europe to be dominated exclusively by Latin civilization."*[104]

In contemporary Poland—despite the emergence of a Polish state that is almost entirely ethnically Polish and Catholic—civilizational fundamentalists have resurrected Koneczny's Orientalist fears as part of their discourse on civilizational dangers, especially in connection with their criticism of the EU. Critics say that a European federation must be formed within the framework of Latin civilization or it will not survive. The civilizational struggle described by Koneczny is an ongoing one; for his heirs it takes the form of Latin Poland combating various Oriental elements of the EU agenda: "Byzantine" German hegemony, the threat of "Turanian" Turkey gaining entry, and Islamic ("Arabic," in Konecznian civilizational terms) immigration.

"Universalism" or political federation is not necessarily the problem. Koneczny hailed the efforts of Charlemagne, who was crowned Holy Roman Emperor by the Pope on Christmas Day in 800 A.D.; however, he deemed the Byzantine and other eastern empires as oppressive. The key difference, according to Koneczny, was that Charlemagne allowed for sociopolitical pluralism and understood that "the best path to unity is in the recognition of variety."[105] The Ottonian German empire, which according to Koneczny was Byzantinized under the influence of Theophano, had nothing in common with the Carolingian empire "either genetically or spiritually."[106] This is a key for the Konecznian critique of the EU. Koneczny saw room for a "free union" of sorts in Europe, which became the ideal for many Polish "Euroskeptics." These critics do not reject "Europe"; rather, they reject a European Union that is dominated by Byzantinism in the form of German hegemony. They support an association that allows for "unity in variety" within an "organic" union. In Konecznian terms, this is the opposite of the "mechanical uniformity" and "monotony" that is characteristic of Byzantine civilization.[107]

For those who adhere to Koneczny's theories, it is impossible to discuss the European Union as a manifestation of a "Unified Europe." Civilizational differences within the Union make this out of the question. Just as an individual person or a society "cannot be civilized in two ways," neither can federations of states.[108] From a Konecznian perspective, Byzantinism crushes civil society and national integrity. Dominated by "Byzantine" Germany, the EU represents an "Oriental" entity that is alien and hostile to Latin civilization, and therefore, the Polish nation. Moreover, the EU facilitates the immigration of Muslims, who represent a civilizational threat that Koneczny largely ignored.[109] Paweł Skibiński contends that "the civilizational situation in Germany does not remain without meaning for the whole European continent, if we pay attention to the leading role that Germany plays in the European Union."[110] Images accompanying commentary entitled "The German Question" by the editor (Jan Engelgard) of Myśl Polska exemplify the mistrust of Germany still held by Konecznian fundamentalists. The faces of three persons are featured: a Teutonic Knight in the rear, then a German soldier from World War II, and Chancellor Angela Merkel in the forefront.[111]

Taking a quintessentially Orientalist approach, Koneczny asserted that "[e]verywhere in the East the moral element is subordinated to material strength. In Byzantium, this is linked with the attribution of superiority to form over content, and accompanied by a strong impulse to uniformity; Byzantinism does not understand unity without uniformity."[112] For Polish Euroskeptics this means a loss of autonomy and national identity. In Konecznian terms, this also means a loss of Latin—the only authentic "European" civilization—identity. Expressing the concerns of those Polish nationalists who share Koneczny's logic, Piotr Bezat predicts that "if Byzantine civilization finally succeeds in seizing all of Europe for itself, then it will not be anything other than a purely geographical meaning of the word."[113]

For Koneczny, the emergence of an authoritarian Prussian state in modern times was a turning point in the history of Byzantine civilization. This "Byzantinization" of Germany culminated in the unification of the modern empire by Otto von Bismarck, whom Koneczny dubbed "the greatest Byzantinist in all of world History."[114] The unified German state also represented yet another failed synthesis of East and West. From a Konecznian perspective, all mixtures of East and West are lethal because the "Orient" acts as a poison that kills the civilizational ideals of the West. The "lower" civilization pollutes the "higher," yet the resulting artificial fusion can persist as a horrible monstrosity, such as the Byzantine Empire, the unified German state, . . . or the European Union.

Over fifty years ago, Anton Hilckman provided a Konecznian interpretation of the problem of European unification:

> It is not the Imperial idea, of which the Germans felt themselves to be the bearers, which now appears as the truly Western idea: but something quite different, the idea of a federal Europe conceived as a brotherhood of nations, equally free and with equal rights. The Imperial idea, on the other hand, originated much more in the Byzantine world.[115]

For persons viewing the world through a Konecznian lens, Germany remains the "main bastion of Byzantine civilization in Europe."[116] In the civilizational fundamentalist journal the *Nowy Przegląd Wszechpolski*, an editorial from 2002 (one year prior to the Polish referendum on European Union membership) claimed that the EU

> is a tool of the masons—above all German—to deprive Europe of its identity, or of Latin civilization. It is a continuation of the thousand-year policy of the German elites, educated in the Byzantine civilization, aiming to subordinate the Roman Catholic Church. The union also includes the spirit of the Jewish civilization.[117]

Together these collectivist civilizations purportedly seek to weaken personalism in Latin civilization, especially in Poland. Włodzimierz Bojarski has described the EU as a renewed German threat—"a new era of *Drang nach Osten*"—that takes the form of the "politico-economic neocolonial directive of the European Union"[118]

Maciej Giertych states succinctly the binary relationship between Latin and Byzantine civilizations: "Byzantine civilisation developed in contrast to the Roman West."[119] Most threatening to Poland, he adds that "in the East of Germany, Byzantine influences always dominated. In the West, particularly in the Rhineland, there was more Latin influence. The return of the capital from Bonn to Berlin [decided in 1991 and completed by 1999] is likely to be civilisationally, an unwelcome development."[120] "Today," Giertych warned in 2008, "the role of . . . the Prussian, and thus Byzantine, spirit in Germany is immense."[121]

Giertych's writings in opposition to Polish membership in the EU (before the referendum in 2003) were extensive, and as a member of European Parliament (2004–9) he continued to voice his skepticism.[122] In a vivid example of the essentializing of the "other" that Koneczny inspires, Giertych described "Byzantine" German tendencies in the following way:

> While in Rome and now in the Latin civilisation, unity of purpose unites but methods and forms may be very different, in Byzantium and now in Germany, a state imposed uniformity is the norm. . . . We tend to be

impressed by German efficiency. We often envy them. We dream of having such law and order, such functionality and such affluence as they have.[123]

This peculiar lure of Byzantinism described by Giertych was identified fifty years earlier by Anton Hilckman. He warned the Latin world that

> Byzantium stood, it is true, for centuries high above the West: an admired, envied and imitated model.... [T]he fact that Byzantium was superior to the West in external culture was the source of an immence [sic] danger for all the Western European peoples. All of them fell under the spell of the Byzantine temptation—and this temptation meant the danger of a very harmful influence.[124]

Today, the "spell" and "temptation" of Byzantium—in the view of those Euroskeptics applying a Konecznian civilizational paradigm to the contemporary world—take the form of the German-dominated EU.

Consistently applying Konecznian reasoning, Maciej Giertych has frequently focused his missives in his journal *Opoka w Kraju* on "German Byzantinism" as a reason to fear the European Union.[125] In a special issue from April 2003, just prior to the Polish EU membership referendum in June, Giertych reminded readers of the long history of German plans in the modern era to dominate a unified Europe, from Bismarck to the European Union. He asked at one point: "Have the German plans changed so much?" He responded that "[t]he EU is of course closer to the proposition of [Friedrich] Naumann than the method of Hitler."[126] But in the article "*Co teraz?*" (What Now?), written after the Polish "yes" vote, Giertych proposed a general plan for a civilizational rearguard action:

> We ought to politically organize the weakened forces of Christian Europe to a counteroffensive. We ought to restore its soul to Europe, and this can only be a Christian soul. For the time being, Brussels is governed by atheistic, liberal, and Masonic forces.... We have been a Christian bulwark, we have defended the Pope before the German emperors ... Vienna before the Turks, and all of Europe before Bolshevism and Hitlerism. Today we have to restore to Europe its Christian soul—we will work in this direction.[127]

In a special issue of his journal from May 2004, he provided a more specific "Program for LPR Deputies to the European Parliament" that targeted creeping Byzantinism. It stressed the belief in "traditional, Christian values and Latin civilization, on which Poland and Europe were built"; it also pledged that delegates "will defend Poland and all of Europe against the growing influence of Germany, which aims to force Europe under its hegemony."[128]

For Giertych, the Byzantine nature of the EU bureaucracy is painfully obvious. Equally clear are the civilizational tensions within the EU between "Latin"

Poland and "Byzantine" Germany. His 2005 booklet, *Z nadzieją w przyszłość* (With Hope for the Future), includes a lengthy explanation of the history of Latin-Byzantine tensions in Europe. Giertych emphasized that since the EU is dominated by Germany, it is essentially a Byzantine institution that represents a threat to Latin Poland. Poland, he predicted, will have to bear a messianic burden once again—seemingly a "predestined" role within the EU—as the bastion of Catholicism and Latin civilization in Europe.[129] Later, in his 2007 booklet, *Civilisations at War in Europe*, Giertych explains fully the civilizational implications of Polish membership in the EU:

> Our strength lies in diversity, in the readiness to criticize the government and we should defend these values against the German intention of regulating everything from above—today from Brussels, rather than from Berlin. The overregulation so prevalent in the European Union is obviously of Byzantine and not of Latin origin.[130]

Giertych summarized the problem in his booklet *Quo vadis Europa?* (2009): "The Byzantine way of thinking dominated the politics of the Order of the Teutonic Knights, the Prussian kings and the most famous Prussian chancellors. This mentality requires that the state be primarily successful and not necessarily ethical."[131]

Andrzej Horodecki is another Konecznian pundit who consistently tags the German-dominated EU with the perjorative "Byzantine" label. As a frequent columnist for the weekly *Myśl Polska*, but more importantly as an editor and contributor to the journal *Nowy Przegląd Wszechpolski,* he has produced a plethora of essays about contemporary issues. He has cogently applied a Konecznian paradigm to various aspects of the EU "problem": (1) German Byzantinism and its domination of the Union;[132] (2) the potential entry of "Turanian"—and Islamic—Turkey into the EU;[133] (3) the growing "threat" of Islamic immigrants—who primarily represent the "Arabic" civilization—and the poor historical record of Byzantine civilization in combating the spread of Islam; (4) the separation of Kosovo, with its primarily Islamic population, from Serbia, and its recognition by much of the international community as an independent state;[134] (5) the destruction of independent Polish farming;[135] and (6) the loss of Polish national identity within the EU.

In his arguments against the European Union, Horodecki frequently restates the fundamental Konecznian law: "Civilizational syntheses are not possible." He reminds readers that Koneczny's works were banned during the Communist period, but that his "science of civilizations" can provide Poles a guide to policy making today, especially in its warning to avoid civilizational mashups.[136] Before Polish entry into the EU, Horodecki cited Koneczny in explaining the unique ties to the land that are nurtured by Poles and other peoples within Latin civilization. He asserted that Byzantine Germans, and by extension, the EU—or what Horodecki terms "Paneuropa Deutschland"—do not share these concerns. Horodecki fears that "the EU aims for the liquidation of the agricultural population in Poland—the last country where Latin civilization still has healthy roots and branches."[137] Moreover, Horodecki warned before the accession vote that if Poland joined the EU this would lead to "the factual liquidation of the Polish nation and its state."[138] He has urged Poles to explore an alternative to the EU, which he has dubbed "the Fourth German Reich."[139] Following Koneczny's logic, he envisions Polish cooperation with "its neighbors in the area that are from the same Latin civilization."[140]

This resistance to the EU has been given historical gravitas by the term "Nowy Grunwald," which Horodecki uses in his rhetoric.[141] Teresa Bloch, editor of the fundamentalist monthly *Nowy Przegląd Wszechpolski*, highlighted the victory at Grunwald among the list of historical turning points at which Poles saved Latin civilization; others include the Battle of Legnica against the Mongols (1241), the defense of Vienna against the Turks (1683), and the Battle of Warsaw (1920)—the "miracle on the Vistula"—against the Bolsheviks.[142] As Poles debated membership in the EU, she wrote about the long and bloody relations between Byzantine Germany and Latin Poland, wondering: "Will the referendum on the matter of entering the Union be a second Grunwald?"[143]

A variant of this theme is Horodecki's vision of the European Union as a joint Byzantine-Jewish threat to Latin civilization.[144] In essence, his argument is that since the EU is not founded on the principles of Latin civilization, it is anti-European. He succinctly concludes that "[t]he European Union is de facto the Anti-European Union."[145] Using Konecznian terminology, Horodecki has reminded readers that the EU was designed by "collectivist civilizations . . . Byzantine and Jewish" and is inherently "incompatible with the personalism of the Latin civilization of Poles."[146] In several articles, Horodecki vividly recounts the plots to eliminate the elite of Latin civilization during the twentieth century.[147] He has argued that the concept of an "open society" associated with the EU is the latest threat—"a tool of the Byzantine and Jewish enemies of our civilization."[148] Ultimately, Horodecki believes, this is a life-and-death struggle for Poles: "For us the *greatest matter* is the desire of Germany to eliminate—in this, or in another way—the Polish Republic from the map of Europe . . . this is *the logical result* of civilizational differences."[149] Citing Koneczny, he has warned that the inferior, collectivist, Byzantine part of Germany, formerly Prussia, seeks "the strengthening of the hegemony of Byzantinized Germany" over Europe.[150]

Horodecki's criticism in 2005 of the draft European constitution centered not only on its "atheistic character," but also on its lack of emphasis on natural law and other concepts dear to Koneczny and his followers.[151] He was not alone; Jerzy Bajda complained that the preamble of the draft EU constitution discussed Europe as a creator of civilization, but that it did not say that "this specific European civilization is Latin civilization, which was able to emerge only in the spiritual climate of the Catholic Church (Koneczny)."[152] The overarching concern about the EU, stated in Konecznian terms, is that Poland needs to be "free from the influences of foreign civilizations, states, and international organizations."[153] This does not reflect "any national egoism, but *civilizational soundness*, which is at the same time responding to the *civilizational utopia* known as the European Union."[154]

CATHOLIC TOTALISM

Stopping Byzantinism and other alien civilizational influences from destroying Latin civilization in Poland requires a renewed commitment to civilizational purity and a return to what Koneczny called a "totality of ethics" in both private and public lives.[155] The ethical and religious components in civilizational fundamentalist rhetoric reflect the concerns of "Catholic totalism" that Koneczny had envisioned decades ago. As Maciej Giertych wrote in 1996, "We want a Catholic state, Catholic educational institutions, Catholic health services, Catholic culture."[156]

The problematic relationship between national identity and religion is identified by Maria Janion as one of the "postcolonial symptoms" that she sees in Poland.[157] It was evident in the 1990s in the debates surrounding the preamble to the Polish constitution. Geneviève Zubrzycki points out that the pitting of ethnic and civic visions of nationhood against one another took place "in a setting that one might expect to be unproblematic: an ethnically homogeneous country with no significant national minorities or border disputes."[158] Yet the "Catholic Right" insisted that the preamble refer to Christian values that would indicate not only an ethnic homogeneity, but also a cultural one.[159] Many Polish fundamentalists reject what one critic calls "Multi-Kulti civilization."[160] Others have chafed at proclamations of the "historical necessity" for Poles to accept the EU and globalization in general, comparing them to the tenets of Marxist historical determinism.[161]

The European Union is consistently identified as an enemy of the Polish nation, since it represents values at odds with "Polishness."[162] Moreover, the EU facilitates the immigration of Muslims, who represent a civilizational threat that Koneczny largely ignored.[163] However, Koneczny did discuss the issue of immigration in more general terms: "Immigration may even change the civilisation of a given area if the immigrants arrive with a strong consciousness of possessing a high-level civilisation of their own; immigrants whose civilisation is slight after a certain time adopt the civilisation of the new country."[164] Koneczny was also concerned that newcomers from other civilizations might not be able to assimilate.[165]

Konecznian fundamentalists frequently complain about the EU's shortcomings in dealing with the influx into Europe of peoples from other civilizations. Jan Bodakowski worries that "Euro bureaucrats and not Poles will decide about Poland and Poles," warning that an EU constitution would allow "the EU and not Poland to issue visas. This will . . . allow a terrorist from Africa living in old Europe to travel to Poland."[166] Maciej Giertych fears that the EU will not stress Christian values, and will allow Islam to gain greater influence in Europe. He calls for the civilizational purity of the EU, noting that the most important function of the Polish representatives in the European parliament is "the defense of a Christian identity for Europe," which is a "defense also of the identity of Poland."[167]

As examined in chapter 5, the discourse of Konecznian fundamentalism reflects a real sense of impotence in defending Polish sovereignty. This often manifests itself as a desire to return gender roles to their "natural" order. Agnieszka Graff identifies a wartime mentality evident in this sort of rhetoric, in which "the prevailing category has been 'crisis' and need of 'renewal,' as well as 'moral purification.'"[168] She also detects a "crisis of masculinity" that can be traced to the loss of independence in the eighteenth century,[169] and more recently to "the pressures of globalization, and the resulting diminution of Poland's autonomy as a nation-state."[170] Having a history of precarious sovereignty, it is not surprising that some Poles are anxious about the EU. Civilizational fundamentalists can thus demonize the supranational organization as another threat to Polish independence. Moreover, the EU represents a civilizational challenge to Poland's traditional Catholic values. Prior to Poland's admission to the EU, Włodzimierz Bojarski warned that Polish membership in the union would lead to a moral collapse evident in "abortion, euthanasia, homosexual unions, drug addiction, and juvenile depravation."[171] He also expressed a deep mistrust of cultural globalization, fearing the "neocolonial exploitation" of Poland and the "devaluation of fundamental concepts, such as the family" through an "intensive anti-family propaganda" and "the popularization of free unions, divorces, and abortion."[172]

In the concluding chapter, I will analyze the Koneczny revival and Konecznian discourse more thoroughly within the postcolonial context. My analysis will further explain the continued impact of Koneczny's science of civilizations into the twenty-first century. For Polish civilizational fundamentalists who are anxious about Poland's fate, Koneczny's theories from the interwar period help them make sense of complex challenges in today's world.

Konecznian Fundamentalism in the Twenty-First Century

POSTCOLONIAL ANXIETY

Despite Poland's independence, Polish civilizational fundamentalists in the early twenty-first century saw their sovereignty and way of life threatened by the European Union, international capital, and cultural globalization. In this new era of anxiety, Koneczny's ideas once again seemed relevant. Koneczny professed scholarly objectivity, but it is clear that he was deeply concerned with guarding Poland's Latin civilization against the dangers of cultural influences from other, "lesser," "Oriental" civilizations.[1] Poland is not typically discussed in the literature on Orientalism, but in an essay entitled "Said and the Polish Question," Ewa Thompson argues that Edward Said's critique of Orientalism can be legitmately applied to the case of Poland.[2] The "postcolonial resentment" that she also identifies is an additional important factor in the resurgence of nationalist ideologies since 1989.[3]

Koneczny's own works on the "science of civilizations" can be read as expressions of postcolonial anxiety. He examined Poland's fate in the context of its colonial experiences and civilizational struggles throughout the ages. Over the course of the interwar period, Koneczny became more strident in his rhetoric about the threats to Poland, its Latin civilization, and especially its Catholic faith. He saw "Byzantine etatism" on the rise, as well as the alleged growing intellectual influence of Jewish civilization.[4] While Koneczny had once seen hope in Polish-Russian amity,[5] he became hardened in his opinion that a "civilizational boundary" divided the two countries.[6]

Koneczny sought to liberate the "colonized mind" of Poles who had lived under Austrian, German, and Russian rule during the partition period. He worried that "at the turn of the nineteenth and twentieth centuries there began to appear in Poland a new type: a Pole with an ardent Polish heart, prepared for all sorts of sacrifices, even to martyrdom for Poland, but having . . . a Russified brain."[7] This process had to be reversed, and in interwar Poland Koneczny also warned against succumbing to further temptations of alien civilizations. Only Latin civilization, aided by the Catholic Church, had developed the sort of freedoms that characterized modern civil societies. The best exemplar of this civilization, the Polish nation, must defend it and seek to spread its influence. This not only meant resistance to external pressures from "Byzantine" Germany and "Turanian" Russia, but also the challenge of Jewish civilization, which Koneczny also linked directly to the Bolshevik threat.

Koneczny serves as an important authority for many contemporary fundamentalist ideologues.[8] His observations, and those by his admirers today, are reminiscent of the *ressentiment* described by Tamara Hundorova. A term associated with Friedrich Nietzsche and others who grappled with interpretations of identity, the concept has come to assume a broader meaning of "imaginary revenge."[9] Hundorova argues that this "serves as an affirmation of 'the weak' in its relations with 'the strong'" and it is therefore "feasible to also use it in the analysis of postcolonial consciousness, in particular, in the case of the self-assertion of the colonized."[10] Koneczny's strident assertions about Poland's special civilizational status compared to its colonizers' appear as attempts at "imaginary revenge." His example supports Hundorova's contention that "the concept of *ressentiment* allows us to return to the issue of co-existence of anti-colonialism and post-colonialism."[11] Before Polish independence, Koneczny had begun to create a discourse of imaginary dominance that obviated the problem of Poland's occupation by more powerful neighbors. In his fully developed science of civilizations that emerged in the interwar period, Poland became the shining beacon for Latin civilization in its struggle against other, "inferior," and "Orientalized" civilizations.

Koneczny's attacks on modern cosmopolitanism and his yearning for "civilizational purity" are important components of his mood that are also reflected in fundamentalist critiques.[12] Konecznian ideologue Maciej Giertych wonders "whether Europe will be Latin or Byzantine: This is the key question of our times."[13] One pundit, Peter Bein, even commented on the Danish cartoon controversy of 2005–6 from a Konecznian perspective: "Koneczny found civilisations confronted each other in 'wars of ideas.' To survive, a civilisation must defend and promote itself through education of the young. When a civilisation gives up its identity and treats other civilisations as equals, the one wins which is the most demanding of its members."[14] As Bein's commentary exemplifies, Koneczny's theories provide ammunition in the Polish culture wars. Referencing Koneczny's civilizational theory as a way to explain Poland's victimization has also been prevalent. Konecznian historian Dariusz Ratajczak pointed to the usual "civilizational" enemies of Poland:

> Undoubtedly . . . communism is the theoretical creation of Jewish civilization, and in general all totalitarianisms are the effect of a combustible Turanian-Byzantine-Jewish mixture. Also Hitlerism, despite its anti-Jewishness, is the fruit of influences of ideas of Jewish civilization. . . . [I]n the end the notion of the chosen nation taken from the Jews was an element of the Hitlerite worldview.[15]

Fundamentalist opponents to cultural globalization have borrowed heavily from Koneczny's civilizational discourse as a means to rally the defense of Poland and Latin civilization against "threatening others."[16] The message is clear: One must be on guard against one's enemies, either real or imagined.

Koneczny's followers do not perceive the economic and technological exchanges that are associated with globalization as the greatest threats to civilizational purity. Koneczny and they would agree with I. A.Vasilenko's judgment that "[i]n today's world, modernization is by no means equivalent to Westernization."[17] For Koneczny, technological exchange was distinctly different than the homogenization of cultural values. It seems that globalization would not necessarily destroy civilizational identities, as long as the consumer culture did not undermine distinct civilizational values.[18] Even in the material realm, however, exchanges should have limitations. Koneczny's heirs resent economic globalization, too, since it could entail the sale of farmland and other Polish properties to foreigners; in their view, this could eventually lead to the loss of national sovereignty.

Citing Koneczny as a main authority, pundits such as Arkadiusz Maślach denounce the modern globalized liberal state and its bureaucratic tendencies as products of other civilizations. He and other fundamentalist critics bemoan the "sickness" of liberalism and characterize liberal democracy as an artificial and alien imposition on Polish society, in contrast to the sort of natural and organic civil society envisioned by Koneczny in his works.[19] They equate liberal democracy with communism, resenting the rise of "homo democraticus" and the attempts to create a new Poland through "social engineering."[20]

Another reason for the popularity of Koneczny is his devout Catholicism, a faith that many Poles have embraced as an alternative to excessive materialism associated first with Marxism during the People's Republic, and now with the globalized consumer economy that is regarded as equally alien to Polish culture. Koneczny's emphasis on ethical totalism has inspired commentators to apply his theoretical framework to a wide range of contemporary issues, from reproductive rights to environmentalism.[21] For these critics, globalization—especially cultural globalization and the imposition of civilizationally alien values—resembles colonization.[22]

While Polish civilizational fundamentalists today reject Marxist visions of class warfare and Social Darwinist arguments about the survival of the fittest, they make use of Koneczny's theory of civilizational struggle.[23] Citing Koneczny, Andrzej Horodecki bluntly states that any sort of "peaceful coexistence" between different civilizations is impossible.[24] He adds that the "civilizational struggle, which Koneczny describes, cannot at all be spontaneous; rather, it is conducted with premeditation generation after generation."[25] Horodecki has frequently expressed concern about a confrontation with Byzantine Germans, the "neighbors beyond the Oder."[26] He also frets over the "ignorance of the fundamental differences between Latin civilization and Jewish civilization"[27] among Poles. Following Konecznian logic, he points out that the two are incompatible and cannot be partners. He reminds readers of Koneczny's "fundamental historical law: no one can be civilized in two ways—on Monday, Wednesday, and Friday guided by Latin principles, and on Tuesday, Thursday, and Saturday by Jewish or Byzantine principles."[28] From the Konecznian fundamentalist perspective, Poland is confronted with the constant threat of a civilizational struggle for survival.

An age-old civilizational threat to Poland is Byzantinized Germany, which Konecznian fundamentalists argue is using the European Union as a way to fulfill the traditional German goal of dominating Europe. Konecznian critics of the "Byzantine" EU complain about an oppressive bureaucracy in Brussels, coupled with unwanted cultural cosmopolitanism. Writing in 2002, Włodzimierz Bojarski boldly asserted that the EU is the new colonizer in Poland, and that this is all part of the New World Order (*Nowy Porządek Świata*) that seeks to create a new "supertotalitarian government."[29] For Bojarski, the legacy of colonialism and imperialism is still with us today, "rooted deeply in the mentality and culture of many countries."[30] Warning that "the old demons have been awakened," he hypothesizes that the collapse of the communist system simply opened the door for a new wave of colonization.[31] Józef Kossecki opines that in "the twentieth and twenty-first centuries a manifestation of the clash of Latin civilization and the Orient is in the European Union the struggle of the Latin concept of the Europe of Homelands with the typically Byzantine concept of the unification through the Brussels bureaucracy of Europe as one great *legal state* based on the doctrine of positivist law."[32] Kossecki calls for "a thorough *de-Byzantinization*" in Poland.[33]

Konecznian fundamentalists in the twenty-first century argue that "the rebirth of Latin civilization must begin in Poland,"[34] because "the mentality and minds of Poles have not been contaminated by modernism and socialism"[35] too much. As the "*apostle of Latin civilization*,"[36] Poland is destined for a special role in history. But Poland must become civilizationally pure itself before it can fulfill its messianic mission as described by Koneczny: "Our duty and historical mission are one and the same: the promotion of Latin civilization."[37] This message now inspires the new *endeks* as they don their "civilizational armor"[38] to fight for Poland's civilizational integrity. This search for purity is a symptom of postcolonial anxiety, a response to the perceived alien influences, multiculturalism, and hybridity that seeped into Poland with foreign occupation.

POSTCOLONIAL THEORY AND POLAND

The field of postcolonial studies emerged in the 1970s as a way to understand the legacy of European empires. Since its focus has been primarily on the lingering impact of colonialism in Asia and Africa, the field has generally ignored

Poland.[39] Janusz Korek reminds us that postcolonial theories "emerged in connection with leftist discourses and mainly within Marxist circles at the time of the Cold War."[40] This seems to have forestalled robust debate about the postcolonial nature of regions dominated by Soviet imperialism.[41] Korek concludes that the whole field of Slavic and Soviet Studies was "deformed" by the Cold War, excluding it from broader developments in theory.[42]

However, by 1998 Roumiana Deltcheva was writing that "the socio-political dynamics of the region [East Central Europe] indicates that it should be approached as a contemporary post-coloniality."[43] And in a 2007 collection of essays dedicated to the problem of postcolonialism in Central and Eastern Europe, Aleksander Fiut posits that the "omnipresent, although invisible, shadow of empires has undoubtedly left its destructive, pernicious traces" on the region.[44] A leading figure in the debate about the applicability of postcolonial theory to Poland, Ewa Thompson, adds that "it can hardly be denied that the partitions of Poland in the eighteenth century and occupation of Poland by Soviet Russia after the Second World War were forms of colonialism."[45] Thompson and other scholars have also identified the resentment evidenced in nationalist commentary about Poland's colonial past, and the anxiety about threatened sovereignty.[46] When we consider the focus of postcolonial theory, Poland certainly seems a fitting case study. According to Sanjay Seth, "[t]he 'post' in postcolonialism does not indicate the belief that colonialism is dead and buried, a matter of the past with no bearing on the present. Quite the contrary, it is a form of periodization which aggressively signals the centrality of colonialism to the entire historical period after it."[47]

A complicating factor, which Korek and others have noted, is the complex postcolonial perspective in the Polish case: Poland has played both the role of the colonized and the colonizer. As Krzysztof Kowalczyk-Twarowski puts it, the "history of the Polish *Drang nach Osten* from the fourteenth to the eighteenth centuries, and in a limited way up to World War II" possessed a "distinct colonial character."[48] Consequently, in the Polish national consciousness

> it is possible to distinguish two colonial complexes: (1) nostalgia for the borderlands [*kresy*], and (2) the humiliation of the period of partitions, the Hitlerite and Soviet occupations. As a result, the Polish reader today finds himself in an epistemologically exceptionally profitable situation, because he is able to bring to his cultural heritage the mentality of the oppressor as well as that of the oppressed.[49]

Yet Poland's own colonial ventures in the *kresy* are depicted in positive ways by fundamentalist commentators. Włodzimierz Bojarski even opines that "Poland never participated in the madness of imperialism."[50] Likewise, the editor of *Nowy Przegląd Wszechpolski*, Teresa Bloch, can characterize Polish inroads to the east under the Jagiellonians as "peaceful colonization,"[51] while also suggesting that "our powerful neighbors—Germany and Russia—always cooperate against Poland" as part of a larger civilizational war aimed at destroying Latin civilization.[52]

Magdalena Nowicka concedes that "at first glance the exotic postcolonial theory has nothing in common with Polish reality," but she nevertheless underscores the important point that Poland has been under foreign domination at different times in its history.[53] She finds that many Poles do not accept the narrative of a colonized Poland, since it relates to notions of dependency and seems to categorize Poland with underdeveloped countries. Ewa Thompson agrees that many Polish intellectuals dismiss the applicability of postcolonial theory to Poland, since they "associate colonialism with the conquest of Africa and orientalism with the Near and Far East."[54] Roumiana Deltcheva also notes "the refusal of the East Central European intellectual circles to acknowledge their position of subordination."[55] Yet these scholars and others, such as Clare Cavanagh, are convinced that there is a "distinctively Polish but unmistakably postcolonial sensibility"[56] in Poland.

Deltcheva has also posited that one aspect of this "postcolonial sensibility" is the "coexistence of a new wave of nationalistic attitudes, 'cosmopolitanism' as a symbol of 'Europeanness' . . . and prejudice towards and scapegoating of the Other."[57] A 2007 editorial from the fundamentalist journal *Nowy Przegląd Wszechpolski* concisely expresses this mood with its condemnation of the "cult of 'the other.' Another idea, another policy, another organization, another commodity are 'better.'"[58] The author literally demonizes "others" by using the term "satanic intrigue"[59] in reference to the European Union, which has been regarded by Euroskeptic nationalists as merely another manifestation of Poland's exploitation by foreign powers.

Such tension between cosmopolitanism and nationalism is not isolated to Poland; indeed, scholars have detected a "fundamental contradiction"[60] between these two trends in other postcolonial settings. Similar to Deltcheva, Pheng Cheah finds that a "new, post-colonial nationalism" exists alongside a "new, post-colonial cosmopolitanism."[61] This peculiar juxtaposition is fodder for fundamentalist commentary in Poland. For example, Marcin Dybowski— owner of the Antyk publishing house that has reissued Koneczny's books—has insisted that the "threat of the ideology of contemporary cosmopolitanism" to the Polish nation and Latin civilization is more real than the threat of communism during the period of the People's Republic.[62]

This postcolonial anxiety augments the civilizational fundamentalism in Konecznian commentary. Modernity is characterized as civilizationally chaotic, as a "*pluralizmokracji*"[63] that encourages cosmopolitanism. Fundamentalist critics have constructed arguments against this trend by using Konecznian logic. In addressing the issue of foreigners becoming Polish, for example, Adam Wielomski distinguishes between those belonging to Latin civilization and those from other civilizations. He concludes that "an Arab, a Black from the Congo, a Chinese, or a Vietnamese" could never be considered a Pole because of civilizational differences.[64] Konecznian fundamentalist discourse demonstrates what Magdalena Kania terms "the persistence of national resentment and the so-called post-communist mentality, and, related to this, questions about the presence of the Other as a symbolic marker of national boundaries."[65] She correctly asserts that *"thinking* in postcolonial terms offers an interesting and alternative outlook" on these issues.[66]

Writing in 1957, Albert Memmi articulated some of the earliest insights about the process by which cultural "self-discovery" played an important part in freeing the "colonial mind": "Assimilation being abandoned, the colonized's liberation must be carried out through a recovery of self and autonomous dignity. . . . It is in this context that the colonized's xenophobia and even a certain racism, must make their return."[67] The colonized subject regains "self-control" through a process of "self-renewal," which often involves a return to tradition and religion.[68] Scholars have identified similar processes in post-communist societies in Central and Eastern Europe. In a comparative study, Mitja Velikonja found that "extreme integrists" in both Poland and Slovakia have spoken of "an *'arousal from slumber,' 'spiritual regeneration,'* an *'emergence from the catacombs.' "*[69] Memmi explains that "to expect the colonized to open his mind to the world and be a humanist and internationalist would seem to be ludicrous thoughtlessness. He is still regaining possession of himself."[70] We see this very process at work in postcolonial Poland at the start of the twenty-first century, and it is articulated clearly by Konecznian fundamentalist ideologues who call for "the restructuring of consciousness"[71] to overcome the "moral schizophrenia"[72] and civilizational chaos that they believe bedevils Polish society. In the case of Poland, Piotr Jaroszyński submits that "it is not possible to disregard that the period of partitions, of occupation, of foreign governments contributed not only to the colonial exploitation of territories, but above all to the *demoralization* of the people."[73]

CIVILIZATIONAL THREATS AND THE CHALLENGE OF ISLAM

Metaphors of chaos and decline are not uncommon in the rhetoric of postcolonial anxiety, as seen in Adam Wielomski's comment that one of the "clear symptoms of civilizational decadence is thus cosmopolitanism."[74] He defines this as not so much as an understanding of other cultures, but the loss of understanding of one's own culture. "For cosmopolitans," he adds, "a Gothic cathedral and a work by Velazquez are of equal beauty to a Chinese palace or a Zulu war mask."[75] Tolerance and multiculturalism are signs of weakness and confusion, and "cultural relativism" is a symptom of a "spiritual crisis."[76] The source of these problems was identified by Koneczny, he notes, in his "law of laws": "It is not possible to belong to two civilizations simultaneously."[77] In the view of some Konecznian critics, the colonization of Polish consciousness continues today in the form of foreign media interests. Maciej Giertych has complained of both Jewish control of world media[78] and German control of Polish media.[79] For some, this constitutes a form of "neocolonialism" in Poland.[80]

As we have seen, Andrzej Horodecki is a pundit who consistently views the world through a Konecznian lens. He considers globalism a "Byzantine-Jewish civilizational mixture taking the form of a global pseudo-civilization, which aims to construct a so-called 'open society.'"[81] Globalization is labeled a "new totalitarianism," and even "a Satanic totalitarian doctrine."[82] The tool of "the elite of the *world intellectual aristocracy*,'" globalization threatens to undermine the purity of Latin civilization in Poland, where politicians representing Byzantine, Turanian, and Jewish civilizations have been "*practically uncontrolled*."[83] Horodecki is deeply concerned that the "dictatorship of the minority" that allegedly manifested itself in the form of Jewish domination during the communist era will now reemerge.[84] He complains that the "lower" Jewish civilization is already dominating the "higher" Latin civilization. This, he assumes, is one of the "costs" of the transition to democracy.[85] Józef Kossecki also blames the influence of Jewish civilization for the economic ills of the former People's Republic, as well as the vagaries of capitalism in the post-communist era. The common denominator, it is claimed, is the tendency of a priori thinking, which leads to the implementation of preconceived and inflexible economic programs that do not take into account the social realities of a given situation.[86]

Nearly seventy years after Koneczny's death, Poles were once again being urged to return to their "civilizational foundations" as they enter the third millennium.[87] This is especially needed, according to radical activist Kamil Eckhardt, in order to combat the potential "Islamicization of Europe" that he had identified by 2008. This threat manifests itself in various ways: (1) Muslim population growth; (2) European economic stagnation; (3) boundless European tolerance and pacifism; (4) the increasingly aggressive attitude of Muslims in Europe; (5) the Muslim immigrants' lack of desire to assimilate; and (6) their growing radicalization.[88] Maciej Giertych adds that "Islam is not shaping the European Union today [2009], but this will change should Turkey join the Union."[89] But he is more concerned with the issue of Muslim immigrants, and reminds Poles that

> Muslims migrate *en masse* to Christian countries, and there they continue to have many children in spite of the fact that they live among people who deliberately restrict their fertility. . . . Not only do they give birth to Islamic citizens of western countries, but they continue to bring them up in the Islamic faith and norms. . . . The western world stands helpless in face of these challenges.[90]

Even though Maciej Giertych admits that immigration to Poland is a small problem at this time, he nevertheless worries about "people from other civilizations" and their inability to integrate.[91] In his booklet, *Gender Equality and Life Issues in the European Union* (2008), Giertych provides a peculiar twist to his discussion of the immigration problem:

> We observe how in the Muslim and Roma communities this natural co-incidence of sex life and reproduction assures a demographic future and a stability of the family. On the other hand the aging childless feminists complain about everything around them but fail to see their own fault in what is happening.[92]

The fundamental problem in Europe, Giertych believes, is that "Islam is strong spiritually and Christianity is weakening. . . . Only a return to traditional European values, based on natural law, on Roman law and Christian ethic, can ensure a capacity to face the challenge of Islamic influences in Europe. I appeal for a return to these values."[93]

Discourse analyses of LPR rhetoric during the period of its electoral success found the issue of Muslim immigrants to be closely linked to the fear of demographic collapse. Polish women were urged to perform their "natural" national duty by staying at home and raising more children; the defense of Poland's civilizational purity depended on this. In an address from May 2003, Giertych expressed a fear of a biological and cultural collapse due to the declining birthrate and immigration. Multiculturalism, especially in the form of non-Latin immigrants allowed in by lax EU rules, was threatening to destroy the Polish family.[94] Wojciech Wierzejski also explicitly warned in LPR brochures, "We go to war for the family."[95] His suggested response to the threat of immigration is clear: Poles need to increase the fertility of their nation in the face of a perceived existential threat. In this endeavor, Polish women obviously play a central role. Wierzejski also cites Koneczny's "law of expansiveness" and argues that "[o]ur [Latin] civilization has ceased to be expansive."[96] He laments that "our European, Christian culture" has ceased to spread to new lands, while the reverse is taking place: "false tolerance, relativism, and cosmopolitanism" has had an effect on the elites in "our civilization" at a time of expansiveness for our "eternal enemies—Islam and Turanianism."[97]

In March 2008, Maciej Giertych responded to the latest Muslim "threat" to Europe: the recognition of the new state of Kosovo. According to Giertych, "[t]his is a sign of weakness in response to the spread of Islam."[98] This weakness takes many forms, but primarily stems from a lack of civilizational awareness and civilizational purity among Europeans. Moreover, Giertych believes that the Byzantine German-dominated European Union will likely not present an effective response to the Islamic threat. Koneczny had voiced similar concerns about earlier confrontations in his writings, noting that the Byzantine Empire proved ineffective against Islamic expansion. He asserted that over time Islam influenced Byzantine culture, as evidenced in the iconoclastic controversy of the eighth and ninth centuries.[99] Giertych reminds his readers that it is impossible to fully address the "European confrontation with Islam" without understanding the "civilizational aspect" of the question.[100] He warns that civilizational conflicts are

> not won by concessions. One has to be strong oneself and ready to defend one's identity. . . . Lukewarm religiosity in Europe led to lukewarm civilisational awareness. And when one's own civilisation is not being defended, one succumbs to another, more determined in its drive towards victory.[101]

Konecznian fundamentalists have tended to discuss the issue of immigration in terms of civilizational incompatibility, rather than in terms of legal status or civic rights.[102] Andrzej Horodecki defines tolerance of immigrants from other civilizations in this way: "I know that you are a member of another civilization, and therefore—with complete respect—you can live under my roof, but you cannot attain any power."[103] Metaphors of disease and infection from civilizational pollutants, as well as metaphors of war against civilizational foes, are frequently used to describe the threat.[104] The key concern is the preservation of civilizational purity.[105] And Konecznian pundits believe that Poland has a cultural "mission" as a chosen nation, given the responsibility of defending "higher" Latin civilization against "lower" rival civilizations.[106] Krzysztof Nagrodzki employs this Konecznian paradigm in his commentaries on the threats to Poland from "anti-Latin hordes" who are "enemies of our [Latin] civilization."[107] He frets about the susceptibility of the "higher" Latin civilization to "lower" civilizations and fears the dangers of civilizational mixing. He also condemns the "terror of the ideology of 'political correctness'" and the disorienting impact it has on morals in Poland, which has a special role in defending the purity of Latin civilization.[108]

Fundamentalist pundits sometimes uncritically parrot Koneczny, who presented a distorted vision of the Islamic faith. For example, he claimed that "the whole of Moslem [sic] religion derives from the five basic duties of the moral life: prayers, alms, pilgrimages, fasts and participation in holy wars."[109] Koneczny's simplistic analysis, which followed his tendency to essentialize the various "others" he encountered, is also factually wrong in this case. He replaced "profession of faith" with the requirement to take part in holy wars as one of the "pillars" of Islam. This radically shifts one's understanding of Islam, in part because the concept of "jihad" relates more to one's inner struggle with keeping the faith as opposed to the "holy war" cited by Koneczny. Unfortunately, this mistake is often repeated by Konecznian critics in their warnings about a "clash of civilizations" in the twenty-first century.[110]

But the Islamic threat that already worried Paweł Bała and other Konecznian commentators in the first decade of the twenty-first century was not "jihad" or terrorism, but immigration. In his essay, "Eurodżihad," Bała argues that "Latin Civilization (or rather its remnant) finds itself in a state of decay, which attests to the lack of a will for struggle, passivity, decadence, and . . . extreme demoralization."[111] He fears a "demographic catastrophe" will lead to the formation of "ghettoes" of frustrated Arabs in Europe.[112] Ireneusz Białkowski also warned in 2007 about the Islamic threat, quoting Koneczny's dictum: "A civilization must be pure, or it will not be; it is not possible to be civilized in two ways."[113] He sees a looming clash between Islam and Latin civilization as Muslim immigrants become a growing presence in Europe.[114] In his own list of historical "laws," Henryk Nowik refers to Koneczny and cites his law of "intercivilizational conflict." Nowik calls this an "uncompromising conflict," also noting that it is not possible to blend civilizations without falling into a state of acivilization.[115] Interestingly, the idea has been raised that Poland should become not only a "bulwark of Christendom" against the East, but also to the West—due to lax immigration policies of the European Union.[116] But this requires Poles to become more mindful of their civilizational duties in response to the demographic challenge posed by large immigrant families.

Jan Bodakowski also worries that a European constitution would create a legal framework that would allow for the inundation of Europe by immigrants. In his mind, this would lead to "the destruction of the cultural identity of Europe."[117] Zdzisław Zakrzewski argued in 2002 that "the massive influx of colored people from former colonies (Algeria, Morocco, Senegal, India, etc.), as well as seasonal workers . . . (Turkey, Yugoslavia, even Asia)" had already created in Europe a "picture completely unlike" that of earlier eras.[118] He fears that Europe will follow the American model of a "melting pot." Rather than an effective blending—which would be the model for a global society—there is a diminution of the "higher" (Latin) civilization in the United States, which is polluted by immigrant representatives from "lower" (non-Latin) civilizations. In Zakrzewski's judgment, the experiment has led to "moral decline, liberal upbringing, and ethical relativism" in the United States.[119] He wants to avoid a similar fate for Poland.

In his research, Jerzy Nikitorowicz has detected a common theme in pessimistic prognoses about the effects of Muslim immigrants in Europe. Skeptical pundits insist that a multicultural society "appears as a myth" and that the inability of immigrants to fully adjust to life in Europe will prove the failure of "the experiment of the coexistence of cultures."[120] In his analysis of the European identity crisis, Konecznian scholar Henryk Kiereś concludes that a real source of "evil" is the influx of influences from foreign civilizations. He claims that these are too often "uncritically and naively accepted by the European in the name of an alleged civilizational universalism!"[121] Wojciech Szurgot also urges vigilance before the threats from other civilizations, which present different value systems that might undermine the ethical foundation of Latin civilization.[122]

Konecznian scholar Mieczysław Ryba also fears that the influx of Muslim immigrants will lead to the loss of cultural identity throughout Europe.

He maintains that there is "one great truth that the Islamic ideological expansion has revealed. The West has been stuck in materialism and drawn away from religion, has fallen into moral deterioration."[123] Citing Koneczny and his "law" prohibiting civilizational mixing, Ryba reminds his readers that in such cases the "most primitive" civilization emerges victorious. He urges Poles to return to their Latin civilizational roots as a "remedy for the Islamicization of the West. . . . Having a tradition of 'a Christian bulwark' (for example, Jan III Sobieski's Battle for Vienna), we must take a decisive position in the present civilizational confrontation."[124]

Ryba's remarks provide a fitting conclusion to this book. He demonstrates that Feliks Koneczny's "science of civilizations" has become merged with Polish messianism to construct a vision of civilizational purity as a salvation for Poland's (and Europe's) problems in the new century. The Giertychs and other fundamentalists have crafted an ideology that blends Koneczny's theories with interwar *endek* thought and traditional Catholicism. Konecznian civilizational fundamentalism preserves the anachronistic thinking from an era of intolerance and chauvinism within a theoretical framework that has proven remarkably resilient. Once forgotten, Feliks Koneczny is now better known in Poland than during his own lifetime.

Notes

PREFACE

1. Radical nationalist ideologue Jędrzej Giertych (1903–92) embraced Koneczny's theories during the interwar period, and during his postwar exile in England he published several of Koneczny's manuscripts. His son, Maciej (b. 1936), has served as the leading ideologue for the League of Polish Families (Liga Polskich Rodzin, LPR, formed in 2001), as well as a deputy to the European Parliament (2004–9). Maciej's younger brother, Wojciech (b. 1951) is a Catholic priest and was appointed Papal Theologian (Theologian of the Papal Household) in December 2005. Maciej's son, Roman (b. 1971), served briefly (May 2006–August 2007) as Deputy Prime Minister and Minister of Education in a coalition government. A concise and cogent synopsis of Koneczny's "science of civilizations" was delivered in 2012 to an audience at Christendom College in Virginia by Father Giertych. See Wojciech Giertych, "Feliks Koneczny (1862–1949)," *Christendom College*, 14 September 2012, http://www.christendom.edu/news/2012/koneczny.pdf (accessed 9 June 2013).

2. The term *Endecja* refers to the National Democracy political movement led by Roman Dmowski (1864–1939). *Endek* refers to a member of this nationalist movement, and it is also used as an adjective.

3. Rafal Pankowski, *The Populist Radical Right in Poland: The Patriots* (London: Routledge, 2010), 27.

4. For one example, see Anna Zechenter, "Multi-kulti i Feliks Koneczny," *Nasz Dziennik*, 31 October / 1 November 2012, http://www.naszdziennik.pl/wp/13792,multi-kulti-i-feliks-koneczny.html (accessed 13 November 2012).

5. Stanisław Czesław Michałowski, "Wizja cywilizacji łacińskiej i kultury europejskiej na tle myśl Feliksa Konecznego," in *Wspólnota dziedzictwa kulturowego*, ed. Bronisława Dymara (Kraków: Oficyna Wydawnicza "Impuls," 2004), 1:25.

6. Paweł Skrzydlewski, "Życie i myśl Feliksa Konecznego (1 XI 1862–10 II 1949)," *Akademia Górniczo-Hutnicza im. Stanisława Staszica w Krakowie*, http://ciapek.uci.agh.edu.pl/~kwlodarc/tekstyo/pskrzydlewski.html (accessed 28 June 2004).

7. Ireneusz Białkowski, *Idea ścierania się cywilizacji według Feliksa Konecznego a bezpieczeństwo współczesnej Europy: Koncepcje, które powracają jak bumerang* (Krzeszowice: Dom Wydawniczy "Ostoja," 2007), 48.

8. Jacek Barlik, "Czy kres cywilizacji łacińskiej? O historiozofii Feliksa Konecznego (1862–1949)," *Chrześcijanin w Świecie* 18, no. 11/12 (1986): 160.

INTRODUCTION: FELIKS KONECZNY (1862–1949) AND THE SCIENCE OF CIVILIZATIONS

1. Feliks Koneczny, *Polskie logos a ethos: Roztrząsanie o znaczeniu i celu Polski*, 2 vols., 2nd ed. (Komorów: Wydawnictwo Antyk, 1997), 1:9.
2. Ibid., 28.
3. The Polish state was carved up in a series of three partitions in 1772, 1793, and 1795. Portions of its lands were taken by Prussia, Austria, and Russia. The final partition eliminated the indpendent Polish state.
4. Paweł Milcarek, "Feliks Koneczny i jego synteza historii Polski," *Brulion* 13 (1998): 210.
5. Jacek Chrobaczyński, "Kraków przed i w 1914 roku," *Dzieje Najnowsze* 36, no. 3 (2004): 65.
6. Jacek Purchla, *Jak powstał nowoczesny Kraków*, 2nd ed. (Kraków: Wydawnictwo Literackie, 1990), 33, 41.
7. Feliks Koneczny, "Co robić wobec rusinów?" *Świat Słowiański* 4, vol. 1, no. 6 (1908): 588–91.
8. Jacek Purchla, "Kraków i Lwów: zmienność relacji w XIX i XX wieku," in *Kraków i Lwów w cywilizacji europejskiej*, ed. Jacek Purchla (Kraków: Międzynarodowe Centrum Kultury w Krakowie, 2003), 84.
9. Ryszard Polak, "Feliks Koneczny wobec Rosji i jej cywilizacji (cz. I)," *Cywilizacja* 15 (2005): 101.
10. Keely Stauter-Halsted, "Rural Myth and the Modern Nation: Peasant Commemorations of Polish National Holidays, 1879–1910," in *Staging the Past: The Politics of Commemoration in Habsburg Central Europe, 1848 to the Present*, ed. Maria Bucur and Nancy M. Wingfield (West Lafayette, IN: Purdue University Press, 2001), 155–56. See also Keely Stauter-Halsted, *The Nation in the Village: The Genesis of Peasant National Identity in Austrian Poland, 1848–1914* (Ithaca, NY: Cornell University Press, 2001).
11. Stauter-Halsted, "Rural Myth and the Modern Nation," 154–58.
12. Larry Wolff, "Dynastic Conservatism and Poetic Violence in Fin-de-Siècle Cracow: The Habsburg Matrix of Polish Modernism," *American Historical Review* 106, no. 3 (June 2001): 742.
13. Stauter-Halsted, "Rural Myth and the Modern Nation," 154.
14. Ibid., 159.
15. Ibid., 164.
16. Feliks Koneczny, "Konserwatyzm chłopski," *Znak* 37, no. 1–2 (1985): 33.
17. Purchla, "Kraków i Lwów," 82.
18. Purchla, *Jak powstał nowoczesny Kraków*, 50.
19. Ibid., 37.
20. Ibid., 82.
21. Wolff, "Dynastic Conservatism and Poetic Violence in Fin-de-Siècle Cracow," 736.
22. Ibid., 748.
23. Ibid., 751.
24. Piotr Biliński, *Feliks Koneczny (1862–1949): Życie i działalność* (Warsaw: Inicjatywa Wydawnicza 'Ad Astra,' 2001), 59–70.
25. Feliks Koneczny, *Teatr Krakowski*, ed. Kazimierz Gajda (Kraków: Wydawnictwo Naukowe WSP, 1994), 66.

26. Ibid., 204–6. More generally, see also Józef Tarnowski, "Konecznego aksjologia dzieła sztuki teatralnej," in *Feliks Koneczny dzisiaj. Praca zbiorowa,* ed. Jan Skoczyński (Kraków: Księgarnia Akademicka, 2000), 268.

27. Ibid., 285–86.

28. Feliks Koneczny, "Nowiny z historyografii polskiej," *Przegląd powszechny* 13, vol. 52 (1896): 170.

29. This is evident in his review of Gabriela Zapolska's *Małka Szwarcenkopf* (1897), a play about a Jewish woman trapped in an arranged marriage, unable to fulfill her potential. Koneczny complained that the playwright presented this theme without any features unique to the life of a young Jewish woman. See Koneczny, *Teatr Krakowski,* 78.

30. Tarnowski, "Konecznego aksjologia dzieła sztuki teatralnej," 267. See also Koneczny, *Teatr Krakowski,* 54.

31. Feliks Koneczny, "Historia," *Przegląd Powszechny* 50, vol. 200 (1933): 351–52.

32. Purchla, *Jak powstał nowoczesny Kraków,* 75.

33. Chrobaczyński, "Kraków przed i w 1914 roku," 67.

34. Purchla, *Jak powstał nowoczesny Kraków,* 30.

35. Chrobaczyński, "Kraków przed i w 1914 roku," 67.

36. Nathaniel D. Wood, *Becoming Metropolitan: Urban Selfhood and the Making of Modern Cracow* (DeKalb: Northern Illinois University Press, 2010), 25; 124–28.

37. Ibid., 193.

38. I. A. Vasilenko, "Dialogue of Cultures, Dialogue of Civilizations," *Russian Social Science Review* 41, no. 2 (March–April 2000): 6. Vasilenko was especially referring to Francis Fukuyama's triumphalist *The End of History and the Last Man* (1992), in which the author hypothesized that with the end of the Cold War, capitalism and (possibly) liberal democracy would become the only viable models for economic and political development.

39. Biliński, *Feliks Koneczny,* 180.

40. Tadeusz Stanisław Grabowski, obituary for "Feliks Koneczny (1.XI.1862–10. II.1949)," *Kwartalnik Historyczny* 57 (1949): 335.

41. Zbigniew Solak, "Marian Zdziechowski i Klub Słowiański," *Studia Historyczne* 30, no. 2 (1987): 221–23. In 1902, the Club had 45 members. Ibid., 220.

42. Biliński, *Feliks Koneczny,* 79.

43. Feliks Koneczny, *Dzieje Polski za Jagiellonów* (1903; repr., Komorów: Wydawnictwo Antyk-Marcin Dybowski, 1997), 203 ff.

44. For a review of Koneczny's academic work during this period, see Ryszard Jadczak, "Wileński okres Feliksa Konecznego," *Studia Historyczne* 41, no. 3 (1998): 395–406.

45. Selim Chazbijewicz, "Feliks Koneczny i jego filozofia cywilizacji," *Debata* 2, no. 29 (February 2010): 9.

46. Biliński, *Feliks Koneczny,* 131.

47. Ibid., 121.

48. Andrzej Bokiej, *Cywilizacja łacińska. Studium na podstawie dorobku historiozoficznego Feliksa Konecznego* (Legnica: Wyższe Seminarium Duchowne Diecezji Legnickiej, 2000), 43.

49. Feliks Koneczny, *On the Plurality of Civilisations* (London: Polonica Publications, 1962), 323.

50. Zbigniew Pucek, "Koncepcje cywilizacyjne F. Konecznego na tle tez humanistyki przełomu antypozytywistycznego," in *Filozofia i religia w kulturze narodów*

słowiańskich, ed. Tadeusz Chrobak and Zbigniew Stachowski (Rzeszów: Wydawnictwo Wyższej Szkoły Pedagogicznej, 1995), 114.

51. Bokiej, *Cywilizacja łacińska*, 153.
52. Marek N. Jakubowski, *Ciągłość historii i historia ciągłości. Polska filozofia dziejów* (Toruń: Wydawnictwo Uniwersytetu Mikołaja Kopernika, 2004), 214–16.
53. Koneczny later complained about this situation in postwar correspondence to University authorities. See Archiwum Uniwersytetu Jagiellońskiego [Archive of Jagiellonian University], SII 619, "Sprawy Osobowe."
54. Piotr Grabowiec, *Model społeczeństwa obywatelskiego w historiozofii Feliksa Konecznego* (Wrocław: Wydawnictwo Uniwersytetu Wrocławskiego, 2000), 137.
55. Jolanta Kolbuszewska, "Reorientacje w historiografii polskiej przełomie XIX i XX wieku a koncepcje cywilizacyjne Feliksa Konecznego," *Historyka* 32 (2002): 111.
56. Sonia Bukowska, *Filozofia polska wobec problemu cywilizacji. Teoria Feliksa Konecznego* (Katowice: Wydawnictwo Uniwersytetu Śląskiego, 2007), 82.
57. See Feliks Koneczny, *Dzieje Śląska* (1897; repr., Warsaw: Wydawnictwo Antyk, 1999), 125–29.
58. Jan Skoczyński, *Koneczny: Teoria cywilizacji* (Warsaw: Wydawnictwo IFiS PAN, 2003), 162.
59. The title of one of Koneczny's earliest works in civilizational theory is *Polskie logos a ethos*. It was originally published in 1921.
60. Marian Szczęsny, "Rola chrześcijaństwa w tworzeniu cywilizacji łacińskiej według Feliksa Konecznego," *Studia Teologiczne* 20 (2002): 397.
61. Skoczyński, *Koneczny: Teoria cywilizacji*, 63–64.
62. Bokiej, *Cywilizacja łacińska*, 20.
63. Feliks Koneczny, *Etyki a cywilizacje* (1931; repr., Krzeszowice: Dom Wydawniczy "Ostoja," 2004), 5.
64. Koneczny, *Polskie logos a ethos*, 2:526, 479.
65. Feliks Koneczny, "U źródeł kultury polskiej," *Tygodnik Warszawski* 2, no. 51 (25 December 1946): 4.
66. Feliks Koneczny, *Polska między wschodem a zachodem* (1928; repr. Lublin: "Onion," 1996), 47.
67. Ibid., 48.
68. Paweł Skrzydlewski, *Polityka w cywilizacji łacińskiej. Aktualność nauki Feliksa Konecznego* (Lublin: Fundacja Rozwoju Kultury Polskiej, 2002), 77.
69. The phrase is borrowed from the title of Brian Porter's monograph, *When Nationalism Began to Hate: Imagining Modern Politics in Nineteenth-Century Poland* (Oxford: Oxford University Press, 2000).
70. Józef Pawlak, "Feliks Koneczny o rozwoju moralności," in *Rozprawy z etyki*, ed. Józef Pawlak and Włodzimierz Tyburski (Toruń: Wydawnictwo Naukowe UMK, 1999), 139. Pawlak adds that this notion reflects Koneczny's "Europocentrism." Ibid., 144.
71. See Koneczny, *Plurality of Civilisations*, 162.
72. Ibid., 163.
73. Sally Boss, review of *From Sovietology to Postcoloniality: Poland and Ukraine from a Postcolonial Perspective*, ed. Janusz Korek, *Sarmation Review* 28, no. 1 (January 2008), http://www.ruf.rice.edu/~sarmatia/108/281boss.htm (accessed 30 June 2008). Emphasis in the original.

74. Porter, *When Nationalism Began to Hate*, 186. See also Ewa Thompson, "Narodowość i polityka," *Dziennik.pl*, 11 May 2007, http://www.dziennik.pl/dziennik/europa/ar ticle46439/Narodowosc_i_polityka.html (accessed 30 June 2008).

75. Paweł Skrzydlewski, "Prawo stanowione w cywilizacji łacińskiej (na kanwie rozważań F. Konecznego)," *Cywilizacja* 12 (2005): 53.

76. Anna Frątczak, *Feliks Koneczny o państwie i wartościach* (Kraków: Ośrodek Myśli Politycznej; Księgarnia Akademicka, 2003), 98–101.

77. Grabowiec, *Model społeczeństwa obywatelskiego*, 87.

78. Feliks Koneczny, *Prawa dziejowe. Oraz dodatek bizantynizm niemiecki* (London: Wydawnictwa Towarzystwa imienia Romana Dmowskiego, 1982), 31.

79. Anton Hilckman, "Feliks Koneczny and the Comparative Science of Civilisation," in Koneczny, *Plurality of Civilisations*, 10.

80. Feliks Koneczny, *O ład w historii: Z dodatkami o twórczości i wpływie Konecznego*, 4th ed. (Wrocław: Wydawnictwo "Nortom," 2004), 13.

81. Koneczny, *Plurality of Civilisations*, 169.

82. Sonia Bukowska, "Metodologiczne aspekty historiozoficznej koncepcji Feliksa Konecznego," *Folia Philosophica* 18 (2000): 289. For a positive review of Koneczny's methodology, see Józef Kossecki, *Podstawy nowoczesnej nauki porównawczej o cywilizacjach. Socjologia porównawcza cywilizacji* (Katowice: "Śląsk" Sp. z o.o. Wydawnictwo Naukowe, 2003), 11.

83. Ibid., 290.

84. Anton Hilckman, introduction to Koneczny, *Plurality of Civilisations*, 4. Anton Hilckman (1900–1970), who served as the director of an institute for the comparative study of civilizations at the University of Mainz, was an ardent propagator of Koneczny's ideas. While Koneczny fell into disfavor in his homeland, Hilckman became his most important spokesperson in Europe. For his most concise explication of Koneczny's theories, see Anton Hilckman, "Feliks Koneczny und die Vergleichende Kulturwissenschaft," *Saeculum* 3, no. 4 (1952): 571–602.

85. Jan Skoczyński, *Idee historiozoficzne Feliksa Konecznego* (Kraków: Nakładem Uniwersytetu Jagiellońskiego, 1991), 117.

86. Sonia Bukowska, "Feliks Koneczny—indukcyjna nauka o cywilizacji a prawa dziejowe," *Folia Philosophica* 8 (1991): 211.

87. Koneczny, *Polskie logos a ethos*, 1:28.

88. Bukowska, *Filozofia polska wobec problemu cywilizacji*, 131.

89. Koneczny, *Prawa dziejowe*, 174.

90. Ibid., 126.

91. Ibid., 191.

92. Ibid., 205.

93. Zbigniew Kuderowicz, "Koncepcja praw historii w ujęciu Feliksa Konecznego," in Skoczyński, *Feliks Koneczny dzisiaj*, 36.

94. Ibid., 37–38.

95. Koneczny, *Polska między Wschodem a Zachodem*, 51; and *Plurality of Civilisations*, 322.

96. Koneczny, *Plurality of Civilisations*, 320–21.

97. Ibid., 166.

98. Arkadiusz Robaczewski, "Quincunx jako odbicie klasycznej teorii osoby," *Człowiek w Kulturze* 10 (1998): 56.

99. Grabowiec, *Model społeczeństwa obywatelskiego*, 30.
100. Ibid. The term "logos" refers to theory and the term "ethos" refers to practice, or implementation of theory. See Skoczyński, *Koneczny: Teoria cywilizacji*, 33.
101. Bukowska, "Feliks Koneczny—indukcyjna nauka o cywilizacji a prawa dziejowe," 211.
102. Bokiej, *Cywilizacja łacińska*, 187.
103. Koneczny, *Plurality of Civilisations*, 153.
104. Zbigniew Pucek, "Feliks Koneczny: teoria pluralizmu cywilizacyjnego," in *Szkice z historii socjologii polskiej*, ed. Kazimierz Z. Sowa (Warsaw: PAX, 1983), 184.
105. Ibid., 185.
106. Koneczny, *Plurality of Civilisations*, 174.
107. Ibid.
108. Ibid., 175.
109. Koneczny, *Polskie logos a ethos*, 2:375.
110. Koneczny, *Plurality of Civilisations*, 321. Emphasis added.
111. Feliks Koneczny, *Rozwój moralności* (1938; repr., Komorów: Wydawnictwo Antyk, 1997), 111.
112. S. Borzym, H. Floryńska, B. Skarga, and A. Walicki, *Zarys dziejów filozofii polskiej 1815-1918*, ed. Andrzej Walicki (Warsaw: Państwowe Wydawnictwo Naukowe, 1983), 395–97. See also Eugeniusz Wasilewski, "O istocie i sposobach funkcjonowania dobra według Feliksa Konecznego i Mariana Zdziechowskiego," in *Filozofia na Uniwersytecie Stefana Batorego*, ed. Józef Pawlak (Toruń: Uniwersytet Mikołaja Kopernika, 2002), 222.
113. Koneczny, *Plurality of Civilisations*, 316.
114. Ibid.
115. Ibid.
116. Koneczny, *O ład w historii*, 18.
117. Ibid., 17.
118. Janusz Goćkowski, "Konecznego model dziejów powszechnych," in Skoczyński, *Feliks Koneczny dzisiaj*, 27.
119. Letter to Prof. Michał Siedlecki (27 July 1935). Biblioteka Jagiellońska—Oddział Rękopisów [Jagiellonian Library—Manuscript Collection]. Przyb. 128/57.
120. Edward Said, *Orientalism* (New York: Vintage Books, 1994), 69, 65. An Orientalist reading of Koneczny was suggested by Charles T. Evans. The author is grateful for his advice in the early stages of this project. For a discussion of Russian Orientalism, see his "Vasilii Barthold: Orientalism in Russia?" *Russian History / Histoire Russe* 26, no. 1 (Spring 1999): 25–44. Jiří Vykoukal also discusses Koneczny's Orientalism in connection with his views of Russia in "Territorial Contexts of the Polish Reflection of Russia," in *Regions in Central and Eastern Europe: Past and Present*, ed. Tadayuki Hayashi and Fukuda Hiroshi (Tokyo: Slavic Research Center, 2007), 109–20; http://src-h.slav.hokudai.ac.jp/coe21/publish/no15_ses/contents.html (accessed 30 June 2008).
121. Mirosław Filipowicz, *Wobec Rosji. Studia z dziejów historiografii polskiej od końca XIX wieku po II wojnę światową* (Lublin: Instytut Europy Środkowo-Wschodniej, 2000), 17.
122. Grzegorz Kucharczyk, *Mała historia polskiej myśli politycznej* (Dębogóra: Klub Książki Katolickiej, 2007), 316–35.

123. Feliks Koneczny, *Chrześcijaństwo wobec ustrojów życia zbiorowego* (Krzeszowice: Dom Wydawniczy "Ostoja," 2003), 11. Originally published in *Ateneum Kapłańskie* 18, vol. 30 (1932): 131–47, 255–76.

124. Maciej Salamon, "Bizancjum Feliksa Konecznego," in Skoczyński, *Feliks Koneczny dzisiaj*, 168.

125. Feliks Koneczny, *Święci w dziejach narodu polskiego*, 4th ed. (Komorów: Wydawnictwo Antyk, 1997), 9.

126. Pucek, "Feliks Koneczny: teoria pluralizmu cywilizacyjnego," 171.

127. Rafał Stobiecki, "Rosja i Rosjanie w polskiej myśli historycznej XIX i XX wieku," in *Katalog wzajemnych uprzedzeń Polaków i Rosjan*, ed. Andrzej Lazari (Warsaw: Polski Instytut Spraw Międzynarodowych, 2006), 159–60.

128. Attila Melegh, *On the East-West Slope. Globalization, Nationalism, Racism and Discourses on Central and Eastern Europe* (Budapest: Central European University Press, 2006).

129. Koneczny, *Polska między wschodem a zachodem*, 51. This is the text of a speech that was delivered in 1927 at Catholic University in Lublin (KUL) and later published in 1928. For an overview of Koneczny's views on Russia, see Ryszard Polak, "Feliks Koneczny wobec Rosji i jej cywilizacji (cz. I)," *Cywilizacja* 15 (2005): 82–101; and "Konecznego ocena relacji polsko-rosyjskich (cz. II)," *Cywilizacja* 16 (2006): 119–40.

130. Jörn Rüsen, "Some Theoretical Approaches to Intercultural Comparative Historiography," *History and Theory* 35, no. 4 (December 1996): 11.

131. Melegh, *On the East-West Slope*, 39.

132. Syed Farid Alatas, "Eurocentrism and the Role of the Human Sciences in the Dialogue among Civilizations," *European Legacy* 7, no. 6 (2002): 760–62.

133. Vykoukal, "Territorial Contexts of the Polish Reflection of Russia," 113. See also Jiří Vykoukal, "Polské vidění Ruska: příklad negativního stereotypu (IV. Syntézy kanonické i nekanonické)," *Slovanský Přehled* 86, no. 2 (2000): 215–38.

134. Vykoukal, "Territorial Contexts of the Polish Reflection of Russia," 115.

135. Aleksandra Niewiara, "Procesy kategoryzacyjne a kulturowe konstruowanie obrazu 'innego' (Moskwicin-Moskal-Rosjanin)," in Lazari, *Katalog wzajemnych uprzedzeń Polaków i Rosjan*, 70.

136. Janusz Tazbir, *Polska przedmurzem Europy* (Warsaw: Twój Styl, 2004), 151. Interestingly, anti-Austrian sentiment was comparatively muted, since the Habsburg monarchy was Catholic. See ibid., 140–41.

137. Filipowicz, *Wobec Rosji*, 17.

138. Tazbir, *Polska przedmurzem Europy*, 144–45.

139. Stobiecki, "Rosja i Rosjanie w polskiej myśli historycznej," 199.

140. Maria Janion, *Niesamowita Słowiańszczyzna. Fantazmaty literatury* (Kraków: Wydawnictwo Literackie, 2006), 328–29.

141. Jean-François Bayart, *The Illusion of Cultural Identity* (Chicago: University of Chicago Press, 2005), 77.

142. Michał Bohun, "Oblicza obsesji—negatywny obraz Rosji w myśli polskiej," in Lazari, *Katalog wzajemnych uprzedzeń Polaków i Rosjan*, 220.

143. Ibid., 228.

144. Ibid.

145. Koneczny, *O ład w historii*, 33.

146. See Maciej Giertych, "Z nauczania Feliksa Konecznego," *Opoka w Kraju* 21, no. 42 (March 1997), http://opoka.giertych.pl/ (accessed 18 August 2010).
147. Filipowicz, *Wobec Rosji*, 21.
148. Ibid., 22–23.
149. Ibid., 35–38. Wacław Sobieski (1872–1935) also stressed the "civilizational antagonism" of Poland and Russia. See Stobiecki, "Rosja i Rosjanie w polskiej myśli historycznej," 166.
150. Bohun, "Oblicza obsesji," 233. On Kucharzewski and Jasinowski, see also Marek Kornat, *Bolszewizm, totalitaryzm, rewolucja Rosja. Początki sowietologii i studiów nad systemami totalitarnymi w Polsce (1918–1939)*, 2 vols. (Kraków: Księgarnia Akademicka, 2004), 1:259–93, 322–52.
151. Feliks Koneczny, "Potrójna walka o byt," in *Zwierzchnictwo moralności ekonomia i etyka* (Komorów: Wydawnictwo Antyk, 2006), 15.
152. Feliks Koneczny, "Ekonomia i etyka," in *Zwierzchnictwo moralności ekonomia i etyka*, 22.
153. Koneczny, *O ład w historii*, 19–23.
154. Koneczny, *Plurality of Civilisations*, 72.
155. Ibid., 124.
156. Stobiecki, "Rosja i Rosjanie w polskiej myśli historycznej," 175–77.
157. Koneczny, *Święci w dziejach narodu polskiego*, 688–689.
158. Bogumił Grott, "The Conception of 'Roman-Catholic Totalism' in Poland before World War II," *Zeszyty Naukowe Uniwersytetu Jagiellońskiego. Studia Religiologica* 8 (1982): 101–3.
159. Bogumił Grott, "Mediewalizm w koncepcjach Obozu Wielkiej Polski ze studiów nad religijnymi uwarunkowaniami myśli politycznej," *Zeszyty Naukowe Uniwersytetu Jagiellońskiego. Studia Religiologica* 7 (1982): 61.
160. Grabowiec, *Model społeczeństwa obywatelskiego*, 150.
161. Ibid., 187.
162. Koneczny, *Plurality of Civilisations*, 52.
163. Ibid., 57.
164. Ibid., 58.
165. Koneczny, *Święci w dziejach narodu polskiego*, 683–84.
166. Koneczny, *Rozwój moralności*, 317.
167. Feliks Koneczny, *Państwo i prawo w cywilizacji łacińskiej* (Warsaw: Wydawnictwo Antyk, 2001), 5.
168. Ibid., 8.
169. Ibid.
170. Ibid., 10.
171. Ibid., 9.
172. Ibid., 242.
173. Ibid., 17.
174. Ibid., 27.
175. Ibid., 29.
176. Feliks Koneczny, "Ślubowanie i ciąg dalszy," in *Zwierzchnictwo moralności ekonomia i etyka*, 8.
177. Tomasz Wituch, "Religia jako rdzeń cywilizacji," in Skoczyński, *Feliks Koneczny dzisiaj*, 79–84.

178. Koneczny, "Ślubowanie i ciąg dalszy," 8.
179. Feliks Koneczny, "Warunki powodzenia," in *Zwierzchnictwo moralności ekonomia i etyka*, 67.
180. Feliks Koneczny, "Zwierzchnictwo moralności," in *Zwierzchnictwo moralności ekonomia i etyka*, 12.
181. Ibid.,
182. Feliks Koneczny, "Samorządy gospodarcze," in *Zwierzchnictwo moralności ekonomia i etyka*, 29–33.
183. Feliks Koneczny, "Więcej dobrobytu," in *Zwierzchnictwo moralności ekonomia i etyka*, 17.
184. Ibid.
185. Koneczny, *Polskie logos a ethos*, 2:477.
186. Ibid., 472.
187. Ibid., 473.
188. Klaus E. Müller, "Perspectives in Historical Anthropology," in *Western Historical Thinking: An Intercultural Debate*, ed. Jörn Rüsen (New York: Berghahn Books, 2002), 40.
189. Zbigniew Pucek, *Pluralizm cywilizacyjny jako perspektywa myśli socjologicznej* (Kraków: Akademia Ekonomiczna, 1990), 37.
190. Müller, "Perspectives in Historical Anthropology," 39.
191. Krystyna Kurowska, "Feliksa Konecznego nauka o wielości cywilizacji," *Przegląd Humanistyczny* 22, no. 7/8 (1978): 90.
192. Ibid.
193. Koneczny, *Polskie logos a ethos*, 1:308.
194. Ibid., 2:469–70. These comments were published in 1921. Writing later, in 1937, Koneczny developed this position. He explained that in an earlier period (the thirteenth century), "Poland had the historic obligation to spread Catholicism and Latin civilization." See *Święci w dziejach narodu polskiego*, 135. He distinguished peaceful Polish missionary efforts, however, from the Teutonic Knights' use of force in northern Europe. Ibid., 224.
195. Skoczyński, *Idee historiozoficzne Feliksa Konecznego*, 106–7.
196. Bokiej, *Cywilizacja łacińska*, 54–55.
197. Stanisław Jedynak, "Aksjologiczne zagadnienie rozwoju cywilizacji według Feliksa Konecznego." *Przegląd Humanistyczny* 32, no. 3 (1988): 124.
198. Stanisław Jedynak, *Naród społeczeństwo państwo* (Warsaw: Wydawnictwo TRIO, 2002), 135.
199. Jolanta Kolbuszewska, "Od historii przez filozofię dziejów po historyczną aksjologię. Przeobrażenia historycznej refleksji Feliksa Konecznego," *Historyka* 34 (2004): 27. Other versions were also published in *Kultura i Historia* 3 (2002) and *Czasopismo Naukowe "Kultura i Historia,"* http://www.kulturaihistoria.umcs.lublin.pl/archives/103 (accessed 25 August 2009).
200. Jedynak, "Aksjologiczne zagadnienie rozwoju cywilizacji według Feliksa Konecznego," 128.

CHAPTER ONE. KEY KONECZNIAN THEMES

1. Koneczny, *Polskie logos a ethos*, 1:44.
2. Ibid., 46.
3. Ibid., 2:612.
4. Ibid., 596. For additional discussion of Koneczny's views on a European federation, see Wiesław Bokajło, "Polnische konzepte einer europäischen föderation. Zwischen den "Vereinigten Staaten von Europa" und dem konföderalen mitteleuropa (1917–1939)," in *Vision Europa: deutsche und polnishce föderationspläne des 19. Und frühen 20. Jahrhunderts*, ed. Heinz Duchhardt and Małgorzata Morawiec (Mainz: Veröffentlichungen des Instituts für Europäische Geschichte Mainz. Universalgeschichte Beiheft, 60. Verlag Philipp von Zabern, 2003), 87–90.
5. Koneczny, *Rozwój moralności*, 214.
6. Koneczny, *Polskie logos a ethos*, 2:477.
7. Koneczny, *Plurality of Civilisations*, 312.
8. Koneczny, *Prawa dziejowe*, 335.
9. Joanna Nowak, "Jedność w rozmaitości—czyli o romantycznych korzeniach koncepcji narodu Feliksa Konecznego," *Sprawy Narodowościowe* 30 (2007): 85.
10. Hilckman, "Feliks Koneczny and the Comparative Science of Civilisation," 28.
11. Ibid., 30.
12. Koneczny, *Polskie logos a ethos*, 2:555.
13. Feliks Koneczny, *Tło cywilizacyjne odsieczy wiedeńskiej* (Warsaw: Milla, 1999), 34.
14. Ibid., 35.
15. Radosław Brzózka, "Polityka międzynarodowa w cywilizacji łacińskiej," *Cywilizacja* 4/5 (2003): 29.
16. Ibid., 30.
17. Ibid., 34.
18. Ibid., 35.
19. Koneczny, *Plurality of Civilisations*, 310–11. Emphasis in the original.
20. Bogumił Grott, *Nacjonalizm Chrześcijański: Narodowo-katolicka formacja ideowa w II Rzeczypospolitej na tle porównawczym*, 2nd ed. (Kraków: Wydawnictwo "Ostoja," 1996), 85.
21. Grott, "Mediewalizm w koncepcjach Obozu Wielkiej Polski," 61.
22. See Grott, "The Conception of 'Roman-Catholic Totalism' in Poland before World War II," 101–7.
23. Bogumił Grott, "Chrześcijańskie i świeckie inspiracje w doktrynach nacjonalizmu polskiego," *Przegląd Humanistyczny*, no. 4 (1994): 85–86.
24. Feliks Koneczny, *Prawa dziejowe*, 119.
25. Koneczny, *Tło cywilizacyjne odsieczy wiedeńskiej*, 33.
26. Koneczny, *Polskie logos a ethos*, 2:473–74.
27. Ibid., 593.
28. Koneczny, *Plurality of Civilisations*, 208.
29. Ibid., 216.
30. Bokiej, *Cywilizacja łacińska*, 22. Also see Józef Misiek, "O wielości cywilizacyj—refleksje metodologiczne," in Skoczyński, *Feliks Koneczny dzisiaj*, 56.
31. Kurowska, "Feliksa Konecznego nauka o wielości cywilizacji," 81.
32. Koneczny, "O kierunek polskości," *Cywilizacja* 4/5 (2003): 220. Originally published in *Tęcza* 2, no. 21 (26 May 1928): 1–2.

33. Jacques Semelin, *Purify and Destroy: The Political Uses of Massacre and Genocide*, trans. Cynthia Schoch (New York: Columbia University Press, 2007), 33.

34. Koneczny, *Rozwój moralności*, 214.

35. Stefan Zabieglik, "Feliksa Konecznego teoria cywilizacji," *Toruński Przegląd Filozoficzny* 5/6 (2003): 118.

36. Marian Bębenek, "Paradygmat polityki w cywilizacji łacińskiej," in Skoczyński, *Feliks Koneczny dzisiaj*, 86–88.

37. Koneczny, *Rozwój moralności*, 27.

38. Koneczny, *Prawa dziejowe*, 119.

39. Ibid., 124–25.

40. Feliks Koneczny, *Kościół w Polsce wobec cywilizacji* (Krzeszowice: Dom Wydawniczy "Ostoja," 2005), 16.

41. Koneczny, *Prawa dziejowe*, 99.

42. Feliks Koneczny, "Państwo a metody życia zbiorowego," in *Napór orientu na zachód i inne pisme o życiu społecznym* (Warsaw: Wydawnictwo "Hobbysta," 2004), 70.

43. Feliks Koneczny, "Harmider etyk," in *O cywilizację łacińską* (Krzeszowice: Dom Wydawniczy "Ostoja," 2006), 44.

44. Feliks Koneczny, "Czy polityka należy do cywilizacji?" in *Napór orientu na zachód i inne pisme o życiu społecznym*, 76.

45. Feliks Koneczny, "Rodowód monizmu prawniczego," in *O cywilizację łacińską*, 49. Also republished in *Człowiek w Kulturze* 10 (1998): 213–25.

46. Koneczny, *Rozwój moralności*, 27.

47. Feliks Koneczny, "Polskie Logos a Ethos," *Tygodnik Warszawski* 3, no. 27 (6 July 1947): 4.

48. Koneczny, *Plurality of Civilisations*, 320.

49. Robert Piotrowski, *Problem filozoficzny ładu społecznego a porównawcza nauka o cywilizacjach* (Warsaw: Dialog, 2003), 79.

50. Ibid., 69.

51. Ibid., 125.

52. Ibid., 129.

53. Ibid., 128.

54. Ibid., 123.

55. Koneczny, *Państwo i prawo w cywilizacji łacińskiej*, 47.

56. Ibid., 158. Koneczny also wanted greater freedom for private schools and Church schools to determine curriculum. See Ryszard Jadczak, "Feliks Koneczny o państwie i jego roli w wychowaniu," in *Wychowanie a polityka. Między wychowaniem narodowym a państwowym*, ed. Witold Wojdyła (Toruń: Uniwersytet Mikołaja Kopernika, 1999), 76.

57. Koneczny, *Państwo i prawo w cywilizacji łacińskiej*, 174.

58. Ibid., 66.

59. Koneczny, *Rozwój moralności*, 31.

60. Koneczny, *Państwo i prawo w cywilizacji łacińskiej*, 102.

61. Koneczny, *O ład w historii*, 17.

62. Skoczyński, *Idee historiozoficzne Feliksa Konecznego*, 42.

63. Bokiej, *Cywilizacja łacińska*, 151–152.

64. Koneczny, *Etyki a cywilizacje*, 9.

65. Pucek, "Feliks Koneczny: teoria pluralizmu cywilizacyjnego," 175.

66. Rüsen, "Some Theoretical Approaches," 13.

67. Koneczny, *O ład w historii*, 10.
68. Pucek, "Feliks Koneczny: teoria pluralizmu cywilizacyjnego," 175. Emphasis added.
69. Ibid., 177.
70. Jörn Rüsen, "Introduction: Historical Thinking as Intercultural Discourse," in *Western Historical Thinking: An Intercultural Debate*, ed. Jörn Rüsen (New York: Berghahn Books, 2002), 2.
71. Piotrowski, *Problem filozoficzny ładu społecznego*, 67. Artur Soboń also connects the productivity of a given society with its civilizational levels of "the capitalization of time." See Artur Soboń, "Koncepcja historiozoficzna Feliksa Konecznego," http://ciapek.uci.agh.edu.pl/~kwlodarc/tekstyo/asobon.html (accessed 28 June 2004).
72. Koneczny, *Polskie logos a ethos*, 2:472–73.
73. Pucek, "Feliks Koneczny: teoria pluralizmu cywilizacyjnego," 177.
74. Ibid., 176.
75. Rüsen, "Some Theoretical Approaches," 12.
76. Kurowska, "Feliksa Konecznego nauka o wielości cywilizacji," 85.
77. Bokiej, *Cywilizacja łacińska*, 26.
78. Koneczny, *Plurality of Civilisations*, 292.
79. Ibid., 294.
80. Feliks Koneczny, "Samorząd gminy wieskiej," in *Zwierzchnictwo moralności ekonomia i etyka* (Komorów: Wydawnictwo Antyk, 2006), 45.
81. Koneczny, "Samorządy gospodarcze," 32.
82. Koneczny, *Etyki a cywilizacje*, 36. See also Koneczny, *Chrześcijaństwo wobec ustrojów życia zbiorowego*, 26.
83. Grabowiec, *Model społeczeństwa obywatelskiego*, 82.
84. Koneczny, *Etyki a cywilizacje*, 38.
85. Koneczny, *Plurality of Civilisations*, 297.
86. Ibid., 302.
87. Feliks Koneczny, *Polskie logos a ethos*, 1:12–13.
88. Jolanta Kolbuszewska, "Konecznego koncepcja dziejów Rosji," in Skoczyński, *Feliks Koneczny dzisiaj*, 188.
89. Koneczny, *Plurality of Civilisations*, 278.
90. Ibid., 271.
91. Hilckman, "Feliks Koneczny and the Comparative Science of Civilisation," 27.
92. Kolbuszewska, "Konecznego koncepcja dziejów Rosji," 192–93. See also Koneczny, *Dzieje Rosji od najdawniejszych do najnowszych czasów* (Warsaw: Wydawnictwo M. Arcta, 1921). This theme of the organization of society by the state for military conquest is more thoroughly developed by Koneczny in *Polskie logos a ethos*, 2:349–51.
93. Grabowiec, *Model społeczeństwa obywatelskiego*, 196.
94. Ibid., 155–56. On Koneczny's distinction between "bureaucracy" and "administration," see also "Administracja obywatelska," *Niedziela* 17, no. 22 (1–7 June 1947): 175. For a lengthy discussion of Poland's adminstrative history, see *Dzieje administracji w Polsce* (1924; repr., Warsaw: Wydawnictwo Antyk, 1999).
95. Koneczny, *Polskie logos a ethos*, 2:549.
96. Ibid., 550.
97. Koneczny, "Potrójna walka o byt," 14.
98. Ibid., 15.
99. Koneczny, *Prawa dziejowe*, 119.

100. Koneczny, *O ład w historii*, 18.
101. Felix Koneczny, *Głos w sprawie ludowej* (Kraków: Drukarnia Uniwersytetu Jagiellońskiego, 1896), 121.
102. Koneczny, *Plurality of Civilisations*, 159.
103. Koneczny, "O kierunek polskości," 218. For a concise discussion of Koneczny's concept of "nation," see Leszek Gawor, "Feliksa Konecznego koncepcja narodu," in *Charakter narodowy i religia*, ed. Kazimierz Wiliński (Lublin: Wydawnictwo Uniwersytetu Marii Curie-Skłodowskiej, 1997): 35–42.
104. Nowak, "Jedność w rozmaitości," 81.
105. Ibid., 80–81.
106. Koneczny, *Plurality of Civilisations*, 306.
107. Ibid., 307.
108. Ibid., 314.
109. Koneczny, *O ład w historii*, 5.
110. Ibid.
111. Ibid., 5–6.
112. Ibid., 7.
113. Zabieglik, "Feliksa Konecznego teoria cywilizacji," 123–24.
114. Piotrowski, *Problem filozoficzny ładu społecznego*, 48ff.
115. Koneczny, *Rozwój moralności*, 120.
116. Ibid., 123.
117. Ibid.
118. Piotrowski, *Problem filozoficzny ładu społecznego*, 49.
119. Jan Skoczyński, "Logos i ethos w teorii cywilizacji," in *Rozmyślania o cywilizacji*, ed. J. Baradziej and J. Goćkowski (Kraków: Wydawnictwo Baran i Suszczyński, 1997), 138.
120. Koneczny, *Plurality of Civilisations*, 170.
121. Ibid., 172.
122. Koneczny, *Rozwój moralności*, 94.
123. Ibid., 111.
124. Ibid., 125.
125. Ibid.
126. Piotrowski, *Problem filozoficzny ładu społecznego*, 48–49.
127. Ibid., 61–63.
128. Koneczny, *Plurality of Civilisations*, 289.
129. Ibid., 285.
130. See "O nierówności religii," *Tygodnik Warszawski* 2, no. 35 (1 September 1946): 4.
131. Grabowiec, *Model społeczeństwa obywatelskiego*, 81.
132. Koneczny, *O ład w historii*, 10.
133. Koneczny, *Plurality of Civilisations*, 246.
134. Koneczny, "Przemienność sił," in *Zwierzchnictwo moralności ekonomia i etyka* (Komorów: Wydawnictwo Antyk, 2006), 91.
135. Koneczny, "Ekonomia i etyka," 24.

CHAPTER TWO. CLASSICISM AND MEDIEVALISM IN KONECZNIAN THOUGHT

1. Robaczewski, "Quincunx jako odbicie klasycznej teorii osoby," 44–45.
2. Koneczny, *Plurality of Civilisations*, 163–64.
3. Koneczny, *O ład w historii*, 11.
4. Koneczny, *Plurality of Civilisations*, 164–65.
5. Ibid., 165.
6. Christopher Dawson, *Dynamics of World History* (Wilmington, DE: ISI Books, 2002), 67.
7. Ibid.
8. Ibid.
9. Ricardo Duchesne, "Defending the Rise of Western Culture against Its Multicultural Critics," *European Legacy* 10, no. 5 (2005): 471. On the role of Greek farmers and the historiography of this issue, see Victor Davis Hanson, *The Other Greeks: The Family Farm and the Agrarian Roots of Western Civilization*, 2nd ed. (Berkeley: University of California Press, 1999).
10. Szczęsny, "Rola chrześcijaństwa w tworzeniu cywilizacji łacińskiej," 393.
11. Ibid., 397.
12. Dawson, *Dynamics of World History*, 68–69.
13. Ibid., 70.
14. Arnold Toynbee, *Reconsiderations*, vol. 12, *A Study of History* (New York: Oxford University Press, 1964), 389.
15. Koneczny, *Plurality of Civilisations*, 299. Emphasis added.
16. Ibid., 303.
17. Bokiej, *Cywilizacja łacińska*, 43.
18. Feliks Koneczny, *Cywilizacja bizantyńska* (London: Wydawnictwa Towarzystwa imienia Romana Dmowskiego, 1973), 43.
19. Ibid., 47.
20. Ibid., 52. Jaroslav Krejčí describes Alexander's efforts as "perhaps the first attempt at socio-cultural integration on a multi-civilizational scale. We can consider it to be the first rehearsal of globalization." See *The Paths of Civilization: Understanding the Currents of History* (New York: Palgrave Macmillan Press, 2004), 148.
21. Koneczny, *Cywilizacja bizantyńska*, 61.
22. Ibid., 37.
23. Ibid., 38.
24. Ibid.
25. Ibid.
26. Bokiej, *Cywilizacja łacińska*, 93–94.
27. Koneczny, *Cywilizacja bizantyńska*, 69.
28. Ibid., 100.
29. Ibid.
30. Ibid.
31. Ibid., 119.
32. Ibid., 117.
33. Koneczny—as well as nationalist publicists in the interwar period—also generally distinguished between the Roman law of the Republican period and later Byzantine

practices. See Tomasz Banach, "Prawo rzymskie w publicystyce obozu narodowego Polski międzywojennej," *Myśl Polska*, no. 32–33 (6–13 August 2006), http://www .myslpolska.icenter.pl/ (accessed 12 September 2006).

34. Koneczny, *Cywilizacja bizantyńska*, 101.
35. Ibid., 102.
36. Ibid., 116. Emphasis added.
37. Bokiej, *Cywilizacja łacińska*, 96ff.
38. Koneczny, *Cywilizacja bizantyńska*, 157.
39. Koneczny, *Polska między wschodem a zachodem*, 2.
40. Ibid., 51.
41. Pucek, "Feliks Koneczny: teoria pluralizmu cywilizacyjnego," 158–59.
42. Koneczny, *Prawa dziejowe*, 100.
43. Leszek Gawor, *O wielości cywilizacji: Filozofia społeczna Feliksa Konecznego* (Lublin: Wydawnictwo Uniwersytetu Marii Curie-Skłodowskiej, 2002), 124.
44. Koneczny, *Rozwój moralności*, 26.
45. Koneczny, *Cywilizacja bizantyńska*, 135.
46. Ibid., 164.
47. Michael McCormick, "Byzantium's Role in the Formation of Early Medieval Civilization: Approaches and Problems," *Illinois Classical Studies* 12, no. 2 (Fall 1987): 207.
48. Koneczny, *Cywilizacja bizantyńska*, 159–160.
49. Ibid., 163.
50. Małgorzata Dąbrowska, "La vision moscoutaire de Byzance et le byzantinisme allemande de Koneczny ou Byzance sans Byzance," *Organon* 28–30 (1999–2001): 259–60. See also Salamon, "Bizancjum Feliksa Konecznego," 181.
51. Koneczny, *Cywilizacja bizantyńska*, 163.
52. Ibid., 221.
53. Ibid., 223–224.
54. Feliks Koneczny, *Bizantynizm niemiecki* (Warsaw: Milla, 2002), 8.
55. Bokiej, *Cywilizacja łacińska*, 185.
56. Koneczny, *Chrześcijaństwo wobec ustrojów życia zbiorowego*, 24.
57. Koneczny, *Bizantynizm niemiecki*, 7.
58. Ibid., 9.
59. Ibid., 12.
60. Ibid., 10.
61. Koneczny, *Cywilizacja bizantyńska*, 53.
62. Ibid., 84.
63. Koneczny, *Polskie logos a ethos*, 2:323.
64. Koneczny, *Cywilizacja bizantyńska*, 61.
65. Ibid., 18.
66. Koneczny, *Polskie logos a ethos*, 2:321–22.
67. Ibid., 322.
68. Koneczny, *Cywilizacja bizantyńska*, 24.
69. Ibid., 22.
70. Koneczny, *Plurality of Civilisations*, 300.
71. Koneczny, *Cywilizacja bizantyńska*, 166.
72. Ibid., 139.

73. Ibid., 138.
74. Ibid., 150.
75. Ibid., 123. And if caesaropapism was the first feature of the new civilization to appear, then Koneczny pointed to "a priority of form over content" as the second. This relates in part to the introduction of Persian court ceremony. Ibid., 128–31.
76. Ibid., 140.
77. Ibid., 121.
78. Koneczny, *Plurality of Civilisations*, 151.
79. Koneczny, *Chrześcijaństwo wobec ustrojów życia zbiorowego*, 45.
80. Ibid., 44–45.
81. Ibid., 20.
82. Koneczny, *Cywilizacja bizantyńska*, 132.
83. Koneczny, *Święci w dziejach narodu polskiego*, 62–63. According to Paweł Milcarek, Koneczny portrayed the saints as "pioneers of ethics and civilization" who personified the pursuit of "total ethics" in Latin civilization. See "Świętość w dziejach ludzkich w ujęciu Feliksa Konecznego," in Skoczyński, *Feliks Koneczny dzisiaj*, 225–30.
84. Koneczny, *Plurality of Civilisations*, 306.
85. Ibid., 306–7.
86. Ibid., 276.
87. Ibid., 303.
88. Koneczny, *Rozwój moralności*, 209.
89. Witold Wojdyło and Grzegorz Radomski, "W obronie niezależności narodu. Ruch narodowy w Polsce wobec wspólnot wyższego rzędu oraz idei integracyjnych w Europie w XX w.," *Przegląd Humanistyczny* 50, no. 3 (2006): 91–92.
90. Grott, "Mediewalizm w koncepcjach Obozu Wielkiej," 68.
91. Rafał Łętocha, *Katolicyzm a idea narodowa. Miejsce religii w myśli obozu narodowego lat okupacji* (Lublin: Fundacja *Servire Veritati* Instytut Edukacji Narodowej, 2002), 94.
92. Ewa Maj, *Związek Ludowo-Narodowy, 1919–1928. Studium z dziejów myśli politycznej* (Lublin: Wydawnictwo Uniwersytetu Marii Curie-Skłodowskiej, 2000), 112–13, 117.
93. Elizabeth Emery and Laura Morowitz, *Consuming the Past: The Medieval Revival in fin-de-siècle France* (Burlington, VT: Ashgate Publishing Company, 2003), 4.
94. Ibid.
95. Laura Morowitz, "Anti-Semitism, Medievalism and the Art of the Fin-de-Siecle," *Oxford Art Journal* 20, no. 1 (1997): 38.
96. Ibid., 35.
97. Emery and Morowitz, *Consuming the Past*, 4.
98. Ibid., 16.
99. Ibid., 19.
100. Ibid., 24.
101. Paul Robichaud, *Making the Past Present: David Jones, the Middle Ages and Modernism* (Washington, DC: Catholic University of America Press, 2007), 5.
102. Stefan Goebel, *The Great War and Medieval Memory. War, Remembrance and Medievalism in Britain and Germany, 1914–1940* (Cambridge: Cambridge University Press, 2007), 16.

103. Ibid., 13.

104. Robichaud, *Making the Past Present*, 140.

105. Ibid., 117.

106. Koneczny, *Rozwój moralności*, 277. Koneczny referenced the neo-Thomist papal encyclicals of the late nineteenth century in other works. See Koneczny, *Prawa dziejowe*, 26.

107. Grabowiec, *Model społeczeństwa obywatelskiego*, 90.

108. Koneczny, *Prawa dziejowe*, 40.

109. Koneczny's debt to Aristotelian Thomism is frequently pointed out in the context of his emphasis on commensurability among the existential values of the quincunx, which calls for harmony and balance between the material and spiritual. See Gawor, *O wielości cywilizacji*, 43; Ryszard Polak, *Cywilizacje a moralność w myśli Feliksa Konecznego* (Lublin: Fundacja *Servire Veritati* Instytut Edukacji Narodowej, 2001), 31, 35; and Mieczysław Ryba, "Człowiek, naród, państwo w cywilizacji łacińskiej," *Cywilizacja* 1 (2002): 8; http://cywilizacja.ien.pl/?id=77 (accessed 27 August 2009).

110. Koneczny, *Plurality of Civilisations*, 149.

111. Tracey Rowland, *Culture and the Thomist Tradition: After Vatican II* (London: Routledge, 2003), 40–41.

112. Wojciech Szurgot, *Prawo jako fundament cywilizacji łacińskiej w myśli Feliksa Konecznego* (Krzeszowice: Dom Wydawniczy "Ostoja," 2007), 20.

113. Soboń, "Koncepcja historiozoficzna Feliksa Konecznego."

114. Frątczak, *Feliks Koneczny o państwie i wartościach*, 29–30.

115. Ibid., 100.

116. Grabowiec, *Model społeczeństwa obywatelskiego*, 27.

117. Koneczny, *Polskie logos a ethos*, 2:567.

118. Peter Kivisto, "The Brief Career of Catholic Sociology," *Sociological Analysis* 50, no. 4 (Winter 1989): 351.

119. Polak, *Cywilizacje a moralność w myśli Feliksa Konecznego*, 82.

120. On this matter, see Bogumił Grott, *Nacjonalizm i religia. Proces zespalania nacjonalizmu z katolicyzmem w jedną całość ideową w myśli Narodowej Demokracji 1926–1939* (Kraków: Nakładem Uniwersytetu Jagiellońskiego, 1984), 140–41; and Łętocha, *Katolicyzm a idea narodowa*, 92–94.

121. Robichaud, *Making the Past Present*, 103.

122. Ibid., 112.

123. Alice Chandler, *A Dream of Order: The Medieval Ideal in Nineteenth-Century English Literature* (Lincoln: University of Nebraska Press, 1971), 1.

124. Robichaud, *Making the Past Present*, 114.

125. Charles Dellheim, "Interpreting Victorian Medievalism," in *History and Community: Essays in Victorian Medievalism*, ed. Florence S. Boos (New York: Garland Publishing, Inc., 1992), 53.

126. Kivisto, "The Brief Career of Catholic Sociology," 355. Kivisto is referring to Ross's article, "Sociology and the Catholic" in *American Catholic Sociological Review* 1, no. 1 (March 1940): 6–9.

127. Frątczak, *Feliks Koneczny o państwie i wartościach*, 111–14.

128. Chandler, *A Dream of Order*, 3.

129. Ibid., 7.

CHAPTER THREE. CIVILIZATIONAL THREATS TO POLAND

1. Koneczny, *Cywilizacja bizantyńska*, 264.
2. Grzegorz Kucharczyk also identifies this peculiar feature of Koneczny's Orientalism. See *Mała historia polskiej myśli politycznej*, 331–32.
3. Bokiej, *Cywilizacja łacińska*, 138.
4. Koneczny, *Cywilizacja bizantyńska*, 225.
5. Małgorzata Dąbrowska, "Przemoskwiona wizja Bizancjum a niemiecki bizantynizm Konecznego," in Skoczyński, *Feliks Koneczny dzisiaj*, 157, 160, 162.
6. Arnold Toynbee, review of Matthew Melko, *The Nature of Civilizations*, in *History and Theory* 10, no. 2 (1971): 250.
7. Todd Kontje, *German Orientalisms* (Ann Arbor: University of Michigan Press, 2004), 12.
8. Iver B. Neumann, *Uses of the Other: "The East" in European Identity Formation* (Minneapolis: University of Minnesota Press, 1999), 207.
9. Jan Skoczyński attributes the origin of this term to the French philosopher Edgar Quinet (1803–75). See *Koneczny: Teoria cywilizacji*, 142. Also see Skoczyński, *Idee historiozoficzne Feliksa Konecznego*, 113. Rafał Łętocha points out that other Polish nationalists of the interwar period and war years, such as J. Cieszkowski, discussed the Byzantinism of Germany. See Łętocha, *Katolicyzm a idea narodowa*, 67–70, 285.
10. Feliks Koneczny, *Dzieje Polski za Piastów* (1902; repr., Komorów: Wydawnictwo Antyk, 1997), 36.
11. Dąbrowska, "Przemoskwiona wizja Bizancjum," 161; Koneczny, "Bizantynizm niemiecki," in *Prawa dziejowe*, 353.
12. K. Ciggaar, "Theophano: An Empress Reconsidered," in *The Empress Theophano: Byzantium and the West at the Turn of the First Millenium*, ed. Adelbert Davids (New York: Cambridge University Press, 1995), 51.
13. Rosamond McKitterick, "Ottonian Intellectual Culture in the Tenth Century and the Role of Theophano," in Davids, *The Empress Theophano*, 169.
14. This is the title of one of Koneczny's articles on the theme of German Byzantinism. See Feliks Koneczny, "Dwoistość Niemiec," *Myśl Narodowa* 10, no. 53 (21 December 1930): 799–800. See also Koneczny, *Bizantynizm niemiecki*, 15.
15. Koneczny, *Bizantynizm niemiecki*, 16.
16. Ibid.
17. Ibid., 23.
18. Karl Leyser, "*Theophanu divina gratia imperatrix augusta*: Western and Eastern Emperorship in the Later Tenth Century," in Davids, *The Empress Theophano*, 15.
19. Ciggaar, "Theophano: An Empress Reconsidered," 49.
20. Judith Herrin, "Theophano: Considerations on the Education of a Byzantine Princess," in Davids, *The Empress Theophano*, 81.
21. Ibid., 64.
22. Odilo Engels, "Theophano, the Western Empress from the East," in Davids, *The Empress Theophano*, 33–36.
23. Ibid., 41.
24. Herrin, "Theophano: Considerations on the Education of a Byzantine Princess," 84.
25. Ibid., 85.
26. Leyser, "*Theophanu divina gratia imperatrix augusta*," 27.

27. McKitterick, "Ottonian Intellectual Culture in the Tenth Century and the Role of Theophano," 187.
28. Hilckman, "Feliks Koneczny and the Comparative Science of Civilization," 29–30.
29. Koneczny, *Bizantynizm niemiecki*, 24–25. Many of these themes of East-West conflict are presented in Koneczny's "Napór Orient na Zachód" (1937), which has been reprinted in *Napór orientu na zachód i inne pisma o życiu społecznym* (Warsaw: Wydawnictwo "Hobbysta," 2004), 5–22. For more on German Byzantinism, see Justyna M. Krauze, "Die byzantinische Zivilisation im philosophischen Denken von Feliks Koneczny und ihre Wiederspiegelung am Hofe Wilhelms II: ein Versuch," *Studia Niemcoznawsze* 22 (2001): 239–57.
30. Koneczny, *Chrześcijaństwo wobec ustrojów życia zbiorowego*, 27.
31. Bukowska, *Filozofia polska wobec problemu cywilizacji*, 58.
32. Koneczny, *Tło cywilizacyjne odsieczy wiedeńskiej*, 34.
33. Bokiej, *Cywilizacja łacińska*, 135.
34. Bukowska, *Filozofia polska wobec problemu cywilizacji*, 118–19.
35. Feliks Koneczny, *Tadeusz Kościuszko na setną rocznicę zgonu naczelnika. Życie, czyny, duch* (Poznań: Wielkopolska Księgarnia Nakładowa Karola Rzepeckiego, 1918), 15–16. Here Koneczny draws a distinction between Poland and Lithuania prior to their union.
36. Feliks Koneczny, *Teoria Grunwaldu* (Warsaw: Milla, 1999), 5–8. On Koneczny's intellectual debt to St. Augustine, see also Koneczny, *Plurality of Civilisations*, 275; Grabowiec, *Model społeczeństwa obywatelskiego*, 151; Frątczak, *Feliks Koneczny o państwie i wartościach*, 100; Bukowska, *Filozofia polska wobec problemu cywilizacji*, 126; and Kolbuszewska, "Od historii przez filozofię dziejów po historyczną aksjologię," 29.
37. Kontje, *German Orientalisms*, 182.
38. Ibid., 183.
39. Koneczny, *Cywilizacja bizantyńska*, 282.
40. Koneczny, *Teoria Grunwaldu*, 9.
41. Ibid., 15.
42. Ibid., 9.
43. Ibid.
44. Ibid., 11.
45. Ibid.
46. Ibid., 13–14.
47. Ibid., 15.
48. Andrzej Wierzbicki, *Naród-Państwo w polskiej myśli historycznej dwudziestolecia międzywojennego* (Wrocław: Wydawnictwo Polskiej Akademii Nauk, 1978), 80–87.
49. Brzózka, "Polityka międzynarodowa w cywilizacji łacińskiej," 28–29. See also Koneczny, *Święci w dziejach narodu polskiego*, 230–48.
50. Paweł Gondek, "Rola Kościoła w kulturze polskiej: na marginesie prac Feliksa Konecznego," *Człowiek w Kulturze* 10 (1998): 92.
51. Maciej Giertych, *Z nadzieją w przyszłość* (Warsaw: Maciej Giertych, 2005), 62. At *Opoka w Kraju*, http://opoka.giertych.pl/ (accessed 26 August 2011).
52. Kontje, *German Orientalisms*, 184.
53. Ibid.
54. Ibid.

55. Ibid., 184–185.
56. Goebel, *The Great War and Medieval Memory*, 135.
57. Patrice M. Dabrowski, *Commemorations and the Shaping of Modern Poland* (Bloomington: Indiana University Press, 2004), 161.
58. Ibid., 162.
59. Goebel, *The Great War and Medieval Memory*, 135.
60. Dabrowski, *Commemorations and the Shaping of Modern Poland*, 164–65.
61. Ibid., 168.
62. Stauter-Halsted, "Rural Myth and the Modern Nation," 158.
63. Kontje, *German Orientalisms*, 208.
64. Ibid.
65. Ibid., 185.
66. Ibid.
67. Goebel, *The Great War and Medieval Memory*, 127.
68. Ibid., 129.
69. Ibid., 130.
70. Ibid., 133.
71. Ibid., 134–35.
72. Ibid., 141.
73. Akta Starostwa Grodzkiego w Krakowie StGKr. 220, teczka 460. Towarzystwo Słowianstwo (1912–1918) 1929–1938, k. 1517. "Sekcja Łużycka Towarzystwa Słowiańskiego w Krakowie." Odezwa (nd). Archiwum Narodowe w Krakowie [National Archive in Kraków].
74. Ibid., k. 1519–1521. Letter from Henryk Zeman to Władysław Pałosz (23 January 1933).
75. Biliński, *Feliks Koneczny*, 44.
76. Feliks Koneczny, "Cztery posiedzenia Klubu Słowiańskiego," *Świat Słowiański* 1, vol. 2, no. 11–12 (1905): 418–19.
77. Andrzej Wierzbicki, *Spory o polską duszę. Z zagadnień charakterologii narodowej w historiografii polskiej XIX i XX w* (Warsaw: Instytut Historii Polskiej Akademii Nauk, 1993), 251.
78. Włodzimierz Pawluczuk, "My i oni. Przyczynek do fenomenologii dyskursu międzycywilizacyjnego," *Przegląd Humanistyczny* 50, no. 5–6 (2006): 187.
79. Ezequiel Adamovsky, "Euro-Orientalism and the Making of the Concept of Eastern Europe in France, 1810–1880," *Journal of Modern History* 77 (September 2005): 591.
80. Stobiecki, "Rosja i Rosjanie w polskiej myśli historycznej," 179.
81. Selim Chazbijewicz, "Polemika z koncepcją cywilizacji turańskiej Feliksa Konecznego (komunikat)," in *Tradycje duchowe Europy Środkowej i Wschodniej*, ed. Selim Chazbijewicz and Józef Kwapiszewski (Słupsk: Wyższa Szkoła Pedagogiczna w Słupsku, 1999), 81.
82. Hilckman, "Feliks Koneczny and the Comparative Science of Civilisation," 26.
83. Koneczny, *Plurality of Civilisations*, 320.
84. Koneczny, *Polska między wschodem a zachodem*, 45. In Poland today, Koneczny is the scholarly authority most frequently cited by nationalists who embrace the notion of "Latin civilization." Andrzej Walicki believes that the concept, which connotes a civilizational separation of Poles from Russians, is attractive to those

who seek to eradicate the legacy of Russian domination during the Communist era. Walicki attributes Koneczny's renaissance in post-Communist Poland to this phenomenon. See Andrzej Walicki, *Rosja, katolicyzm, i sprawa polska* (Warsaw: Prószyński i S-ka, 2002), 366–67.

85. Mieczysław Ryba, "Polska w XX wieku a cywilizacje," *Człowiek w Kulturze* 10 (1998): 100.

86. Jedynak, "Aksjologiczne zagadnienia rozwoju cywilizacji według Feliksa Konecznego," 126.

87. For Koneczny's explanation of the civilizational variety in Slavdom, see "Różnolitość cywilizacyjna Słowiańszczyzny," *Przegląd Powszechny* 42, vol. 168 (1925): 257–82; 43, vol. 169 (1926): 21–46.

88. Bohun, "Oblicza obsesji," 210–12.

89. See Andrew Kier Wise, "The Search for Slavic Unity: Aleksander Lednicki and the Russian Revolution of 1905," *Polish Review* 42, no. 1 (1997): 29–44.

90. One scholar has compared the impact of the failure of the 1905 revolution among Poles to the devastation felt among Europeans after the failed revolutions of 1848. Poles were forced to reevaluate their "romantic nationalism" and tradition of rebellion. Realism replaced idealism, and with this change came a new cultural and spiritual outlook. Koneczny's reinterpretation of Russia's past and its relationship with Poland is part of this story. See Thomas Burek, "1905, nie 1918," in *Problemy literatury polskiej lat 1890–1939*, seria I, ed. Hanna Kirchner and Zbigniew Żabicki (Wrocław: Wydawnictwo Polskiej Akademii Nauk, 1972), 77–105.

91. Filipowicz, *Wobec Rosji*, 66.

92. Sygn. III 7351—Korespondencja Józefa Korzeniowskiego, historyka. T. 30, k. 38. Biblioteka Narodowa w Warszawie [National Library in Warsaw].

93. Biliński, *Feliks Koneczny*, 80.

94. Filipowicz, *Wobec Rosji*, 16–17. Writing the introduction in December 1916 to the first volume of his multivolume history of Russia, Koneczny commented on his freedom from Russian censorship. See Feliks Koneczny, *Dzieje Rosji*, vol. 1, *Do roku 1449* (Warsaw: Skład Główny w Księgarni E. Wende i Spółka, 1917), vii–viii.

95. Feliks Koneczny, "Czy będzie sąd? Artykuł polski," *Świat Słowiański* 1, vol. 2, no. 11 (1905): 343; "Czego chce rząd rosyjski?" *Świat Słowiański* 2, vol. 1, no. 1 (1906): 1. In a later work otherwise characterized by a negative interpretation of the course of Russian history, Koneczny recalled the heady days of hope in 1905. See *Dzieje Rosji od najdawniejszych do najnowszych czasów*, 282–83. See also Biliński, *Feliks Koneczny*, 92–94.

96. For a more thorough discussion of these events, see Andrew Kier Wise, *Aleksander Lednicki: A Pole among Russians, a Russian among Poles. Polish-Russian Reconciliation in the Revolution of 1905* (Boulder, CO: East European Monographs, 2003).

97. Feliks Koneczny, "Propaganda zgody z Rosyą," *Świat Słowiański* 1, vol. 2, no. 10 (1905): 265, 271. See also Łukasz Nadolski, "Wątki historyczne w publicystyce Feliksa Konecznego na łamach 'Świata Słowiańskiego,'" in Skoczyński, *Feliks Koneczny dzisiaj*, 62.

98. In a letter to Oswald Balzer from 8 December 1904, Koneczny opined: "One cannot have Slavdom without Poland, but it is also certain that Poland cannot do without Slavdom." See Sygn. 7676 II—Korespondencja Oswalda Balzera. T. XVIII, k. 22. Biblioteka Zakładu Narodowego im. Ossolińskich we Wrocławiu [Library of the

Ossoliński National Institute in Wrocław]. For expressions of a similar sentiment, also see Feliks Koneczny, "Przed konferencyą praską," *Świat Słowiański* 4, vol. 1, no. 7 (1908): 631; and "Po konferencyi praskiej," *Świat Słowiański* 4, vol. 2, no. 8–9 (1908): 708.

99. Koneczny, "Czego chce rząd rosyjski?," 2.
100. Kolbuszewska, "Od historii przez filozofię dziejów po historyczną aksjologię," 26.
101. Feliks Koneczny, "Problem zgody z Rosyą," *Świat Słowiański* 3, vol. 2, no. 10 (1907): 216.
102. Feliks Koneczny, "Słowianoznawstwo a słowianofilstwo (Przemówienie na założenie 'Towarzystwa Słowiańskiego' w Krakowie)," *Świat Słowiański* 9, vol. 1, no. 2 (1913): 67.
103. Koneczny now saw the Turanian-Jewish amalgam threatening Poland and all of Europe. See *Cywilizacja bizantyńska*, 393–94.
104. Feliks Koneczny, *Cywilizacja żydowska* (London: Wydawnictwa Towarzystwa imienia Romana Dmowskiego, 1974), 390. In his introduction, Jędrzej Giertych notes that Koneczny claimed to have most of this book finished by 1934, when his *Plurality of Civilisations* was completed. Giertych gives 1943 as the final date of completion, with a few changes added after that. Ibid., 8.
105. Koneczny, *Polskie logos a ethos*, 2:561.
106. Koneczny, *Dzieje Rosji*, 1:vi.
107. Jedynak, "Aksjologiczne zagadnienia rozwoju cywilizacji według Feliksa Konecznego," 127.
108. Feliks Koneczny, *Dzieje Rosji*, vol. 2, *Litwa a Moskwa w latach 1449–1492* (Wilno: Wileńskie Towarzystwo Przyjaciół Nauk, 1929), 2–6. This book was harshly reviewed by Kazimierz Chodynicki, who called into question Koneczny's knowledge of the Russian language, his broad generalizations about Muscovite culture, his introduction of the term "Letuwa" to designate the non-Slavic populations of Lithuania, and his accentuation of "Turanian" aspects of Muscovite culture at the expense of Byzantine cultural influences that were more generally recognized by scholars. See *Kwartalnik Historyczny* 44 (1930): 386–408. For Koneczny's response, and Chodynicki's final reply, see *Kwartalnik Historyczny* 50 (1936): 175–78, and *Kwartalnik Historyczny* 50 (1936): 584–92. On Koneczny's peculiar distinction between "Letuwa" and "Lithuania," see "Letuwa a Litwa," *Przegląd Powszechny* 39, vol. 155–156 (1922): 38–45.
109. Koneczny, *Dzieje Rosji*, 2:83.
110. Feliks Koneczny, *Dzieje Rosji*, vol. 3, *Schyłek Iwana III, 1492–1505* (London: Wydawnictwa Towarzystwa imienia Roman Dmowskiego, 1984), 202.
111. Koneczny, *Plurality of Civilisations*, 318. Emphasis in the original.
112. Koneczny, *Polskie logos a ethos*, 1:28.
113. Ibid., 2:400.
114. Koneczny, *Polska między wschodem a zachodem*, 50–51. According to Koneczny, throughout history there had been many failed attempts at a synthesis between east and west. Alexander the Great, the Roman Empire, the Byzantine Empire, and most recently Poland had failed to merge two distinct civilizations. In Koneczny's judgment, all such attempts only served to "orientalize" (and therefore diminish) the west. See Koneczny, *Polskie logos a ethos*, 2:319–65.
115. Koneczny, *Dzieje Rosji*, 1:161.
116. As Michał Bohun notes, "It is curious that Koneczny nearly completely ignored the

Byzantine element in the history of Russia." See "Oblicza obsesji," 230. Koneczny consistently minimized Byzantine influence in Russian history, concluding that "Byzantium became only a secondary civilizational force for Rus'; its main source became, unfortunately, Turanianism." See Koneczny, *Prawa dziejowe*, 328. Notably, he argued that Germany is quite "Byzantine" in its culture. "There is no comparison," he concluded: "there is more Byzantinism in the history of the Germans than the Rus!" See Koneczny, *Polskie logos a ethos*, 2:348.

117. Feliks Koneczny, *Dzieje Rosji*, 1:2–3.
118. Koneczny, *Dzieje Rosji*, 3:103. Published only in 1984, the manuscript was completed in 1930. In a text written during the Nazi occupation of Kraków, Koneczny noted that Russia currently had a "Turanian-Jewish mixture"—Bolshevism—which had very nearly created an "a-civilized state." Koneczny, *Prawa dziejowe*, 208.
119. Kuderowicz, "Koncepcja praw historii w ujęciu Feliksa Konecznego," 38.
120. Koneczny, *Dzieje Rosji*, 1:161.
121. Koneczny, *Dzieje Rosji*, 3:103.
122. Koneczny, *Plurality of Civilisations*, 320.
123. Ibid., 271.
124. Kolbuszewska, "Konecznego koncepcja dziejów Rosji," 189. Kolbuszewska therefore places Koneczny in the Eurasianist school of historiography. See also Biliński, *Feliks Koneczny*, 117.
125. Koneczny, *Dzieje Rosji*, 1:132, 232–33.
126. Koneczny, *Plurality of Civilisations*, 297.
127. Koneczny, *Dzieje Rosji*, 3:104.
128. Koneczny, *Dzieje Rosji od najdawniejszych do najnowszych czasów*, 66.
129. Ibid., 83.
130. Ibid., 98.
131. Feliks Koneczny, "Geneza uroszczeń Iwana III do Rusi litewskiej," *Ateneum Wileńskie* 3 (1925–26): 19–20.
132. Koneczny, *Dzieje Rosji*, 2:118. Koneczny even denied Zoe's influence on court ceremony. Turanian influences, not Byzantine, prevailed in this area, too. Ibid., 119.
133. Koneczny, *Dzieje Rosji*, 3:103. In a typically derogatory comment, Koneczny notes that these servitors simply embraced a new language without dropping their Turanian ways. He asserted that a new language had no special meaning for the Mongols, since Asians in general had no concept of national identity.
134. Koneczny noted that after Ivan IV's conquest of Kazan in 1552 there was a considerable influx of migrants into the Muscovite heartland. This served to "Orientalize" Muscovy even more. Koneczny, *Dzieje Rosji od najdawniejszych do najnowszych czasów*, 96–100.
135. Koneczny, *Cywilizacja bizantyńska*, 341.
136. Koneczny, *Prawa dziejowe*, 333.
137. Koneczny, *Polskie logos a ethos*, 2:357.
138. Koneczny, *Dzieje Rosji od najdawniejszych do najnowszych czasów*, 191.
139. Ibid., 191–92.
140. Koneczny, *Cywilizacja żydowska*, 407–9.
141. Ibid., 388.
142. Jan M. Małecki, "Cracow Jews in the 19th Century: Leaving the Ghetto," *Acta Poloniae Historica* 76 (1997): 91.
143. Ibid.

144. Brian Porter, "Antisemitism and the Search for a Catholic Identity," in *Antisemitism and Its Opponents in Modern Poland*, ed. Robert Blobaum (Ithaca, NY: Cornell University Press, 2005), 104.
145. Ibid., 106.
146. Ibid., 106–7.
147. Dariusz Libionka, "Antisemitism, Anti-Judaism, and the Polish Catholic Clergy during the Second World War, 1939–1945," in Blobaum, *Antisemitism and Its Opponents in Modern Poland*, 235.
148. Ibid.
149. Ibid., 237.
150. Szymon Rudnicki, "Anti-Jewish Legislation in Interwar Poland," in Blobaum, *Antisemitism and its Opponents in Modern Poland*, 155–57. Marshal Józef Piłsudski (1867–1935) was a Polish revolutionary and military leader who served as head of state for Poland from 1918 to 1922. Retired from politics but dismayed by the inefficiency of the Republic's parliamentary system, he marched on Warsaw with the support of military units loyal to him and forced the resignation of the government and the president in May 1926. He assumed leadership of the military, rather than the presidency, and was the de facto ruler of Poland until his death.
151. Biliński, *Feliks Koneczny*, 128.
152. Rudnicki, "Anti-Jewish Legislation in Interwar Poland," 166.
153. Ibid., 165.
154. Joanna Beata Michlic, *Poland's Threatening Other: The Image of the Jew from 1880 to the Present* (Lincoln: University of Nebraska Press, 2006), 112–13.
155. Rudnicki, "Anti-Jewish Legislation in Interwar Poland," 166.
156. Ibid., 170.
157. William W. Hagen, "Before the 'Final Solution': Toward a Comparative Analysis of Political Anti-Semitism in Interwar Germany and Poland," *Journal of Modern History* 68, no. 2 (1996): 360.
158. Ibid., 371.
159. Ibid.
160. Ibid., 361.
161. Ibid., 372–74.
162. Ronald Modras, "The Interwar Polish Catholic Press on the Jewish Question," *Annals of the American Academy of Political and Social Science* 548 (November 1996): 182.
163. Ibid., 184.
164. Ibid., 180.
165. Libionka, "Antisemitism, Anti-Judaism, and the Polish Catholic Clergy," 239.
166. Ibid., 240. Emphases in the original.
167. Porter, "Antisemitism and the Search for a Catholic Identity," 115.
168. Łętocha, *Katolicyzm a idea narodowa*, 88–89.
169. Ibid., 284–285.
170. Piotrowski, *Problem filozoficzny ładu społecznego*, 84.
171. Bukowska, *Filozofia polska wobec problemu cywilizacji*, 96.
172. Koneczny, *Cywilizacja żydowska*, 12.
173. Koneczny, *Państwo i prawo w cywilizacji łacińskiej*, 8. Emphasis added.
174. Michlic, *Poland's Threatening Other*, 86–88.

175. Anna Landau-Czajka, "The Image of the Jew in the Catholic Press during the Second Republic," in *Polin: Studies in Polish Jewry*, vol. 8, *Jews in Independent Poland, 1918–1939*, ed. Antony Polonsky, Ezra Mendelsohn and Jerzy Tomaszewski (London: Littman Library of Jewish Civilization, 1994), 167.

176. Koneczny, *Cywilizacja żydowska*, 352–63.

177. Ibid., 311.

178. Ibid., 353.

179. Jerzy Jedlicki, "Resisting the Wave: Intellectuals against Antisemitism in the Last Years of the 'Polish Kingdom,'" in Blobaum, *Antisemitism and Its Opponents in Modern Poland*, 61.

180. Ibid., 63.

181. Ibid., 61.

182. Robert Blobaum, introduction to *Antisemitism and Its Opponents in Modern Poland*, 6.

183. Michlic, *Poland's Threatening Other*, 92–93.

184. Feliks Koneczny, "Problem Polski obok Prus," *Świat Słowiański* 9, vol. 1, no. 3 (1913): 170.

185. Alexander Victor Prusin, *Nationalizing a Borderland: War, Ethnicity, and Anti-Jewish Violence in East Galicia, 1914–1920* (Tuscaloosa: University of Alabama Press, 2005), 67.

186. Koneczny, *Cywilizacja żydowska*, 354–55.

187. Ibid., 374–375.

188. Michlic, *Poland's Threatening Other*, 115.

189. Ibid., 97.

190. Ibid., 114, 124.

191. Malgorzata Domagalska, "Antisemitic Discourse in Polish Nationalist Weeklies Between 1918 and 1939," *East European Jewish Affairs* 36, no. 2 (December 2006): 191.

192. Ibid., 192.

193. Ibid.

194. Ibid.

195. Ibid.

196. Michlic, *Poland's Threatening Other*, 100, 171. Emphases added.

197. Koneczny, *Państwo i prawo w cywilizacji łacińskiej*, 8.

198. Koneczny referred to this as the "Shylock method." See Koneczny, *Państwo i prawo w cywilizacji łacińskiej*, 37. In his analyses, Adolf Nowaczyński used the term "Shylockracja." See Małgorzata Domagalska, *Antysemityzm dla inteligencji? Kwestia żydowska w publicystyce Adolfa Nowaczyńskiego na łamach "Myśli Narodowej" (1921–1934) i "Prosto z mostu" (1935–1939) (na tle porównawczym)* (Warsaw: Żydowski Instytut Historyczny, 2004), 180, 182.

199. Koneczny, *Cywilizacja żydowska*, 176.

200. Koneczny, *Plurality of Civilisations*, 275.

201. Koneczny, *Polskie logos a ethos*, 2:539. Ewa Maj has explored commentary by nationalist ideologues who also saw a similarity in Jewish and German desires for "domination of the world, for the disruption of the existing social and political order, for the weakening of Christianity as the moral foundation of European nations." See Maj, *Związek Ludowo-Narodowy*, 194.

202. Koneczny, *Cywilizacja żydowska*, 352–63. For a recent Konecznian analysis of

German-Jewish plots for the creation of a "state within a state," see Andrzej Leszek Szcześniak, *Judeopolonia: żydowskie państwie polskim* (Radom: Polskie Wydawnictwo Encyklopedyczne, 2004).

203. Koneczny, *Prawa dziejowe*, 161.
204. Koneczny, *Cywilizacja żydowska*, 363.
205. Ibid., 389. For similar commentary, also see Koneczny, *Prawa dziejowe*, 208ff.
206. Landau-Czajka, "Image of the Jew in the Catholic Press," 160.
207. Łętocha, *Katolicyzm a idea narodowa*, 251–53.
208. Dariusz Ratajczak, "O cywilizacjach," *dariuszratajczak.blogspot.com,* http://dari uszratajczak.blogspot.com/2009/01/o-cywilizacjach.html (accessed 26 May 2009).
209. Andrzej Horodecki, "Sejmowe słodycze," *Myśl Polska,* no. 1–2 (5–12 January 2003), http://www.myslpolska.icenter.pl/ (accessed 26 March 2005).
210. Koneczny, *Cywilizacja żydowska*, 125. For further commentary, see Bokiej, *Cywilizacja łacińska*, 99–100; and Anna Tylki-Szymańska, "Kościół katolicki wobec cywilizacji w Europie według teorii Feliksa Konecznego," *Studia nad Rodziną* 7, no. 2 (2003): 190.
211. Łętocha, *Katolicyzm a idea narodowa*, 250–51.
212. Koneczny, *Cywilizacja żydowska*, 120. Koneczny used other controversial sources in his work. For example, he extensively cited Rev. Stanisław Trzeciak (1873–1944). Trzeciak's *Mesjanizm a kwestia żydowska* (1934) "belonged to the 'classics' of interwar antisemitic literature….He was a national and international 'expert' on the 'Jewish question,' his international fame resting on his activitiy in the Nazi-sponsored Institut zur Erforschung der Judenfrage (Institute for Research of the Jewish Question), headquartered in Erfurt." See Libionka, "Antisemitism, Anti-Judaism, and the Polish Catholic Clergy," 257.
213. Tadeusz Zieliński, *Hellenizm a Judaizm*, 2 vols. (Warsaw: Wydawnictwo J. Mortkowicza, 1927), 1:2.
214. Ibid.
215. Ibid., 3.
216. Ibid.
217. See Grott, *Nacjonalizm i religia*, 128–29; Grott, *Nacjonalizm Chrześcijański*, 82–83; and Łętocha, *Katolicyzm a idea narodowa*, 250–51. It bears mentioning that Jędrzej Giertych, a leading ideologue of the *endek* youth in the 1930s and publisher of Koneczny's works in postwar London, also denied any Jewish-Christian ties in the traditional sense. See Artur Domosławski, "Saga rodu Giertychów—część II," *gazeta.pl,* http://serwisy.gazeta.pl/kraj/1,62905,1074233.html (accessed 10 June 2005). Originally published in *Gazeta Wyborcza,* 18 October 2002.
218. Feliks Koneczny, "Geneza Judeocentryzmu," *Myśl Narodowa* 9, no. 1 (6 January 1929): 4.
219. Ibid.
220. Ibid., 5
221. Koneczny, *Cywilizacja żydowska*, 372.
222. Ibid., 386.
223. Ibid.
224. Koneczny, *Cywilizacja bizantyńska*, 327.
225. Koneczny, *Cywilizacja żydowska*, 17. For a concise discussion, see Feliks Koneczny, *Protestantyzm w życiu zbiorowym* (Warszawa: Wydawnictwo "Milla," n.d), 16–18. This work was originally published in 1938.

226. Ibid., 43. Likewise, Judaism is "a defective religion." Ibid., 32.
227. Koneczny, *Plurality of Civilisations*, 252.
228. Koneczny, *Cywilizacja żydowska*, 177.
229. Koneczny, *Prawa dziejowe*, 23–24.
230. Koneczny, *Plurality of Civilisations*, 252.
231. Koneczny, *Cywilizacja żydowska*, 38.
232. Koneczny, *Plurality of Civilisations*, 252. Koneczny notes that a third source, the kabbalah, was later added to the mix.
233. Koneczny, *Cywilizacja żydowska*, 39.
234. Ibid., 176. For Koneczny's discussion of this "sickness" in the form of excessive legislation and bloated government, see " 'Elephantiasis' prawodawcza," *Myśl Narodowa* 12, no. 55 (18 December 1932): 798–801.
235. Ibid., 32.
236. Libionka, "Antisemitism, Anti-Judaism, and the Polish Catholic Clergy," 236.
237. Feliks Koneczny, *Religie a cywilizacje* (Krzeszowice: Dom Wydawniczy "Ostoja," 2004), 10.
238. Ibid., 39.
239. Koneczny, *Plurality of Civilisations*, 284. Another civilizational theorist from the time, Arnold Toynbee, regarded Jews as "fossilized relics." See Arnold Toynbee, *A Study of History* (London: Oxford University Press, 1935), 1:51.
240. Koneczny, *Cywilizacja żydowska*, 256–57.
241. Ibid., 180.
242. Ibid., 397.
243. Ibid., 405.
244. Ibid., 100, 105, and 108.
245. Koneczny, *Plurality of Civilisations*, 256.
246. Łętocha, *Katolicyzm a idea narodowa*, 248.
247. Koneczny, *Cywilizacja żydowska*, 40.
248. Ibid., 163–67.
249. Ibid., 153. See also Feliks Koneczny, "Nauka a cywilizacje," in *O cywilizację łacińską* (Krzeszowice: Dom Wydawniczy "Ostoja," 2006), 16.
250. Ibid., 141.
251. Ibid., 153.
252. Koneczny, *Rozwój moralności*, 347.
253. Koneczny, "Nauka a cywilizacje," 15.
254. Koneczny, *Cywilizacja żydowska*, 43.
255. Ibid.
256. Koneczny, "Nauka a cywilizacje," 16.
257. Koneczny, *Rozwój moralności*, 348.
258. Koneczny, *Cywilizacja żydowska*, 161.
259. Ibid., 383.
260. Ibid., 236, 257. See also Koneczny, *Prawa dziejowe*, 76.
261. Alan E. Steinweis, *Studying the Jew: Scholarly Antisemitism in Nazi Germany* (Cambridge, MA: Harvard University Press, 2006), 29.
262. Ibid., 46–49.
263. Ibid., 75.
264. Zieliński, *Hellenizm a Judaizm*, 2:86.
265. Ibid., 1:133.

266. Ibid., 174.
267. Steinweis, *Studying the Jew*, 80.
268. Ibid., 81.
269. Zieliński, *Hellenizm a Judaizm*, 2:36.
270. Steinweis, *Studying the Jew*, 82.
271. Szurgot, *Prawo jako fundament cywilizacji łacińskie*, 46.
272. Katarzyna Stańczak-Wiślicz, "W pułapce kołobłędu, czyli antysemityzm uczo-
    nego," *Nigdy Więcej* 16 (Winter–Spring 2008): 19.
273. Feliks Koneczny, "Amoralność życia gospodarczego," in *O sprawach ekonomicznych*
    (Kraków: Wydawnictwo WAM, 2000), 121–22. This essay was originally published
    in 1933.
274. Koneczny discussed the role of Jews in the Polish rural economy in detail in *Skrót
    do dziejów włościaństwa w Polsce* (Wilno: Nakładem Księgarni Jozefa Zawadzkiego,
    1921). See especially 38–50.
275. Koneczny, *Cywilizacja bizantyńska*, 334–35.
276. This refers to the period from 1648 to 1667, during which the Polish-Lithuanian
    Commonwealth endured rebellions and invasions. The Swedish invasion was the
    backdrop for volume 2 (*Potop*, The Deluge) of Henryk Sienkiewicz's trilogy of his-
    torical novels set in the seventeenth century, which was published in 1886.
277. Koneczny, *Święci w dziejach narodu polskiego*, 412–13.
278. Koneczny, *Polska między wschodem a zachodem*, 47.
279. Ibid.
280. Koneczny, *Kościół w Polsce wobec cywilizacji*, 15–16.
281. Koneczny, *Plurality of Civilisations*, 322. Emphasis in original.

CHAPTER FOUR. KONECZNY'S INTELLECTUAL CONTEXT AND LEGACY

1. Leopold von Ranke (1795–1886) was a prominent German historian and advocate
    of the scientific method in historical research; he emphasized the critical use of
    primary sources in order to explain events as they actually happened.
2. Kolbuszewska, "Reorientacje w historiografii polskiej," 112.
3. Ibid., 119, 123.
4. Ibid., 119.
5. Andrzej F. Grabski, "Feliks Koneczny a mutacja modernistyczna w historiografii
    polskiej," in Skoczyński, *Feliks Koneczny dzisiaj*, 11–15. See also Jolanta Kolbusze-
    wska, "Przełom antypozytywistyczny czy mutacja modernistyczna? Rozważania o
    przemianach w historiografii schyłku XIX i początku XX wieku," in "Między mod-
    ernizmem a postmodernizmem w historiografii," ed. Jan Pomorski, special issue,
    Res Historica 19 (2005): 53.
6. Kolbuszewska, "Przełom antypozytywistyczny czy mutacja modernistyczna?,"
    48–49.
7. Michał Graban, "Supremacja sił duchowych w cywilizacji łacińskiej," in Skoczyński,
    Feliks Koneczny dzisiaj, 146.
8. Koneczny, *O ład w historii*, 7.

9. Graban, "Supremacja sił duchowych w cywilizacji łacińskiej," 154.
10. Chazbijewicz, "Feliks Koneczny i jego filozofia cywilizacji," 9.
11. Milcarek, "Feliks Koneczny i jego synteza historii Polski," 224–25.
12. Chazbijewicz, "Feliks Koneczny i jego filozofia cywilizacji," 9.
13. Kolbuszewska, "Reorientacje w historiografii polskiej," 117–18.
14. Ibid., 124.
15. Koneczny, *Etyki a cywilizacje*, 7.
16. Kuderowicz, "Koncepcja praw historii w ujęciu Feliksa Konecznego," 40.
17. Koneczny, *O ład w historii*, 17.
18. Bokiej, *Cywilizacja łacińska*, 19.
19. Bukowska, *Filozofia polska wobec problemu cywilizacji*, 8–9.
20. Skoczyński, *Idee historiozoficzne Feliksa Konecznego*, 12, 23–34.
21. Bukowska, *Filozofia polska wobec problemu cywilizacji*, 21.
22. Pucek, "Feliks Koneczny: teoria pluralizmu cywilizacyjnego,"157–58.
23. Bukowska, *Filozofia polska wobec problemu cywilizacji*, 125.
24. Kolbuszewska, "Reorientacje w historiografii polskiej," 121.
25. Ibid. Here Kolbuszewska is citing *Prawa dziejowe*.
26. Ibid.
27. Ibid., 124.
28. Bukowska, *Filozofia polska wobec problemu cywilizacji*, 31–33.
29. Joachim Diec, *Cywilizacje bez okien. Teoria Mikołaja Danilewskiego i późniejsze koncepcje monadycznych formacji socjokulturowych* (Kraków: Wydawnictwo Uniwersytetu Jagiellońskiego, 2002), 139. See Erazm Majewski, *Nauka o cywilizacjyi*, vol. 2, *Teorya człowieka i cywilizacji* (Warsaw: E. Wende i S-ka, 1910), http://www.prawia.org/ksiazki/majewski/majewski2f.html (accessed 23 August 2009); and Grażyna Szumera, *Cywilizacja w myśli polskiej: Poglądy filozoficzno-społeczne Erazma Majewskiego* (Katowice: Wydawnictwo Uniwersytetu Śląskiego, 2007), 155.
30. Koneczny, *Plurality of* Civilisations, 58–59.
31. Robert Piotrowski, "Dwie doktryny cywilizacyjne. Koneczny a Majewski," *Archiwum Historii Filozofii i Myśli Społecznej* 52 (2007): 219.
32. Ibid., 224.
33. Toynbee, *A Study of History*, 1:150.
34. Vasilenko, "Dialogue of Cultures, Dialogue of Civilizations," 7.
35. Toynbee, *A Study of History*, 1:151.
36. Andrzej Piskozub, "Feliks Koneczny (1862–1949) jako pionier nauki o cywilizacji w Polsce," *Kultura i Edukacja*, no. 1 (1999): 135–36.
37. Bukowska, *Filozofia polska wobec problemu cywilizacji*, 139.
38. Pucek, "Feliks Koneczny: teoria pluralizmu cywilizacyjnego," 155.
39. Skoczyński, *Koneczny. Teoria cywilizacji*, 179.
40. Pucek, "Feliks Koneczny: teoria pluralizmu cywilizacyjnego," 157.
41. Piotr Bezat, *Teoria cywilizacji Feliksa Konecznego* (Krzeszowice: Dom Wydawniczy "Ostoja," 2004), 12.
42. Koneczny, *Plurality of Civilisations*, 325. Emphasis in original.
43. Dawson, *Dynamics of World History*, 42.
44. Ibid., 43–44.
45. Ibid., 80.
46. Ibid.

47. Janusz Mucha, "Sociology in Eastern Europe or East European Sociology: Historical and Present," Institute of Sociology, Academia Sinica, Taiwan, 7; http://www.ios .sinica.edu.tw/cna/download/5b_Mucha_2.pdf (accessed 24 August 2009). Text of a paper delivered at "Challenges for Sociology in an Unequal World: Conference of the Council for National Associations" (Taiwan, 23–25 March 2009).

48. Dawson, *Dynamics of World History*, 81.

49. Ibid.

50. Ibid., 81–83.

51. Ibid., 238. This passage comes from "Bolshevism and the Bourgeoisie" (1932).

52. Ibid., 241–42. This passage also comes from "Bolshevism and the Bourgeoisie" (1932).

53. Skoczyński, *Idee historiozoficzne Feliksa Konecznego*, 12.

54. Ibid., 23–24.

55. Ibid., 31.

56. Ibid., 32.

57. Ibid.

58. Piotrowski, *Problem filozoficzny ładu społecznego*, 16.

59. Othmar F. Anderle, "A Plea for Theoretical History," *History and Theory* 4, no. 1 (1964): 30.

60. Ibid.

61. Ibid., 31.

62. Ibid.

63. Ibid., 34.

64. Ibid.

65. John Lukacs, *Historical Consciousness: The Remembered Past* (New Brunswick, NJ: Transaction Publishers, 1994), 260.

66. Skoczyński, *Idee historiozoficzne Feliksa Konecznego*, 129–33.

67. Mucha, "Sociology in Eastern Europe or East European Sociology," 7.

68. Pucek, "Feliks Koneczny: teoria pluralizmu cywilizacyjnego," 159.

69. Ibid.

70. Ibid., 173.

71. Ibid.

72. Piskozub, "Feliks Koneczny (1862–1949) jako pionier nauk," 137.

73. Mucha, "Sociology in Eastern Europe or East European Sociology," 8.

74. Ibid., 8–9.

75. Ibid., 9.

76. Stanisław Jojczyk, "Relacja państwo-społeczeństwo u Feliksa Konecznego," in Skoczyński, *Feliks Koneczny dzisiaj*, 247.

77. Skoczyński, *Idee historiozoficzne Feliksa Konecznego*, 53–57. For more on Durkheim, see also 65 and 90.

78. See Goćkowski, "Konecznego model dziejów powszechnych," 21–34.

79. On Kurnatowski, see Andrew Kier Wise, "Jerzy Kurnatowski and Polish Solidarism," *Polish Review* 46, no. 3 (2001): 327–44.

80. Bokiej, *Cywilizacja łacińska*, 120.

81. Skoczyński, *Idee historiozoficzne Feliksa Konecznego*, 105.

82. Jedynak, *Naród społeczeństwo państwo*, 132.

83. Skoczyński, *Idee historiozoficzne Feliksa Konecznego*, 103.

84. Ibid., 61–63.
85. Ibid., 72.
86. Ibid., 83.
87. Ibid., 103–4.
88. Jean Floud, Review of Koneczny's *The Plurality of Civilisations*, *History & Theory* 4, no. 2 (1965): 271.
89. Anton Hilckman, "Feliks Koneczny and the Comparative Science of Civilisation," 11. Koneczny claimed that there are seven civilizations. Four are ancient: Brahman, Jewish, Chinese, and Turanian. Three developed in the Middle Ages: Byzantine, Latin, and Arabic.
90. Maciej Giertych, "Z nauczania Feliksa Konecznego," *Opoka w Kraju* 18, no. 39 (June 1996), http://opoka.giertych.pl/owk18.htm (accessed 30 June 2008).
91. Augustyn Baran, "Głębie i mielizny Feliksa Konecznego," *Athenaeum* 8 (2002): 173–75.
92. Goćkowski, "Konecznego model dziejów powszechnych," 27.
93. Bębenek, "Paradygmat polityki w cywilizacji łacińskiej," 90–91.
94. Kuderowicz, "Koncepcja praw historii w ujęciu Feliksa Konecznego," 41.
95. Jan Skoczyński, "Trzecia droga (O metodzie historiozoficznej Feliksa Konecznego)," *Historyka* 18 (1988): 68.
96. Jedynak, "Aksjologiczne zagadnienie rozwoju cywilizacji według Feliksa Konecznego," 127.
97. Bukowska, "Metodologiczne aspekty historiozoficznej koncepcji Felksa Konecznego," 296.
98. Jan Wróbel, "Bobrzyński miał rację, ale był za łagodny. Jan Wróbel rozmawia z Henrykiem Samsonowiczem," *Dziennik.pl.* http://www.dziennik.pl/dziennik/eu ropa/46814.html (accessed 29 August 2009). Originally published in *Europa*, no. 49 (9 March 2005).
99. Wojciech Wierzejski, "Prymat etyki, zwierzchnictwo moralności," *Blog Wojciecha Wierzejskiego* (19 November 2006), http://wierzejski.blog.onet.pl/2,ID150782916, index.html (accessed 17 December 2007).
100. Bokiej, *Cywilizacja łacińska*, 9.
101. Jedynak, "Aksjologiczne zagadnienie rozwoju cywilizacji według Feliksa Konecznego," 127.
102. Konrad Niklewicz, "Maciej Giertych znów szokuje eurodeputowanych," *Gazeta Wyborcza*, 16 February 2007, http://www.gazetawyborcza.pl/gazetawyborcza /2029020,76842,3923332.html (accessed 1 March 2007).
103. Mucha, "Sociology in Eastern Europe or East European Sociology, 9.
104. Semelin, *Purify and Destroy*, 27.
105. Leonidas Donskis, *Forms of Hatred: The Troubled Imagination in Modern Philosophy and Literature* (Amsterdam: Rodopi, 2003), 7.
106. Neumann, *Uses of the Other*, 17.
107. Rüsen, "Some Theoretical Approaches," 6.
108. Rüsen, "Introduction: Historical Thinking as Intercultural Discourse," 2.
109. Ibid., 3.
110. Rüsen, "Some Theoretical Approaches," 6.
111. Ibid., 7.
112. For a related discussion on Toynbee, see Paul Rich, "Civilisations in European and

World History: A Reappraisal of the Ideas of Arnold Toynbee, Fernand Braudel and Marshall Hodgson," *European Legacy* 7, no. 3 (2002): 333.

113. Jacinta O'Hagan, "A 'Clash of Civilizations'?" in *Contending Images of World Politics*, ed. Greg Fry and Jacinta O'Hagan (New York: St. Martin's Press, 2000), 139.

114. Rüsen, "Some Theoretical Approaches," 7.

115. Adamovsky, "Euro-Orientalism," 591.

116. Alatas, "Eurocentrism," 760.

117. Adamovsky, "Euro-Orientalism," 623. Adamovsky is referring to David Cannadine's *Ornamentalism: How the British Saw Their Empire* (Oxford: Oxford University Press, 2001).

118. Alatas, "Eurocentrism," 762.

119. Ibid.

120. Donskis, *Forms of Hatred*, xiii.

121. Ibid., 232.

122. Rüsen, "Some Theoretical Approaches," 11.

123. Koneczny, *Plurality of Civilisations*, 101.

124. Ibid., 102.

125. Ibid., 129.

126. Koneczny, *Rozwój moralności*, 14–15.

127. Ibid., 74.

128. Koneczny, *Plurality of Civilisations*, 106.

129. Robert Piotrowski also critically appraises Koneczny's sources, noting that he primarily used secondary sources (an unavoidable methodology in such syntheses) and accounts by European travelers, such as missionaries, officers, or colonial officials. Of the 162 sources cited in *Plurality of Civilisations*, Piotrowski finds almost one-fourth (39) are travel accounts or memoirs, while the rest are mainly anthropological and sociological texts or works on religion. Twenty-three sources deal with philosophy broadly understood, including historiosophical works. See Piotrowski, *Problem filozoficzny ładu społecznego*, 6. Koneczny's selection of source materials and the conclusions drawn from them is thus representative of the duality of the Polish colonial experience; his superior attitude to other civilizations is derived in part from the imperial projects of other Europeans, even while he chafes at German, Russian, and Jewish domination and strives to prove the superiority of Latin civilization in his theories.

130. Koneczny, *Plurality of Civilisations*, 184.

131. See ibid., 185–86. Here Koneczny discusses cases from Brazil and Central Asia.

132. Ibid., 196–97. Emphasis in the original.

133. In the Konecznian system there is a hierarchy of languages. Koneczny contended that language can help or hinder civilizational progress: "Is a language incapable of forming a fairly involved compound sentence a suitable tool for the expression of abstractions? For where abstractions cannot be exactly and conveniently formulated, how…can the higher reaches of knowledge be cultivated in such a language?" (ibid., 244). A moribund society can benefit by embracing a new language. As Koneczny asserted, the "*newly* adopted language carries forward an *old* civilisation.…The historical importance of languages is thus extreme, and their influence incomparably greater than that of race. And what was out of place in the case of race is entirely in order in referring to languages: *there exists a hierarchy of languages*,

according to the degree of their capacity for development [emphases in original]."
(ibid., 245).

134. Bukowska, *Filozofia polska wobec problemu cywilizacji*, 43–45.
135. Pucek, "Feliks Koneczny: teoria pluralizmu cywilizacyjnego," 173.
136. Bukowska, *Filozofia polska wobec problemu cywilizacji*, 120.
137. Rüsen, "Some Theoretical Approaches," 10.
138. Ibid., 11.
139. Kolbuszewska, "Od historii przez filozofię dziejów po historyczną aksjologię," 24.
140. Brzózka, "Polityka międzynarodowa w cywilizacji łacińskiej," 26.
141. Ibid., 28.
142. Gondek, "Rola Kościoła w kulturze polskiej," 91–92.
143. Bukowska, *Filozofia polska wobec problemu cywilizacji*, 132–33. See also Pawlak, "Feliks Koneczny o rozwoju moralności," 141.
144. Skoczyński, *Idee historiozoficzne Feliksa Konecznego*, 114.
145. Ibid.
146. Pucek, *Pluralizm cywilizacyjny jako perspektywa myśli socjologicznej*, 109.
147. Wituch, "Religia jako rdzeń cywilizacji," 79.
148. Koneczny, *O ład w historii*, 10.
149. Koneczny, *Państwo i prawo w cywilizacji łacińskiej*, 15.
150. Bokiej, *Cywilizacja łacińska*, 53–54.
151. Koneczny, *Prawa dziejowe*, 45.
152. Gawor, *O wielości cywilizacji*, 119–20.
153. Ibid., 137–38.
154. Clare A. Simmons, introduction to *Medievalism and the Quest for the "Real" Middle Ages*, ed. Clare A. Simmons (London: Frank Cass, 2001), 12.
155. Ibid.
156. Ibid., 16
157. Ibid., 17.
158. Norman F. Cantor, *Inventing the Middle Ages: The Lives, Works, and Ideas of the Great Medievalists of the Twentieth Century* (New York: Quill, William Morrow & Co., 1991), 43.
159. Koneczny, *Rozwój moralności*, 205.
160. Sonia Bukowska, "Feliksa Konecznego historiozoficzna refleksja nad narodem," *Folia Philosophica* 20 (2002): 244.
161. Stefan Auer, *Liberal Nationalism in Central Europe* (London: Routledge Curzon, 2004), 57.
162. Ryba, "Człowiek, naród, państwo w cywilizacji łacińskiej."
163. Koneczny, *Teoria Grunwaldu*, 23.
164. Ibid., 25.
165. Bukowska, *Filozofia polska wobec problemu cywilizacji*, 68.
166. See his essay on *The Use and Abuse of History* (1873).
167. Bukowska, *Filozofia polska wobec problemu cywilizacji*, 68.
168. Skoczyński, *Idee historiozoficzne Feliksa Konecznego*, 110–12.
169. Koneczny, *Państwo i prawo w cywilizacji łacińskiej*, 132.
170. Piotrowski, *Problem filozoficzny ładu społecznego*, 44, 69, 128. For examples, see Koneczny, *Prawa dziejowe*, 119, 124–25.
171. Ratajczak, "O cywilizacjach."

172. Ibid.
173. Koneczny, *Cywilizacja bizantyńska*, 17.
174. Waldemar Ceran, *Historia i bibliografia rozumowana bizantynologii polskiej (1800–1998)* (Łódź: Wydawnictwo Uniwersytetu Łódzkiego, 2001), 1:343.
175. Bokiej, *Cywilizacja łacińska*, 90.
176. Salamon, "Bizancjum Feliksa Konecznego," 170, 174–75, 178.
177. Dąbrowska, "La vision moscoutaire de Byzance," 258. Dąbrowska is very critical of Koneczny's work, noting his poor research on the Byzantine world and his insistence on its Asiatic features.
178. See Averil Cameron, "Byzance dans le débat sur l'orientalisme," in *Byzance en Europe*, ed. Marie-France Auzépy (Saint-Denis: Presses Universitaires de Vincennes, 2003), 235.
179. Dimiter G. Angelov, "The Making of Byzantinism," Kokkalis Program on Southeastern and East-Central Europe (Harvard University, John F. Kennedy School of Government), http://www.hks.harvard.edu/kokkalis/GSW1/GSW1/01%20Angelov.pdf (accessed 30 June 2008).
180. Ibid.
181. Ibid.
182. Ibid.
183. McCormick, "Byzantium's Role in the Formation of Early Medieval Civilization," 209.
184. Bokiej, *Cywilizacja łacińska*, 71–80.
185. Said, *Orientalism*, 290.
186. Koneczny, *Plurality of Civilisations*, 300.
187. Said, *Orientalism*, 70.
188. Piotr Jaroszyński, "Anton Adam Hilckman: Polacy i Niemcy," in *Naród ma trwać!* (Warszawa: Dom Polski, 2006), 218.
189. Anton Hilckman, "Introduction," 6.
190. Piotr Jaroszyński, *Polska i Europa* (Lublin: Instytut Edukacji Narodowej, 1999), 28.
191. Anton Hilckman, "Introduction," 7.
192. Anton Hilckman, "Rusia y Europa. Aspectos culturales," *Razón y Fe. Revista Hispano-Americana de Cultura* 155, no. 708 (1957): 17.
193. Ibid., 22.
194. Said, *Orientalism*, 300.
195. Anton Hilckman, "Qu'est-ce que l'occident? Essai d'un exposé de la doctrine européenne de Feliks Koneczny," *Sacrum Poloniae millennium: rozprawy, szkice, materialy, historyczne* 12 (1966): 535. Emphasis in original.
196. Hilckman, "Feliks Koneczny and the Comparative Science of Civilisation," 27. Emphases in original.
197. Koneczny, *Rozwój moralności*, 207.
198. Koneczny, *Plurality of Civilisations*, 318.
199. Ibid.
200. Bukowska, *Filozofia polska wobec problemu cywilizacji*, 8.
201. S. L. Shneiderman, "'High' Anti-Semitism Revived," *Midstream* 22 (August/September 1976): 76–81.
202. Piskozub, "Feliks Koneczny (1862–1949) jako pionier," 137.
203. Shneiderman, "'High' Anti-Semitism Revived," 80.

204. Koneczny, *Cywilizacja żydowska*, 340–342.
205. Ibid., 9. Koneczny was also alive at the time of the 11 August 1945 attacks that killed five Jews in Kraków. Rumors of ritual murder by Jews served as the pretext; this was also the justification cited for the pogrom in Kielce on 4 July 1946, in which forty-two Jews died of injuries suffered. See Bożena Szaynok, "The Role of Antisemitism in Postwar Polish-Jewish Relations," in Blobaum, *Antisemitism and Its Opponents in Modern Poland*, 272. See also Michlic, *Poland's Threatening Other*, 210.
206. Richard Pipes, "Polish Sovietology in the Lead-up to the Cold War," *Journal of Cold War Studies* 13, no. 2 (Spring 2011): 189.
207. Ibid., 190.
208. Joanna Michlic, "The Soviet Occupation of Poland, 1939–41, and the Stereotype of the Anti-Polish and Pro-Soviet Jew," *Jewish Social Studies: History, Culture, Society*, n.s., 13, no. 3 (Spring/Summer 2007): 140.
209. Koneczny, *Cywilizacja żydowska*, 8.
210. Ibid., 9.
211. Tomasz Zarycki, "Polska i jej regiony a debata postkolonialna," in *Oblicze polityczne regionów Polski*, ed. M. Dajnowicz (Białystok: Wyższa Szkoła Finansów i Zarządzania, 2008), 41.
212. Wierzbicki, *Naród-Państwo w polskiej myśli historycznej*, 14–15.
213. Wierzbicki, *Spory o polską duszę*, 252. The reference is to Feliks Koneczny's *Polskie logos a ethos*, 2 vols.
214. Peter Childs and R. J. Patrick Williams, *An Introduction to Post-Colonial Theory* (London: Prentice Hall / Harvester Wheatsheaf, 1997), 110.
215. Janion, *Niesamowita Słowiańszczyzna*, 7ff.
216. While Koneczny highlighted the avaricious behavior of the Russian, German, and Austrian empires in relation to Poland's dismemberment in the eighteenth century, he did not judge Polish expansionism so harshly. Historian Stephen Velychenko points out that Koneczny characterized the Polish role in the *kresy* as benign, if not beneficial. He explains that "Koneczny introduced the term 'Jagiellonian idea' into general histories of Poland, which seemed aptly to summarize the amalgam of messianic/nationalistic ideas characteristic of late nineteenth- and early twentieth-century Polish thought." See Stephen Velychenko, *National History as Cultural Process: A Survey of the Interpretations of Ukraine's Past in Polish, Russian, and Ukrainian Historical Writing from the Earliest Times to 1914* (Edmonton: Canadian Institute of Ukrainian Studies Press, University of Alberta, 1992), 43. Koneczny described the peaceful Polish-Lithuanian union as "the most beautiful example for other European nations." See Koneczny, *Święci w dziejach narodu polskiego*, 335.
217. Tomasz Zarycki, "Uses of Russia: The Role of Russia in the Modern Polish National Identity," *East European Politics and Societies* 18, no. 4 (2004): 625.
218. Melegh, *On the East-West Slope*, 9.
219. Ibid., 29. Emphasis in original.
220. Tomasz Banach, "Rzymski ideał prawa w katolickim państwie narodu polskiego," *Cywilizacja: o nauce, moralności, sztuce i religii* 12 (2005): 77.
221. Andrzej Horodecki, "O zdrowiu w cywilizacji łacińskiej," *Nowy Przegląd Wszechpolski* 10, no. 3–4 (2003), http://www.npw.pl/ARCHIWUM_NPW/2003_03_04/PIS-Horodecki_o_zdrowiu.html (accessed 28 November 2008). Emphasis in the original.

222. Koneczny, *Teatr Krakowski*, 41.
223. Feliks Koneczny, "O pierwotnej polskości Rusi Czerwonej," *Świat Słowiański* 9, vol. 1, no. 4 (1913): 228.
224. Skrzydlewski, *Polityka w cywilizacji łacińskiej*, 81–85.
225. Ibid., 100.
226. Mariusz Kowalski, "Electoral Behaviour in Poland as the Effect of the 'Clash of Civilization,'" *Geografický Časopis* 54, no. 3 (2002): 219–37; "Polaryzacja zachowań wyborczych w Polsce jako rezultat cywilizacyjnego rozdarcia kraju," in *Przestrzeń wyborcza Polski*, ed. Mariusz Kowalski (Warsaw: Oddział Akademicki PTG, Instytut Geografii i Przestrzennego Zagospodarowania PAN, 2003), 11–48; and "Regional Differentiation of Electoral Behaviour in Countries of Central and Eastern Europe as the Effect of the 'Civilisation Clash,'" *Revista Română de Geografie Politică* 3, no. 1 (2001): 77–90.
227. Andrzej Chodubski, "Uwarunkowania cywilizacyjne przystąpienia Polski do Unii Europejskiej," in *Polska między zachodem a wschodem w dobie integracji europejskiej*, ed. Maria Marczewska-Rytko (Lublin: Wydawnictwo Uniwersytetu Marii Curie-Skłodowskiej, 2001), 22.
228. Jan Kieniewicz, *Wprowadzenie do historii cywilizacji Wschodu i Zachod* (Warsaw: Wydawnictwo Akademickie Dialog, 2003), 354, 357, 361, 364, and 367–68.
229. Ibid., 368.
230. Ibid., 140.
231. Ibid., 147.
232. Jan Kieniewicz, "East and West: Civilisations and Their History," *Wydział Orientalistyczny Uniw. Warszawskiego*, http://www.orient.uw.edu.pl/pl/iss/jk-main.htm (accessed 20 March 2006). See also Jan Kieniewicz, "Is Dialogue Between Civilizations Possible?" *Uniwersytet Warszawski. Instytut Badań Interdyscyplinarnych "Artes Liberales,"* http://www.obta.uw.edu.pl/~zoja/Kieniewiczdialog_cywilizacji_ang%5B1%5D.pdf (accessed 27 August 2009).
233. Arkady Rzegocki, "Mirosława Dzielskiego rozważania o cywilizacji," *Ośrodek Myśli Politycznej*, http://www.omp.org.pl/index.php?module=subjects&func=viewpage&pageid=56 (accessed 23 June 2006).
234. Ibid.
235. Mirosław Dzielski, "Powrót cywilizacji," in *Odrodzenie ducha—budowa wolności. Pisma zebrane*, ed. Grzegorz Łuczkiewicz (Kraków: Znak, 1995), 277.
236. Rzegocki, "Mirosława Dzielskiego rozważania o cywilizacji."
237. Miłowit Kuniński, "Mirosław Dzielski—polityka polska w perspektywie cywilizacyjnej," *Ośrodek Myśli Politycznej*, http://www.omp.org.pl/index.php?module=subjects&func=viewpage&pageid=54 (accessed 23 June 2006). Also in Skoczyński, *Feliks Koneczny dzisiaj*, 133–44.
238. See Romuald Piekarski, "Prymat etyki w życiu publicznym. Dyskusja tezy Konecznego," in Skoczyński, *Feliks Koneczny dzisiaj*, 236n13.
239. Rzegocki, "Mirosława Dzielskiego rozważania o cywilizacji."
240. Miłowit Kuniński, "Mirosław Dzielski—polityka polska w perspektywie cywilizacyjnej."
241. Mirosław Dzielski, "Kilka uwag o obyczaju złej pracy w Polsce," in *Odrodzenie ducha—budowa wolności*, 121.
242. However, "Dzielski did not share Koneczny's conviction that the penetration of

different civilizations is not possible and he reckoned that neighboring civilizations would have a strong effect on one another." See Miłowit Kuniński, "Liberalizm chrześcijański. W 15. rocznicę śmierci Mirosława Dzielskiego," *onet.pl—Tygodnik Powszechny*, http://tygodnik.onet.pl/0,1201178,druk.html (accessed 19 June 2006).

243. Miłowit Kuniński, "Obalić komunizm...i co dalej?" *Ośrodek Myśli Politycznej*, http://www.omp.org.pl/index.php?module=subjects&func=viewpage&pageid=55 (accessed 23 June 2006).

244. See Mirosław Dzielski, "Szkice o polityce polskiej," in *Odrodzenie ducha—budowa wolności*, 345–73.

245. Dzielski, "Powrót cywilizacji," 276.

246. Rzegocki, "Mirosława Dzielskiego rozważania o cywilizacji." See also Mirosław Dzielski, "Polityka polska dziś," in *Odrodzenie ducha—budowa wolności*, 321.

247. Kossecki, *Podstawy nowoczesnej nauki porównawczej o cywilizacjach*, 11.

248. Koneczny continued to embrace this notion after the war; in 1946 he wrote that Catholics demanded total ethics so that morality would play a role in politics. See Feliks Koneczny, "Religia sprawą najbardziej publiczną," *Tygodnik Warszawski* 2, no. 42 (20 October 1946): 3.

249. Gondek, "Rola Kościoła w kulturze polskiej," 94.

250. Ibid.

251. Ibid., 96.

252. Radosław Brzózka, "Czytajmy Feliksa Konecznego," *Cywilizacja* 1 (2002): 68.

253. Mieczyslaw Ryba, "O cywilizacjach," http://home.chello.no/~jskorups/KMFK/mieczyslaw_ryba3.htm (accessed 25 August 2009). On Krąpiec and Koneczny, also see Piotr Jaroszyński, "Ojca M.A. Krąpca bój o polską kulturę (cz. 2)," *Nasz Dziennik*, 21–22 May 2008.

254. Radosław Brzózka, "Wybitny pedagog," *Nasz Dziennik*, 16 May 2008.

255. Brzózka, "Czytajmy Feliksa Konecznego," 68.

256. Mieczysław Ryba, "O ludzką politykę," *Nasz Dziennik*, 16 May 2008.

257. Mirosław Król, "Pomagał zrozumieć człowieka i jego dzieje," *Nasz Dziennik*, 16 May 2008.

258. Henryk Kiereś, *Człowiek i cywilizacja* (Lublin: Wydawnictwo Fundacja *Servire Veritati* Instytut Edukacji Narodowej, 2007), 144.

259. Ibid., 9–10.

260. Krzysztof Nagrodzki, "Analiza współczesności kard. Josepha Ratzingera," *Myśl Polska*, no. 37–38 (11–18 September 2005), http://www.myslpolska.icenter.pl/ (accessed 28 January 2006).

CHAPTER FIVE. THE KONECZNIAN REVIVAL

1. Karol Brandt, "Niezapomniany Feliks Koneczny," *Myśl Polska*, no. 31–32 (2–9 August 2009), http://www.myslpolska.org/node/10210 (accessed 21 August 2009]. See also Kamila Baranowska, "Zapomniany poprzednik Huntingtona," *Rzeczpospolita*, 11 February 2009, http://www.rp.pl/artykul/261642.html? (accessed 27 February 2009).

2. Ewa Maj, "Sposoby zaprzeczania Zagładzie Żydów: przypadek środowisk neoendeckich," *Forum Żydzi- Chrześcijanie-Muzułmanie*, 14 October 2003, http://www

.znak.org.pl/?lang1=pl&page1=studies&subpage1=studies00&infopassid1=83&scr
tl=sn (accessed 12 August 2010).

3. Brandt, "Niezapomniany Feliks Koneczny."

4. Maciej Kociuba, "Tożsamość kulturowa cywilizacji europejskiej. O potrzebie aksjologicznej 'metanoi,'" *Annales Universitatis Mariae Curie-Skłodowska. Lublin—Polonia. Sectio I. Wydział Filozofii i Socjologii UMCS* 27, no. 3 (2002): 52, 60.

5. Jedynak, "Aksjologiczne zagadnienie rozwoju cywilizacji według Feliksa Konecznego," 126.

6. Jedynak, *Naród społeczeństwo państwo*, 137.

7. Ibid., 138. Emphasis added.

8. Ibid., 140.

9. Andrzej Horodecki, "Wobec zamachu na patriotyzm," *Nasza witryna*, http://www
.naszawitryna.pl/jedwabne_297.html (accessed 7 May 2008). Originally published
in *Myśl Polska*, no. 24–25 (22 June 2001) and in *Nowy Przegląd Wszechpolski* 8,
no. 1–2 (2001), http://www.npw.pl/ARCHIWUM_NPW/2001_01_02/PIS-Horo
decki_Wobec-zamachu.html (accessed 21 June 2006). As a frequent contributor
to the weekly *Myśl Polska* and as an editor and contributor to the monthly *Nowy
Przegląd Wszechpolski*, Horodecki has produced dozens of essays that apply Koneczny's civilizational paradigm to myriad contemporary problems. They consistently reflect the sort of postcolonial themes that scholars have identified in other
contexts: resentment about the legacies of past colonial periods; the fear of new
colonial threats; the rejection of cultural elements that are alien; and the defense of
one's own authentic cultural traditions.

10. Michał Wolnicki, "Grudniowe przemyślenia," *Ojczyzna.pl*, http://www.ojczyzna
.pl/Arch-Teksty/WOLNICKI__Grudniowe-Przemyslenia.htm (accessed 29 March
2005).

11. Mirosław Dakowski, "Potencjały rozpraszające a instynkt samozachowawczy narodów (cywilizacja według Feliksa Konecznego)," *Strona Mirosława Dakowskiego*, 12 March 2007, http://dakowski.pl/index.php?option=com_content&t
ask=view&id=47&Itemid=49 (accessed 23 August 2009).

12. Ibid.

13. Ibid.

14. Maciej Giertych, "Z nauczania Feliksa Konecznego," *Opoka w Kraju* 18, no. 39
(June 1996), http://opoka.giertych.pl/owk18.htm (accessed 27 July 2011).

15. Giertych, *Z nadzieją w przyszłość*, 72.

16. Katarzyna Stępień, "Historia—*lux veritatis*. Rozmowa z Marcinem Dybowskim,
Wydawcą dzieł Feliksa Konecznego," *Człowiek w Kulturze* 10 (1998): 253.

17. Katarzyna Surmiak-Domańska, "Ja, grzesznik. Anatomia fundamentalisty," *gazeta.pl—Gazeta Wyborcza*, 7 April 2006, http://serwisy.gazeta.pl/
df/2029020,34471,3267990.html (accessed 1 March 2007).

18. Piotr Sutowicz, "Feliks Koneczny i jego nauka historii," *Nowe Życie: Donośląskie
Pismo Katolickie*, no. 4 (2002), http://nowezycie.archidiecezja.wroc.pl/num
ery/042002/09.html (accessed 25 August 2009).

19. Editorial, "Zaufajmy duchowi świętemu," *Nowy Przegląd Wszechpolski* 12, no. 5–6
(2005), http://www.npw.pl/ARCHIWUM_NPW/2005_05_06/WST-Red_Zaufa-
jmy_duchowi.html (accessed 21 June 2006).

20. Wojciech Reszczyński, "Cywilizacje, Ordnung i kapelusze," *Nasz Dziennik*,

19 February 2009, http://www.naszdziennik.pl/index.php?typ=dd&dat=200902 19&id=main (accessed 3 March 2009).

21. Wojciech Reszczyński, "Media a odpowiedzialność za audytorium," *Radio Maryja*, http://www.radiomaryja.pl/artykuly.php?id=98202 (accessed 24 August 2009). Originally published in *Nasz Dziennik*, 21 November 2008.

22. Established in 1998, *Nasz Dziennik* "quickly became the most influential religious paper in Poland" and sells an estimated 200,000 copies every day. The daily is closely linked to *Radio Maryja*, which since its founding in 1991 has been formally run by the Order of Holy Redeemer (Ojcowie Redemptoryści), but is really managed by its director, Father Tadeusz Rydzyk. See Stanisław Burdziej, "Voice of the Disinherited? Religious Media after the 2005 Presidential and Parliamentary Elections in Poland," *East European Quarterly* 42, no. 2 (June 2008): 208. Koneczny is frequently referenced in *Nasz Dziennik* and *Radio Maryja* commentaries, including those by Father Rydzyk. See Rafał Maszkowski, "Inny świat—obraz Żydów w Radiu Maryja," *Kwartalnik Historii Żydów*, no. 4 (2006): 671.

23. Rafał Maszkowski, "Otwarte społeczeństwo i jego radio," *Stowarzyszenie Nigdy Więcej*, http://www.nigdywiecej.org/index2.php?option=com_content&do_pdf=1&id=91 (accessed 26 August 2009).

24. "Teoria cywilizacji. Spotkanie na temat teorii cywilizacji Feliksa Konecznego," *Stowarzyszenie Patriotyczne Serenissima*, 8 October 2004, http://www.serenissima.org.pl/Patriotyzm/Patriotyzm.html (accessed 27 July 2011).

25. Mirosław Dakowski, "60-ciolecie śmierci Feliksa Konecznego," *Strona Mirosława Dakowskiego*, 17 February 2009, http://dakowski.pl/index.php?option=com_content&task=view&id=972&Itemid=49 (accessed 24 August 2009).

26. Ibid.

27. Mirosław Dakowski, "Nie potępiajmy Konecznego!" *Myśl Polska*, 23 February 2007, http://www.myslpolska.org/?idx=janek_art&lusterko=193442 (accessed 16 March 2007).

28. Piotr Jaroszyński, "Feliks Koneczny—wielki nieobecny," in *Przywracanie pamięci* (Warsaw: Dom Polski, 2007), 114.

29. Sebastian Pasławski, "Feliks Koneczny. Nadal aktualny," *Prawy.pl*, http://www.prawy.pl/?action=print&dz=felietony&id=21835&subdz= (accessed 16 March 2007).

30. Ibid.

31. Włodzimierz Bojarski, *Dokąd Polsko? Wobec globalizacji i integracji europejskiej* (Warsaw: Inicjatywa Wydawnicza "ad astra," 2002), 88.

32. Ibid., 110.

33. Giertych, *Z nadzieją w przyszłość*, 5. See also Maciej Giertych, "Stronnictwo Narodowe," *Opoka w Kraju* 12, no. 33 (May 1995): 1–3, http://opoka.giertych.pl/owk12.htm (accessed 30 June 2008).

34. Grzegorz Tokarz, *Ruch narodowy w Polsce w latach 1989–1997* (Wrocław: Wydawnictwo Uniwersytetu Wrocławskiego, 2002), 97.

35. Andrzej Horodecki, "Czas próby polskich sumień trwa," *Nowy Przegląd Wszechpolski* 7, no. 11–12 (2000), http://www.npw.pl/ARCHIWUM_NPW/2000_11_12/PIS-Horodecki_czas-proby-czas-trwania.html (accessed 24 June 2006). Jerzy Pawlas has similar fears about Germans gaining ownership of lands from old German territories. "Ziemi nie przybywa," *Radio Pomost* (20 May 2005), http://www

.radiopomost.com/index.php?option=news&task=viewarticle&sid=3628 (accessed 24 June 2006).

36. Andrzej Horodecki, "Polsko, szanuj swoją wiarę i wolność!" *Nowy Przegląd Wszechpolski* 10, no. 5–6 (2003), http://www.npw.pl/ARCHIWUM_NPW/2003_05_06/ TMS-Horodecki_Polsko_szanuj.html (accessed 13 September 2006).

37. Andrzej Horodecki, "Projekt Konstytucji Rzeczpospolitej Polskiej," *Nowy Przegląd Wszechpolski* 10, no. 9–10 (2003), http://www.npw.pl/ARCHIWUM_NPW/2003_09_10/TMS-Horodecki_Projekt-konstytucji-rzecpospolitej.html (accessed 21 June 2006).

38. Jan Piwowarski, "Oddolne zorganizowanie się Polaków warunkiem przetrwania Narodu i Państwa Polskiego," *Nowy Przegląd Wszechpolski* 8, no. 5–6 (2001), http://www.npw.pl/ARCHIWUM_NPW/2001_05_06/TMS-Piwowarski_Oddolne-orga nizowanie-sie.html (accessed 21 June 2006).

39. Ibid.

40. Maciej Giertych, "Agro-środowisko pożądane," *Opoka w Kraju* 42, no. 63 (August 2002): 3, http://opoka.giertych.pl/42.pdf (accessed 28 August 2009). Also see "Wieś ma być zniszczona," *Opoka w Kraju*. Numer specjalny, poświęcony referendum w sprawie akcesji do Unii Europejskiej, 44, no. 65 (April 2003): 7–8, http://opoka. giertych.pl/44.pdf (accessed 30 June 2008); and "Zniszczyć rolnictwo!" *Opoka w Kraju* 15, no. 36 (December 1995): 5, http://opoka.giertych.pl/owk15.htm (accessed 30 June 2008).

41. Ewa Maj, "Polska mitologia historyczna w myśli politycznej Narodowej Demokracji w XX wieku: model realizacji idei," in *Wizje i realia. Studia nad realizacją polskiej myśli politycznej XX wieku*, ed. Waldemar Paruch and Krystyna Trembicka (Lublin: Wydawnictwo Uniwersytetu Marii Curie-Skłodowskiej, 2002), 212.

42. Nick Baron and Peter Gatrell, "Population Displacement, State-Building, and Social Identity in the Lands of the Former Russian Empire, 1917–23," *Kritika: Explorations in Russian and Eurasian History* 4, no. 1 (2003): 86.

43. Ibid.

44. Tokarz, *Ruch narodowy w Polsce*, 97.

45. Joanna Kurczewska, Anna Horolets, and Monika Trojanowska-Strzęboszewska, with the collaboration of Mirosław Bieniecki, *The European Dilemma: Institutional Patterns and Politics of 'Racial' Discrimination. Project Report: Work Package 6. Discourse Analysis of Politics: LPR's Rhetoric* (Warsaw: Institute of Public Affairs, 2005), 29. http://www.isp.org.pl/files/11297950200606281001164194296.pdf (accessed 30 June 2008).

46. Ray Taras, "Poland's Accession into the European Union: Parties, Policies and Paradoxes," *Polish Review* 48, no. 1 (2003): 12. Responding to these fears, the Polish government successfully negotiated with the EU for a special transition period concerning the sale of farmland to foreigners.

47. Mirella Eberts, "The Catholic Church and Poland's Accession to the European Union," in *Redefining Europe*, ed. Joseph Drew (Amsterdam: Rodopi, 2005), 175.

48. Horodecki, "Czas próby polskich sumień trwa."

49. Andrzej J. Horodecki, "Walka cywilizacyjna," *Nowy Przegląd Wszechpolski* 8, no. 3–4 (2001), http://www.npw.pl/ARCHIWUM_NPW/2001_03_04/TMS-Horo decki_Walka-Cywilizacyjna.html (accessed June 21, 2006).

50. Dariusz Kosiur, "Są w Ojczyźnie ważne sprawy," *polskawalczaca.com*, http://www

.polskawalczaca.com/viewtopic.php?t=322 (accessed 28 August 2009).

51. Andrzej J. Horodecki, "Przez wieś do odbudowy cywilizacji łacińskiej w Polsce," *Nowy Przegląd Wszechpolski* 7, no. 9–10 (2000), http://www.npw.pl/ARCHIWUM_ NPW/2000_09_10/PIS-Horodecki_PRzez-wies-do-odbudowy.html (accessed 21 June 2006). Emphasis in the original.

52. Pawlas, "Ziemi nie przybywa."

53. Piotr Jaroszyński, "Pytanie o przyszłość polskich Ziem Odzyskanych," in *Ocalić polskość!* (Lublin: Wydawnictwo Instytut Edukacji Narodowej, 2001), http://www .polonica.net/OcalicPolskosc2.htm (accessed 3 June 2003).

54. Piotr Jaroszyński, "Stosunek do ziemi w różnych cywilizacjach," *Klub Myśli Feliksa Konecznego,* http://home.chello.no/~jskorups/KMFK/piotr_jaroszynski7.htm (accessed 1 October 2002).

55. Ibid.

56. Pawlas, "Ziemi nie przybywa."

57. Jaroszyński, "Stosunek do ziemi."

58. Ibid.

59. Magdalena Nowicka, "Rzeczpospolita postkolonialna," *Gazeta Wyborcza,* 10 October 2007, http://wyborcza.pl/1,76506,4431065.html (accessed 4 May 2010).

60. Židas Daskalovski, "Go East! Racism and the EU," *ce-review.org* 2, no. 24 (19 June 2000), http://www.ce-review.org/00/24/daskalovski24.html (accessed 15 February 2003).

61. Włodzimierz Bojarski, "Uwagi do program nowej ewangelizacji," *Internetowa Gazeta Katolików* (April 2004), http://www.krajski.com/955wbkos.htm (accessed 6 December 2007).

62. Mariusz Kowalski, "Kaszuby, Kociewie—cywilizacja łacińska," *Nasze Kaszuby,* http://www.naszekaszuby.pl/modules/newbb/viewtopic.php?viewmode=flat&order=ASC&topic_id=272&forum=3&move=prev&topic_time=1102780633 (accessed 4 October 2006). Originally published in *Najwyższy Czas!,* no. 25 (19 June 2004).

63. Giertych, *Z nadzieją w przyszłość,* 5.

64. Maciej Giertych, "Nie oddawać pola," *Opoka w Kraju* 49, no. 70 (May 2004): 2, http://opoka.giertych.pl/owk49.htm (accessed 19 March 2005). Also published in *Myśl Polska,* no. 23 (6 June 2004), http://www.myslpolska.icenter.pl/ (accessed 19 March 2005).

65. Piotr Jaroszyński, *Europa bez Ojczyzn?* (Warsaw: Dom Polski, 2002), 8.

66. Ibid.

67. Jaroszyński, *Polska i Europa,* 56.

68. Ibid., 100.

69. Piotr Jaroszyński, *W nowogródzkiej stronie* (Warsaw: Dom Polski, 2004), 128.

70. Bukowska, *Filozofia polska wobec problemu cywilizacji,* 129.

71. Anna Cieslik and Maykel Verkuyten, "National, Ethnic and Religious Identities: Hybridity and the Case of the Polish Tatars," *National Identities* 8, no. 2 (June 2006): 79. A popular concept associated with postcolonial thought, "hybridity" is generally used "to criticise ethnic boundaries and essentialisms, and to valorise mixture and change." It represents an alternative to "the exclusionary and racist consequences of social categorisations, such as national, religious and ethnic ones." Ibid., 78.

72. Piotrowski, *Problem filozoficzny ładu społecznego,* 43.

73. Skoczyński, *Idee historiozoficzne Feliksa Konecznego,* 109–10.

74. Ibid., 111.
75. Adam Wielomski, "Euro-barbarzyństwo," *Nasza Witryna*, www.iyp.org/polish/his tory/antypolonizmy/europa_432.html (accessed 15 Februay 2003).
76. Ibid.
77. Ibid.
78. Viranjini Munasinghe, "Nationalism in Hybrid Spaces: The Production of Impurity out of Purity," *American Ethnologist* 29, no. 3 (2002): 672.
79. See Andrzej J. Horodecki, "Bez dyskusji," *Myśl Polska*, no. 36 (5 September 2004), http://www.myslpolska.icenter.pl/ (accessed 19 March 2005).
80. Elżbieta Holz, "Kuc—czy pony? Cywilizacja łacińska a współczesne postawy polskiego środowiska jeździeckiego," *Nowy Przegląd Wszechpolski* 9, no. 1–2 (2002), http://www.npw.pl/ARCHIWUM_NPW/2002_01_02/OKW-Kuc_czy_pony.htm (accessed 21 June 2006).
81. Tomasz Jaźwiński, "Rządowa deklaracja w sprawie moralności i etyki nie ma znaczenia," *Myśl Polska*, no. 9 (2 March 2003), http://www.myslpolska.icenter.pl/ (accessed 26 March 2005). Also see Andrzej J. Horodecki, "Ciemności europejskie," *Nowy Przegląd Wszechpolski* 11, no. 5–6 (2004), http://www.npw.pl/ARCHIWUM_NPW/2004_05_06/OKW-Horodecki_CIEMNOZCI-EUROPEJSKIE.html (accessed 21 June 2006).
82. Editorial, "Jan Paweł II odnowiciel," *Nowy Przegląd Wszechpolski* 13, no. 5–6 (2006): 1, http://www.npw.pl/pdf/npw.2006.5–6.pdf (accessed 27 August 2009).
83. Adrian Nikiel, "Eko-filozofia czy ekologia chrześcijańska?" *Wydawnictwo "Zielone Brygady,"* http://www.zb.eco.pl/publication/eko-filozofia-czy-ekologia-chrzescijan ska-p217511 (accessed 6 May 2009).
84. Mieczysław Ryba, "Liberalny Rzym i barbarzyńcy," *Radio Pomost*, 24 March 2004, http://www.radiopomost.com/test/index.php?option=news&task=viewarticle& sid=1834 (accessed 26 August 2009).
85. Ibid.
86. Neil McInnes, "The Great Doomsayer: Oswald Spengler Reconsidered," *National Interest*, no. 48 (Summer 1997): 70–71.
87. Ibid., 71.
88. Mirosław Dakowski, "Poglądy Samuela Huntington—plagiat oraz "odwrócenie kota ogonem" dorobku Feliksa Konecznego," *Strona Mirosława Dakowskiego*, http://dakowski.pl/index.php?option=com_content&task=view&id=48&Itemid=49 (accessed 23 August 2009). See also Mirosław Dakowski, "Wojny o energię," *Wydawnictwo "Zielone Brygady,"* http://zb.eco.pl/zb/183/military.htm (accessed 30 June 2004). A longer version is also available at "Nośniki energii a geopolityka," *Rurociągi: Polish Pipeline Journal*, http://www.rurociagi.com/spis_art/2004_2–3/ nosniki.htm (accessed 12 September 2006).
89. Biliński, *Feliks Koneczny*, 184.
90. Koneczny, *Chrześcijaństwo wobec ustrojów życia zbiorowego*, 5–6.
91. Rich, "Civilisations in European and World History," 331.
92. Ibid.
93. O'Hagan, "A 'Clash of Civilizations'?," 136.
94. Ibid., 138.
95. Ibid., 137.
96. Ibid.

97. Ibid., 139.
98. Koneczny, *Prawa dziejowe*, 164–65.
99. Kuderowicz, "Koncepcja praw historii w ujęciu Feliksa Konecznego," 42.
100. O'Hagan, "A 'Clash of Civilizations'?," 142.
101. Ibid.
102. Ibid., 145.
103. Ibid., 146.
104. Ibid.
105. Ibid., 139.
106. Ibid., 140.
107. Ibid.
108. See Jan Skoczyński, "Huntington i Koneczny," in Skoczyński, *Feliks Koneczny dzisiaj*, 103–10; Leszek Gawor, "Konecznego i Huntingtona wizja cywilizacyjnego pluralizmu," *Toruński Przegląd Filozoficzny* 5/6 (2003): 31–42; Jan Skoczyński, "Huntington and Koneczny (An Attempt to Compare)," *Canadian Slavonic Papers* 41, no. 2 (June 1999): 207–16; and Piotrowski, *Problem filozoficzny ładu społecznego*, 191–205.
109. Samuel P. Huntington, *Who Are We? The Challenges to America's National Identity* (New York: Simon & Schuster, 2004), 310.
110. O'Hagan, "A 'Clash of Civilizations'?," 141.
111. Ibid.
112. Huntington, *Who Are We?*, 171.
113. Mislav Kukoc, "Reshaped Regional Multiculturalism in the Post-Communist Europe," *Europe: Expectations and Reality*, http://www.unesco.org/most/faltan.htm (accessed 25 August 2009).
114. Vasilenko, "Dialogue of Cultures, Dialogue of Civilizations," 7.
115. Ibid., 10.
116. Ibid., 20.
117. Ibid.
118. Ibid., 22.
119. Andrzej Horodecki, "Totalna walka z cywilizacją łacińską, część II," *Nowy Przegląd Wszechpolski* 9, no. 5–6 (2002), http://www.npw.pl/ARCHIWUM_NPW/2002_05_06/PIS-Horodecki__Totalna-Walka.htm (accessed 21 June 2006).
120. Quoted in Biliński, *Feliks Koneczny*, 150. Originally published as "Czterdzieści tez zasadniczych," *Trybuna Narodu* 2, no. 19 (8 May 1927): 2–3. Also republished in *Arcana* 86–87, no. 2/3 (2009); and also at *forum.michalkiewicz.pl*, 1 May 2009, http://www.forum.michalkiewicz.pl/viewtopic.php?f=4&t=12381 (accessed 10 August 2011).
121. Ibid., 151.
122. Tokarz, *Ruch narodowy w Polsce*, 99–100.
123. Robaczewski, "Quincunx jako odbicie klasycznej teorii osoby," 46.
124. Skoczyński, *Koneczny: Teoria cywilizacji*, 70–71.
125. Koneczny, *Plurality of Civilisations*, 216. Emphasis in original.
126. Skoczyński, *Idee historiozoficzne Feliksa Konecznego*, 126.
127. Nagrodzki, "Analiza współczesności kard. Josepha Ratzingera." The notion of "lower" civilizations overcoming "higher" ones is frequently discussed in Konecznian analyses. It encapsulates Social Darwinian notions of "survival of the fittest,"

a fear of "others," and the centrality of cultural traditions in one's identity. See An-drzej Horodecki, "Wojna światów," *Myśl Polska*, no. 49–50 (4–11 December 2005), http://www.myslpolska.icenter.pl/ (accessed 28 January 2006).

128. See Henryk Nowik, "Ekshortacja Jana Pawła II *Kościół w Europie* w kontekście his-toriozoficznym," *Nowy Przegląd Wszechpolski* 11, no. 1–2 (2004), http://www.npw .pl/ARCHIWUM_NPW/2004_01_02/ZRE-Nowik_Ekshortacja-jana-pawla.html (accessed 21 June 2006); and the editorial, "Jan Paweł II odnowiciel."

129. Maciej Giertych, "Z nauczania Feliksa Konecznego," *Opoka w Kraju*, 11, no. 32 (March 1995): 6, http://opoka.giertych.pl/ (accessed 15 August 2010).

130. Jarosław Paszyński, "Tożsamość Polski a cywilizacje," *Człowiek w Kulturze* 10 (1998): 85.

131. Donskis, *Forms of Hatred*, xiii.

132. Ibid., 2.

133. Wojciech Giertych, "Niewykorzystany kapitał?" *W drodze*, no. 3 (2008), http://www.mateusz.pl/goscie/wdrodze/nr415/04-wdr.htm (accessed 28 November 2008).

134. See Wojciech Giertych, "The Moral Natural Law: Problems and Prospects," *Catholic Online*, 25 February 2007, http://www.catholic.org/featured/headline.php?ID=4093 (accessed 26 February 2007). Koneczny advocated natural law over positivist law, fitting with his insistence on the primacy of ethics and morality in public life. In his view, ethical considerations should shape the law, rather than the reverse. Koneczny closely associated Judaism with the latter view, frequently criticizing Jews' adher-ence to "the letter of the law" rather than ethics. The debate about the distinction between natural law and positive law emerged in the controversy over the preamble for the constitution in the late 1990s. Geneviève Zubrzycki summarizes the distinc-tions: "Natural law stipulates that there is a normative system given in nature; that norms are not subject to change in time or place. The logic of positive law is dif-ferent: it is the law that defines the normative system; norms are a human creation and therefore are subject to change and interpretation. The law could then define norms that are against natural law or humanity." See Geneviève Zubrzycki, "'We, the Polish Nation': Ethnic and Civic Visions of Nationhood in Post-Communist Constitutional Debates," *Theory and Society* 30, no. 5 (2001): 667.

135. Ryszard Montusiewicz, "Jezus i judaizm. Z ks. Prof. Romualdem Jakubem Wekslerem-Waszkinelem rozmawia Ryszard Montusiewicz," *Forum: Żydzi-Chrześcijanie-Muzułmanie*, http://znak.org.pl/?lang1=pl&page1=pressreview&su bpage1=pressreview00&infopassid1=3669&scrt1=sn (accessed 21 August 2009). Weksler-Waszkinel was born to a Jewish family in 1943 near Wilno (Vilnius). Be-fore her death, his mother asked a Christian family to raise him. They did, but when he decided to become a priest they were shocked. He is also critical of Tadeusz Zieliński, whose *Hellenizm a judaizm* (1927) was a source for Koneczny's commen-tary in his posthumously published *Cywilizacja żydowska*.

136. Andrzej Horodecki, "Polowanie na Polskę," *Myśl Polska*, no. 13 (28 March 2004), http://www.myslpolska.icenter.pl/ (accessed 22 March 2005).

137. Ks. Romuald Jakub Weksler-Waszkinel, "Antysemityzm bez Żydów," *Miesięcznik "Znak,"* December 2008, http://www.tezeusz.pl/cms/tz/index.php?id=3773 (ac-cessed 5 January 2010). For a Konecznian critique of Vatican II, see Andrzej Horo-decki, "Wobec dziedzictwa wiary," *Nowy Przegląd Wszechpolski* 14, no. 1–2 (2007): 26, http://www.npw.pl/pdf/npw.2007.1–2.pdf (accessed 27 August 2009).

138. Romuald Jakub Weksler-Waszkinel, "Księdza Stanisława Musiała zmagania z pamięcią," *Zagłada Żydów. Studia i Materiały* 2 (2006): 443. For further commentary on Koneczny, see also Romuald Jakub Weksler-Waszkinel, "A Breakthrough in the Teachings of the Church on Jews and Judaism," in *Imaginary Neighbors: Mediating Polish-Jewish Relations after the Holocaust*, ed. Dorota Glowacka and Joanna Zylinska (Lincoln: University of Nebraska Press, 2007), 227. Emphases in original.

139. See Józef Życiński, "Siła słabych," *Gazeta Wyborcza*, 5 April 2007, http://www .gazetawyborcza.pl/gazetawyborcza/2029020,79328,4042232.html (accessed 15 April 2007).

140. Joanna B[eata] Michlic, "Antisemitism in Contemporary Poland. Does It Matter? And for Whom Does It Matter?" In *Rethinking Poles and Jews: Troubled Past, Brighter Future*, ed. Robert Cherry and Annamaria Orla-Bukowska (Lanham, MD: Rowman & Littlefield Publishers, Inc., 2007), 160.

141. Joanna Michlic and Antony Polonsky, "Catholicism and the Jews in Post-Communist Poland," in *Jews, Catholics, and the Burden of History*, ed. Eli Lederhendler (Oxford: Oxford University Press, 2006), 40–41.

142. Michlic, *Poland's Threatening Other*, 269.

143. Weksler-Waszkinel, "Antysemityzm bez Żydów."

144. Joanna Tokarska-Bakir, *Legendy o krwi. Antropologia przesądu (z cyklu: obraz osobliwy)* (Warsaw: Wydawnictwo W.A.B., 2008), 492.

145. Stefan Kurowski, "'Dziewiąta cywilizacja' w działaniu (1)," *Zaprasza.net*, http://za prasza.net/a_y.php?article_title=kurowski&mid=5707 (accessed 25 August 2009).

146. Andrzej Szydlik, "Globalizm kontra...globalizm," http://www.man.pl/~nowa/ nowa/Artykuly/anszydl2.html (accessed 29 June 2004).

147. Szcześniak, *Judeopolonia*, 55. On alleged German plans for a Jewish state during World War II, see Edward Gigilewicz, *Lublinland: państwo żydowskie w planach III Rzeszy* (Radom: Polskie Wydawnictwo Encyklopedyczne, 2004).

148. Zbigniew Lignarski, "Talmud ze swastyką w tle?" *Archipelag-Instytut Norwida*, 20 May 2009, http://archipelag.org.pl/newsdesk_info.php?newsPath=4&newsdesk_ id=4 (accessed 21 November 2009).

149. Ibid.

150. Kurczewska, Horolets, and Trojanowska-Strzęboszewska, *The European Dilemma*, 79–81.

151. Andrzej Horodecki, "Rozum zagrożony," *Nowy Przegląd Wszechpolski* 14, no. 5–6 (2007): 39, http://www.npw.pl/pdf/npw.2007.5-6.pdf (accessed 27 August 2009).

152. Andrzej Horodecki, "Nie ma patriotyzmu bez personalizmu," *Nowy Przegląd Wszechpolski* 11, no. 1–2 (2004), http://www.npw.pl/ARCHIWUM_NPW/2004_01_02/ PIS-Horodecki_nie-ma-patriotyzmu.html (accessed 21 June 2006).

153. Koneczny, *Polska między wschodem a zachodem*, 2.

154. Horodecki, "Walka cywilizacyjna."

155. Horodecki, "Wobec zamachu na patriotyzm." Koneczny devoted an entire chapter ("The Dejudaized Jew") of *Cywilizacja żydowska* to this problem. See Koneczny, *Cywilizacja żydowska*, 395–406. Kamil Sawczak also refers to Koneczny's thoughts on this issue. See Sawczak, "Poglądy: o rozwiązaniu kwestii żydowskiej," Referat wygłoszony na II Konferencji Konecznańskiej, Kraków, 9.02.2008, *Nacjonalista. pl—Portal Narodowo-Radykalny*, http://www.nacjonalista.org/artykuly.php?id=88 (accessed 2 April 2008).

156. Koneczny, *Polska między wschodem a zachodem*, 51.
157. Koneczny, "Warunki powodzenia," 67.
158. Andrzej Horodecki, "Walka cywilizacyjna."
159. Witold Kowalski, "Cztery cywilizacje," *Nowy Przegląd Wszechpolski* 14, no. 5–6 (2007): 48. http://www.npw.pl/pdf/npw.2007.5–6.pdf (accessed 9 December 2009).
160. Ibid.
161. Ibid., 49.
162. Ibid.
163. Adam Wielomski, "Unia Europejska jako wyzwanie historiozoficzne," *Konserwatyzm.pl (Klub Zachowawczo-Monarchistyczny)*, http://konserwatyzm.pl/content/view/1046/143/ (accessed 30 June 2008).
164. Martin W. Lewis and Kären E. Wigen, *The Myth of Continents: A Critique of Metageography* (Berkeley: University of California Press, 1997), 76.
165. Rafał Dobrowolski, "Teoria historiozoficzna prof. Feliksa Konecznego," *My, Nowe Pokolenie!* 2, no. 15 (2003), http://infopatria.pl/index.php/artykul/13/0/310 (accessed 2 November 2009). Here Dobrowolski seemingly is referring to Koneczny's essay "Napór Orientu na Zachód," which was first published in *Kultura i Cywilizacja* (1937), 1–24.
166. Adam Wielomski, "Unia Europejska jako wyzwanie historiozoficzne." .
167. These various tropes borrow much from the rhetoric of Polish interwar anti-Semitism. For analyses of this trend, see Agnieszka Graff, "Gej, czyli Żyd ... i co dalej?" in *Rykoszetem: Rzecz o płci, seksualności i narodzie* (Warsaw: Wydawnictwo W.A.B, 2008): 110–42; Agnieszka Graff, "We Are (Not All) Homophobes: A Report from Poland," *Feminist Studies* 32, no. 2 (2006): 434–49; and Gregory E. Czarnecki, "Analogies of Pre-War Anti-Semitism and Present-Day Homophobia in Poland," *Beyond the Pink Curtain: Everyday Life of LGBT people in Eastern Europe*, ed. Roman Huhar and Judit Takács (Ljubljana: Mirovni Institut, 2007), 327–44. Available online at *Homepage of Judit Takács*, http://www.policy.hu/takacs/books/isbn9616455459/ (accessed 26 September 2010). Also see Adam Ostolski, "Żydzi, geje i wojna cywilizacji," *Kobiety Kobietom*, 2 June 2005, http://kobiety-kobietom.com/queer/art.php?art=2249 (accessed 20 August 2010). Ostolski places this phenomenon within the context of Feliks Koneczny's "clash of civilizations" theory and its appeal to fundamentalists who advocate traditional gender roles.
168. Jaroszyński, *W nowogródzkiej stronie*, 148.
169. Ibid., 141, 144, 150.
170. Teresa Zawojska, "O narodzie w cywilizacji łacińskiej," *Człowiek w Kulturze* 16 (2004): 288.
171. Jarosław Tomasiewicz, *Ugrupowania neoendeckie w III Rzeczypospolitej* (Toruń: Wydawnictwo Adam Marszałek, 2003), 261.
172. Wiesław Koneczny, "O prof. Feliksie Konecznym (1862–1949) (wspomnienia wnuka)," *Arcana* 4, no. 1 (1998): 143, 146. Koneczny was a "traditionalist" who even refused to embrace the reforms to Polish spelling that were introduced in 1936. Ibid., 148.
173. Grabowiec, *Model społeczeństwa obywatelskiego*, 116.
174. Paweł Skrzydlewski, "Rodzina w cywilizacji łacińskiej a wolność człowieka. Na kanwie rozważań Feliksa Konecznego," *Człowiek w Kulturze* 11 (1998): 210.
175. Ibid., 231–232.

176. Feliks Koneczny, "Młodzież jako rzekoma rękojmia przyszłości," in *O pajdokracji* (Warsaw: Wydawnictwo "Slowa," 1912), 30.
177. Koneczny, *Chrześcijaństwo wobec ustrojów życia zbiorowego*, 8.
178. Koneczny, *Rozwój moralnośc*, 141.
179. Grabowiec, *Model społeczeństwa obywatelskiego*, 115–21.
180. Gondek, "Rola Kościoła w kulturze polskiej," 95.
181. Jerzy Bajda, "Ku odnowionej Polsce," *Radio Maryja—Katolicka Głos w Twoim Domu*, 7 January 2006, http://www.radiomaryja.pl/artykuly.php?id=2 (accessed 21 August 2010). Originally published in *Nasz Dziennik*, 7 January 2006.
182. Agnieszka Graff, "Gender, Sexuality, and Nation—Here and Now: Reflections on the Gendered and Sexualized Aspects of Contemporary Polish Nationalism," in *Intimate Citizenships: Gender, Sexualities, Politics*, ed. Elzbieta H. Oleksy (New York: Routledge, 2009), 139.
183. Ibid.
184. Ibid.
185. Tamar Mayer, "Gender Ironies of Nationalism: Setting the Stage," in *Gender Ironies of Nationalism: Sexing the Nation*, ed. Tamar Mayer (London: Routledge, 2000), 10.
186. Agnieszka Graff, "The Land of Real Men and Real Women: Gender and E.U. Accession in Three Polish Weeklies," *Journal of the International Institute* 15, no. 1 (Fall 2007): 11.
187. Catarina Kinnvall, "Globalization and Religious Nationalism: Self, Identity, and the Search for Ontological Security," *Political Psychology* 25, no. 5 (October 2004): 742–44.
188. Ibid., 747.
189. Koneczny, *Państwo i prawo w cywilizacji łacińskiej*, 118.
190. Graff, "Land of Real Men and Real Women," 10.
191. Ibid., 11.
192. Quoted in Tomasiewicz, *Ugrupowania neoendeckie w III Rzeczypospolitej*, 261.
193. Graff, "Gender, Sexuality, and Nation," 141.
194. Eberts, "The Catholic Church and Poland's Accession to the European Union," 170.
195. Maciej Giertych, "Miejsce dla religii," *Opoka w Kraju*, Numer specjalny, poświęcony referendum w sprawie akcesji do Unii Europejskiej, 44, no. 65 (April 2003): 5. Available online at http://opoka.giertych.pl/44.pdf (accessed 30 June 2008).
196. Graff, "Land of Real Men and Real Women," 10.
197. Kinnvall, "Globalization and Religious Nationalism," 762.
198. Maciej Giertych, "Traditional Catholicism in Polish Public life," *Prof. Maciej Giertych*, http://giertych.eu/?sr=!czytaj&dz=7&id=178 (accessed 29 August 2010).
199. Wanda Nowicka, "The Struggle for Abortion Rights in Poland," in *SexPolitics: Reports from the Front Lines*, ed. Richard Parker, Rosalind Petchesky, and Robert Sember (New York: Sexuality Policy Watch, 2007), 169–72. Available online at http://www.sxpolitics.org/frontlines/book/pdf/sexpolitics.pdf (accessed 26 September 2010).
200. Graff, "Gender, Sexuality, and Nation," 135.
201. Rachel Alsop and Jenny Hockey, "Women's Reproductive Lives as a Symbolic Resource in Central and Eastern Europe," *European Journal of Women's Studies* 8, no. 4 (November 2001): 461.
202. Nowicka, "Struggle for Abortion Rights in Poland," 167–168.

203. Agnieszka Graff, "A Different Chronology: Reflections on Feminism in Contemporary Poland," in *Third Wave Feminism: A Critical Exploration*, ed. Stacy Gillis, et al. (London: Palgrave, 2007), 151.
204. Graff, "Gender, Sexuality, and Nation," 141.
205. Barbara Bubula, "Na manowcach społeczeństwa obywatelskiego," *Magazyn Obywatel*, no. 4 (2001), http://www.obywatel.org.pl/index.php?module=subjects&func =viewpage&pageid=1039 (accessed 3 March 2007).
206. Katarzyna Gawlicz, "Płeć i naród. Dyskurs dotyczący aborcji w "Naszym Dzienniku" a konstruowanie tożsamości narodowej," in *Kobiety, feminizm i media*, ed. Edyta Zierkiewicz and Izabela Kowalczyk (Poznań: Konsola, 2005), 112.
207. Maciej Giertych, *Gender Equality and Life Issues in the European Union* (Brussels: Maciej Giertych, 2008), 20. Available online at *Opoka w Kraju*, http://opoka.gier tych.pl/ (accessed 27 September 2010).
208. Anne-Marie Kramer, "The Polish Parliament and the making of Politics through Abortion: Nation, Gender and Democracy in the 1996 Liberalization Amendment," *International Feminist Journal of Politics* 11, no. 1 (2009): 83.
209. Ibid., 96.
210. Gawlicz, "Płeć i naród," 102.
211. Ibid., 105.
212. Ibid., 106.
213. Koneczny, *Plurality of Civilisations*, 132.
214. Koneczny, *Chrześcijaństwo wobec ustrojów życia zbiorowego*, 34.
215. Koneczny, *Plurality of Civilisations*, 278.
216. Bajda, "Ku odnowionej Polsce."
217. Koneczny, *Plurality of Civilisations*, 95.
218. Skrzydlewski, "Prawo stanowione w cywilizacji łacińskiej," 54.
219. Bajda, "Ku odnowionej Polsce."
220. Giertych, *Gender Equality and Life Issues*, 23.
221. See Ewa Hauser, "Traditions of Patriotism, Questions of Gender: The Case of Poland," *Genders* 22 (Fall 1995): 78–104. In a series of three partitions of Poland (1772, 1793, and 1795), the great powers of Russia, Austria, and Prussia eliminated Poland as an independent state. Polish political independence was revived in 1918, as a result of World War I and subsequent peace treaties.
222. Nowicka, "The Struggle for Abortion Rights in Poland," 178.
223. Sabina Witkowska, "Liga stawia na kobiety!," *Aspekt Polski*, 1 October 2006, http:// www.aspektpolski.pl/index.php?option=com_content&task=view&id=918&Ite mid=30 (accessed 19 August 2010).
224. Alsop and Hockey, "Women's Reproductive Lives," 460.
225. Barbara Einhorn and Charlotte Sever, "Gender and Civil Society in Central and Eastern Europe," *International Feminist Journal of Politics* 5, no. 2 (2003): 175.
226. Nowicka, "Struggle for Abortion Rights in Poland," 178.
227. Gawlicz, "Płeć i naród," 112.
228. Kramer, "The Polish Parliament and the Making of Politics through Abortion," 82.
229. Giertych, *Gender Equality and Life Issues*, 20.
230. Ibid., 22.
231. Nira Yuval-Davis, *Gender and Nation* (London: Sage Publications, 1997), 22.
232. Ibid., 26.

233. Alsop and Hockey, "Women's Reproductive Lives," 460.
234. Nira Yuval-Davis, "Women, Globalization and Contemporary Politics of Belonging," *Gender, Technology, and Development* 13, no. 1 (2009): 2.
235. Mayer, "Gender Ironies of Nationalism," 6.
236. Yuval-Davis, "Women, Globalization and Contemporary Politics of Belonging," 9.
237. Jaroszyński, *Polska i Europa*, 41–45.
238. "Mamy wielką wolę zmian," *Aspekt Polski*, 31 May 2006, http://aspektpolski.pl//index2.php?option=com_content&task=view&id=791&Itemid (accessed 22 June 2006).
239. Kramer, "The Polish Parliament and the making of Politics through Abortion," 96.
240. Tomasiewicz, *Ugrupowania neoendeckie w III Rzeczypospolitej*, 260.
241. Gawlicz, "Płeć i naród," 107.
242. Ryszard Polak, "Status kobiety w różnych cywilizacjach," *Cywilizacja* 21 (2007): 74.
243. Alsop and Hockey, "Women's Reproductive Lives," 462.
244. Nowicka, "Struggle for Abortion Rights in Poland," 182.
245. Ibid., 179.
246. Horodecki, "Przez wieś do odbudowy cywilizacji łacińskiej w Polsce."
247. Andrzej J. Horodecki, "Co nam zamyka oczy i uszy?" *Nowy Przegląd Wszechpolski* 11, no. 7–8 (2004), http://www.npw.pl/ARCHIWUM_NPW/2004_07_08/PIS-Horodecki_co-nam-zamyka.html (accessed 21 June 2006).
248. Andrzej Horodecki, "De profundis clamavi ad te, domine ..." *Nowy Przegląd Wszechpolski* 12, no. 1–2 (2005), http://www.npw.pl/ARCHIWUM_NPW/2005_01_02/OKW-Horodecki_de.html (accessed 21 June 2006).
249. Piotr Jaroszyński, "Media: między ideologią a biznesem," *Nasz Dziennik*, 6–7 June 2009, http://www.naszdziennik.pl/index.php?dat=20090606&typ=my&id=my51.txt (accessed 21 August 2010).
250. Graff, "Gender, Sexuality, and Nation," 133.
251. Ibid.
252. Anika Keinz, "European Desires and National Bedrooms? Negotiating 'Normalcy' in Postsocialist Poland," *Central European History* 44 (2011): 100.
253. Horodecki, "Przez wieś do odbudowy cywilizacji łacińskiej w Polsce."
254. Horodecki, "Projekt Konstytucji Rzeczpospolitej Polskiej."
255. Horodecki, "Sejmowe słodycze."
256. Dariusz Tarnowski, "Polska między Wschodem i Zachodem—za życia prof. Feliksa Konecznego i dziś," Referat wygłoszony na konferencji poświęconej profesorowi Feliksowi Konecznemu, zorganizowanej przez Narodowe Odrodzenie Polski 10 lutego 2007 w Krakowie, *Nacjonalista.pl—Portal Narodowo-Radykalny*, http://www.nacjonalista.org/artykuly.php?id=54&licz=1 (accessed 28 August 2009).
257. Andrzej Horodecki, "My, szarzy ludzie..." *Nowy Przegląd Wszechpolski* 15, no. 1–2 (2008): 50, http://www.npw.pl/pdf/npw.2008.1-2.pdf (accessed 27 August 2009).
258. Maciej Giertych, "Rozumienie świata a podziały cywilizacyjne prof. dr hab. Maciej Giertych," *Nasza witryna*, http://www.naszawitryna.pl/jedwabne_497.html (accessed 6 November 2007). Originally published in *Nasz Dziennik*, 6 February 2001.
259. Koneczny, *Państwo i prawo w cywilizacji łacińskiej*, 54.
260. Koneczny, *Prawa dziejowe*, 120.
261. Tomasiewicz, *Ugrupowania neoendeckie w III Rzeczypospolitej*, 253.
262. Skrzydlewski, "Rodzina w cywilizacji łacińskiej," 233.

263. Maciej Giertych, *Civilisations at War in Europe* (Brussels: Maciej Giertych, 2007), 4.

264. Maciej Giertych, "Z nauczania Feliksa Konecznego," *Opoka w Kraju* 12, no. 33 (May 1995): 4, http://opoka.giertych.pl/ (accessed 30 June 2008).

265. Ibid. For a scholarly analysis of the magazine's history and its content, see Anna Szwed, " 'Opoka w Kraju' (The Bedrock in a Country). The Magazine's Monograph," *Annales Universitatis Mariae Curie-Skłodowska, Lublin-Polonia, Sectio K (Politologia)* 20, no. 1 (2013): 251–70.

266. Giertych, *Civilisations at War in Europe*, 7.

267. Maciej Giertych, "Z nauczania Feliksa Konecznego," *Opoka w Kraju* 21, no. 42 (March 1997): 9, http://opoka.giertych.pl/ (accessed 18 August 2010).

268. Mayer, "Gender Ironies of Nationalism," 7.

269. Bajda, "Ku odnowionej Polsce."

270. Ibid.

271. Giertych, *Civilisations at War in Europe*, 30.

272. Ibid.

273. Giertych, *Gender Equality and Life Issues*, 26.

274. Ibid.

275. Maciej Giertych, *European Values* (Brussels: Maciej Giertych, 2007), 3. Available online at *Opoka w Kraju*, http://opoka.giertych.pl/ (accessed 27 September 2010).

276. Giertych, "Traditional Catholicism in Polish public life."

277. Giertych, *Civilisations at War in Europe*, 13.

278. Koneczny, *Plurality of Civilisations*, 85.

279. Koneczny, *Państwo i prawo w cywilizacji łacińskiej*, 118.

280. Koneczny, *Plurality of Civilisations*, 84.

281. Maciej Giertych, "Kobieta pracująca zarobkowo," *Opoka w Kraju* 29, no. 50 (March 1999), http://opoka.giertych.pl/owk29.htm (accessed 19 August 2010).

282. Ibid.

283. Ibid.

284. Giertych, *Gender Equality and Life Issues*, 15.

285. Ibid., 16.

286. Ibid.

287. Ibid., 23.

288. Ibid., 28.

289. Ibid., 17–18.

290. Ibid., 26.

291. This term is used by other scholars. See Jakubowski, *Ciągłość historii i historia ciągłości*, 258.

292. Giertych, *Civilisations at War in Europe*, 4.

293. A review of Polish press reports collected by the Jewish Historical Institute (Warsaw) from February to April 2007 indicates that over fifty articles appeared in reaction to the Giertych booklet during those months. Analysis focused mainly on Giertych's comments about Jews, and the terms "shock" or "shocking" were commonly used. See "Monitoring prasy," 02–2007, 03–2007, and 04–2007, Żydowski Instytut Historyczny (Jewish Historical Institute), Warsaw. Few of these press reports, however, discussed Koneczny in any detail. More recently, however, articles in *Nigdy Więcej* 16 (Winter–Spring 2008) have discussed Koneczny's anti-Semitism. See Katarzyna Stańczak-Wiślicz, "W pułapce kołobłędu, czyli antysemityzm

uczonego," *Nigdy Więcej* 16 (Winter–Spring 2008): 18–20; and Stefan Zgliczyński, "Od 'obrony cywilizacji' do 'ostatecznego rozwiązania,'" *Nigdy Więcej* 16 (Winter–Spring 2008): 21.

294. Dinah A. Spritzer, "Jews are a Detriment to Europe, Polish Politician Says," *Jerusalem Post*, 19 February 2007, http://www.jpost.com/servlet/Satellite?cid=117035989 2598&pagename=JPArticle%2FShowFull (accessed 6 January 2010).

295. Ibid.

296. Maciej Giertych, "Wojna cywilizacji w Europie," *Opoka w Kraju* 61, no. 82 (April 2007): 1, http://opoka.giertych.pl/owk61.htm (accessed 30 June 2008).

297. Ibid., 2.

298. Maszkowski, "Otwarte społeczeństwo i jego radio."

299. "Bronię naszej cywilizacji przed polityką bez etyki," *Gazeta Lubuska*, 31 March/1 April 2007, in "Monitoring prasy," 03–2007, 777; Żydowski Instytut Historyczny (Jewish Historical Institute), Warsaw.

300. Ibid.

301. Ibid.

302. Giertych, *Civilisations at War in Europe*, 23.

303. Ibid., 24. Giertych has warned elsewhere about the need to prevent pollution by foreign civilizational elements. See "Rozumienie świata a podziały cywilizacyjne prof. dr hab. Maciej Giertych."

304. Editorial, "Czy jestem Polakiem?" *Nowy Przegląd Wszechpolski* 13, no. 1–2 (2006), http://www.npw.pl/ARCHIWUM_NPW/2006_01_02/index.html (accessed 20 June 2006).

305. See Bogdan Gancarz, "Koneczny—prekursor Huntingtona," *Rzeczpospolita*, http://www.rzeczpospolita.pl/dodatki/opinie_070222/opinie_a_4.html (accessed 26 August 2009).

306. Brandt, "Niezapomniany Feliks Koneczny."

307. Piotr Bezat, *Poglądy polityczno-prawne Feliksa Konecznego* (Krzeszowice: Dom Wydawniczy "Ostoja," 2004), 54.

308. Dakowski, "Nie potępiajmy Konecznego!"

309. Piotr Jaroszyński, "Koneczny o tożsamości Zachodu," in *Przywracanie pamięci*, 119. Emphasis in original.

310. Ibid. Emphasis in original.

CHAPTER SIX. KONECZNIAN FUNDAMENTALISM IN POLITICS

1. Kurczewska, Horolets, and Trojanowska-Strzęboszewska, *The European Dilemma*, 49.

2. See Jędrzej Giertych, *Nacjonalizm chrześcijański*, 3rd ed. (Krzeszowice: Dom Wydawniczy "Ostoja," 2004).

3. Piotr Piesiewicz, *Myśl ideowo-polityczna Jędrzeja Giertycha*, 2nd ed. (Krzeszowice: Dom Wydawniczy "Ostoja", 2006), 26–28.

4. Ibid., 36.

5. Ibid., 34.

6. Jarosław Tomasiewicz, "Neo-nationalism in Poland," http://adnikiel.republika.pl/neo.html (accessed 24 April 2004).

7. Andrzej Walicki, "The Troubling Legacy of Roman Dmowski," *East European Politics and Societies* 14, no. 1 (Winter 2000): 31–32.
8. Ibid., 32.
9. Ibid., 39–40.
10. Maciej Giertych, "Stronnictwo Narodowe."
11. Maciej Giertych, "Teolog domu papieskiego," *Opoka w Kraju* 55, no. 76 (December 2005): 16, http://opoka.giertych.pl/55.pdf (accessed 15 August 2010). Maciej proudly declared that his brother was named on 1 December 2005 as "Theologian of the Papal Household." Wojciech has used Koneczny's civilizational theories in his theological works. See Wojciech Giertych, "The Moral Natural Law." He received extensive press coverage in 2009 for his comments on gender and sin. For a brief account, see Carol Glatz, "Women, Men Experience Sin Differently, Papal Theologian Says," *Catholic News Service*, 19 February 2009, http://www.catholicnews.com/data/stories/cns/0900774.htm (accessed 26 September 2010).
12. Ulrich Schmid, "Eine glückliche Familie. Die Giertychs und ihre Ideologie," *Osteuropa* 56, no. 11–12 (November–December 2006): 69. Also see Ulrich M. Schmid, "Hüter der polnischen Kultur; Wes Geistes Kind ist der polnische Bildungsminister?" *Neue Zürcher Zeitung*, 1 December 2006; and Knut Krohn, "Auch Darwin ist des Teufels," *Stuttgarter Zeitung*, 13 March 2007.
13. Maciej Giertych, "Rok Konecznego," *Opoka w Kraju* 29, no. 50 (March 1999), http://opoka.giertych.pl/owk29.htm (accessed 30 June 2008).
14. Peter Oliver Loew, "Zwillinge zwischen Endecja und Sanacja. Die neue polnische Rechtsregierung und ihre historischen Wurzeln," *Eurozine* (2005), http://www.eurozine.com/articles/2006-01-12-loew-de.html (accessed 26 August 2009). Originally published in *Osteuropa*, no. 11 (2005), 3.
15. Giertych, "Rok Konecznego."
16. Horodecki, "My, szarzy ludzie . . . , "45. Horodecki even argues that Koneczny's *Logos and Ethos* should be assigned in high schools. See "Odwieczny problem," *Myśl Polska*, 22 September 2002, http://www.myslpolska.icenter.pl/ (accessed 26 March 2005).
17. See Andrzej J. Horodecki, "Projekt Konstytucji Rzeczpospolitej Polskiej środowisk patriotycznych skupionych wokół 'Nowego Przeglądu Wszechpolskiego,'" *Nowy Przegląd Wszechpolski* 12, no. 7–8 (2005), http://www.npw.pl/ARCHIWUM_NPW/2005_07_08/PiS-Horodecki_konstytucja.html (accessed 30 June 2008). Emphases in the original.
18. Tomasiewicz, *Ugrupowania neoendeckie w III Rzeczypospolitej*, 74–75, 115.
19. Wituch, "Religia jako rdzeń cywilizacji," 79.
20. Andrzej Horodecki, "Wilki w owczarni," *Myśl Polska*, no. 43 (24 October 2004), http://www.myslpolska.icenter.pl/ (accessed 25 March 2005). Koneczny's warnings about civilizational mixing are frequently repeated in fundamentalist commentary about the dangers of alien influences. Piotr Bezat even argues that "[w]ithout civilizational mixture there cannot be revolution." See *Poglądy polityczno-prawne Feliksa Konecznego*, 51.
21. Andrzej Horodecki, "Powrót polskości," *Myśl Polska*, no. 39 (24 September 2006), http://www.myslpolska.org/?idx=artykul&src=98030 (accessed 6 October 2006).
22. Ryba, "Polska w XX wieku a cywilizacje," 97.
23. Scholars contradict the implication here that the communist regime in Poland was

totalitarian in nature. Rather, it can be classified as an "authoritarian" regime that tolerated some level of dissent and societal independence. See Sarah L. de Lange and Simona Guerra, "The League of Polish Families between East and West, Past and Present," *Communist and Post-Communist Studies* 42 (2009): 530.

24. Tomasiewicz, *Ugrupowania neoendeckie w III Rzeczypospolitej*, 47–48.

25. Tokarz, *Ruch narodowy w Polsce*, 17.

26. For example, see Józef Kossecki, "Zderzenie cywilizacji łacińskiej i orientu w świetle nauki porównawczej o cywilizacjach i cybernetyki społecznej," *Strona Ruchu Obrony Rodziny i Jednostki,* http://74.125.93.132/search?q=cache:9Xt5CQr_gJcJ:rorij. free.ngo.pl/Zderzenie%2520cywilizacji.doc+kossecki+zderzenie+orientu&cd=1& hl=en&ct=clnk&gl=us (accessed 22 September 2006).

27. Tomasiewicz, *Ugrupowania neoendeckie w III Rzeczypospolitej*, 52–53. See also Maciej Giertych, "Mój życiorys," *Opoka w Kraju* 14, no. 35 (October 1995), http://opoka.giertych.pl/owk14.htm (accessed 30 June 2008).

28. Maciej Giertych, "Moja teczka w SB," *Opoka w Kraju* 32, no. 53 (December 1999), http://opoka.giertych.pl/owk32.htm (accessed 30 June 2008).

29. T. David Curp, "'Roman Dmowski Understood': Ethnic Cleansing as Permanent Revolution," *European History Quarterly* 35, no. 3 (2005): 405.

30. Ibid., 413.

31. Ibid., 420.

32. Ibid., 405.

33. See Lukasz Hirszowicz, "Antisemitism in Today's Poland," *Soviet Jewish Affairs* 12, no. 1 (1982): 55–65.

34. Bezat, *Poglądy polityczno-prawne Feliksa Konecznego*, 49.

35. De Lange and Guerra, "The League of Polish Families," 530–31.

36. Jan Józef Lipski, "Dwie ojczyzny—dwa patriotyzmy. Uwagi o megalomanii narodowej i ksenofobii Polaków," *My—mankurty,* http://www.mankurty.com/statti/dwie%20ojczyzny.pdf (accessed 24 August 2009). This article has been reprinted in *Gazeta Wyborcza,* 26 September 2006, and in an abridged English-language translation as "Two Fatherlands; Two Patriotisms," in *Between East and West: Writings from Kultura,* ed. Robert Kostrzewa (New York: Hill and Wang, 1990), 52–71.

37. Jan Skoczyński, "Człowiek bez tożsamości. Rozmowa Józefa Barana z prof. Janem Skoczyńskim," in *O globalizmie na spokojnie,* ed. Anna Frątczak (Kraków: Wydawnictwo "Zielone Brygady," 2005), 41.

38. Sergiusz Kowalski and Magdalena Tulli, *Zamiast procesu. Raport o mowie nienawiści* (Warsaw: Instytut Studiów Politycznych PAN, 2003), 486.

39. Tomasiewicz, *Ugrupowania neoendeckie w III Rzeczypospolitej*, 61–62. See also Alina Cała, *Żyd—wróg odwieczny? Antysemityzm w Polsce i jego źródła* (Warsaw: Wydawnictwo Nisza, 2012), 512, 563–65.

40. Kazimierz Janusz, *Konfrontacje Rosja-Zachód. Zderzenie dwóch cywilizacji* (1974; repr., Komorów: Wydawnictwo Antyk Marcin Dybowski, 1997), 23. For a more complete discussion of Janusz's debt to Koneczny, see Jiří Vykoukal, "Rusko v 'druhém oběhu' aneb Střet civilizací po polsku," *Soudobé dějiny* 9, no. 3–4 (2002): 593–601.

41. Janusz, *Konfrontacje Rosja-Zachód*, 27, 98, 120.

42. Located near the University, one banner in the exhibit quoted an entry for 14 November 1968 from Stefan Kisielewski's diary that describes proceedings of the 5th

Party Congress as "Byzantine" in nature. Józef Kossecki devotes an entire chapter of his book to an analysis of the Byzantine nature of communist Poland ("red Byzantinism")—especially its bureaucratizing tendencies—and its lingering civilizational impact in Poland today. See Kossecki, *Podstawy nowoczesnej nauki porównawczej o cywilizacjach,* 141–62.

43. Koneczny, *Plurality of Civilisations,* 120, fn. 22.
44. Ibid., 136.
45. Tomasiewicz, *Ugrupowania neoendeckie w III Rzeczypospolitej,* 330.
46. "Prof. Maciej Giertych kandydatem województwa świętokrzyskiego w prawyborach prezydenckich," *Serwis internetowy Ligi Polskich Rodzin,* 9 October 2004, http://www.lpr.pl/?sr=!czytaj&id=1033&dz=region&x=92&pocz=693&gr= (accessed 28 March 2005).
47. Tokarz, *Ruch narodowy w Polsce,* 13–14.
48. Ibid., 26.
49. Szurgot, *Prawo jako fundament cywilizacji łacińskiej,* 7.
50. Michał Poradowski, *Dzieje cywilizacji europejskiej* (Wrocław: Wydawnictwo Nortom, 2007), 17–18.
51. Ibid., 20.
52. Ibid.
53. Tomasiewicz, *Ugrupowania neoendeckie w III Rzeczypospolitej,* 219.
54. Ibid.
55. Bębenek, "Paradygmat polityki w cywilizacji łacińskiej," 90.
56. Stefan Zgliczyński, *Antysemityzm po polsku* (Warsaw: Instytut Wydawniczy Książka i Prasa, 2008), 114.
57. Jaroszyński, *Polska i Europa,* 125.
58. Tokarz, *Ruch narodowy w Polsce,* 29–30.
59. Małgorzata Olszewska, "Krew tej ziemi. Wszechpolaków portret zbiorowy," *onet. pl Tygodnik Powszechny* 15 May 2006, http://tygodnik.onet.pl/0,1335465,druk. html (accessed 19 June 2006). This stress on Koneczny is evident at the local MW chapters elsewhere. The MW site at http://free4web.pl/NewsList/122494, described meetings in 2005–6 at which there were lectures on Koneczny's theory of civilizations, the role of women in Latin civilization, the EU from a civilizational perspective, etc.
60. De Lange and Guerra, "The League of Polish Families," 536–38.
61. Tomasiewicz, *Ugrupowania neoendeckie w III Rzeczypospolitej,* 9.
62. De Lange and Guerra, "The League of Polish Families," 536–38.
63. Stanisław Stojanowski-Han, "LPR—przyczyny klęski," *Myśl Polska,* no. 5 (3 February 2008).
64. Kurczewska, Horolets, and Trojanowska-Strzęboszewska, *The European Dilemma,* 10.
65. Reply to Artur Domosławski's article in the readers' forum, found at *gazeta.pl,* http://serwisy.gazeta.pl/forum/72,2.html?f=521&w=3243518 (accessed 10 June 2005).
66. Jerzy Tomaszewski, "From Internationalism to Nationalism? Poland 1944–96," in *Nationalism and Internationalism in the Post-Cold War Era,* ed. Kjell Goldmann, Ulf Hannerz, and Charles Westin (London: Routledge, 2000), 81.

67. De Lange and Guerra, "The League of Polish Families," 529.

68. Ibid.

69. Ibid., 531.

70. Ibid. This phrase is borrowed by the authors from B. Crawford and A. Lijpart, "Old Legacies, New Institutions: Explaining Political and Economic Trajectories in Post-Communist Regimes," in *Liberalization and Leninist Legacies: Comparative Perspectives on Democratic Transition*, ed. B. Crawford and A. Lijphart (Berkeley: University of California Press, 1997), 22.

71. Kurczewska, Horolets, and Trojanowska-Strzęboszewska, *The European Dilemma*, 73.

72. Hanna Kwiatkowska, "Conflict between the Image of the Jews and the Self-Image of the Poles in the Light of the Articles Published in 'Nasz Dziennik' 1998–2003," *Scripta Judaica Cracoviensia* 2 (2003): 91.

73. Daria Łatkowska, "Ocalić cywilzację [sic] łacińską," *LPR Górny Śląsk*, 8 June 2006, http://www.lprtychy.iap.pl/index.html?id=39750&site_id=39235 (accessed 18 June 2006).

74. Ibid.

75. Wojciech Wierzejski, *Naród, młodzież, idea: zbiór narodowej publicystyki z lat 1997–2000* (Krzeszowice: Dom Wydawnicy "Ostoja", 2001), 40–41.

76. Adam Wielomski, "Globalizatorzy," *Myśl Polska*, no. 18–19 (2–9 May 2004), http://www.myslpolska.icenter.pl/ (accessed 22 March 2005).

77. Marcin Olbrycht, "Wojciech Wierzejski," *Wszechpolak: Pismo Młodzieży Narodowej* 115 (June 2004): 6.

78. Ibid., 7.

79. Jan Piwowarski, "Program polityczny PLN," *Nowy Przegląd Wszechpolski* 11, no. 5–6 (2004), http://www.npw.pl/ARCHIWUM_NPW/2004_05_06/PIS-Piwowarski_Program-polityczny-PLN.html (accessed 21 June 2006).

80. Ibid.

81. See *Młodziez [sic] Wszechpolska—Legnica*, http://web.pertus.com.pl/~mwszechp/literatura.html (accessed 5 July 2006), and *Młodzież Wszechpolska—Jelenia Góra*, http://www.mwjelenia.republika.pl/ksiazki.html (accessed 5 July 2006).

82. Anna Fostakowska, "Wszechpolki—rozmowy kontrolowane," *gazeta.pl*, 11 February 2005. http://serwisy.gazeta.pl/kraj/1,62906,2547356.html?as=1&ias=5 (accessed 10 June 2005).

83. Adam Łącki, "Obóz we Wrocławiu," *MW Koło Lubań*, 5 May 2006, http://free4web.pl/NewsList/89149 (accessed 5 July 2006). Also at *Młodzież Wszechpolska—Dolny Śląsk*, http://www.ds.wszechpolacy.pl/ (accessed 5 July 2006).

84. "Śladem myśli Feliksa Konecznego—Bialska Wszechnica," *Serwis internetowy Ligi Polskich Rodzin* http://www.lpr.pl/?sr=!czytaj&id=2849&dz=region&x=3&pocz=499&gr= (accessed 8 July 2011).

85. "III Wszechnica Narodowa," *Młodzież [sic] Wszechpolska—koło Radom*, 21 May 2005, http://radom.wszechpolacy.pl/ (accessed 5 July 2006).

86. Paweł Kusak, "Dziedzictwo Konecznego," *Młodzież Wszechpolska*, http://www.ma.wszechpolacy.pl/podstrony/!czytaj.php?id=1542&dz=artykuly&x=0&pocz= (accessed 5 July 2006). As MW member Paweł Kusak points out in his essay: "For a Catholic, such as Koneczny, man consists of spirit and body, and all humans must possess an Aristotelian form and content."

87. Mitja Velikonja, "Slovenian and Polish Religio-National Mythologies: A Comparative Analysis," *Religion, State & Society* 31, no. 3 (2003): 248. Emphases in original.
88. "Prawdziwa Tożsamość Europy," *Obóz Narodowo-Radykalny*, 30 December 2010, http://www.onr.h2.pl/index.php?option=com_content&task=view&id=221&Ite mid=104# (accessed 28 May 2011). For a broader application of Koneczny's theories to the problem of Poland's civilizational enemies, see "Właściwa wizja zjednocznonej Europy," *Obóz Narodowo-Radykalny*, 30 December 2010, http://www .onr.h2.pl/index.php?option=com_content&view=article&id=223:waciwa-wizja-zjednoczonej-europy-&catid=54:unia-europejska (accessed 28 May 2011).
89. The Stephen Roth Institute for the Study of Contemporary Antisemitism and Racism reported in 2007 that the NOP was "the most aggressively antisemitic organization in Poland." See *Antisemitism Worldwide 2007—Poland*, http://www.tau.ac.il/ Anti-Semitism/asw2007/poland.html (accessed 12 August 2010).
90. Piotr Kudzia and Grzegorz Pawelczyk, "The Training of Polish Neo-fascists," *Forum Żydzi-Polacy-Chrześcijanie*, http://www.forum-znak.org.pl/print.php?t=przeglad &id=1852&1=en (accessed 25 August 2009). Also see "Szkolenia polskich neofaszystów," *Forum Żydzi-Polacy-Chrześcijanie*, http://www.forum-znak.org.pl/ print.php?t=przeglad&id=1852&1=pl (accessed 25 August 2009). Originally published as "Biało-Polacy," *Wprost*, no. 20 (18 May 2003): 34–36.
91. Andrzej J. Horodecki, "Ciemności europejskie." In this essay Horodecki specifically calls for Koneczny's works to be required reading in religious education classes in middle schools.
92. Marcin Jendrzejczak, "Nacjonalizm bizantyjski," *Prawica.net*, 28 June 2007, http:// www.prawica.net/node/7547 (accessed 8 July 2010). Several dozen people reportedly attended the conference. Topics of speeches included: Dariusz Tarnowski, "Polska między Wschodem a Zachodem"; Bartosz Biernat, "Cywilizacja Łacińska a Cywilizacja Zachodu"; and Zbigniew Lignarski, "Talmud a ideologia III Rzeszy." See *Nacjonalista.pl—Portal Narodowy-Radykalny*, http://www.nacjonalista.org/ galeria.php?id=110 (accessed 20 November 2009). Also see Lignarski, "Talmud ze swastyką w tle?"
93. Tarnowski, "Polska między Wschodem i Zachodem."
94. Ibid.
95. Sawczak, "O rozwiązaniu kwestii żydowskiej."
96. See Modras, "The Interwar Polish Catholic Press on the Jewish Question," 179–80.
97. In his book on "Jewish civilization," Koneczny discussed this issue. See Koneczny, *Cywilizacja żydowska*, 383–84.
98. Sawczak, "O rozwiązaniu kwestii żydowskiej."
99. Stańczak-Wiślicz, "W pułapce kołobłędu, czyli antysemityzm uczonego," 18.
100. Ibid.
101. "Kraków: III Konferencja Konecznańska," *Narodowe Odrodzenie Polski*, 5 March 2009, http://www.nop.org.pl/?artykul_id=824 (accessed 20 November 2009).
102. "Kraków: VIII Konferencja Konecznańska," *Narodowe Odrodzenie Polski/National Rebirth of Poland*, 24 February 2014, http://www.nop.org.pl/2014/02/24/krakow -viii-konferencja-konecznanska/ (accessed 17 June 2014). On 22 February 2014, the LPR hosted a similar conference and gravesite memorial in Kraków. See "Konferencja poświęcona prof. Feliksowi Konecznemu, 22.02.2014," *Liga Polskich Rodzin*

Serwis Internetowy, 1 March 2014, http://www.lpr.pl/2014/03/01/konferencja-po-swiecona-prof-feliksowi-konecznemu-22022014/ (accessed 17 June 2014).

103. For a brief overview of the nationalist critique of the EU, see Tokarz, *Ruch narodowy w Polsce*, 167–77. Tokarz also discusses the Konecznian inspiration for fundamentalists' vision of a civilizational conflict among the Latin, Byzantine, Turanian, and Jewish civilizations in Europe.

104. Bojarski *Dokąd Polsko?*, 89. He is quoting from Koneczny, *Polskie logos a ethos*, 2: 612. Emphasis in original.

105. Bokiej, *Cywilizacja łacińska*, 119.

106. Koneczny, *Cywilizacja bizantyńska*, 224–25.

107. Bokiej, *Cywilizacja łacińska*, 120.

108. Bezat, *Teoria cywilizacji Feliksa Konecznego*, 26. Koneczny asserted that in Germany Catholics found it difficult to identify with Byzantine civilization, because of its caesaropapism. Nevertheless, he asserted that strong Byzantine influences were present in Germany from the tenth century onward. See Koneczny, *Tło cywilizacyjne odsieczy wiedeńskiej*, 34.

109. In "Koneczny o cywilizacji arabskiej," Giertych points out that Koneczny primarily focused on the Latin, Byzantine, Turanian, and Jewish civilizations. *Opoka w Kraju* 59, no. 80 (October 2006): 5–7, http://opoka.giertych.pl/owk59.htm (accessed 30 June 2008). The "Islamic threat," facilitated by lax EU immigration policies, is also analyzed from a Konecznian perspective by Białkowski in *Idea ścierania się cywilizacji według Feliksa Konecznego*.

110. Paweł Skibiński, "Bizancjum na zachodzie. Niemcy w historiozofii Feliksa Konecznego," *Fronda* 17/18 (1999): 43.

111. Jan Engelgard, "Kwestia niemiecka," *Myśl Polska*, no. 35 (2 September 2007), http://www.myslpolska.org/?article=506 (accessed 15 September 2007).

112. Koneczny, *Plurality of Civilisations*, 271.

113. Bezat, *Teoria cywilizacji Feliksa Konecznego*, 88.

114. Koneczny, *Cywilizacja bizantyńska*, 364.

115. Hilckman, "Introduction," 6.

116. Ratajczak, "O cywilizacjach."

117. Editorial, "Egzamin dla każdego z nas," *Nowy Przegląd Wszechpolski* 9, no. 5–6 (2002), http://www.npw.pl/ARCHIWUM_NPW/2002_05_06/WST-Red_Egza min.htm (accessed 21 June 2006).

118. Bojarski, *Dokąd Polsko?*, 134.

119. Giertych, *Civilisations at War in Europe*, 19.

120. Ibid., 20.

121. Maciej Giertych, "Konfrontacja z islamem," *Opoka w Kraju* 66, no. 87 (March 2008): 5, http://opoka.giertych.pl/66.pdf (accessed 30 June 2008).

122. Poles overwhelmingly voted "yes" in the referendum, with over 77% supporting membership in the EU. The turnout was 58.85% of the registered voters, well above the constitutional requirement of 50%. See Aleks Szczerbiak, "Referendum Briefing No. 5: The Polish EU Accession Referendum, 7–8 June 2003," *Sussex European Institute: Opposing Europe Research Network*, http://www.sussex.ac.uk/polces/docu ments/poland5.pdf, 6–9.

123. Giertych, *Civilisations at War in Europe*, 21.

124. Hilckman, "Feliks Koneczny and the Comparative Science of Civilisation," 29.

125. See "Europa łacińska," *Opoka w Kraju* 40, no. 61 (December 2001), http://opoka
.giertych.pl/owk40.htm (accessed 30 June 2008), which deals with the EU and civilizational identity; and "Bizantynizm niemiecki," which deals with Koneczny's concept of German Byzantinism explicitly.

126. Maciej Giertych, "Korzenie UE," *Opoka w Kraju*, Numer specjalny, poświęcony referendum w sprawie akcesji do Unii Europejskiej, 44, no. 65 (April 2003), http://
opoka.giertych.pl/owk44.htm (accessed 30 June 2008). Also in this issue are
"Superpaństwo," in which Giertych expresses a general fear of globalization; and
"Geopolityka," in which he reiterates his fears of German hegemony (via the EU).

127. Maciej Giertych, "Co teraz?" *Opoka w Kraju* 45, no. 66 (July 2003), http://opoka
.giertych.pl/owk45.htm (accessed 30 June 2008).

128. Maciej Giertych, "Program dla posłów LPR do Parlamentu Europejskiego," *Opoka
w Kraju* 49, no. 70 (May 2004), http://opoka.giertych.pl/owk49.htm (accessed 30
June 2008).

129. Giertych, *Z nadzieją w przyszłość*, 23, 29–32.

130. Giertych, *Civilisations at war in Europe*, 22.

131. Maciej Giertych, *Quo vadis Europa?* (Brussels: Maciej Gertych, 2009), 9, http://
opoka.giertych.pl/quo_vadis_ang.pdf (accessed 26 September 2010).

132. Polish opposition to Byzantinism is crucial, he believes. See Andrzej Horodecki,
"Kościół wobec personalizmu i gromadnościowości: Konsekwencje lekceważenia
grzechu pierworodnego," *Nowy Przegląd Wszechpolski* 11, no. 3–4 (2004), http://
www.npw.pl/ARCHIWUM_NPW/2004_03_04/ZRE-Horodecki_KOSCIOL-WO
BEC.html (accessed 30 June 2008).

133. See Horodecki, "Wilki w owczarni."

134. Andrzej Horodecki, "Teraz Serbia," *Myśl Polska* (n.d.), http://www.myslpolska.
org/?article=803 (accessed 30 June 2008). Addressing the recognition of Kosovo,
Horodecki argues that the creation of an Islamic "Great Albania" will pave the way
for "Islamic pressure on Europe" that will grow and become wider with Turkish
entry to the EU. He also sees this as a way to extend German power into the region.

135. See Andrzej Horodecki, "Ecce Polonia," *Myśl Polska*, no. 17 (25 April 2004); and
"Piastowskie korzenie," *Myśl Polska*, no. 34–35 (20–27 August 2006).

136. Horodecki, "Wobec zamachu na patriotyzm."

137. Andrzej Horodecki, "Totalna walka z cywilizacją łacińską, część I," *Nowy
Przegląd Wszechpolski* 9, no. 3–4 (2002), http://www.npw.pl/ARCHIWUM_
NPW/2002_03_04/PIS-Horodecki_Totalna-walka-z-CL.htm (accessed 30 June
2008).

138. Horodecki, "Totalna walka z cywilizacją łacińską, część II." He also repeats here his
warning that the "liquidation of Polish agricultural society—the final base of Latin
civilization" by the CSP ("Centralne Siły Polityczne," or "Central Political Powers")
will be one of the costs of entry to the EU.

139. See Andrzej Horodecki, "Gra o wytrwałość," *Myśl Polska*, 27 October 2002, and
Andrzej Horodecki, "Nowa Enigma IV Rzeszy," *Myśl Polska*, 8 December 2002.

140. Andrzej Horodecki, "Prominentna aprobata proceduru," *Myśl Polska*, 7–14 April
2002. In his analysis of the EU, Włodzimierz Bojarski proposes a similar alliance
of Poland, the Czech Republic, Hungary, and Croatia, along with other "Latin" nations that might create a bloc to oppose both German and Russian hegemony over
the region. See *Dokąd Polsko?*, 88–91.

141. Andrzej Horodecki, "Nowy Grunwald," *Myśl Polska*, no. 3 (19 January 2003). He is referring to the victory of Poles and allied forces over the Teutonic Knights at the Battle of Grunwald in 1410.
142. Teresa Bloch, "85. rocznica osiemnastej bitwy decydującej o losach świata," *Nowy Przegląd Wszechpolski* 12, no. 9–10 (2005), http://www.npw.pl/ARCHIWUM_NPW/2005_09_10/HiW-Bloch_85_rocznica.html (accessed 21 June 2006).
143. Teresa Bloch, "Dwa oblicza unii. Unie polsko-litewskie a Unia Europejska," *Nowy Przegląd Wszechpolski* 9, no. 3–4 (2002), http://www.npw.pl/ARCHIWUM_NPW/2002_03_04/HIW-Bloch_Dwa-oblicza-unii.htm (accessed 21 June 2006).
144. See Andrzej Horodecki, "Restrukturyzacja świadomości," *Myśl Polska*, no. 4 (26 January 2003); and Andrzej Horodecki, "Kurort Europa," *Myśl Polska*, no. 5 (2 February 2003).
145. Andrzej Horodecki, "Unia antyeuropejska," *Myśl Polska*, no. 23 (8 June 2003).
146. Ibid.
147. See Andrzej Horodecki, "Wychowanie do wolności w prawdzie," *Nowy Przegląd Wszechpolski* 11, no. 9–10 (2004), http://www.npw.pl/ARCHIWUM_NPW/2004_09_10/PIS-Horodecki_wychowanie-do-wolnosci.html (accessed 30 June 2008).
148. Andrzej Horodecki, "Neototalitaryzm," *Myśl Polska*, no. 44–45 (2–9 November 2003). http://www.myslpolska.icenter.pl/ (accessed 22 March 2005). See also Horodecki, "Kościół wobec personalizmu i gromadnościowości."
149. Andrzej Horodecki, "W cieniu wyborów," *Myśl Polska*, no. 41 (9 October 2005). Emphases in the original.
150. Ibid.
151. See Andrzej Horodecki, "O powrót do Bożej czasoprzestrzeni odniesienia," *Nowy Przegląd Wszechpolski* 12, no. 9–10 (2005), http://www.npw.pl/ARCHIWUM_NPW/2005_09_10/HiW-Horodecki_O_powrot_do_bozej.html (accessed 30 June 2008).
152. Jerzy Bajda, "Konstytucja Europejska: ocena moralna," *Instytut Studiów nad Rodziną* (n.d.), http://www.isnr.uksw.edu.pl/teksty/Bajda/ocena%20konst%20UE.htm (accessed 30 June 2008).
153. Editorial, "Czy jestem Polakiem?"
154. Ibid. Emphases in the original.
155. Koneczny, *Cywilizacja bizantyńska*, 403.
156. Tomasiewicz, *Ugrupowania neoendeckie w III Rzeczypospolitej*, 265.
157. Janion, *Niesamowita Słowiańszczyzna*, 323–24.
158. Zubrzycki, "'We, the Polish Nation,'" 635.
159. Ibid., 637.
160. Michał Wolnicki, "Co nas czeka?" *Ojczyzna.pl* (18 December 2001), http://www.ojczyzna.pl/Arch-Teksty/WOLNICKI__Co-nas-czeka.htm (accessed 29 March 2005).
161. Tomasz Jaźwiński, "'(Nie)konieczność historyczna' jednej Europy," *Myśl Polska*, no. 36–37 (3–10 September 2006), http://www.myslpolska.org/ (accessed 6 October 2006).
162. Gawlicz, "Płeć i naród," 108-9.
163. Giertych, "Koneczny o cywilizacji arabskiej," 5–7.
164. Koneczny, *Plurality of Civilisations*, 203.

165. Koneczny, *Prawa dziejowe*, 162–63
166. Jan Bodakowski, "Euro konstytucja czyli wstęp do czerwonego terroru," *Nacjonalista.pl—portal narodowo-radykalny* (23 October 2007), http://nacjonalista.pl/ar tykuly.php?id=70 (accessed 9 January 2008).
167. Maciej Giertych, "Pożytki," *Opoka w Kraju* 49, no. 70 (May 2004): 5. http://opoka .giertych.pl/49.pdf (accessed 28 August 2009).
168. Graff, "Gender, Sexuality, and Nation," 142.
169. Ibid.
170. Graff, "Land of Real Men and Real Women," 10.
171. Bojarski, *Dokąd Polsko?*, 98.
172. Ibid., 110–11.

CONCLUSION: KONECZNIAN FUNDAMENTALISM IN THE TWENTY-FIRST CENTURY

1. Skrzydlewski, *Polityka w ciwilizacji łacińskiej*, 77.
2. Ewa Thompson, "Said a sprawa Polska," *Dziennik.pl*, 29 June 2005, http://www.dzi ennik.pl/dziennik/europa/article47614/Said_a_sprawa_polska.html (accessed 30 June 2008). Originally published in *Europa*, no. 65 (29 June 2005).
3. Ewa Thompson, "Sarmatyzm i postkolonializm," *Dziennik.pl*, 18 November 2006, http://www.dziennik.pl/dziennik/europa/article46218/Sarmatyzm_i_postkolo nializm.html (accessed 30 June 2008). Originally published in *Europa*, no. 137 (18 November 2006).
4. Koneczny, *Rozwój moralności*, 213–14.
5. Nadolski, "Wątki historyczne w publicystyce Feliksa Konecznego," 61–63.
6. Koneczny, *Polskie logos a ethos*, 2:360.
7. Koneczny, *Polska między wschodem a zachodem*, 46. In 1905, Koneczny worked closely with these same people in the Slavic Club in Kraków.
8. See Loew, "Zwillinge zwischen Endecja und Sanacja."
9. Tamara Hundorova, "Postcolonial *Ressentiment*—the Ukrainian Case," in *From Sovietology to Postcoloniality: Poland and Ukraine from a Postcolonial Perspective*, ed. Janusz Korek (Huddinge: Södertörns högskola, 2007), 103.
10. Ibid., 104.
11. Ibid., 105.
12. Poland's debate about "a return to Europe" also brought forth new scholarly works with a civilizational perspective. See Stanisław Piskor, *Na moście Europy* (Katowice: Wydawca Towarzystwo Zachęty Kultury, 1992). Piskor's analysis has some similarities with the Konecznian worldview. For example, he sees Byzantine civilization as an Orientalized rival of western civilization. See Piskor, *Na moście Europy*, 25–27, 37–38, and 69–70.
13. Giertych, "Konfrontacja z islamem," 7.
14. Peter Bein, "Wojna o cywilizacje. Operation Danish Cartoons—A Battle in the War of Civilizations." *now@ on-line* (March 2008), http://nowaonline.strefa.pl/66_ Bein_P_2.htm (accessed 24 October 2008). Also at *Zaprasza.net.* http://zaprasza .net/a_y.php?article_title=koneczny&mid=22348 (accessed 25 August 2009).
15. Ratajczak, "O cywilizacjach."

16. Bruce Mazlish's judgment on the reception of Samuel Huntington's *The Clash of Civilizations* (New York: Simon and Schuster, 1996) seems relevant here: "Its importance is in inverse proportion to its scholarly worth, but that is often the case with an argument that catches the public mood. With the Cold War over in the early 1990s, a powerful need was felt in some quarters for a substitute enemy that would allow for a black-and-white conflict such as existed in relation to communism." See *Civilization and its Contents* (Stanford: Stanford University Press, 2004), 115.

17. Vasilenko, "Dialogue of Cultures, Dialogue of Civilizations," 7.

18. Diec, *Cywilizacje bez okien*, 168.

19. Arkadiusz Maślach, "Czy Polska potrzebuje społeczeństwa obywatelskiego?" *Magazyn Obywatel*, no. 4 (2003), http://www.obywatel.org.pl/index.php?module=subje cts&func=viewpage&pageid=363 (accessed 3 March 2007).

20. Marian Miszalski, "W kręgu 'inżynierii społecznej.' Kolejny 'nowy człowiek'— homo democraticus? *Niedziela—Tygodnik Katolicki*, http://www.niedziela.pl/ artykul_w_niedzieli.php?doc=ed200115&nr=16 (access 24 June 2006). Originally published in *Niedziela—Tygodnik Katolicki*. *Edycja łódzka* 15 (2001).

21. Paweł Zawadzki, "Feliks Koneczny, postać bardzo niewygodna," *Wydawnictwo "Zielone Brygady"* 2, no. 182 (April 2003), http://www.zb.eco.pl/publication/feliks -koneczny-postac-bardzo-niewygodna-p172811 (accessed 4 May 2009).

22. Andrzej Solak, "Tradycjonalizm 'politycznie poprawny,'" *Myśl Polska*, 28 April 2002, http://www.myslpolska.icenter.pl/ (accessed 25 March 2005).

23. Kociuba, "Tożsamość kulturowa cywilizacji europejskiej," 52.

24. Andrzej Horodecki, "Między myśleniem a świadomością," *Nowy Przegląd Wszechpolski* 13, no. 1–2 (2006), http://www.npw.pl/ARCHIWUM_NPW/2006_01_02/2 .html (accessed 20 June 2006).

25. Horodecki, "O zdrowiu w cywilizacji łacińskiej."

26. Horodecki, "Walka cywilizacyjna."

27. Ibid.

28. Ibid.

29. Włodzimierz Bojarski, "Czy kolonializm przeminął?" *Nasza Witryna*, http://www .naszawitryna.pl/europa_343.html (accessed 11 May 2010). First published in *Nasz Dziennik*, 20 February 2002.

30. Ibid.

31. Ibid.

32. Kossecki, "Zderzenie cywilizacji łacińskiej i orientu." Emphasis in the original.

33. Kossecki, *Podstawy nowoczesnej nauki porównawczej o cywilizacjach*, 162. Emphasis in the original.

34. Horodecki, "Kościół wobec personalizmu i gromadnościowości."

35. Paweł Bała, "Eurodżihad," *Organizacja Monarchistów Polskich oddział Lublin*, (http://www.omp.lublin.pl/artykuly.php?autor=3&artykul=0) (accessed 4 January 2010).

36. Horodecki, "Wychowanie do wolności w prawdzie." Emphasis in the original.

37. Koneczny, *Prawa dziejowe*, 324. Koneczny's "neo-messianism" is noted by many scholars; see Bukowska, "Feliksa Konecznego historiozoficzna refleksja nad narodem," 247. On Koneczny's romanticism, see Nowak, "Jedność w rozmaitości," 75–94.

38. Editorial, "Miłość przebija pancerze," *Nowy Przegląd Wszechpolski* 14, no. 1–2 (2007): 1, http://www.npw.pl/pdf/npw.2007.1–2.pdf (accessed 27 August 2009).

39. Commenting in 2001, David Chioni Moore stated that in his view, "at least two features of this giant [post-Soviet] sphere are significant for currently constituted postcolonial studies: first, how extraordinarily postcolonial the societies of the former Soviet regions are, and, second, how extraordinarily little attention is paid to this fact, at least in these terms." See "Is the Post- in Postcolonial the Post- in Post-Soviet? Toward a Global Postcolonial Critique," *PMLA* 116, no. 1 (2001): 114. For other useful commentary, see Bogusław Bakuła, "Kolonialne i postkolonialne aspekty polskiego dyskursu kresoznawczego (zarys problematyki)," *Teksty Drugie*, no. 6 (2006): 11–33; Dariusz Skórczewski, "Postkolonialna Polska—project (nie) możliwy," *Teksty Drugie*, no. 1–2 (2006): 100–112; and Zarycki, "Polska i jej regiony a debata postkolonialna," 31–48.

40. Janusz Korek, "Central and Eastern Europe from a Postcolonial Perspective," in Korek, *From Sovietology to Postcoloniality*, 8.

41. Dariusz Skórczewski adds that the Soviet Union skillfully masked its own imperialism while criticizing others. See "Dlaczego Polska powinna upomnieć się o swoją postkolonialność," *Znak* 59, no. 9 (2007): 149.

42. Korek, "Central and Eastern Europe from a Postcolonial Perspective," 6.

43. Roumiana Deltcheva, "The Difficult Topos In-Between. The East Central European Cultural Context as a Post-Coloniality," *Sarmatian Review* 18, no. 3 (September 1998): 557.

44. Aleksander Fiut, "In the Shadow of Empires. Postcolonialism in Central and Eastern Europe—Why Not?" In Korek, *From Sovietology to Postcoloniality*, 33.

45. Ewa Thompson, "The Surrogate Hegemon in Polish Postcolonial Discourse," *Ewa M. Thompson's Homepage*, 1, http://www.owlnet.rice.edu/~ethomp/The%20Surrogate%20Hegemon.pdf (accessed 27 June 2010).

46. Thompson, "Said a sprawa Polska." Thompson also cites resentment of the "armia moherowych beretów" (army of mohair berets)—the elderly women listeners of *Radio Maryja* (Radio Maria)—as another product of colonialism. See "Sarmatyzm i postkolonializm."

47. Sanjay Seth, "A 'Postcolonial World'?" In *Contending Images of World Politics*, ed. Greg Fry and Jacinta O'Hagan (New York: St. Martin's Press, 2000), 215.

48. Krzysztof Kowalczyk-Twarowski, "Imperialne przestworza, spolegliwi tubylcy: Polska, Rosja, RPA," *Er(r)go* 8, no. 1 (2004): 174.

49. Ibid., 174–75.

50. Bojarski, *Dokąd Polsko?*, 19.

51. Teresa Bloch, "Miejsce wschodnich rubieży w dziejach ojczystych," *Nowy Przegląd Wszechpolski* 14, no. 3–4 (2007): 16, http://www.npw.pl/pdf/npw.2007.3–4.pdf (accessed 9 December 2009).

52. Teresa Bloch, "Nie wszystko stracone," *Nowy Przegląd Wszechpolski* 11, no. 5–6 (2004), http://www.npw.pl/ARCHIWUM_NPW/2004_05_06/HIW-Bloch_Nie wszystko-stracone.html (accessed 21 June 2006).

53. Magdalena Nowicka, "Rzeczpospolita postkolonialna."

54. Thompson, "The Surrogate Hegemon," 1.

55. Deltcheva, "The Difficult Topos In-Between," 557.

56. Clare Cavanagh, "Postcolonial Poland," *Common Knowledge* 10, no. 1 (Winter 2004): 88.

57. Deltcheva, "The Difficult Topos In-Between," 557.
58. Editorial, "O wyjście z chaosu," *Nowy Przegląd Wszechpolski*, vol. 14, no. 3–4 (2007): 1, http://www.npw.pl/pdf/npw.2007.3–4.pdf (accessed 9 December 2009).
59. Ibid.
60. Michael L. Miller and Scott Ury, "Cosmopolitanism: The End of Jewishness?" *European Review of History—Revue européenne d'histoire* 17, no. 3 (2010): 337.
61. Ibid., 344.
62. Stępień, "Historia—*lux veritatis*," 249. In 2004 there was debate in Polish media about the Antyk bookstore, located since 1997 in the basement of All Saints Church in Warsaw at the edge of the remnant of the Jewish ghetto established under German occupation in World War II. The Church bears a commemorative plaque recalling its role in sheltering Jews during the Holocaust. Until its closing in 2006, the Antyk bookstore was the main outlet for reprints (published by the Antyk press) of Koneczny's works. Fundamentalists defended the bookstore's selection of titles. Stanisław Krajski rebuffed the allegations by "so-called intellectuals" that the bookstore was selling anti-Semitic publications (such as Koneczny's *Cywilizacja żydowska*, which was reissued by Antyk publishers in 2001). He believed that this was part of an anti-Catholic and anti-Polish assault on "fundamental values." He warned of a "new ideological censor" and the specter of a "new totalitarianism." See Żydowski Instytut Historyczny (Jewish Historical Institute), Warsaw, "Monitoring prasy" (2004). Stanisław Krajski, "Czy grozi nam nowy totalitaryzm?" *Nasz Dziennik*, 2 January 2004. When discussing the legal charges brought against him, Marcin Dybowski, the owner of Antyk Publishing and Antyk Bookstore, referred to himself as a victim of a "Nazi-communist style persecution." See Żydowski Instytut Historyczny (Jewish Historical Institute), Warsaw. "Monitoring prasy" (2004). Jakub Rzekanowski, "Antysemityzm. Antyk kontratakuje: Lekcja miłosierdzia," *Trybuna* (Warsaw), 13/14 December 2003.
63. Horodecki, "Ciemności europejskie." Emphasis in original.
64. Adam Wielomski, "Metecy," *Myśl Polska*, 2–9 June 2002, http://www.myslpolska .icenter.pl/ (accessed 25 March 2005). The title of the article alludes to the residential aliens (metics) in ancient Greek city-states.
65. Magdalena Kania, " 'Here comes the Rest': A Sociological Perspective on Postcolonial Rethinking of the 'Second World'—the Case of Poland," *Postcolonial Europe* (2009), http://postcolonial-europe.eu/index.php?option=com_content&view=ar ticle&id=85%3Ahere-comes-the-rest-a-sociological-perspective-on-postcolonial -rethinking-of-the-second-world-the-case-of-poland&catid=45%3Aattitudes&Ite mid=65&lang=en (accessed 27 August 2009).
66. Ibid. Emphasis in the original.
67. Albert Memmi, *The Colonizer and the Colonized*, expanded ed. (Boston: Beacon Press, 1991), 128–30.
68. Ibid., 135.
69. Velikonja, "Slovenian and Polish Religio-National Mythologies," 248. Emphases in the original.
70. Memmi, *The Colonizer and the Colonized*, 135.
71. Horodecki, "Restrukturyzacja świadomości."
72. Horodecki, "Rozum zagrożony," 39.
73. Jaroszyński, *Europa bez Ojczyzn?*, 21. Emphasis added.
74. Wielomski, "Unia Europejska jako wyzwanie historizoficzne."

75. Ibid.
76. Ibid.
77. Ibid.
78. Maciej Giertych, "Polityka zagranicza," *Opoka w Kraju* 17, no. 38 (April 1996), http://opoka.giertych.pl/owk17.htm (accessed 30 June 2008). This is the text of an address delivered on 16 March 1996 at a meeting of the "Bloc for Poland." An expression of postcolonial resentment, Giertych's xenophobia was explicitly expressed during this period. Also see Giertych, "Stronnictwo Narodowe."
79. Giertych, *Quo vadis Europa?*, 24.
80. See Wacław Kiczora, "Wiedzieć, aby rozumieć, rozumieć, aby ocalić własne państwo. Część II," *Nowy Przegląd Wszechpolski* 11, no. 5–6 (2004), http://www.npw.pl/ARCHIWUM_NPW/2004_05_06/PIS-Kiczora_WIEDZIEC-ABY-RO ZUMIEC-cz2.html (accessed 21 June 2006).
81. Andrzej Horodecki, "Gdzie jest inicjatywna polityka Polska?" *Nowy Przegląd Wszechpolski* 7, no. 5–6 (2000), http://www.npw.pl/ARCHIWUM_NPW/2000_05_06/ TMS-Horodecki_Gdzie-jest-inicjatywna.htm (accessed 21 June 2006).
82. Piwowarski, "Oddolne zorganizowanie się Polaków." Also see Horodecki, "Neototalitaryzm."
83. Horodecki, "Totalna walka z cywilizacją łacińską, część I." Emphases in original.
84. Horodecki, "Wobec zamachu na patriotyzm."
85. Horodecki, "Totalna walka z cywilizacją łacińską, część II."
86. Kossecki, *Podstawy nowoczesnej nauki porównawczej o cywilizacjach*, 48–49, and 120.
87. Jaroszyński, *Europa bez Ojczyzn?*, 18.
88. Kamil Eckhardt, "Islamizacja Europy," *Najwyższy CZAS! Pismo Konserwatywno-liberalne*, 15 January 2008, http://nczas.com/publicystyka/islamizacja-europy/ (accessed 15 March 2008).
89. Giertych, *Quo vadis Europa?*, 34.
90. Ibid.
91. Giertych, *Z nadzieją w przyszłość* , 44.
92. Giertych, *Gender Equality and Life Issues*, 23. For a peculiarly Konecznian perspective on gender issues, see Polak, "Status kobiety w różnych cywilizacjach," 61–75.
93. Giertych, *Quo vadis Europa?* 40.
94. Kurczewska, Horolets, and Trojanowska-Strzęboszewska, *The European Dilemma*, 32.
95. Ibid., 33.
96. Wierzejski, *Naród, młodzież, idea*, 40.
97. Ibid.
98. Giertych, "Konfrontacja z islamem," 1.
99. Koneczny, *Święci w dziejach narodu polskiego*, 8.
100. Giertych, "Konfrontacja z islamem," 2.
101. Giertych, *Quo vadis Europa?*, 27.
102. Kurczewska, Horolets, and Trojanowska-Strzęboszewska, *The European Dilemma*, 82–84.
103. Andrzej Horodecki, "W cieniu afer," *Myśl Polska*, no. 31 (3 August 2003), http:// www.myslpolska.icenter.pl/ (accessed 26 March 2005).

104. Kurczewska, Horolets, and Trojanowska-Strzęboszewska, *The European Dilemma*, 42–46.
105. Ibid., 37, 52.
106. Ibid., 51–53.
107. Krzysztof Nagrodzki, "Barbaria wsączalna," *Myśl Polska*, no. 40 (7 October 2007).
108. Krzysztof Nagrodzki, "Wojna światów," *Myśl Polska*, no. 49–50 (4–11 December 2005), http://www.myslpolska.icenter.pl/ (accessed 28 January 2006).
109. Koneczny, *Plurality of Civilisations*, 266. Writing in 1931, Koneczny had made the same mistake in a discussion of the "five fundamental obligations of moral life" for a devout Muslim. See Koneczny, *Etyki a cywilizacje*, 19.
110. See Kossecki, *Podstawy nowoczesnej nauki porównawczej o cywilizacjach*, 171.
111. Bała, "Eurodżihad."
112. Ibid.
113. Białkowski, *Idea ścierania się cywilizacji według Feliksa Konecznego*, 55.
114. Ibid., 60–63.
115. Nowik, "Ekshortacja Jana Pawła II Kościół w Europie w kontekście historiozoficznym."
116. Jendrzejczak, "Nacjonalizm bizantyski."
117. Bodakowski, "Euro konstytucja czyli wstęp do czerwonego terroru."
118. Zdzisław Zakrzewski, "Miejsce Polski w świecie XXI wieku," *Tygodnik Internetowy*, 26 July 2002, http://www.polskiejutro.com/art/a.php?p=miejsce_polski (accessed 28 March 2005).
119. Ibid.
120. Jerzy Nikitorowicz, "Prognozy Nowej Europy w kontekście realizowania zadań edukacji międzykulturowej," in *Etniczność i obywatelskość w nowej Europie. Konteksty edukacji międzykulturowej*, ed. Jerzy Nikitorowicz, Dorota Misiejuk, and Mirosław Sobecki (Białystok: Trans Humana, 2007), 21.
121. Kiereś, *Człowiek i cywilizacja*, 171.
122. Szurgot, *Prawo jako fundament cywilizacji łacińskiej*, 72.
123. Mieczysław Ryba, "Islam w natarciu," *Dla Polski*, http://www.dlapolski.pl/islam (accessed 25 August 2009).
124. Ibid.

Bibliography

ARCHIVAL COLLECTIONS

Kraków
Archiwum Uniwersytetu Jagiellońskiego (Archive of Jagiellonian University)
Biblioteka Jagiellońska—Oddział Rękopisów (Jagiellonian Library—Manuscript Collection)
Archiwum Narodowe w Krakowie (National Archive in Kraków)

Warsaw
Biblioteka Narodowa (National Library)
Żydowski Instytut Historyczny (Jewish Historical Institute)

Wrocław
Biblioteka Zakładu Narodowego im. Ossolińskich (Ossolineum Library)

BOOKS AND PAMPHLETS BY FELIKS KONECZNY

Bizantynizm niemiecki. 1927. Reprint, Warsaw: Milla, 2002.
Chrześcijaństwo wobec ustrojów życia zbiorowego. 1932. Reprint, Krzeszowice: Dom Wydawniczy "Ostoja," 2003.
Cywilizacja bizantyńska. London: Wydawnictwa Towarzystwa imienia Romana Dmowskiego, 1973.
Cywilizacja żydowska. London: Wydawnictwa Towarzystwa imienia Romana Dmowskiego, 1974.
Dzieje administracji w Polsce. 1924. Reprint, Warsaw: Wydawnictwo Antyk, 1999.
Dzieje Polski za Piastów. 1902. Reprint, Komorów: Wydawnictwo Antyk, 1997.
Dzieje Polski za Jagiellonów. 1903. Reprint, Komorów: Wydawnictwo Antyk, 1997.
Dzieje Rosji. Vol. 1, *Do roku 1449*. Warsaw: Skład Główny w Księgarni E. Wende i Spółka, 1917.
Dzieje Rosji. Vol. 2, *Litwa a Moskwa w latach 1449–1492*. Wilno: Wileńskie Towarzystwo Przyjaciół Nauk, 1929.
Dzieje Rosji. Vol. 3, *Schyłek Iwana III, 1492–1505*. London: Wydawnictwa Towarzystwa imienia Romana Dmowskiego, 1984.

Dzieje Rosji od najdawniejszych do najnowszych czasów. Wydanie skrócone. Warsaw: Wydawnictwo M. Arcta, 1921.

Dzieje Śląska. 1897. Reprint, Warsaw: Wydawnictwo Antyk, 1999.

Etyki a cywilizacje. 1931. Reprint, Krzeszowice: Dom Wydawniczy "Ostoja," 2004.

Głos w sprawie ludowej. Kraków: Drukarnia Uniwersytetu Jagiellońskiego, 1896.

Kościół w Polsce wobec cywilizacji. 1928. Reprint, Krzeszowice: Dom Wydawniczy "Ostoja," 2005.

Napór orientu na zachód i inne pisme o życiu społecznym. Warsaw: Wydawnictwo "Hobbysta," 2004.

O cywilizację łacińską. Krzeszowice: Dom Wydawniczy "Ostoja," 2006.

O ład w historii: Z dodatkami o twórczości i wpływie Konecznego. Introduction by Jędrzej Giertych. 4th ed. Wrocław: Wydawnictwo "Nortom," 2004.

On the Plurality of Civilisations. Translated by Jędrzej Giertych. Introduction by Anton Hilckman. Preface by Arnold Toynbee. London: Polonica Publications, 1962. First published in Polish as *O wielości cywilizacyj* (Kraków: Gebethner i Wolf, 1935).

O pajdokracji. Warsaw: Wydawnictwo "Slowa," 1912.

O sprawach ekonomicznych. Kraków: Wydawnictwo WAM, 2000.

Państwo i prawo w cywilizacji łacińskiej. Warsaw: Wydawnictwo Antyk, 2001.

Polska między wschodem a zachodem. 1928. Reprint, Lublin: Onion, 1996.

Polskie logos a ethos: Roztrząsanie o znaczeniu i celu Polski. 2 vols., 1921. 2nd ed. Komorów: Wydawnictwo Antyk, 1997.

Prawa dziejowe. Oraz dodatek bizantynizm niemiecki. London: Wydawnictwa Towarzystwa imienia Romana Dmowskiego, 1982.

Protestantyzm w życiu zbiorowym. 1938. Reprint, Warsaw: Wydawnictwo "Milla," n.d.

Religie a cywilizacje. 1926. Reprint, Krzeszowice: Dom Wydawniczy "Ostoja," 2004.

Rozwój moralności. 1938. Reprint, Warsaw: Wydawnictwo Antyk, 1997.

Skrót do dziejów włościaństwa w Polsce. Wilno: Nakładem Księgarni Jozefa Zawadzkiego, 1921.

Święci w dziejach narodu polskiego. 1937. 4th ed. Komorów: Wydawnictwo Antyk, 1997.

Tadeusz Kościuszko na setną rocznicę zgonu naczelnika. Życie, czyny, duch. Poznań: Wielkopolska Księgarnia Nakładowa Karola Rzepeckiego, 1918.

Teatr Krakowski. Edited by Kazimierz Gajda. Kraków: Wydawnictwo Naukowe WSP, 1994.

Teoria Grunwaldu. 1910. Reprint, Warsaw: Milla, 1999.

Tło cywilizacyjne odsieczy wiedeńskiej. 1933. Reprint, Warsaw: Milla, 1999.

Zwierzchnictwo moralności ekonomia i etyka. Komorów: Wydawnictwo Antyk, 2006.

ARTICLES BY FELIKS KONECZNY

"Administracja obywatelska." *Niedziela* 17, no. 22 (1–7 June 1947): 175.

"Co robić wobec rusinów?" *Świat Słowiański* 4, vol. 1, no. 6 (1908): 577–96.

"Czego chce rząd rosyjski?" *Świat Słowiański* 2, vol. 1, no. 1 (1906): 1–7.

"Czterdzieści tez zasadniczych." *Trybuna Narodu* 2, no. 19 (8 May 1927): 2–3.

"Cztery posiedzenia Klubu Słowiańskiego." *Świat Słowiański* 1, vol. 2, no. 11 (1905): 411–20.

"Czy będzie sąd? Artykuł polski." *Świat Słowiański* 1, vol. 2, no. 11 (1905): 339–46.

"Dwoistość Niemiec." *Myśl Narodowa* 10, no. 53 (21 December 1930): 799–800.

"Ekonomia i etyka." *Niedziela* 17, no. 13 (30 March–5 April 1947): 97–98.

"'Elephantiasis' prawodawcza." *Myśl Narodowa* 12, no. 55 (18 December 1932): 798–801.

"Geneza Judeocentryzmu." *Myśl Narodowa* 9, no. 1 (6 January 1929): 3–6.

"Geneza uroszczeń Iwana III do Rusi litewskiej." *Ateneum Wileńskie* 3 (1925–26): 1–72.

"Historia." *Przegląd Powszechny* 50, vol. 200 (1933): 351–75.

"Konserwatyzm chłopski." *Znak* 37, no. 1–2 (1985): 33–46.

"Letuwa a Litwa." *Przegląd Powszechny* 39, vol. 155–56 (1922): 38–45.

"Nowiny z historyografii polskiej." *Przegląd Powszechny* 13, vol. 52 (1896): 169–90; vol. 54 (1896): 396–418.

"O kierunek polskości." 1928. Reprint, *Cywilizacja* 4/5 (2003): 217–21.

"O nierówności religii." *Tygodnik Warszawski* 2, no. 27 (1 September 1946): 4.

"O pierwotnej polskości Rusi Czerwonej." *Świat Słowiański* 9, vol. 1, no. 4 (1913): 212–36.

"Po konferencyi praskiej." *Świat Słowiański* 4, vol. 2, no. 8–9 (1908): 707–13.

"Polemika z Kazimierzem Chodynickim." *Kwartalnik Historyczny* 50 (1936): 175–78.

"Polskie Logos a Ethos." *Tygodnik Warszawski* 3, no. 27 (6 July 1947): 4.

"Potrójna walka o byt." *Niedziela* 17, no. 4 (26 January–1 February 1947): 25.

"Problem Polski obok Prus." *Świat Słowiański* 9, vol. 1, no. 3 (1913): 164–70.

"Problem zgody z Rosyą." *Świat Słowiański* 3, vol. 2, no. 10 (1907): 209–21.

"Propaganda zgody z Rosyą." *Świat Słowiański* 1, vol. 2, no. 10 (1905): 259–73.

"Przed konferencyą praską." *Świat Słowiański* 4, vol. 1, no. 7 (1908): 631–40.

"Przemienność sił." *Niedziela* 18, no. 20 (16 May 1948): 178.

"Religia sprawą najbardziej publiczną." *Tygodnik Warszawski* 2, no. 42 (20 October 1946): 3.

"Rodowód monizmu prawniczego." 1936. Reprint, *Człowiek w Kulturze* 10 (1998): 213–25.

"Różnolitość cywilizacyjna Słowiańszczyzny." *Przegląd Powszechny* 42, vol. 168 (1925): 257–82; 43, vol. 169 (1926): 21–46.

"Samorząd gminy wiejskiej." *Niedziela* 17, no. 38 (21–27 September 1947): 303.

"Samorządy gospodarcze." *Niedziela* 17, no. 28 (13–19 August 1947): 223–24.

"Słowianoznawstwo a słowianofilstwo. (Przemówienie na założenie 'Towarzystwa Słowiańskiego' w Krakowie)." *Świat Słowiański* 9, vol. 1, no. 2 (1913): 61–79.

"Ślubowanie i ciąg dalszy." *Niedziela* 16, no. 46 (17–23 November 1946): 365.

"U źródeł kultury polskiej." *Tygodnik Warszawski* 2, no. 51 (25 December 1946): 4.

"Warunki powodzenia." 1947. Reprint, *Cywilizacja* 4/5 (2003): 204–7.

"Więcej dobrobytu." *Niedziela* 17, no. 10 (9–15 February 1947): 75.

"Zwierzchnictwo moralności." *Niedziela* 17, no. 1 (5–11 January 1947): 1–2.

SCHOLARLY BOOKS AND ARTICLES

Adamovsky, Ezequiel. "Euro-Orientalism and the Making of the Concept of Eastern Europe in France, 1810-1880." *Journal of Modern History* 77 (September 2005): 591–628.

Alatas, Syed Farid. "Eurocentrism and the Role of the Human Sciences in the Dialogue among Civilizations." *European Legacy* 7, no. 6 (2002): 759–70.

Alsop, Rachel, and Jenny Hockey. "Women's Reproductive Lives as a Symbolic Resource in Central and Eastern Europe." *European Journal of Women's Studies* 8, no. 4 (November 2001): 455–72.

Anderle, Othmar F. "A Plea for Theoretical History." *History and Theory* 4, no. 1 (1964): 27–56.

Angelov, Dimiter G. "The Making of Byzantinism." Kokkalis Program on Southeastern and East-Central Europe (Harvard University, John F. Kennedy School of Government) http://www.hks.harvard.edu/kokkalis/GSW1/GSW1/01%20Angelov.pdf (accessed 30 June 2008).

Auer, Stefan. *Liberal Nationalism in Central Europe*. London: Routledge Curzon, 2004.

Auzépy, Marie-France, ed. *Byzance en Europe*. Saint-Denis: Presses Universitaires de Vincennes, 2003.

Bakuła, Bogusław. "Kolonialne i postkolonialne aspekty polskiego dyskursu kresoznawczego (zarys problematyki)." *Teksty Drugie*, no. 6 (2006): 11–33.

Banach, Tomasz. "Rzymski ideał prawa w katolickim państwie narodu polskiego." *Cywilizacja* 12 (2005): 71–75.

Baran, Augustyn. "Głębie i mielizny Feliksa Konecznego." *Athenaeum* 8 (2002): 173–75.

Barlik, Jacek. "Czy kres cywilizacji łacińskiej? O historiozofii Feliksa Konecznego (1862–1949)." *Chrześcijanin w Świecie* 18, no. 11/12 (1986): 150–62.

Baron, Nick, and Peter Gatrell. "Population Displacement, State-Building, and Social Identity in the Lands of the Former Russian Empire, 1917–23." *Kritika: Explorations in Russian and Eurasian History* 4, no. 1 (2003): 51–100.

Bayart, Jean-François. *The Illusion of Cultural Identity*. Chicago: University of Chicago Press, 2005.

Bezat, Piotr. *Poglądy polityczno-prawne Feliksa Konecznego*. Krzeszowice: Dom Wydawniczy "Ostoja," 2004.

———. *Teoria cywilizacji Feliksa Konecznego*. Krzeszowice: Dom Wydawniczy "Ostoja," 2004.

Bębenek, Marian. "Paradygmat polityki w cywilizacji łacińskiej." In Skoczyński, *Feliks Koneczny dzisiaj*, 85–92.

Białkowski, Ireneusz. *Idea ścierania się cywilizacji według Feliksa Konecznego a bezpieczeństwo współczesnej Europy. Koncepcje, które powracają jak bumerang*. Krzeszowice: Dom Wydawniczy "Ostoja," 2007.

Biliński, Piotr. *Feliks Koneczny (1862–1949): Życie i działalność*. Warsaw: Inicjatywa Wydawnicza "Ad Astra," 2001.

Blobaum, Robert, ed. *Antisemitism and Its Opponents in Modern Poland*. Ithaca, NY: Cornell University Press, 2005.

———. Introduction to Blobaum, *Antisemitism and Its Opponents in Modern Poland*, 1–19.

Bohun, Michał. "Oblicza obsesji—negatywny obraz Rosji w myśli polskiej." In *Katalog wzajemnych uprzedzeń Polaków i Rosjan*, edited by Andrzej Lazari, 203–302. Warsaw: Polski Instytut Spraw Międzynarodowych, 2006.

Bokajło, Wiesław. "Polnische Konzepte einer europäschen Föderation. Zwischen den 'Vereinigten Staaten von Europa' und dem konföderalen Mitteleuropa (1917–

1939)." In *Vision Europa. Deutsche und polnische Föderationspläne des 19. und frühen 20*, edited by Heinz Duchhardt and Małgorzata Morawiec, 85–116. Mainz: Verlag Philipp von Zabern, 2003.

Bokiej, Andrzej. *Cywilizacja łacińska. Studium na podstawie dorobku historiozoficznego Feliksa Konecznego*. Legnica: Wyższe Seminarium Duchowne Diecezji Legnickiej, 2000.

Borzym, Stanisław, H. Floryńska, B. Skarga, and A. Walicki. *Zarys dziejów filozofii polskiej 1815–1918*. Edited by Andrzej Walicki. Warsaw: Państwowe Wydawnictwo Naukowe, 1983.

Boss, Sally. Review of *From Sovietology to Postcoloniality: Poland and Ukraine from a Postcolonial Perspective*, edited by Janusz Korek. *Sarmation Review* 28, no. 1 (January 2008). http://www.ruf.rice.edu/~sarmatia/108/281boss.htm (accessed 30 June 2008).

Brzózka, Radosław. "Czytajmy Feliksa Konecznego." *Cywilizacja* 1 (2002): 65–69.

———. "Polityka międzynarodowa w cywilizacji łacińskiej." *Cywilizacja* 4/5 (2003): 26–40.

Bukowska, Sonia. "Feliksa Konecznego historiozoficzna refleksja nad narodem." *Folia Philosophica* 20 (2002): 239–50.

———. "Feliks Koneczny—indukcyjna nauka o cywilizacji a prawa dziejowe." *Folia Philosophica* 8 (1991): 201–15.

———. *Filozofia polska wobec problemu cywilizacji. Teoria Feliksa Konecznego*. Katowice: Wydawnictwo Uniwersytetu Śląskiego, 2007.

———. "Metodologiczne aspekty historiozoficznej koncepcji Felksa Konecznego." *Folia Philosophica* 18 (2000): 287–99.

Burdziej, Stanisław. "Voice of the Disinherited? Religious Media after the 2005 Presidential and Parliamentary Elections in Poland." *East European Quarterly* 42, no. 2 (June 2008): 207–21.

Burek, Thomas. "1905, nie 1918." In *Problemy literatury polskiej lat 1890–1939*, seria I, edited by Hanna Kirchner and Zbigniew Zabicki, 77–105. Wrocław: Wydawnictwo Polskiej Akademii Nauk, 1972.

Cała, Alina. *Żyd—wróg odwieczny? Antysemityzm w Polsce i jego źródła*. Warsaw: Wydawnictwo Nisza, 2012.

Cameron, Averil. "Byzance dans le débat sur l'orientalisme." In Auzépy, *Byzance en Europe*, 235–50.

Cantor, Norman F. *Inventing the Middle Ages: The Lives, Works, and Ideas of the Great Medievalists of the Twentieth Century*. New York: Quill, William Morrow & Co., 1991.

Cavanagh, Clare. "Postcolonial Poland." *Common Knowledge* 10, no. 1 (Winter 2004): 82–92.

Ceran, Waldemar. *Historia i bibliografia rozumowana bizantynologii polskiej (1800–1998)*. Vol. 1. Łódź: Wydawnictwo Uniwersytetu Łódzkiego, 2001.

Chandler, Alice. *A Dream of Order: The Medieval Ideal in Nineteenth-Century English Literature*. Lincoln: University of Nebraska Press, 1971.

Chazbijewicz, Selim. "Polemika z koncepcją cywilizacji turańskiej Feliksa Konecznego (komunikat)." In *Tradycje duchowe Europy Środkowej i Wschodniej*, edited by Selim Chazbijewicz and Józef Kwapiszewski, 79–82. Słupsk: Wyższa Szkoła Pedagogiczna w Słupsku, 1999.

Childs, Peter, and R. J. Patrick Williams. *An Introduction to Post-Colonial Theory*. London: Prentice Hall / Harvester Wheatsheaf, 1997.

Chodubski, Andrzej. "Uwarunkowania cywilizacyjne przystąpienia Polski do Unii Europejskiej." In *Polska między zachodem a wschodem w dobie integracji europejskiej*, edited by Maria Marczewska-Rytko, 21–34. Lublin: Wydawnictwo Uniwersytetu Marii Curie-Skłodowskiej, 2001.

Chodynicki, Kazimierz. "Polemika z Feliksem Konecznym." *Kwartalnik Historyczny* 50 (1936): 584–92.

———. Review of Koneczny Feliks, *Litwa a Moskwa w latach 1449–1492 Kwartalnik Historyczny* 44 (1930): 386–408.

Chrobaczyński, Jacek. "Kraków przed i w 1914 roku." *Dzieje Najnowsze* 36, no. 3 (2004): 63–78.

Cieslik, Anna, and Maykel Verkuyten. "National, Ethnic and Religious Identities: Hybridity and the Case of the Polish Tatars." *National Identities* 8, no. 2 (June 2006): 77–93.

Ciggaar, K. "Theophano: An Empress Reconsidered." In Davids, *The Empress Theophano*, 49–63.

Curp, T. David. "'Roman Dmowski Understood': Ethnic Cleansing as Permanent Revolution." *European History Quarterly* 35, no. 3 (2005): 405–27.

Czarnecki, Gregory E. "Analogies of Pre-War Anti-Semitism and Present-Day Homophobia in Poland." In *Beyond the Pink Curtain: Everyday Life of LGBT People in Eastern Europe*, edited by Roman Huhar and Judit Takács, 327–44. Ljubljana: Mirovni Institut, 2007. http://www.policy.hu/takacs/books/isbn9616455459/ (accessed 26 September 2010).

Dąbrowska, Małgorzata. "Byzance, source de stéréotypes dans la conscience des Polonais." In Auzépy, *Byzance en Europe*, 43–54.

———. "Cywilizacja bizantyńska, czyli świat średniowiecznych Rzymian." In *Koneczny. Teoria cywilizacji*, edited by Jan Skoczyński, 323–45. Warsaw: Wydawnictwo IFiS PAN, 2003.

———. "Przemoskwiona wizja Bizancjum a niemiecki bizantynizm Konecznego." In Skoczyński, *Feliks Koneczny dzisiaj*, 155–66.

———. "La vision moscoutaire de Byzance et le byzantinisme allemand de Koneczny ou Byzance sans Byzance." *Organon* 28–30 (1999–2001): 257–68.

Dabrowski, Patrice M. *Commemorations and the Shaping of Modern Poland*. Bloomington: Indiana University Press, 2004.

Daskalovski, Židas. "Go East! Racism and the EU." *ce-review.org* 2, no. 24 (19 June 2000). http://www.ce-review.org/00/24/daskalovski24.html (accessed 15 February 2003).

Davids, Adelbert. ed. *The Empress Theophano: Byzantium and the West at the Turn of the First Millenium*. New York: Cambridge University Press, 1995.

Dawson, Christopher. *Dynamics of World History*. Edited by John J. Mulloy. Introduction by Dermot Quinn. Wilmington, DE: ISI Books, 2002.

De Lange, Sarah L., and Simona Guerra. "The League of Polish Families between East and West, Past and Present." *Communist and Post-Communist Studies* 42 (2009): 527–49.

Dellheim, Charles. "Interpreting Victorian Medievalism." In *History and Community: Essays in Victorian Medievalism*, edited by Florence S. Boos, 39–58. New York: Garland Publishing, Inc., 1992.

Deltcheva, Roumiana. "The Difficult Topos In-Between. The East Central European Cultural Context as a Post-Coloniality." *Sarmatian Review* 18, no. 3 (September 1998): 557–62.

Diec, Joachim. *Cywilizacje bez okien. Teoria Mikołaja Danilewskiego i późniejsze koncepcje monadycznych formacji socjokulturowych.* Kraków: Wydawnictwo Uniwersytetu Jagiellońskiego, 2002.

Domagalska, Malgorzata. "Antisemitic Discourse in Polish Nationalist Weeklies Between 1918 and 1939." *East European Jewish Affairs* 36, no. 2 (December 2006): 191–97.

———. *Antysemityzm dla inteligencji? Kwestia żydowska w publicystyce Adolfa Nowaczyńskiego na łamach "Myśli Narodowej" (1921–1934) i "Prosto z mostu" (1935–1939) (na tle porównawczym).* Warsaw: Żydowski Instytut Historyczny, 2004.

Donskis, Leonidas. *Forms of Hatred: The Troubled Imagination in Modern Philosophy and Literature.* Amsterdam: Rodopi, 2003.

Duchesne, Ricardo. "Defending the Rise of Western Culture against Its Multicultural Critics." *European Legacy* 10, no. 5 (2005): 455–84.

Dzielski, Mirosław. *Odrodzenie ducha—budowa wolności. Pisma zebrane.* Edited by Grzegorz Łuczkiewicz. Introduction by Miłowit Kuniński. Kraków: Znak, 1995.

Eberts, Mirella. "The Catholic Church and Poland's Accession to the European Union." In *Redefining Europe*, edited by Joseph Drew, 165–80. Amsterdam: Rodopi, 2005.

Einhorn, Barbara, and Charlotte Sever. "Gender and Civil Society in Central and Eastern Europe." *International Feminist Journal of Politics* 5, no. 2 (2003): 163–90.

Emery, Elizabeth, and Laura Morowitz. *Consuming the Past: The Medieval Revival in Fin-de-siècle France.* Burlington, VT: Ashgate Publishing Company, 2003.

Engels, Odilo. "Theophano, the Western Empress from the East." In Davids, *The Empress Theophano*, 28–48.

Evans, Charles T. "Vasilii Barthold: Orientalism in Russia?" *Russian History / Histoire Russe* 26, no. 1 (Spring 1999): 25–44.

Filipowicz, Mirosław. *Wobec Rosji. Studia z dziejów historiografii polskiej od końca XIX wieku po II wojnę światową.* Lublin: Instytut Europy Środkowo-Wschodniej, 2000.

Fiut, Aleksander. "In the Shadow of Empires. Postcolonialism in Central and Eastern Europe—Why Not?" In Korek, *From Sovietology to Postcoloniality*, 33–40.

Floud, Jean. Review of Koneczny's *The Plurality of Civilisations. History & Theory* 4, no. 2 (1965): 271–75.

Frątczak, Anna. *Feliks Koneczny o państwie i wartościach.* Kraków: Ośrodek Myśli Politycznej; Księgarnia Akademicka, 2003.

Gawlicz, Katarzyna. "Płeć i naród. Dyskurs dotyczący aborcji w 'Naszym Dzienniku' a konstruowanie tożsamości narodowej." In *Kobiety, feminizm i media*, edited by Edyta Zierkiewicz and Izabela Kowalczyk, 99–115. Poznań: Konsola, 2005.

Gawor, Leszek. "Feliksa Konecznego koncepcja narodu." In *Charakter narodowy i religia*, edited by Kazimierz Wiliński, 35–42. Lublin: Wydawnictwo Uniwersytetu Marii Curie-Skłodowskiej, 1997.

———. "Konecznego i Huntingtona wizja cywilizacyjnego pluralizmu." *Toruński Przegląd Filozoficzny* 5/6 (2003): 31–42.

———. *O wielości cywilizacji: Filozofia społeczna Feliksa Konecznego.* Lublin: Wydawnictwo Uniwersytetu Marii Curie-Skłodowskiej, 2002.

Glowacka, Dorota, and Joanna Zylinska, eds. *Imaginary Neighbors: Mediating Polish-Jewish Relations after the Holocaust.* Lincoln: University of Nebraska Press, 2007.

Goćkowski, Janusz. "Konecznego model dziejów powszechnych." In Skoczyński, *Feliks Koneczny dzisiaj*, 21–34.

Goebel, Stefan. *The Great War and Medieval Memory: War, Remembrance and Medievalism in Britain and Germany, 1914–1940.* Cambridge: Cambridge University Press, 2007.

Gondek, Paweł. "Rola Kościoła w kulturze polskiej: na marginesie Feliksa Konecznego." *Człowiek w Kulturze* 10 (1998): 87–96.

Graban, Michał. "Supremacja sił duchowych w cywilizacji łacińskiej." In Skoczyński, *Feliks Koneczny dzisiaj*, 145–54.

Grabowiec, Piotr. *Model społeczeństwa obywatelskiego w historiozofii Feliksa Konecznego.* Wrocław: Wydawnictwo Uniwersytetu Wrocławskiego, 2000.

Grabowski, Tadeusz Stanisław. "Feliks Koneczny (1.XI.1862–10.II.1949)." *Kwartalnik Historyczny* 57 (1949): 334–37.

Grabski, Andrzej F. "Feliks Koneczny a mutacja modernistyczna w historiografii polskiej." In Skoczyński, *Feliks Koneczny dzisiaj*, 11–20.

Graff, Agnieszka. "A Different Chronology: Reflections on Feminism in Contemporary Poland." In *Third Wave Feminism: A Critical Exploration*, edited by Stacy Gillis et al., 142–55. 2nd ed. London: Palgrave, 2007.

———. "Gender, Sexuality, and Nation—Here and Now: Reflections on the Gendered and Sexualized Aspects of Contemporary Polish Nationalism." In *Intimate Citizenships: Gender, Sexualities, Politics*, edited by Elzbieta H. Oleksy, 133–46. New York: Routledge, 2009.

———. "The Land of Real Men and Real Women: Gender and E.U. Accession in Three Polish Weeklies." *Journal of the International Institute* 15, no. 1 (Fall 2007): 10–11.

———. *Rykoszetem: Rzecz o płci, seksualności i narodzie.* Warsaw: Wydawnictwo W.A.B, 2008.

———. "We Are (Not All) Homophobes: A Report from Poland." *Feminist Studies* 32, no. 2 (2006): 434–49.

Grott, Bogumił. "Chrześcijańskie i świeckie inspiracje w doktrynach nacjonalizmu polskiego." *Przegląd Humanistyczny*, no. 4 (1994): 79–91.

———. "The Conception of 'Roman-Catholic Totalism' in Poland before World War II." *Zeszyty Naukowe Uniwersytetu Jagiellońskiego. Studia Religiologica* 8 (1982): 101–7.

———. "Mediewalizm w koncepcjach Obozu Wielkiej Polski ze studiów nad religijnymi uwarunkowaniami myśli politycznej." *Zeszyty Naukowe Uniwersytetu Jagiellońskiego. Studia Religiologica* 7 (1982): 55–70.

———. *Nacjonalizm Chrześcijański: Narodowo-katolicka formacja ideowa w II Rzeczypospolitej na tle porównawczym.* 2nd ed. Kraków: Wydawnictwo "Ostoja," 1996.

———. *Nacjonalizm i religia. Proces zespalania nacjonalizmu z katolicyzmem w jedną całość ideową w myśli Narodowej Demokracji 1926–1939.* Kraków: Nakładem Uniwersytetu Jagiellońskiego, 1984.

Hagen, William W. "Before the 'Final Solution': Toward a Comparative Analysis of Political Anti-Semitism in Interwar Germany and Poland." *Journal of Modern History* 68, no. 2 (1996): 351–81.

Hanson, Victor Davis. *The Other Greeks: The Family Farm and the Agrarian Roots of Western Civilization.* 2nd ed. Berkeley: University of California Press, 1999.

Hauser, Ewa. "Traditions of Patriotism, Questions of Gender: The Case of Poland." *Genders* 22 (Fall 1995): 78–104.

Herrin, Judith. "Theophano: Considerations on the Education of a Byzantine Princess." In Davids, *The Empress Theophano*, 64–85.

Hilckman, Anton. "Feliks Koneczny and the Comparative Science of Civilisation." In Feliks Koneczny, *On the Plurality of Civilisations*, 8–32. London: Polonica Publications, 1962.

———. "Feliks Koneczny und die Vergleichende Kulturwissenschaft." *Saeculum* 3, no. 4 (1952): 571–602.

———. Introduction to Koneczny, *On the Plurality of Civilisations*, 1–7. London: Polonica Publications, 1962.

———. "Qu'est-ce que l'occident? Essai d'un exposé de la doctrine européenne de Feliks Koneczny." *Sacrum Poloniae millennium: rozprawy, szkice, materialy, historyczne* 12 (1966): 477–559.

———. "Rusia y Europa. Aspectos culturales." *Razón y Fe. Revista Hispano-Americana de Cultura* 155, no. 708 (1957): 9–24.

Hirszowicz, Lukasz. "Antisemitism in Today's Poland." *Soviet Jewish Affairs* 12, no. 1 (1982): 55–65.

Hundorova, Tamara. "Postcolonial *Ressentiment*—the Ukrainian Case." In Korek, *From Sovietology to Postcoloniality*, 103–13.

Huntington, Samuel P. *The Clash of Civilizations and the Remaking of the World Order.* New York: Simon & Schuster, 1996.

———. *Who Are We? The Challenges to America's National Identity.* New York: Simon & Schuster, 2004.

Jadczak, Ryszard. "Feliks Koneczny o państwie i jego roli w wychowaniu." In *Wychowanie a polityka. Między wychowaniem narodowym a państwowym*, edited by Witold Wojdyła, 69–82. Toruń: Wydawnictwo Uniwersytetu Mikołaja Kopernika, 1999.

———. "Wileński okres Feliksa Konecznego." *Studia Historyczne* 41, no. 3 (1998): 395–406.

Jakubowski, Marek N. *Ciągłość historii i historia ciągłości. Polska filozofia dziejów.* Toruń: Wydawnictwo Uniwersytetu Mikołaja Kopernika, 2004.

Janion, Maria. *Niesamowita Słowiańszczyzna. Fantazmaty literatury.* Kraków: Wydawnictwo Literackie, 2006.

Janusz, Kazimierz. *Konfrontacje Rosja-Zachód: Zderzenie dwóch cywilizacji.* 1974. Reprint, Komorów: Wydawnictwo Antyk Marcin Dybowski, 1997.

Jedlicki, Jerzy. "Resisting the Wave: Intellectuals against Antisemitism in the Last Years of the 'Polish Kingdom.'" In Blobaum, *Antisemitism and Its Opponents in Modern Poland*, 60–80.

Jedynak, Stanisław. "Aksjologiczne zagadnienie rozwoju cywilizacji według Feliksa Konecznego." *Przegląd Humanistyczny* 32, no. 3 (1988): 121–29.

———. *Naród społeczeństwo państwo.* Warsaw: Wydawnictwo TRIO, 2002.

Jojczyk, Stanisław. "Relacja państwo-społeczeństwo u Feliksa Konecznego." In Skoczyński, *Feliks Koneczny dzisiaj*, 245–54.

Kania, Magdalena. "'Here comes the Rest': A Sociological Perspective on Postcolonial Rethinking of the 'Second World'—the Case of Poland." *Postcolonial Europe.* http://postcolonial-europe.eu/index.php (accessed 27 August 2009).

Kieniewicz, Jan. "East and West: Civilisations and Their History." Wydział Orientalistyczny Uniw. Warszawskiego, http://www.orient.uw.edu.pl/pl/iss/jk-main.htm (accessed 20 March 2006)

———. "Is Dialogue between Civilizations Possible?" Uniwersytet Warszawski. Instytut Badań Interdyscyplinarnych "Artes Liberales." http://www.obta.uw.edu.pl/~zoja/Kieniewiczdialog_cywilizacji_ang%5B1%5D.pdf (accessed 27 August 2009).

———. *Wprowadzenie do historii cywilizacji Wschodu i Zachodu*. Warsaw: Wydawnictwo Akademickie Dialog, 2003.

Keinz, Anika. "European Desires and National Bedrooms? Negotiating 'Normalcy' in Postsocialist Poland." *Central European History* 44 (2011): 92–117.

Kiereś, Henryk. *Człowiek i cywilizacja*. Lublin: Wydawnictwo Fundacja *Servire Veritati* Instytut Edukacji Narodowej, 2007.

Kinnvall, Catarina. "Globalization and Religious Nationalism: Self, Identity, and the Search for Ontological Security." *Political Psychology* 25, no. 5 (October 2004): 741–67.

Kivisto, Peter. "The Brief Career of Catholic Sociology." *Sociological Analysis* 50, no. 4 (Winter 1989): 351–61.

Kociuba, Maciej. "Tożsamość kulturowa cywilizacji europejskiej. O potrzebie aksjologicznej 'metanoi.'" *Annales. Sectio I. Wydział Filozofii i Socjologii UMCS* 27, no. 3 (2002): 37–61.

Kolbuszewska, Jolanta. "Konecznego koncepcja dziejów Rosji." In Skoczyński, *Feliks Koneczny dzisiaj*, 187–98.

———. "Od historii przez filozofię dziejów po historyczną aksjologię. Przeobrażenia historycznej refleksji Feliksa Konecznego." *Czasopismo Naukowe "Kultura i Historia."* http://www.kulturaihistoria.umcs.lublin.pl/archives/103 (accessed 25 August 2009).

———. "Przełom antypozytywistyczny czy mutacja modernistyczna? Rozważania o przemianach w historiografii schyłku XIX i początku XX wieku." In "Między modernizmem a postmodernizmem w historiografii," edited by Jan Pomorski. Special issue, *Res Historica* 19 (2005): 41–54.

——— "Reorientacje w historiografii polskiej przełomie XIX i XX wieku a koncepcje cywilizacyjne Feliksa Konecznego." *Historyka* 32 (2002): 111–25.

Kontje, Todd. *German Orientalisms*. Ann Arbor: University of Michigan Press, 2004.

Korek, Janusz. "Central and Eastern Europe from a Postcolonial Perspective." In Korek, *From Sovietology to Postcoloniality*, 5–22.

———, ed. *From Sovietology to Postcoloniality: Poland and Ukraine from a Postcolonial Perspective*. Huddinge: Södertörns högskola, 2007.

Kornat, Marek. *Bolszewizm, totalitaryzm, rewolucja Rosja. Początki sowietologii i studiów nad systemami totalitarnymi w Polsce (1918–1939)*. 2 vols. Kraków: Księgarnia Akademicka, 2004.

Kossecki, Józef. *Podstawy nowoczesnej nauki porównawczej o cywilizacjach. Socjologia porównawcza cywilizacja*. Katowice: "Śląsk" Sp. z o.o. Wydawnictwo Naukowe, 2003.

Kowalczyk-Twarowski, Krzysztof. "Imperialne przestworza, spolegliwi tubylcy: Polska, Rosja, RPA." *Er(r)go* 8, no. 1 (2004): 173–86.

Kowalski, Mariusz. "Electoral Behaviour in Poland as the Effect of the 'Clash of Civilization.'" *Geografický Časopis* 54, no. 3 (2002): 219–37.

———. "Polaryzacja zachowań wyborczych w Polsce jako rezultat cywilizacyjnego rozdarcia kraju." In *Przestrzeń wyborcza Polski*, edited by Mariusz Kowalski, 11–48. Warsaw: Oddział Akademicki PTG, Instytut Geografii i Przestrzennego Zagospodarowania PAN, 2003.

―――. "Regional Differentiation of Electoral Behaviour in Countries of Central and Eastern Europe as the Effect of the 'Civilisation Clash.'" *Revista Română de Geografie Politică* 3, no. 1 (2001): 77–90.

Kowalski, Sergiusz, and Magdalena Tulli. *Zamiast procesu. Raport o mowie nienawiści.* Warsaw: Instytut Studiów Politycznych PAN, 2003.

Kramer, Anne-Marie. "The Polish Parliament and the Making of Politics through Abortion: Nation, Gender and Democracy in the 1996 Liberalization Amendment." *International Feminist Journal of Politics* 11, no. 1 (2009): 81–101.

Krauze, Justyna M. "Die byzantinische Zivilisation im philosophischen Denken von Feliks Koneczny und ihre Wiederspiegelung am Hofe Wilhelms II: ein Versuch." *Studia Niemcoznawsze* 22 (2001): 239–57.

Krejčí, Jaroslav. *The Paths of Civilization: Understanding the Currents of History.* New York: Palgrave Macmillan Press, 2004.

Kucharczyk, Grzegorz. *Mała historia polskiej myśli politycznej.* Dębogóra: Klub Książki Katolickiej, 2007.

Kuderowicz, Zbigniew. "Koncepcja praw historii w ujęciu Feliksa Konecznego." In Skoczyński, *Feliks Koneczny dzisiaj,* 35–43.

Kuniński, Miłowit. "Mirosław Dzielski—polityka polska w perspektywie cywilizacyjnej." In Skoczyński, *Feliks Koneczny dzisiaj,* 133–44. Also at Ośrodek Myśli Politycznej. http://www.omp.org.pl/artykul.php?artykul=158 (accessed 23 June 2006).

―――. "Obalić komunizm . . . i co dalej?" Ośrodek Myśli Politycznej. http://www.omp.org.pl/index.php?module=subjects&func=viewpage&pageid=55 (accessed 23 June 2006).

Kurczewska, Joanna, Anna Horolets, and Monika Trojanowska-Strzęboszewska. With the collaboration of Mirosław Bienecki. *The European Dilemma: Institutional Patterns and Politics of 'Racial' Discrimination. Project Report: Work Package 6. Discourse Analysis of Politics: LPR's Rhetoric.* Warsaw: Institute of Public Affairs, 2005. http://www.isp.org.pl/files/11297950200606281001164194296.pdf (accessed 30 June 2008).

Kurowska, K. "Feliksa Konecznego nauka o wielości cywilizacji." *Przegląd Humanistyczny* 22, no. 7/8 (1978): 75–90.

Kwiatkowska, Hanna. "Conflict between the Image of the Jews and the Self-Image of the Poles in the Light of the Articles Published in 'Nasz Dziennik' 1998–2003." *Scripta Judaica Cracoviensia* 2 (2003): 89–95.

Landau-Czajka, Anna. "The Image of the Jew in the Catholic Press during the Second Republic." In *Polin: Studies in Polish Jewry,* vol. 8, *Jews in Independent Poland, 1918–1939,* edited by Antony Polonsky, Ezra Mendelsohn, and Jerzy Tomaszewski, 146–75. London: Littman Library of Jewish Civilization, 1994.

Łętocha, Rafał. *Katolicyzm a idea narodowa. Miejsce religii w myśli obozu narodowego lat okupacji.* Lublin: Fundacja *Servire Veritati* Instytut Edukacji Narodowej, 2002.

Lewis, Martin W., and Kären E. Wigen. *The Myth of Continents: A Critique of Metageography.* Berkeley: University of California Press, 1997.

Leyser, Karl. "Theophanu divina gratia imperatrix augusta: Western and Eastern Emperorship in the Later Tenth Century." In Davids, *The Empress Theophano,* 1–27.

Libionka, Dariusz. "Antisemitism, Anti-Judaism, and the Polish Catholic Clergy during the Second World War, 1939–1945." In Blobaum, *Antisemitism and Its Opponents in Modern Poland,* 233–64.

Lukacs, John. *Historical Consciousness: The Remembered Past*. New Brunswick, NJ: Transaction Publishers, 1994.

Maj, Ewa. "Polska mitologia historyczna w myśli politycznej Narodowej Demokracji w XX wieku: model realizacji idei." In *Wizje i realia. Studia nad realizacją polskiej myśli politycznej XX wieku*, edited by Waldemar Paruch and Krystyna Trembicka, 199–217. Lublin: Wydawnictwo Uniwersytetu Marii Curie-Skłodowskiej, 2002.

———. *Związek Ludowo-Narodowy, 1919-1928. Studium z dziejów myśli politycznej*. Lublin: Wydawnictwo Uniwersytetu Marii Curie-Skłodowskiej, 2000.

Majewski, Erazm. *Nauka o cywilizacjyi*. Vol. 2, *Teorya człowieka i cywilizacji*. Warsaw: E. Wende i S-ka, 1910. http://www.prawia.org/ksiazki/majewski/majewski2f.html (accessed 23 August 2009).

Małecki, Jan M. "Cracow Jews in the 19th Century: Leaving the Ghetto." *Acta Poloniae Historica* 76 (1997): 85–96.

Maszkowski, Rafał. "Inny świat—obraz Żydów w Radiu Maryja." *Kwartalnik Historii Żydów*, no. 4 (2006): 669–87.

Mayer, Tamar. "Gender Ironies of Nationalism: Setting the Stage." In *Gender Ironies of Nationalism: Sexing the Nation*, edited by Tamar Mayer, 1–22. London: Routledge, 2000.

Mazlish, Bruce. *Civilization and its Contents*. Stanford, CA: Stanford University Press, 2004.

McCormick, Michael. "Byzantium's Role in the Formation of Early Medieval Civilization: Approaches and Problems." *Illinois Classical Studies* 12, no. 2 (Fall 1987): 207–20.

McInnes, Neil. "The Great Doomsayer." *National Interest*, no. 48 (1997): 65–77.

McKitterick, Rosamond. "Ottonian Intellectual Culture in the Tenth Century and the Role of Theophano." In Davids, *The Empress Theophano*, 169–93.

Melegh, Attila. *On the East-West Slope. Globalization, Nationalism, Racism and Discourses on Central and Eastern Europe*. Budapest: Central European University Press, 2006.

Memmi, Albert. *The Colonizer and the Colonized*. Expanded ed. Boston: Beacon Press, 1991.

Michałowski, Stanisław Czesław. "Wizja cywilizacji łacińskiej i kultury europejskiej na tle myśl Feliksa Konecznego." In *Wspólnota dziedzictwa kulturowego*, edited by Bronisława Dymara, 1:19–51. Kraków: Oficyna Wydawnicza "Impuls," 2004.

Michlic, Joanna Beata. "Antisemitism in Contemporary Poland. Does It Matter? And for Whom Does It Matter?" In *Rethinking Poles and Jews: Troubled Past, Brighter Future*, edited by Robert Cherry and Annamaria Orla-Bukowska, 155–68. Lanham, MD: Rowman and Littlefield Publishers, Inc., 2007.

———. *Poland's Threatening Other: The Image of the Jew from 1880 to the Present*. Lincoln: University of Nebraska Press, 2006.

———. "The Soviet Occupation of Poland, 1939–1941, and the Stereotype of the Anti-Polish and Pro-Soviet Jew." *Jewish Social Studies: History, Culture, Society*, n.s., 13, no. 3 (Spring/Summer 2007): 135–76.

Michlic, Joanna Beata, and Antony Polonsky. "Catholicism and the Jews in Post--Communist Poland." In *Jews, Catholics, and the Burden of History*, edited by Eli Lederhendler, 35–64. Oxford: Oxford University Press, 2006.

Milcarek, Paweł. "Feliks Koneczny i jego synteza historii Polski." *Brulion* 13 (1998): 209–32.

————. "Świętość w dziejach ludzkich w ujęciu Feliksa Konecznego." In Skoczyński, *Feliks Koneczny dzisiaj*, 225–30.

Miller, Michael L., and Scott Ury. "Cosmopolitanism: The End of Jewishness?" *European Review of History—Revue européenne d'histoire* 17, no. 3 (2010): 337–59.

Misiek, Józef. "*O wielości cywilizacyj*—refleksje metodologiczne." In Skoczyński, *Feliks Koneczny dzisiaj*, 45–58.

Modras, Ronald. "The Interwar Polish Catholic Press on the Jewish Question." *Annals of the American Academy of Political and Social Science* 548 (November 1996): 169–90.

Moore, David Chioni. "Is the Post- in Postcolonial the Post- in Post-Soviet? Toward a Global Postcolonial Critique." *PMLA* 116, no. 1 (2001): 111–28.

Morowitz, Laura. "Anti-Semitism, Medievalism and the Art of the Fin-de-Siecle." *Oxford Art Journal* 20, no. 1 (1997): 35–49.

Mucha, Janusz. "Sociology in Eastern Europe or East European Sociology: Historical and Present." Institute of Sociology, Academia Sinica, Taiwan. http://www.ios .sinica.edu.tw/cna/download/5b_Mucha_2.pdf (accessed 24 August 2009).

Müller, Klaus E. "Perspectives in Historical Anthropology." In *Western Historical Thinking: An Intercultural Debate*, edited by Jörn Rüsen, 33–52. New York: Berghahn Books, 2002.

Munasinghe, Viranjini."Nationalism in Hybrid Spaces: The Production of Impurity out of Purity." *American Ethnologist* 29, no. 3 (2002): 663–92.

Nadolski, Łukasz. "Wątki historyczne w publicystyce Feliksa Konecznego, na łamach "Świata Słowiańskiego." In Skoczyński, *Feliks Koneczny dzisiaj*, 59–66.

Neumann, Iver B. *Uses of the Other: "The East" in European Identity Formation*. Minneapolis: University of Minnesota Press, 1999.

Niewiara, Aleksandra. "Procesy kategoryzacyjne a kulturowe konstruowanie obrazu 'innego' (Moskwicin-Moskal-Rosjanin)." In *Katalog wzajemnych uprzedzeń Polaków i Rosjan*, edited by Andrzej Lazari, 49–72. Warsaw: Polski Instytut Spraw Międzynarodowych, 2006.

Nikitorowicz, Jerzy. "Prognozy Nowej Europy w kontekście realizowania zadań edukacji międzykulturowej." In *Etniczność i obywatelskość w nowej Europie. Konteksty edukacji międzykulturowej*, edited by Jerzy Nikitorowicz, Dorota Misiejuk, and Mirosław Sobecki, 15–29. Białystok: Trans Humana, 2007.

Nowak, Joanna. "Jedność w rozmaitości—czyli o romantycznych korzeniach koncepcji narodu Feliksa Konecznego." *Sprawy Narodowościowe* 30 (2007): 75–94.

Nowicka, Wanda. "The Struggle for Abortion Rights in Poland." In *SexPolitics: Reports from the Front Lines*, edited by Richard Parker, Rosalind Petchesky, and Robert Sember, 167–196. New York: Sexuality Policy Watch, 2007. http://www.sxpolitics. org/frontlines/book/pdf/sexpolitics.pdf (accessed 26 September 2010).

O'Hagan, Jacinta. "A 'Clash of Civilizations'?" In *Contending Images of World Politics*, edited by Greg Fry and Jacinta O'Hagan, 135–49. New York: St. Martin's Press, 2000.

Ostolski, Adam. "Żydzi, geje i wojna cywilizacji." *Kobiety Kobietom*, 2 June 2005. http:// kobiety-kobietom.com/queer/art.php?art=2249 (accessed 20 August 2010).

Pankowski, Rafal. *The Populist Radical Right in Poland: The Patriots*. London: Routledge, 2010.

Paszyński, Jarosław. "Tożsamość Polski a cywilizacje." *Człowiek w Kulturze* 10 (1998): 79–85

Pawlak, Józef. "Feliks Koneczny o rozwoju moralności." In *Rozprawy z etyki*, edited by Józef Pawlak and Włodzimierz Tyburski, 137–44. Toruń: Wydawnictwo UMK, 1999.

Pawluczuk, Włodzimierz. "My i oni. Przyczynek do fenomenologii dyskursu między-cywilizacyjnego." *Przegląd Humanistyczny* 50, no. 5–6 (2006): 185–95.

Piekarski, Romuald. "Prymat etyki w życiu publicznym. Dyskusja tezy Konecznego." In Skoczyński, *Feliks Koneczny dzisiaj*, 231–43.

Piesiewicz, Piotr. *Myśl ideowo-polityczna Jędrzeja Giertycha*. 2nd ed. Krzeszowice: Dom Wydawniczy "Ostoja," 2006.

Piotrowski, Robert. "Dwie doktryny cywilizacyjne. Koneczny a Majewski." *Archiwum Historii Filozofii i Myśli Społecznej* 52 (2007): 217–30.

———. *Problem filozoficzny ładu społecznego a porównawcza nauka o cywilizacjach*. Warsaw: Dialog, 2003.

Pipes, Richard. "Polish Sovietology in the Lead-up to the Cold War." *Journal of Cold War Studies* 13, no. 2 (Spring 2011): 175–93.

Piskor, Stanisław. *Na moście Europy*. Katowice: Wydawca Towarzystwo Zachęty Kultury, 1992.

Piskozub, Andrzej. "Feliks Koneczny (1862–1949) jako pionier nauki o cywilizacji w Polsce." *Kultura i Edukacja*, no. 1 (1999): 130–42.

Polak, Ryszard. *Cywilizacje a moralność w myśli Feliksa Konecznego*. Lublin: Fundacja Servire Veritati Instytut Edukacji Narodowej, 2001.

———. "Feliks Koneczny wobec Rosji i jej cywilizacji (cz. I)." *Cywilizacja* 15 (2005): 82–101.

———. "Konecznego ocena relacji polsko-rosyjskich (cz. II)." *Cywilizacja* 16 (2006): 119–40.

———. "Status kobiety w różnych cywilizacjach." *Cywilizacja* 21 (2007): 61–75.

Porter, Brian. "Antisemitism and the Search for a Catholic Identity." In Blobaum, *Antisemitism and Its Opponents in Modern Poland*, 103–23.

———. *When Nationalism Began to Hate: Imagining Modern Politics in Nineteenth-Century Poland*. Oxford: Oxford University Press, 2000.

Prusin, Alexander Victor. *Nationalizing a Borderland: War, Ethnicity, and Anti-Jewish Violence in East Galicia, 1914–1920*. Tuscaloosa: University of Alabama Press, 2005.

Pucek, Zbigniew. "Feliks Koneczny: teoria pluralizmu cywilizacyjnego." In *Szkice z historii socjologii polskiej*, edited by Kazimierz Z. Sowa, 155–88. Warsaw: PAX, 1983.

———. "Koncepcje cywilizacyjne F. Konecznego na tle tez humanistyki przełomu antypozytywistycznego." In *Filozofia i religia w kulturze narodów słowiańskich*, edited by Tadeusz Chrobak and Zbigniew Stachowski, 113–27. Rzeszów: Wydawnictwo Wyższej Szkoły Pedagogicznej, 1995.

———. *Pluralizm cywilizacyjny jako perspektywa myśli socjologicznej*. Kraków: Akademia Ekonomiczna, 1990.

Purchla, Jacek. *Jak powstał nowoczesny Kraków*. 2nd ed. Kraków: Wydawnictwo Literackie, 1990.

———, ed. *Kraków i Lwów w cywilizacji europejskiej*. Kraków: Międzynarodowe Centrum Kultury w Krakowie, 2003.

Rich, Paul. "Civilisations in European and World History: A Reappraisal of the Ideas of Arnold Toynbee, Fernand Braudel and Marshall Hodgson." *European Legacy* 7, no. 3 (2002): 331–42.

Robaczewski, Arkadiusz. "Quincunx jako odbicie klasycznej teorii osoby." *Człowiek w Kulturze* 10 (1998): 43–48.

Robichaud, Paul. *Making the Past Present: David Jones, the Middle Ages, and Modernism*. Washington, DC: Catholic University of America Press, 2007.

Rowland, Tracey. *Culture and the Thomist Tradition: After Vatican II*. London: Routledge, 2003.

Rudnicki, Szymon. "Anti-Jewish Legislation in Interwar Poland." In Blobaum, *Antisemitism and Its Opponents in Modern Poland*, 148–70.

Rüsen, Jörn. "Introduction: Historical Thinking as Intercultural Discourse." In Rüsen, *Western Historical Thinking*, 1–11.

———. "Some Theoretical Approaches to Intercultural Comparative Historiography." *History and Theory* 35, no. 4 (December 1996): 5–22.

———, ed. *Western Historical Thinking: An Intercultural Debate*. New York: Berghahn Books, 2002.

Ryba, Mieczysław. "Człowiek, naród, państwo w cywilizacji łacińskiej." *Cywilizacja* 1 (2002): 7–14. http://cywilizacja.ien.pl/?id=77 (accessed 27 August 2009).

———. "Polska w XX wieku a cywilizacje." *Człowiek w Kulturze* 10 (1998): 97–105.

Rzegocki, Arkady. "Mirosława Dzielskiego rozważania o cywilizacji." Ośrodek Myśli Politycznej. http://www.omp.org.pl/index.php?module=subjects&func=viewpage&pageid=56 (accessed 23 June 2006).

Said, Edward. *Orientalism*. New York: Vintage Books, 1994.

Salamon, Maciej. "Bizancjum Feliksa Konecznego." In Skoczyński, *Feliks Koneczny dzisiaj*, 167–86.

Schmid, Ulrich. "Eine glückliche Familie. Die Giertychs und ihre Ideologie." *Osteuropa* 56, no. 11–12 (November–December 2006): 69–80.

Semelin, Jacques. *Purify and Destroy: The Political Uses of Massacre and Genocide*. Translated by Cynthia Schoch. New York: Columbia University Press, 2007.

Seth, Sanjay. "A 'Postcolonial World'?" In *Contending Images of World Politics*, edited by Greg Fry and Jacinta O'Hagan, 214–26. New York: St. Martin's Press, 2000.

Shneiderman, S. L. "'High' Anti-Semitism Revived." *Midstream* 22 (August/September 1976): 76–81.

Simmons, Clare A. Introduction to *Medievalism and the Quest for the "Real" Middle Ages*, edited by Clare A. Simmons, 1–28. London: Frank Cass, 2001.

Skibiński, Paweł. "Bizancjum na zachodzie. Niemcy w historiozofii Feliksa Konecznego." *Fronda* 17/18 (1999): 22–47.

Skoczyński, Jan. "Człowiek bez tożsamości. Rozmowa Józefa Barana z prof. Janem Skoczyńskim. In *O globalizmie na spokojnie*, edited by Anna Frątczak, 37–41. Kraków: Wydawnictwo "Zielone Brygady," 2005.

———, ed. *Feliks Koneczny dzisiaj. Praca zbiorowa*. Kraków: Księgarnia Akademicka, 2000.

———. "Huntington and Koneczny (an Attempt to Compare)." *Canadian Slavonic Papers* 41, no. 2 (1999): 207–16.

———. "Huntington i Koneczny." In Skoczyński, *Feliks Koneczny dzisiaj*, 102–10.

———. *Idee historiozoficzne Feliksa Konecznego*. Kraków: Nakładem Uniwersytetu Jagiellońskiego, 1991.

———. *Koneczny. Teoria cywilizacji*. Warsaw: Wydawnictwo IFiS PAN, 2003.

———. "Logos i ethos w teorii cywilizacji." In *Rozmyślania o cywilizacji*, edited by J. Baradziej and J. Goćkowski, 137–42. Kraków: Wydawnictwo Baran i Suszczyński, 1997.

———. "Trzecia droga (o metodzie historiozoficznej Feliksa Konecznego)." *Historyka* 18 (1988): 57–70.

Skórczewski, Dariusz. "Dlaczego Polska powinna upomnieć się o swoją postkolonialność." *Znak* 59, no. 9 (2007): 145–53.

———. "Postkolonialna Polska—project (nie)możliwy." *Teksty Drugie*, no. 1–2 (2006): 100–112.

Skrzydlewski, Paweł. *Polityka w cywilizacji łacińskiej. Aktualność nauki Feliksa Konecznego.* Lublin: Fundacja Rozwoju Kultury Polskiej, 2003.

———. "Prawo stanowione w cywilizacji łacińskiej (na kanwie rozważań F. Konecznego)." *Cywilizacja* 12 (2005): 47–60.

———. "Rodzina w cywilizacji łacińskiej a wolność człowieka: na kanwie rozważań Feliksa Konecznego." *Człowiek w Kulturze* 11 (1998): 203-233.

——— "Życie i myśl Feliksa Konecznego (1 XI 1862–10 II 1949)." *Akademia Górniczo-Hutnicza im. Stanisława Staszica w Krakowie.* http://ciapek.uci.agh.edu.pl/~kwlodarc/tekstyo/pskrzydlewski.html (accessed 28 June 2004).

Solak, Zbigniew. "Marian Zdziechowski i Klub Słowiański." *Studia Historyczne* 30, no. 2 (1987): 219–39.

Stauter-Halsted, Keely. *The Nation in the Village: The Genesis of Peasant National Identity in Austrian Poland, 1848–1914.* Ithaca, NY: Cornell University Press, 2001.

———. "Rural Myth and the Modern Nation: Peasant Commemorations of Polish National Holidays, 1879–1910." In *Staging the Past: The Politics of Commemoration in Habsburg Central Europe, 1848 to the Present,* edited by Maria Bucur and Nancy M. Wingfield, 153–77. West Lafayette, IN: Purdue University Press, 2001.

Steinweis, Alan E. *Studying the Jew: Scholarly Antisemitism in Nazi Germany.* Cambridge, MA: Harvard University Press, 2006.

The Stephen Roth Institute for the Study of Contemporary Antisemitism and Racism. *Antisemitism Worldwide 2007—Poland.* http://www.tau.ac.il/Anti-Semitism/asw2007/poland.html (accessed 12 August 2010).

Stobiecki, Rafał. "Rosja i Rosjanie w polskiej myśli historycznej XIX i XX wieku." In *Katalog wzajemnych uprzedzeń Polaków i Rosjan,* edited by Andrzej Lazari, 159–202. Warsaw: Polski Instytut Spraw Międzynarodowych, 2006.

Szaynok, Bożena. "The Role of Antisemitism in Postwar Polish-Jewish Relations." In Blobaum, *Antisemitism and Its Opponents in Modern Poland,* 65–83.

Szczerbiak, Aleks. "Referendum Briefing No. 5: The Polish EU Accession Referendum, 7–8 June 2003." *Sussex European Institute: Opposing Europe Research Network.* http://www.sussex.ac.uk/polces/documents/poland5.pdf (accessed 28 June 2004)

Szczęsny, Marian. "Rola chrześcijaństwa w tworzeniu cywilizacji łacińskiej według Feliksa Konecznego." *Studia Telogiczne* 20 (2002): 377–400.

Szumera, Grażyna. *Cywilizacja w myśli polskiej: poglądy filozoficzno-społeczne Erazma Majewskiego.* Katowice: Wydawnictwo Uniwersytetu Śląskiego, 2007.

Szurgot, Wojciech. *Prawo jako fundament cywilizacji łacińskiej w myśli Feliksa Konecznego.* Krzeszowice: Dom Wydawniczy "Ostoja," 2007.

Szwed, Anna. "'Opoka w Kraju' (The Bedrock in a Country): The Magazine's Monograph." *Annales Universitatis Mariae Curie-Skłodowska, Lublin-Polonia, Sectio K (Politologia)* 20, no. 1 (2013): 251–70.

Taras, Ray. "Poland's Accession into the European Union: Parties, Policies and Paradoxes." *Polish Review* 48, no. 1 (2003): 3–19.

Tarnowski, Józef. "Konecznego aksjologia dzieła sztuki teatralnej." In Skoczyński, *Feliks Koneczny dzisiaj*, 265–72.

Tazbir, Janusz. *Polska przedmurzem Europy*. Warsaw: Twój Styl, 2004.

Tokarska-Bakir, Joanna. *Legendy o krwi. Antropologia przesądu (z cyklu: obraz osobliwy)*. Warsaw: Wydawnictwo W.A.B., 2008.

Tokarz, Grzegorz. *Ruch narodowy w Polsce w latach 1989–1997*. Wrocław: Wydawnictwo Uniwersytetu Wrocławskiego, 2002.

Tomasiewicz, Jarosław. *Ugrupowania neoendeckie w III Rzeczypospolitej*. Toruń: Wydawnictwo Adam Marszałek, 2003.

Tomaszewski, Jerzy. "From Internationalism to Nationalism? Poland, 1944–96." In *Nationalism and Internationalism in the Post-Cold War Era*, edited by Kjell Goldmann, Ulf Hannerz, and Charles Westin, 67–86. London: Routledge, 2000.

Toynbee, Arnold. *A Study of History*. Vol. 1. London: Oxford University Press, 1935.

———. *Reconsiderations*. Vol. 12, *A Study of History*. New York: Oxford University Press, 1964.

———. Review of Matthew Melko, *The Nature of Civilizations* (Boston: Porter Sargent, 1969). *History and Theory* 10, no. 2 (1971): 246–53.

Tylki-Szymańska, Anna. "Kościół katolicki wobec cywilizacji w Europie według teorii Feliksa Konecznego." *Studia nad Rodziną* 7, no. 2 (2003): 187–92.

Vasilenko, I. A. "Dialogue of Cultures, Dialogue of Civilizations." *Russian Social Science Review* 41, no. 2 (March–April 2000): 5–22.

Velikonja Mitja. "Slovenian and Polish Religio-National Mythologies: A Comparative Analysis." *Religion, State & Society* 31, no. 3 (2003): 233–60.

Velychenko, Stephen. *National History as Cultural Process: A Survey of the Interpretations of Ukraine's Past in Polish, Russian, and Ukrainian Historical Writing from the Earliest Times to 1914*. Edmonton: Canadian Institute of Ukrainian Studies Press, University of Alberta, 1992.

Vykoukal, Jiří. "Polské vidění Ruska: příklad negativního stereotypu (IV. Syntézy kanonické i nekanonické)." *Slovanský Přehled* 86, no. 2 (2000): 215–38.

———. "Rusko v 'druhém oběhu' aneb Střet civilizací po polsku." *Soudobé dějiny* 9, no. 3–4 (2002): 593–601.

———. "Territorial Contexts of the Polish Reflection of Russia." In *Regions in Central and Eastern Europe: Past and Present*, edited by Tadayuki Hayashi and Fukuda Hiroshi, 109–20. Tokyo: Slavic Research Center, 2007. http://src-h.slav.hokudai.ac.jp/coe21/publish/no15_ses/contents.html (accessed 30 June 2008).

Walicki, Andrzej. *Rosja, katolicyzm, i sprawa polska*. Warsaw: Prószyński i S-ka, 2002.

———. "The Troubling Legacy of Roman Dmowski." *East European Politics and Societies* 14, no. 1 (Winter 2000): 12–46.

Wasilewski, Eugeniusz. "O istocie i sposobach funkcjonowania dobra według Feliksa Konecznego i Mariana Zdziechowskiego." In *Filozofia na Uniwersytecie Stefana Batorego*, edited by Józef Pawlak, 212–22. Toruń: Wydawnictwo Uniwersytetu Mikołaja Kopernika, 2002.

Weksler-Waszkinel, Romuald Jakub. "Antysemityzm bez Żydów." *Miesięcznik "Znak,"* December 2008. http://www.tezeusz.pl/cms/tz/index.php?id=3773 (accessed 5 January 2010).

——— "A Breakthrough in the Teachings of the Church on Jews and Judaism." In *Imaginary Neighbors: Mediating Polish-Jewish Relations after the Holocaust*, edited by

Dorota Glowacka and Joanna Zylinska, 225–35. Lincoln: University of Nebraska Press, 2007.

———. "Księdza Stanisława Musiała zmagania z pamięcią." *Zagłada Żydów. Studia i Materiały* 2 (2006): 438–58.

Wierzbicki, Andrzej. *Naród-Państwo w polskiej myśli historycznej dwudziestolecia międzywojennego.* Wrocław: Wydawnictwo Polskiej Akademii Nauk, 1978.

———. *Spory o polską duszę. z zagadnień charakterologii narodowej w historiografii polskiej XIX i XX w.* Warsaw: Instytut Historii Polskiej Akademii Nauk, 1993.

Wise, Andrew Kier. *Aleksander Lednicki: A Pole among Russians, a Russian among Poles. Polish-Russian Reconciliation in the Revolution of 1905.* Boulder, CO: East European Monographs, 2003.

———. "Jerzy Kurnatowski and Polish Solidarism." *Polish Review* 46, no. 3 (2001): 327–44.

———. "The Search for Slavic Unity: Aleksander Lednicki and the Russian Revolution of 1905." *Polish Review* 42, no. 1 (1997): 29–44.

Wituch, Tomasz. "Religia jako rdzeń cywilizacji." In Skoczyński, *Feliks Koneczny dzisiaj,* 79–84.

Wojdyło, Witold, and Grzegorz Radomski. "W obronie niezależności narodu. Ruch narodowy w Polsce wobec wspólnot wyższego rzędu oraz idei integracyjnych w Europie w XX w." *Przegląd Humanistyczny* 50, no. 3 (2006): 83–97.

Wolff, Larry. "Dynastic Conservatism and Poetic Violence in Fin-de-Siecle Cracow: The Habsburg Matrix of Polish Modernism." *American Historical Review* 106, no. 3 (June 2001): 735–64.

Wood, Nathaniel D. *Becoming Metropolitan: Urban Selfhood and the Making of Modern Cracow.* DeKalb: Northern Illinois University Press, 2010.

Yuval-Davis, Nira. *Gender and Nation.* London: Sage Publications, 1997.

———. "Women, Globalization and Contemporary Politics of Belonging." *Gender, Technology, and Development* 13, no. 1 (2009): 1–19.

Zabieglik, Stefan. "Feliksa Konecznego teoria cywilizacji." *Toruński Przegląd Filozoficzny* 5/6 (2003): 109–28.

Zarycki, Tomasz. "Polska i jej regiony a debata postkolonialna." In *Oblicze polityczne regionów Polski,* edited by M. Dajnowicz, 31–48. Białystok: Wyższa Szkoła Finansów i Zarządzania, 2008.

———. "Uses of Russia: The Role of Russia in the Modern Polish National Identity." *East European Politics and Societies* 18, no. 4 (2004): 595–627.

Zawojska, Teresa. "O narodzie w cywilizacji łacińskiej." *Człowiek w Kulturze* 16 (2004): 282–88.

Zgliczyński, Stefan. *Antysemityzm po polsku.* Warsaw: Instytut Wydawniczy Książka i Prasa, 2008.

Zieliński, Tadeusz. *Hellenizm a Judaizm.* 2 vols. Warsaw: Wydawnictwo J. Mortkowicza, 1927.

Zubrzycki, Geneviève. "'We, the Polish Nation': Ethnic and Civic Visions of Nationhood in Post-Communist Constitutional Debates." *Theory and Society* 30, no. 5 (2001): 629–69.

ARTICLES AND COMMENTARY FROM THE POPULAR PRESS AND WEBSITES

"III Wszechnica Narodowa." *Młodziez [sic] Wszechpolska—koło Radom*, 21 May 2005. http://radom.wszechpolacy.pl/ (accessed 5 July 2006).

Bajda, Jerzy. "Konstytucja Europejska: ocean moralna." *Instytut Studiów nad Rodziną*. http://www.isnr.uksw.edu.pl/teksty/Bajda/ocena%20konst%20UE.htm (accessed 30 June 2008).

————. "Ku odnowionej Polsce." *Radio Maryja—Katolicka Głos w Twoim Domu*, 7 January 2006. http://www.radiomaryja.pl/artykuly.php?id=2 (accessed 21 August 2010).

Bała, Paweł. "Eurodżihad." *Organizacja Monarchistów Polskich oddział Lublin*. (http://www.omp.lublin.pl/artykuly.php?autor=3&artykul=0) (accessed 4 January 2010).

Banach, Tomasz. "Prawo rzymskie w publicystyce obozu narodowego Polski międzywojennej." *Myśl Polska*, no. 32–33 (6–13 August 2006). http://www.mysl polska.icenter.pl/ (accessed 12 September 2006).

Baranowska, Kamila. "Zapomniany poprzednik Huntingtona." *Rzeczpospolita*, 11 February 2009. http://www.rp.pl/artykul/261642.html? (accessed 27 February 2009).

Bein, Peter. "Wojna o cywilizacje. Operation Danish Cartoons—A Battle in the War of Civilizations." *now@ on-line*, March 2008. http://nowaonline.strefa.pl/66_ Bein_P_2.htm (accessed 24 October 2008). Also at *Zaprasza.net*. http://zaprasza .net/a_y.php?article_title=koneczny&mid=22348 (accessed 25 August 2009).

Bloch, Teresa. "85. rocznica osiemnastej bitwy decydującej o losach świata." *Nowy Przegląd Wszechpolski* 12, no. 9–10 (2005). http://www.npw.pl/ARCHIWUM_ NPW/2005_09_10/HiW-Bloch_85_rocznica.html (accessed 21 June 2006).

————. "Dwa oblicza unii. Unie polsko-litewskie a Unia Europejska." *Nowy Przegląd Wszechpolski* 9, no. 3–4 (2002). http://www.npw.pl/ARCHIWUM_ NPW/2002_03_04/HIW-Bloch_Dwa-oblicza-unii.htm (accessed 21 June 2006).

————. "Miejsce wschodnich rubieży w dziejach ojczystych." *Nowy Przegląd Wszechpolski* 14, no. 3–4 (2007): 16–19. http://www.npw.pl/pdf/npw.2007.3-4.pdf (accessed 9 December 2009).

————. "Nie wszystko stracone." *Nowy Przegląd Wszechpolski* 11, no. 5–6 (2004). http://www.npw.pl/ARCHIWUM_NPW/2004_05_06/HIW-Bloch_Nie-wszystko-stra cone.html (accessed 21 June 2006).

Bodakowski, Jan. "Euro konstytucja czyli wstęp do czerwonego terroru." *Nacjonalista. pl—portal narodowo-radykalny*. http://nacjonalista.pl/artykuly.php?id=70 (accessed 9 January 2008).

Bojarski, Włodzimierz. "Czy kolonializm przeminął?" *Nasza Witryna*. http://www.na szawitryna.pl/europa_343.html (accessed 11 May 2010). First published in *Nasz Dziennik*, 20 February 2002.

————. *Dokąd Polsko? Wobec globalizacji i integracji europejskiej*. Warsaw: Inicjatywa Wydawnicza "ad astra," 2002.

————. "Uwagi do programu nowej ewangelizacji." *Internetowa Gazeta Katolików*. http://www.krajski.com/955wbkos.htm (accessed 6 December 2007).

Brandt, Karol. "Niezapomniany Feliks Koneczny." *Myśl Polska*, no. 31–32 (2–9 August 2009). http://www.myslpolska.org/node/10210 (accessed 21 August 2009).

Brzózka, Radosław. "Wybitny pedagog." *Nasz Dziennik*, 16 May 2008.

Bubula, Barbara. "Na manowcach społeczeństwa obywatelskiego." *Magazyn Obywatel,* no. 4 (2001). http://www.obywatel.org.pl/index.php?module=subjects&func=view page&pageid=1039 (accessed 3 March 2007).

Chazbijewicz, Selim. "Feliks Koneczny i jego filozofia cywilizacji." *Debata* 2, no. 29 (February 2010): 7–10.

Dakowski, Mirosław. "60-ciolecie śmierci Feliksa Konecznego." *Strona Mirosława Dakowskiego,* 17 February 2009. http://dakowski.pl/index.php?option=com_conte nt&task=view&id=972&Itemid=49 (accessed 24 August 2009).

———. "Nie potępiajmy Konecznego!" *Myśl Polska,* 23 February 2007. http://www .myslpolska.org/?idx=janek_art&lusterko=193442 (accessed 16 March 2007).

———. "Nośniki energii a geopolityka." *Rurociągi: Polish Pipeline Journal.* http://www .rurociagi.com/spis_art/2004_2-3/nosniki.htm (accessed 12 September 2006).

———. "Poglądy Samuela Huntingtona—plagiat oraz odwrócenie kota ogonem dorob-ku Feliksa Konecznego." *Strona Mirosława Dakowskiego.* http://dakowski.pl/index. php?option=com_content&task=view&id=48&Itemid=49 (accessed 23 August 2009).

———. "Potencjały rozpraszające a instynkt samozachowawczy narodów." *Strona Mirosława Dakowskiego,* 12 March 2007. http://dakowski.pl/index.php?op tion=com_content&task=view&id=47&Itemid=49 (accessed 23 August 2009).

———. "Wojny o energię." Wydawnictwo "Zielone Brygady." http://zb.eco.pl/zb/183/ military.htm (accessed 30 June 2004).

Dobrowolski, Rafał. "Teoria historiozoficzna prof. Feliksa Konecznego." *My, Nowe Pokolenie!* 2, no. 15 (2003). http://www.infopatria.pl/art.php?art=293 (accessed 7 April 2007).

Domosławski, Artur. "Saga rodu Giertychów." *gazeta.pl.* http://serwisy.gazeta.pl/ kraj/1,62905,1062309.html (accessed 10 June 2005).

———. "Saga rodu Giertychów—część II." *gazeta.pl.* http://serwisy.gazeta.pl/ kraj/1,62905,1074233.html (accessed 10 June 2005).

Eckhardt, Kamil. "Islamizacja Europy." *Najwyższy CZAS! Pismo Konserwatywno-li-beralne,* 15 January 2008. http://nczas.com/publicystyka/islamizacja-europy/ (accessed 3 July 2014).

Editorial. "Czy jestem Polakiem?" *Nowy Przegląd Wszechpolski* 13, no. 1-2 (2006). http://www.npw.pl/ARCHIWUM_NPW/2006_01_02/index.html (accessed 20 June 2006).

———. "Egzamin dla każdego z nas." *Nowy Przegląd Wszechpolski* 9, no. 5–6 (2002). http://www.npw.pl/ARCHIWUM_NPW/2002_05_06/WST-Red_Egzamin.htm (accessed 21 June 2006).

———. "Jan Paweł II odnowiciel." *Nowy Przegląd Wszechpolski* 13, no. 5–6 (2006): 1. http://www.npw.pl/pdf/npw.2006.5-6.pdf (accessed 27 August 2009).

———. "Miłość przebija pancerze." *Nowy Przegląd Wszechpolski* 14, no. 1–2 (2007): 1. http://www.npw.pl/pdf/npw.2007.1-2.pdf (accessed 27 August 2009).

———. "O wyjście z chaosu." *Nowy Przegląd Wszechpolski* 14, no. 3–4 (2007): 1. http:// www.npw.pl/pdf/npw.2007.3-4.pdf (accessed 27 August 2009).

———. "Zaufajmy duchowi świętemu." *Nowy Przegląd Wszechpolski* 12, no. 5–6 (2005). http://www.npw.pl/ARCHIWUM_NPW/2005_05_06/WST-Red_Zaufajmy_duch owi.html (accessed 21 June 2006)

Engelgard, Jan. "Kwestia niemiecka." *Myśl Polska,* no. 35 (2 September 2007).

Fostakowska, Anna. "Wszechpolki—rozmowy kontrolowane." *gazeta.pl*, 11 February 2005. http://serwisy.gazeta.pl/kraj/1,62906,2547356.html?as=1&ias=5 (accessed 10 June 2005).

Gancarz, Bogdan. "Koneczny—prekursor Huntingtona." *Rzeczpospolita*. http://www.rzeczpospolita.pl/dodatki/opinie_070222/opinie_a_4.html (accessed 26 August 2009).

Giertych, Jędrzej. *Nacjonalizm chrześcijański*. 3rd ed. Krzeszowice: Dom Wydawniczy "Ostoja," 2004.

Giertych, Maciej. "Agro-środowisko pożądane." *Opoka w Kraju* 42, no. 63 (August 2002): 3–5. http://opoka.giertych.pl/42.pdf (accessed 28 August 2009).

———. "Bizantynizm niemiecki." *Opoka w Kraju* 40, no. 61 (December 2001). http://opoka.giertych.pl/owk40.htm (accessed 30 June 2008).

———. *Civilisations at War in Europe*. Brussels: Maciej Giertych, 2007. Also online at *Opoka w Kraju*. http://opoka.giertych.pl/.

———. "Co teraz?" *Opoka w Kraju* 45, no. 66 (July 2003): 1–3. http://opoka.giertych.pl/45.pdf (accessed 30 June 2008).

———. "Europa łacińska." *Opoka w Kraju* 40, no. 61 (December 2001): 13. http://opoka.giertych.pl/40.pdf (accessed 30 June 2008).

———. *European Values*. Brussels: Maciej Giertych, 2007. Also online at *Opoka w Kraju*. http://opoka.giertych.pl/.

———. *Gender Equality and Life Issues in the European Union*. Brussels: Maciej Giertych, 2008. Also online at *Opoka w Kraju*. http://opoka.giertych.pl/.

———. "Geopolityka." *Opoka w Kraju*, Numer specjalny, poświęcony referendum w sprawie akcesji do Unii Europejskiej, 44, no. 65 (April 2003): 12–14. http://opoka.giertych.pl/44.pdf (accessed 30 June 2008).

———. "Kobieta pracująca zarobkowo." *Opoka w Kraju* 29, no. 50 (March 1999). http://opoka.giertych.pl/owk29.htm (accessed 19 August 2010).

———. "Koneczny o cywilizacji arabskiej." *Opoka w Kraju* 59, no. 80 (October 2006): 5–7. http://opoka.giertych.pl/59.pdf (accessed 30 June 2008).

———. "Konfrontacja z islamem." *Opoka w Kraju* 66, no. 87 (March 2008): 1–10. http://opoka.giertych.pl/66.pdf (accessed 30 June 2008).

———. "Korzenie UE." *Opoka w Kraju* 44, no. 65 (April 2003): 2–3. http://opoka.giertych.pl/44.pdf (accessed 30 June 2008).

———. "Miejsce dla religii." *Opoka w Kraju*, Numer specjalny, poświęcony referendum w sprawie akcesji do Unii Europejskiej, 44, no. 65 (April 2003): 5–7. http://opoka.giertych.pl/44.pdf (accessed 30 June 2008).

———. "Moja teczka w SB." *Opoka w Kraju* 32, no. 53 (December 1999). http://opoka.giertych.pl/owk32.htm (accessed 30 June 2008).

———. "Mój życiorys." *Opoka w Kraju* 14, no. 35 (October 1995). http://opoka.giertych.pl/owk14.htm (accessed 30 June 2008).

———. "Nie oddawać pola." *Myśl Polska*, no. 23 (6 June 2004). http://www.myslpolska.icenter.pl/ (accessed 19 March 2005). First published in *Opoka w Kraju* 49, no. 70 (May 2004).

———. "Polityka zagraniczna." *Opoka w Kraju* 17, no. 38 (April 1996). http://opoka.giertych.pl/owk17.htm (accessed 30 June 2008).

———. "Program dla posłów LPR do Parlamentu Europejskiego." *Opoka w Kraju* 49, no. 70 (May 2004). http://opoka.giertych.pl/owk49.htm (accessed 30 June 2008).

———. *Quo vadis Europa?* Brussels: Maciej Gertych, 2009. Also online at http://opoka
.giertych.pl/quo_vadis_ang.pdf

———. "Rok Konecznego." *Opoka w Kraju* 29, no. 50 (March 1999). http://opoka.gier
tych.pl/owk29.htm (accessed 30 June 2008).

———. "Rozumienie świata a podziały cywilizacyjne prof. dr hab. Maciej Giertych."
Nasza witryna. http://www.naszawitryna.pl/jedwabne_497.html (accessed 6 November 2007). First published in *Nasz Dziennik*, 6 February 2001.

———. "Stronnictwo Narodowe." *Opoka w Kraju* 12, no. 33 (May 1995). http://opoka
.giertych.pl/owk12.htm (accessed 30 June 2008).

———. "Superpaństwo." *Opoka w Kraju* 44, no. 65 (April 2003). http://opoka.giertych
.pl/owk44.htm (accessed 30 June 2008).

———. "Teolog domu papieskiego." *Opoka w Kraju* 55, no. 76 (December 2005): 16.
http://opoka.giertych.pl/55.pdf (accessed 15 August 2010).

———. "Traditional Catholicism in Polish Public Life." *Prof. Maciej Giertych.* http://
giertych.eu/?sr=!czytaj&dz=7&id=178 (accessed 29 August 2010).

———. "Wieś ma być zniszczona." *Opoka w Kraju.* Numer specjalny, poświęcony
referendum w sprawie akcesji do Unii Europejskiej, 44, no. 65 (April 2003): 7–8.
http://opoka.giertych.pl/44.pdf (accessed 30 June 2008).

———. "Wojna cywilizacji w Europie." *Opoka w Kraju* 61, no. 82 (April 2007): 1–2.
http://opoka.giertych.pl/61.pdf (accessed 30 June 2008).

———. "Wybory do Parlamentu Europejskiego," *Opoka w Kraju* 49, no. 70 (May 2004):
5. http://opoka.giertych.pl/49.pdf (accessed 28 August 2009).

———. *Z nadzieją w przyszłość.* Warsaw: Maciej Giertych, 2005. Also online at *Opoka
w Kraju.* http://opoka.giertych.pl/

———. "Z nauczania Feliksa Konecznego." *Opoka w Kraju* 11, no. 32 (March 1995); 12,
no. 33 (May 1995); 13, no. 34 (September 1995); 15, no. 36 (December 1995); 16,
no. 37 (February 1996); 17, no. 38 (April 1996); 18, no. 39 (June 1996); 19, no. 40
(September 1996); 21, no. 42 (March 1997). http://opoka.giertych.pl/ (accessed 3
July 2014).

———. "Zniszczyć rolnictwo!" *Opoka w Kraju* 15, no. 36 (December 1995). http://opo
ka.giertych.pl/owk15.htm (accessed 30 June 2008).

Giertych, Wojciech. "Feliks Koneczny (1862–1949)." *Christendom College*, 14 September 2012. http://www.christendom.edu/news/2012/koneczny.pdf (accessed 9 June
2013).

———. "The Moral Natural Law: Problems and Prospects." *Catholic Online*, 25 February 2007. http://www.catholic.org/featured/headline.php?ID=4093 (accessed 26
February 2007).

———. "Niewykorzystany kapitał?" *W Drodze*, no. 3 (2008). http://www.mateusz.pl/
goscie/wdrodze/nr415/04-wdr.htm (accessed 28 November 2008).

Gigilewicz, Edward. *Lublinland: państwo żydowskie w planach III Rszeszy.* Radom:
Polskie Wydawnictwo Encyklopedyczne, 2004.

Glatz, Carol. "Women, Men Experience Sin Differently, Papal Theologian Says." *Catholic News Service*, 19 February 2009. http://www.catholicnews.com/data/stories/
cns/0900774.htm (accessed 26 September 2010).

Holz, Elżbieta. "Kuc—czy pony? Cywilizacja łacińska a współczesne postawy polskiego
środowiska jeździeckiego." *Nowy Przegląd Wszechpolski* 9, no. 1–2 (2002). http://
www.npw.pl/ARCHIWUM_NPW/2002_01_02/OKW-Kuc_czy_pony.htm (ac-
cessed 21 June 2006).

Horodecki, Andrzej J. "Bez dyskusji." *Myśl Polska*, no. 36 (5 September 2004). http://www.myslpolska.icenter.pl/ (accessed 19 March 2005).

———. "Ciemności europejskie." *Nowy Przegląd Wszechpolski* 11, no. 5–6 (2004). http://www.npw.pl/ARCHIWUM_NPW/2004_05_06/OKW-Horodecki_CIEM NOZCI-EUROPEJSKIE.html (accessed 21 June 2006).

———. "Co nam zamyka oczy i uszy?" *Nowy Przegląd Wszechpolski* 11, no. 7–8 (2004). http://www.npw.pl/ARCHIWUM_NPW/2004_07_08/PIS-Horodecki_co-nam -zamyka.html (accessed 21 June 2006).

———. "Czas próby polskich sumień trwa." *Nowy Przegląd Wszechpolski* 7, no. 11–12 (2000). http://www.npw.pl/ARCHIWUM_NPW/2000_11_12/PIS-Horodec ki_czas-proby-czas-trwania.html (accessed 21 June 2006).

———. "De profundis clamavi ad te, domine . . ." *Nowy Przegląd Wszechpolski* 12, no. 1–2 (2005). http://www.npw.pl/ARCHIWUM_NPW/2005_01_02/OKW-Horo decki_de.html (accessed 21 June 2006).

———. "Ecce Polonia." *Myśl Polska*, no. 17 (25 April 2004). http://www.myslpolska .icenter.pl/ (accessed 20 March 2005).

———. "Gdzie jest inicjatywna polityka Polska?" *Nowy Przegląd Wszechpolski* 7, no. 5–6 (2000). http://www.npw.pl/ARCHIWUM_NPW/2000_05_06/TMS-Horodec ki_Gdzie-jest-inicjatywna.htm (accessed 21 June 2006).

———. "Gra o wytrwałość." *Myśl Polska*, 27 October 2002. http://www.myslpolska .icenter.pl/ (accessed 20 March 2005).

———. "Kościół wobec personalizmu i gromadnościowości: konsekwencje lekcewa- żenia grzechu pierworodnego." *Nowy Przegląd Wszechpolski* 11, no. 3–4 (2004). http://www.npw.pl/ARCHIWUM_NPW/2004_03_04/ZRE-Horodecki_KOS CIOL-WOBEC.html (accessed 30 June 2008).

———. "Kurort Europa." *Myśl Polska*, no. 5 (2 February 2003). http://www.myslpolska .icenter.pl/ (accessed 22 March 2005).

———. "Między myśleniem a świadomością." *Nowy Przegląd Wszechpolski* 13, no. 1–2 (2006). http://www.npw.pl/ARCHIWUM_NPW/2006_01_02/2.html (accessed 20 June 2006).

———. "My, szarzy ludzie . . ." *Nowy Przegląd Wszechpolski* 15, no. 1–2 (2008): 45–50. http://www.npw.pl/pdf/npw.2008.1-2.pdf (accessed 27 August 2009).

———. "Neototalitaryzm." *Myśl Polska*, no. 44–45 (2–9 November 2003). http://www .myslpolska.icenter.pl/ (accessed 22 March 2005).

———. "Nie ma patriotyzmu bez personalizmu." *Nowy Przegląd Wszechpolski* 11, no. 1–2 (2004). http://www.npw.pl/ARCHIWUM_NPW/2004_01_02/PIS-Horodec ki_nie-ma-patriotyzmu.html (accessed 21 June 2006).

———. "Nowa Enigma IV Rzeszy." *Myśl Polska*, 8 December 2002. http://www.myslpol ska.icenter.pl/ (accessed 20 March 2005).

———. "Nowy Grunwald." *Myśl Polska*, no. 3 (19 January 2003). http://www.myslpol ska.icenter.pl/ (accessed 22 March 2005).

———. "Odwieczny problem." *Myśl Polska*, 22 September 2002, http://www.myslpolska .icenter.pl/ (accessed 26 March 2005).

———. "Odwrócona karta." *Myśl Polska*, no. 40 (1 October 2006). http://www.myslpol ska.org/?article=42 (accessed 30 June 2008).

———. "O powrót do Bożej czasoprzestrzeni odniesienia." *Nowy Przegląd Wszechpolski* 12, no. 9–10 (2005). http://www.npw.pl/ARCHIWUM_NPW/2005_09_10/HiW -Horodecki_O_powrot_do_bozej.html (accessed 30 June 2008).

———. "O zdrowiu w cywilizacji łacińskiej." *Nowy Przegląd Wszechpolski* 10, no. 3–4 (2003). http://www.npw.pl/ARCHIWUM_NPW/2003_03_04/PIS-Horodecki_o_ zdrowiu.html (accessed 28 November 2008).

———. "Papież ponad otchłanią dziejów." *Nowy Przegląd Wszechpolski* 12, no. 5–6 (2005). http://www.npw.pl/ARCHIWUM_NPW/2005_05_06/TMS-Horodec ki_Papiez_ponad.html (accessed 30 June 2008).

———. "Piastowskie korzenie" *Myśl Polska*, no. 34–35 (20–27 August 2006). http:// www.myslpolska.icenter.pl/ (accessed 25 August 2006).

———. "Polowanie na Polskę." *Myśl Polska*, no. 13 (28 March 2004). http://www.mysl -polska.icenter.pl/ (accessed 22 March 2005).

———. "Polsko, szanuj swoją wiarę i wolność!" *Nowy Przegląd Wszechpolski* 10, no. 5–6 (2003). http://www.npw.pl/ARCHIWUM_NPW/2003_05_06/TMS-Horodec ki_Polsko_szanuj.html (accessed 13 September 2006).

———. "Powrót polskości." *Myśl Polska*, no. 39 (24 September 2006). http://www.mysl -polska.org/?idx=artykul&src=98030 (accessed 6 October 2006).

———. "Projekt Konstytucji Rzeczpospolitej Polskiej." *Nowy Przegląd Wszechpolski* 10, no. 9–10 (2003). http://www.npw.pl/ARCHIWUM_NPW/2003_09_10/TMS-Ho rodecki_Projekt-konstytucji-rzecpospolitej.html (accessed 21 June 2006).

———. "Projekt Konstytucji Rzeczpospolitej Polskiej środowisk patriotycznych skupio -nych wokół 'Nowego Przeglądu Wszechpolskiego'." *Nowy Przegląd Wszechpolski* 12, no. 7–8 (2005). http://www.npw.pl/ARCHIWUM_NPW/2005_07_08/PiS-Ho rodecki_konstytucja.html (accessed 30 June 2008).

———. "Prominentna aprobata procederu." *Myśl Polska*, no. 7 (14 April 2002). http:// www.myslpolska.icenter.pl/ (accessed 22 March 2005).

———. "Przez wieś do odbudowy cywilizacji łacińskiej w Polsce." *Nowy Prze- gląd Wszechpolski* 7, no. 9–10 (2000). http://www.npw.pl/ARCHIWUM_ NPW/2000_09_10/PIS-Horodecki_PRzez-wies-do-odbudowy.html (accessed 21 June 2006).

———. "Restrukturyzacja świadomości." *Myśl Polska*, no. 4 (26 January 2003). http:// www.myslpolska.icenter.pl/ (accessed 22 March 2005).

———. "Rozum zagrożony." *Nowy Przegląd Wszechpolski* 14, no. 5–6 (2007): 36–39. http://www.npw.pl/pdf/npw.2007.5-6.pdf (accessed 27 August 2009).

———. "Sejmowe słodycze." *Myśl Polska*, no. 1–2 (5–12 January 2003). http://www .myslpolska.icenter.pl/ (accessed 26 March 2005).

———. "Teraz Serbia." *Myśl Polska*, (n.d.). http://www.myslpolska.org/?article=803 (accessed 30 June 2008).

———. "Totalna walka z cywilizacją łacińską, część I," *Nowy Przegląd Wszechpolski* 9, no. 3–4 (2002). http://www.npw.pl/ARCHIWUM_NPW/2002_03_04/PIS-Horo decki_Totalna-walka-z-CL.htm (accessed 21 June 2006).

———. "Totalna walka z cywilizacją łacińską, część II," *Nowy Przegląd Wszechpolski* 9, no. 5–6 (2002). http://www.npw.pl/ARCHIWUM_NPW/2002_05_06/PIS-Horo decki__Totalna-Walka.htm (accessed 21 June 2006).

———. "Unia antyeuropejska." *Myśl Polska*, no. 23 (8 June 2003). http://www.myslpol ska.icenter.pl/ (accessed 22 March 2005).

———. "Walka cywilizacyjna." *Nowy Przegląd Wszechpolski* 8, no. 3–4 (2001). http:// www.npw.pl/ARCHIWUM_NPW/2001_03_04/TMS-Horodecki_Walka-Cywili zacyjna.html (accessed 21 June 2006).

———. "W cieniu afer." *Myśl Polska*, no. 31 (3 August 2003). http://www.myslpolska.icenter.pl/ (accessed 26 March 2005).
———. "W cieniu wyborów." *Myśl Polska*, no. 41 (9 October 2005). http://www.mysl-polska.icenter.pl/ (accessed 28 January 2006).
———. "Wilki w owczarni." *Myśl Polska*, no. 43 (24 October 2004). http://www.mysl-polska.icenter.pl/ (accessed 25 March 2005).
———. "Wobec dziedzictwa wiary." *Nowy Przegląd Wszechpolski* 14, no. 1–2 (2007): 25–30. http://www.npw.pl/pdf/npw.2007.1-2.pdf (accessed 27 August 2009).
———. "Wobec zamachu na patriotyzm." *Nasza witryna*. http://www.naszawitryna.pl/jedwabne_297.html (accessed 7 May 2008). First published in *Myśl Polska*, no. 24–25 (22 June 2001). Also in *Nowy Przegląd Wszechpolski* 8, no. 1–2 (2001). http://www.npw.pl/ARCHIWUM_NPW/2001_01_02/PIS-Horodecki_Wobec-zamachu.html (accessed 21 June 2006).
———. "Wojna światów." *Myśl Polska*, no. 49–50 (4–11 December 2005). http://www.myslpolska.icenter.pl/ (accessed 28 January 2006).
———. "Wychowanie do wolności w prawdzie." *Nowy Przegląd Wszechpolski* 11, no. 9–10 (2004). http://www.npw.pl/ARCHIWUM_NPW/2004_09_10/PIS-Horodecki_wychowanie-do-wolnosci.html (accessed 30 June 2008).
Jaroszyński, Piotr. *Europa bez Ojczyzn?* Warsaw: Dom Polski, 2002.
———. "Media: między ideologią a biznesem." *Nasz Dziennik*, 6–7 June 2009. http://www.naszdziennik.pl/index.php?dat=20090606&typ=my&id=my51.txt (accessed 21 August 2010).
———. *Naród ma trwać!* Warsaw: Dom Polski, 2006.
———. *Ocalić polskość!* Lublin: Wydawnictwo Instytut Edukacji Narodowej, 2001. Also online at http://www.polonica.net/OcalicPolskosc1.htm (accessed 3 June 2003).
———. "Ojca M.A. Krąpca bój o polską kulturę." *Nasz Dziennik*, 16 May, 21–22 May 2008.
———. *Polska i Europa*. Lublin: Instytut Edukacji Narodowej, 1999. Also online at http://www.polonica.net/PolskaEuropa.htm (accessed 3 June 2003).
———. *Przywracanie pamięci*. Warsaw: Dom Polski, 2007.
———. "Stosunek do ziemi w różnych cywilizacjach." *Klub Myśli Feliksa Konecznego*. http://home.chello.no/~jskorups/KMFK/piotr_jaroszynski7.htm (accessed 1 October 2002).
———. *W nowogródzkiej stronie*. Warsaw: Dom Polski, 2004.
Jaźwiński, Tomasz. "'(Nie)konieczność historyczna' jednej Europy." *Myśl Polska*, no. 36–37 (3–10 September 2006). http://www.myslpolska.org/?idx=artykul&src=97070 (accessed 6 October 2006).
———. "Rządowa deklaracja w sprawie moralności i etyki nie ma znaczenia." *Myśl Polska*, no. 9 (2 March 2003). http://www.myslpolska.icenter.pl/ (accessed 26 March 2005).
Jendrzejczak, Marcin. "Nacjonalizm bizantyski." *Prawica.net*, 28 June 2007. http://www.prawica.net/node/7547 (accessed 30 June 2008).
Kiczora, Wacław. "Wiedzieć, aby rozumieć, rozumieć, aby ocalić własne państwo. Część II." *Nowy Przegląd Wszechpolski* 11, no. 5–6 (2004). http://www.npw.pl/ARCHIWUM_NPW/2004_05_06/PIS-Kiczora_WIEDZIEC-ABY-ROZUMIEC-cz2.html (accessed 21 June 2006).
Koneczny, Wiesław. "O prof. Feliksie Konecznym (1862–1949) (wspomnienia wnuka)." *Arcana* 4, no. 1 (1998): 142–50.

Kosiur, Dariusz. "Są w Ojczyźnie ważne sprawy." *polskawalczaca.com*. http://www
.polskawalczaca.com/viewtopic.php?t=322 (accessed 28 August 2009).

Kossecki, Józef. "Zderzenie cywilizacji łacińskiej i orientu w świetle nauki porównawczej o cywilizacjach i cybernetyki społecznej." *Strona Ruchu Obrony Rodziny i
Jednostki*. http://74.125.93.132/search?q=cache:9Xt5CQr_gJcJ:rorij.free.ngo.pl/
Zderzenie%2520cywilizacji.doc+kossecki+zderzenie+orientu&cd=1&hl=en&c
t=clnk&gl=us (accessed 22 September 2006).

Kowalski, Mariusz. "Kaszuby, Kociewie—cywilizacja łacińska." *Nasze Kaszuby*. http://
www.naszekaszuby.pl/modules/newbb/viewtopic.php?viewmode=flat&or-
der=ASC&topic_id=272&forum=3&move=prev&topic_time=1102780633 (accessed 4 October 2006). First published in *Najwyższy Czas!*, no. 25 (19 June 2004).

Kowalski, Witold. "Cztery cywilizacje." *Nowy Przegląd Wszechpolski* 14, no. 5–6 (2007):
48-49. http://www.npw.pl/pdf/npw.2007.5-6.pdf (accessed 9 December 2009).

Krajski, Stanisław. "Czy grozi nam nowy totalitaryzm?" *Nasz Dziennik*, 2 January 2004.

Krohn, Knut. "Auch Darwin ist des Teufels." *Stuttgarter Zeitung*, 13 March 2007.

Król, Mirosław. "Pomagał zrozumieć człowieka i jego dzieje." *Nasz Dziennik*, 16 May
2008.

Kudzia, Piotr, and Grzegorz Pawelczyk. "The Training of Polish Neo-fascists." *Forum
Żydzi-Polacy-Chrześcijanie*. http://www.forum-znak.org.pl/print.php?t=przeglad
&id=1852&1=en (accessed 25 August 2009).

Kukoc, Mislav. "Reshaped Regional Multiculturalism in the Post-Communist Europe."
Europe: Expectations and Reality. http://www.unesco.org/most/faltan.htm (accessed 25 August 2009).

Kuniński, Miłowit. "Liberalizm chrześcijański. W 15. rocznicę śmierci Mirosława
Dzielskiego." *onet.pl—Tygodnik Powszechny*. http://tygodnik.onet
.pl/0,1201178,druk.html (accessed 19 June 2006).

Kurowski, Stefan. "'Dziewiąta cywilizacja' w działaniu (1)." *Zaprasza.net*. http://zapra
sza.net/a_y.php?article_title=kurowski&mid=5707 (accessed 25 August 2009).

Kusak, Paweł. "Dziedzictwo Konecznego." *Młodzież Wszechpolska*. http://www
.ma.wszechpolacy.pl/podstrony/!czytaj.php?id=1542&dz=artykuly&x=0&pocz=
(accessed 5 July 2006).

Lignarski, Zbigniew. "Talmud a ideologia III Rzeszy." *Nacjonalista.pl—Portal Narodowy-Radykalny*. http://www.nacjonalista.org/galeria.php?id=110 (accessed 20
November 2009).

———. "Talmud ze swastyką w tle?" *Archipelag-Instytut Norwida*, 20 May 2009. http://
archipelag.org.pl/newsdesk_info.php?newsPath=4&newsdesk_id=4 (accessed 21
November 2009).

Lipski, Jan Józef. "Dwie ojczyzny—dwa patriotyzmy. Uwagi o megalomanii narodowej
i ksenofobii Polaków." *My—mankurty*. http://www.mankurty.com/statti/dwie%20
ojczyzny.pdf (accessed 24 August 2009).

Loew, Peter Oliver. "Zwillinge zwischen Endecja und Sanacja. Die neue polnische
Rechtsregierung und ihre historischen Wurzeln." *Eurozine*. http://www.eurozine
.com/articles/2006-01-12-loew-de.html (accessed 26 August 2009). First published in *Osteuropa*, no. 11 (2005).

Łatkowska, Daria. "Ocalić cywilzację [sic] łacińską." *LPR Górny Śląsk*, 8 June 2006.
http://www.lprtychy.iap.pl/index.html?id=39750&site_id=39235 (accessed 18
June 2006).

Łącki, Adam. "Obóz we Wrocławiu." *MW Koło Lubań*, 5 May 2006. http://free4web.pl/ NewsList/89149 (accessed 5 July 2006).

Maj, Ewa. "Sposoby zaprzeczania Zagładzie Żydów: przypadek środowisk neoendeckich." *Forum Żydzi-Polacy-Chrześcijanie*, 14 October 2003. http://www.forum -znak.org.pl/?lang1=pl&page1=studies&subpage1=studies00&infopassid1=83& scrt1=sn (accessed 25 August 2009).

"Mamy wielką wolę zmian." *Aspekt Polski*, 31 May 2006. http://aspektpolski.pl//index2 .php?option=com_content&task=view&id=791&Itemid (accessed 22 June 2006).

Maszkowski, Rafał. "Otwarte społeczeństwo i jego radio." *Stowarzyszenie Nigdy Więcej* [Never Again Association]. http://www.nigdywiecej.org/index2. php?option=com_content&do_pdf=1&id=91 (accessed 26 August 2009).

Maślach, Arkadiusz. "Czy Polska potrzebuje społeczeństwa obywatelskiego?" *Magazyn Obywatel*, no. 4 (2003). http://www.obywatel.org.pl/index.php?module=subjects& func=viewpage&pageid=363 (accessed 3 March 2007).

Miszalski, Marian. "W kręgu 'inżynierii społecznej'. Kolejny 'nowy człowiek'—homo democraticus? *Niedziela—Tygodnik Katolicki*. http://www.niedziela.pl/artykul_w_ niedzieli.php?doc=ed200115&nr=16 (accessed 24 June 2006). First published in *Niedziela—Tygodnik Katolicki. Edycja Łódzka* 15 (2001).

Montusiewicz, Ryszard. "Jezus i judaizm. Z ks. Prof. Romualdem Jakubem Wekslerem-Waszkinelem rozmawia Ryszard Montusiewicz." *Forum: Żydzi-Chrześcijanie-Muzułmanie.* http://znak.org.pl/?lang1=pl&page1=pressreview&subpage1=pressr eview00&infopassid1=3669&scrt1=sn (accessed 21 August 2009).

Nagrodzki, Krzysztof. "Analiza współczesności kard. Josepha Ratzingera." *Myśl Polska*, no. 37–38 (11–18 September 2005). http://www.myslpolska.icenter.pl/ (accessed 28 January 2006).

———. "Barbaria wsączalna." *Myśl Polska*, no. 40 (7 October 2007).

———. "Wojna światów." *Myśl Polska*, no. 49–50 (4–11 December 2005). http://www .myslpolska.icenter.pl/ (accessed 28 January 2006).

Narodowe Odrodzenie Polski, 5 March 2009. http://www.nop.org.pl/?artykul_id=824 (accessed 20 November 2009).

Nikiel, Adrian. "Eko-filozofia czy ekologia chrześcijańska?" Wydawnictwo "Zielone Brygady." http://www.zb.eco.pl/publication/eko-filozofia-czy-ekologia-chrzesci janska-p217511 (accessed 6 May 2009).

Niklewicz, Konrad. "Maciej Giertych znów szokuje eurodeputowanych." *Gazeta Wyborcza*, 16 February 2007. http://www.gazetawyborcza .pl/gazetawyborcza/2029020,76842,3923332.html (accessed 1 March 2007).

Nowicka, Magdalena. "Rzeczpospolita postkolonialna." *Gazeta Wyborcza*, 10 October 2007. http://wyborcza.pl/1,76506,4431065.html (accessed 4 May 2010).

Nowik, Henryk. "Ekshortacja Jana Pawła II Kościół w Europie w kontekście historiozoficznym." *Nowy Przegląd Wszechpolski* 11, no. 1–2 (2004). . http://www.npw .pl/ARCHIWUM_NPW/2004_01_02/ZRE-Nowik_Ekshortacja-jana-pawla.html (accessed 21 June 2006).

Olbrycht, Marcin. "Wojciech Wierzejski." *Wszechpolak: Pismo Młodzieży Narodowej* 115 (June 2004): 4–8.

Olszewska, Małgorzata. "Krew tej ziemi. Wszechpolaków portret zbiorowy." *onet.pl Tygodnik Powszechny*, 15 May 2006. http://tygodnik.onet.pl/0,1335465,druk.html (accessed 19 June 2006).

Pasławski, Sebastian. "Feliks Koneczny. Nadal aktualny." *Prawy.pl*. http://www.prawy.pl /?action=print&dz=felietony&id=21835&subdz= (accessed 16 March 2007).

Pawlas, Jerzy. "Ziemi nie przybywa." *Radio Pomost*. http://www.radiopomost.com/in dex.php?option=news&task=viewarticle&sid=3628 (accessed 24 June 2006).

Piwowarski, Jan. "Oddolne zorganizowanie się Polaków warunkiem przetrwania Narodu i Państwa Polskiego." *Nowy Przegląd Wszechpolski* 8, no. 5–6 (2001). http://www.npw.pl/ARCHIWUM_NPW/2001_05_06/TMS-Piwowarski_Odd olne-organizowanie-sie.html (accessed 21 June 2006).

———. "Program polityczny PLN." *Nowy Przegląd Wszechpolski* 11, no. 5–6 (2004). http://www.npw.pl/ARCHIWUM_NPW/2004_05_06/PIS-Piwowarski_Program -polityczny-PLN.html (accessed 21 June 2006).

Poradowski, Michał. *Dzieje cywilizacji europejskiej*. Wrocław: Wydawnictwo Nortom, 2007.

"Prawdziwa Tożsamość Europy." *Obóz Narodowo-Radykalny*, 30 December 2010. http://www.onr.h2.pl/index.php?option=com_content&task=view&id=221&Item id=104# (accessed 28 May 2011).

Ratajczak, Dariusz. "O cywilizacjach." *dariuszratajczak.blogspot.com*. http://dariusz -ratajczak.blogspot.com/2009/01/o-cywilizacjach.html (accessed 26 May 2009).

Reszczyński, Wojciech. "Cywilizacje, Ordnung i kapelusze." *Nasz Dziennik*, 19 February 2009. http://www.naszdziennik.pl/index.php?typ=dd&dat=20090219&id=main (accessed 3 March 2009).

———. "Media a odpowiedzialność za audytorium." *Radio Maryja*. http://www .radiomaryja.pl/artykuly.php?id=98202 (accessed 24 August 2009). First pub- lished in *Nasz Dziennik*, 21 November 2008.

Ryba, Mieczysław. "Islam w natarciu." *Dla Polski*. http://www.dlapolski.pl/islam (ac- cessed 25 August 2009).

———. "Liberalny Rzym i barbarzyńcy." *Radio Pomost*, 24 March 2004. http://www .radiopomost.com/test/index.php?option=news&task=viewarticle&sid=1834 (accessed 26 August 2009).

———. "O cywilizacjach." http://home.chello.no/~jskorups/KMFK/mieczyslaw_ryba3 .htm (accessed 25 August 2009).

———. "O ludzką politykę." *Nasz Dziennik*, 16 May 2008.

Rzekanowski, Jakub. "Antysemityzm. Antyk kontratakuje: Lekcja miłosierdzia." *Try- buna* (Warsaw), 13/14 December 2003.

Sawczak, Kamil. "Poglądy: o rozwiązaniu kwestii żydowskiej." Referat wygłoszony na II Konferencji Konecznańskiej, Kraków, 9.02.2008. *Nacjonalista.pl—Portal Narodowo-Radykalny*. http://www.nacjonalista.org/artykuly.php?id=88 (accessed 2 April 2008).

Schmid, Ulrich M. "Hüter der polnischen Kultur. Wes Geises Kind ist der polnische Bildungsminister?" *Neue Zürcher Zeitung*, 1 December 2006. http://www.nzz .ch/2006/12/01/fe/articleELVVY.html (accessed 4 December 2007).

Soboń, Artur. "Koncepcja historiozoficzna Feliksa Konecznego." http://ciapek.uci.agh .edu.pl/~kwlodarc/tekstyo/asobon.html (accessed 28 June 2004).

Solak, Andrzej. "Tradycjonalizm 'politycznie poprawny.'" *Myśl Polska*, 28 April 2002. http://www.myslpolska.icenter.pl/ (accessed 25 March 2005).

Spritzer, Dinah A. "Jews are a Detriment to Europe, Polish Politician Says." *Jerusalem Post*, 19 February 2007. http://www.jpost.com/servlet/Satellite?cid=117035989259 8&pagename=JPArticle%2FShowFull (accessed 6 January 2010).

Stańczak-Wiślicz, Katarzyna. "W pułapce kołobłędu, czyli antysemityzm uczonego." *Nigdy Więcej* 16 (Winter–Spring 2008): 18–20.

Stępień, Katarzyna. "Historia—*lux veritatis*. Rozmowa z Marcinem Dybowskim, Wydawcą dzieł Feliksa Konecznego." *Człowiek w Kulturze* 10 (1998): 249–53.

Stojanowski-Han, Stanisław. "LPR—przyczyny klęski." *Myśl Polska*, no. 5 (3 February 2008).

Surmiak-Domańska, Katarzyna. "Ja, grzesznik. Anatomia fundamentalisty." *gazeta.pl—Gazeta Wyborcza*, 7 April 2006. http://serwisy.gazeta.pl/df/2029020,34471,3267990.html (accessed 1 March 2007).

Sutowicz, Piotr. "Feliks Koneczny i jego nauka historii." *Nowe Życie: Donośląskie Pismo Katolickie*, no. 4 (2002). http://nowezycie.archidiecezja.wroc.pl/num ery/042002/09.html (accessed 25 August 2009).

Szcześniak, Andrzej Leszek. *Judeopolonia: żydowskie państwie polskim*. Radom: Polskie Wydawnictwo Encyklopedyczne, 2004.

"Szkolenia polskich neofaszystów." *Forum Żydzi-Polacy-Chrześcijanie*. http://www .forum-znak.org.pl/print.php?t=przeglad&id=1852&l=pl (accessed 25 August 2009). First published as "Biało-Polacy." *Wprost*, no. 20 (18 May 2003): 34–36.

Szydlik, Andrzej. "Globalizm kontra . . . globalizm." http://www.man.pl/~nowa/nowa/ Artykuly/anszydl2.html (accessed 29 June 2004).

"Śladem myśli Feliksa Konecznego—Bialska Wszechnica." *Serwis internetowy Ligi Polskich Rodzin*. http://www.lpr.pl/?sr=!czytaj&id=2849&dz=region&x=3&pocz =499&gr= (accessed 8 July 2011).

Tarnowski, Dariusz. "Polska między Wschodem i Zachodem— za życia prof. Feliksa Konecznego i dziś." Referat wygłoszony na konferencji poświęconej profesorowi Feliksowi Konecznemu, zorganizowanej przez Narodowe Odrodzenie Polski 10 lutego 2007 w Krakowie. *Nacjonalista.pl—Portal Narodowo-Radykalny*. http:// www.nacjonalista.org/artykuly.php?id=54&licz=1 (accessed 28 August 2009).

"Teoria cywilizacji. Spotkanie na temat teorii cywilizacji Feliksa Konecznego." *Stowarzyszenie Patriotyczne Serenissima*, 8 October 2004. http://www.serenissima.org .pl/Patriotyzm/Patriotyzm.html (accessed 27 July 2011).

Thompson, Ewa. "Narodowość i polityka." *Dziennik.pl*, 11 May 2007 http://www .dziennik.pl/dziennik/europa/article46439/Narodowosc_i_polityka.html (accessed 30 June 2008).

———. "Said a sprawa Polska." *Dziennik.pl*, 29 June 2005. http://www.dziennik.pl/ dziennik/europa/article47614/Said_a_sprawa_polska.html (accessed 30 June 2008). First published in *Europa*, no. 65 (29 June 2005).

———. "Sarmatyzm i postkolonializm." *Dziennik.pl*, 18 November 2006. http://www .dziennik.pl/dziennik/europa/article46218/Sarmatyzm_i_postkolonializm.html (accessed 30 June 2008). First published in *Europa*, no. 137 (18 November 2006).

———. "The Surrogate Hegemon in Polish Postcolonial Discourse." *Ewa M. Thompson's Homepage*. http://www.owlnet.rice.edu/~ethomp/The%20Surrogate%20Hege mon.pdf, 1 (accessed 27 June 2010).

Tomasiewicz, Jarosław. "Neo-nationalism in Poland." http://adnikiel.republika.pl/neo .html (accessed 5 August 2009).

Wielomski, Adam. "Euro-barbarzyństwo." *Nasza Witryna*. www.iyp.org/polish/history/ antypolonizmy/europa_432.html (accessed 15 February 2003).

———. "Globalizatorzy." *Myśl Polska*, no. 18–19 (2–9 May 2004). http://www.myslpol ska.icenter.pl/ (accessed 22 March 2005).

———. "Metecy." *Myśl Polska*, 2–9 June 2002. http://www.myslpolska.icenter.pl/ (accessed 25 March 2005).

———. "Unia Europejska jako wyzwanie historizoficzne." *Konserwatyzm.pl (Klub Zachowawczo-Monarchistyczny)*. http://konserwatyzm.pl/content/view/1046/143/ (accessed 30 June 2008).

Wierzejski, Wojciech. *Naród, młodzież, idea: zbiór narodowej publicystyki z lat 1997–2000*. Krzeszowice: Dom Wydawnicy "Ostoja," 2001.

———. "Prymat etyki, zwierzchnictwo moralności." *Blog Wojciecha Wierzejskiego*. http://wierzejski.blog.onet.pl/2,ID150782916,index.html (accessed 17 December 2007).

Witkowska, Sabina. "Liga stawia na kobiety!" *Aspekt Polski*, 1 October 2006. http://www.aspektpolski.pl/index.php?option=com_content&task=view&id=918&Itemid=30 (accessed 19 August 2010).

"Właściwa wizja zjednocznonej Europy." *Obóz Narodowo-Radykalny*, 30 December 2010. http://www.onr.h2.pl/index.php?option=com_content&view=article&id=2 23:waciwa-wizja-zjednoczonej-europy-&catid=54:unia-europejska (accessed 28 May 2011).

Wolnicki, Michał. "Co nas czeka?" *Ojczyzna.pl*. http://www.ojczyzna.pl/Arch-Teksty/WOLNICKI__Co-nas-czeka.htm (accessed 29 March 2005).

———. "Grudniowe przemyślenia." *Ojczyzna.pl*. http://www.ojczyzna.pl/Arch-Teksty/WOLNICKI__Grudniowe-Przemyslenia.htm (accessed 29 March 2005).

Wróbel, Jan. "Bobrzyński miał rację, ale był za łagodny. Jan Wróbel rozmawia z Henrykiem Samsonowiczem." *Dziennik.pl*. http://www.dziennik.pl/dziennik/europa/46814.html (accessed 29 August 2009). First published in *Europa*, no. 49 (9 March 2005).

Zakrzewski, Zdzisław. "Miejsce Polski w świecie XXI wieku." *Tygodnik Internetowy*, 26 July 2002. http://www.polskiejutro.com/art/a.php?p=miejsce_polski (accessed 28 March 2005).

Zawadzki, Paweł. "Feliks Koneczny, postać bardzo niewygodna." *Wydawnictwo "Zielone Brygady"* 2, no. 182 (April 2003). http://www.zb.eco.pl/publication/feliks-koneczny-postac-bardzo-niewygodna-p1728l1 (accessed 4 May 2009).

Zechenter, Anna. "Multi-kulti i Feliks Koneczny." *Nasz Dziennik*, 31 October / 1 November 2012. http://www.naszdziennik.pl/wp/13792,multi-kulti-i-feliks-koneczny.html (accessed 13 November 2012).

Zgliczyński, Stefan. "Od 'obrony cywilizacji' do 'ostatecznego rozwiązania,'" *Nigdy Więcej* 16 (Winter–Spring 2008): 21.

Życiński, Józef. "Siła słabych." *Gazeta Wyborcza*, 5 April 2007. http://www.gazeta wyborcza.pl/gazetawyborcza/2029020,79328,4042232.html (accessed 15 April 2007).

Index

CPSIA information can be obtained
at www.ICGtesting.com
Printed in the USA
LVHW090703111119
636959LV00011B/4101/P